THE STATE AND EDUCATION POLICY

Also available from Continuum

The Great City Academy Fraud, Francis Beckett

Education Policy Unravelled, Dean Garratt and Derek Kassem

Education, Policy and Social Justice, James Avis

The State and Education Policy

The Academies Programme

Edited by Helen M. Gunter

continuum

Continuum International Publishing Group

The Tower Building	80 Maiden Lane
11 York Road	Suite 704
London	New York
SE1 7NX	NY 10038

www.continuumbooks.com

British Library Cataloguing-in-Publication Data
A catalogue record for this book is available from the British Library.

ISBN: 978-1-4411-4311-2 (hardcover)

Library of Congress Cataloging-in-Publication Data
The state and education policy: the academies programme/edited by Helen M. Gunter.
p. cm.
Includes bibliographical references.
ISBN 978-1-4411-4311-2 (hardcover)
1. Education and state—England. 2. Educational evaluation—England. 3. Educational accountability—England. 4. Educational change—England. I. Gunter, Helen. II. Title.
LC93.G7S69 2011
379.41—dc22 2010020578

Typeset by Pindar NZ, Auckland, New Zealand
Printed and bound in Great Britain by the MPG Books Group

Contents

Acknowledgements

I would like to thank the British Educational Leadership Management and Administration Society, particularly Dr Linda Hammersley-Fletcher, and the British Academy, who funded the seminar at the University of Manchester in June 2008 that led to this book. I would like to thank seminar participants for a very stimulating and interesting day.

I would like to give acknowledgement to Professor Stephen Ball, who gave permission to include an edited version of Gorard, S. (2009), 'What are academies the answer to?' *Journal of Education Policy*, 24, (1), 101–13 as Chapter 8 in this collection.

I would like to thank colleagues at Continuum for their support, particularly Alison Baker, the commissioning editor. As a change of government took place in May 2010 I would like to thank the publishers for allowing me to write a Coda regarding policy developments.

I would like to thank Professor Tanya Fitzgerald for reading parts of the book and for her feedback. Most importantly for her friendship and collaborative scholarship.

Finally, I completed editing the major part of the text while working and visiting with Professor John Smyth, University of Ballarat, Australia, in February 2010, and I would like to thank him for his feedback, enthusiasm and intellectual companionship. I dedicate this book to all who believe in and value the importance of a vibrant and inclusive public domain.

Illustrations

Figures

Tables

Abbreviations

AAA	Anti Academies Alliance
ARK	Absolute Return for Kids
ASBM	Advanced School Business Managers
ATL	Association of Teachers and Lecturers
BITC	Business in the Community
BME	Black and minority ethnic
BSF	Building Schools for the Future
BTEC	Business and Technology Education Council
CEA	Cambridge Education Associates
CMO	Charter Management Organization
CTC	City Technology College
DCLG	Department for Communities and Local Government
DCSF	Department for Children, Schools and Families
DETR	Department for the Environment, Transport and the Regions
DfEE	Department for Education and Employment
DfES	Department for Education and Skills
EAL	English as an additional language
ECAC	Every Child a Chance
ECC	Every Child Counts
ECM	Every Child Matters
EMO	Education Management Organization
EOI	Expression of Interest
FMiS	Financial Management in Schools programme
FOIA	Freedom of Information Act
FSM	Free school meals
GCSE	General Certificate of Secondary Education
GMS	Grant-Maintained Status
GNVQ	General National Vocational Qualification
HMC	Headmasters' and Headmistresses' Conference
HOTS	Hands Off Tamworth Schools
HE	Higher Education
ICT	Information and communication technology

KIPP	Knowledge is Power Program
LA	Local Authority
LEA	Local Education Authority
LMS	Local Management of Schools
MP	Member of Parliament
NAEP	National Assessment of Educational Progress
NAGM	National Association of Governors and Managers
NAHT	National Association of Headteachers
NAO	National Audit Office
NASUWT	National Association of Schoolmasters Union of Women Teachers
NCLB	No Child Left Behind
NCSL	National College for School Leadership (from 2009, the National College for Leadership of Schools and Children's Services)
NEET	Not in employment, education or training
NFER	National Foundation for Educational Research
NGC	National Governors' Council
NGO	Non-Governmental Organization
NLE	National Leaders of Education programme
NPD	National Pupil Database
NUT	National Union of Teachers
NRT	National Remodelling Team
OECD	Organisation for Economic Co-operation and Development
OfSTED	Office for Standards in Education
PEF	Private Equity Foundation
PFI	Private Finance Initiative
PISA	Programme for International Student Assessment
PLASC	Pupil Level Annual Schools Census
PwC	PricewaterhouseCoopers
QCA	Qualifications and Curriculum Authority
RE	Religious education
SBD	School business directors
SCC	Staffordshire County Council
SEN	Special educational needs
SENCO	Special educational needs co-ordinator
SHA	Secondary Heads Association
SSAT	Specialist Schools and Academies Trust
SSFA	School Standards and Framework Act

SSP	Specialist Schools Programme
STRB	School Teachers' Review Body
SATs	Standard Attainment Tests
TIMSS	Trends in International Mathematics and Science Study
TUPE	The Transfer of Undertakings (Protection of Employment) Regulations
YPLA	Young People's Learning Agency

Contributors

David Armstrong, PhD, is an Associate Partner at PricewaterhouseCoopers (PwC). Since joining PwC in 1998, David has led a wide range of national research and evaluation assignments on behalf of the Department for Children, Schools and Families (DCSF) and other government departments and agencies. For example, David led PwC's independent review of school leadership, published by DCSF in January 2007, and he is currently finalizing PwC's ongoing longitudinal evaluation of academies, again on behalf of DCSF. He is also currently leading a research project for the Regional Training Unit on the barriers to headship in the north and south of Ireland. Prior to joining PwC, David worked as an academic researcher in Oxford and Belfast, and he completed a PhD in Economics at Warwick University. He has given evidence to a House of Commons select committee on underachievement in secondary education, and he has also acted as an expert adviser to the Northern Ireland Assembly committee for education and industry. He is married with three young children and has absolutely no time or energy for anything else.

Stephen Ball, PhD, FRSA, AcSS, FBA, is the Karl Mannheim Professor of Sociology of Education, Department of Educational Foundations and Policy Studies and Centre for Critical Education Policy Studies, Institute of Education, University of London, and managing editor of the *Journal of Education Policy*. He is currently involved in three projects funded by the Economic and Social Research Council that are focused on: the relationships between philanthropy and education policy (with Carolina Junemann); policy enactments in secondary schools (with Meg Maguire, King's College London, and Annette Braun); and the educational strategies of the black middle class (with Carol Vincent, David Gillborn and Nicola Rollock). He is also working on an international study of the global middle class with colleagues in Spain, Argentina, France, Australia and the US. Recent publications include: *The Education Debate: Policy and Politics in the 21st Century* (2008), Bristol: Policy Press, and *Education Plc: Private Sector Participation in Public Sector Education* (2007), London: Routledge.

Valerie Bunting is a Consultant in the Research, Strategy and Policy Group in PricewaterhouseCoopers (PwC). Prior to joining PwC Valerie worked in the higher education sector, lecturing in social policy. She also spent some time working for a large children's charity. Her doctorate examined user involvement and consultation. Since joining PwC Valerie has been involved in a range of high-profile education evaluations on behalf of the Department for Children, School and Families, including the evaluation of city academies, and high-performing specialist schools. She is currently part of the research team that is evaluating Building Schools for the Future, which is a longitudinal evaluation currently in its fourth year. Her other research interests include equality of opportunity and marginalized groups.

Brian J. Caldwell is Managing Director of Educational Transformations (Australia) and an associate director of the Specialist Schools and Academies Trust, providing support for its international arm – International Networking for Educational Transformation (iNet). From 1998 to 2004 he served as Dean of Education at the University of Melbourne where he is currently Professorial Fellow. His previous appointments include Dean of Education (1989–90) at the University of Tasmania. International work over the last 25 years includes more than 500 presentations, projects and other professional assignments in or for 39 countries. In addition to more than 150 published papers, chapters and monographs, Brian Caldwell is author or co-author of books that helped guide educational reform in several countries, notably the trilogy on self-managing schools. He is Deputy Chair of the board of the Australian Council for Educational Research and a past President and life member of the Australian Council for Educational Leaders.

David Daniels, MBA, MSc, BSc, MCIM, MCIPD, is Principal of the Petchey Academy in Hackney, London, and is currently working towards the completion of a Doctorate in Education at Birmingham University focusing on the ways in which academies use their special characteristics to be 'entrepreneurial' organizations in the way they work, are managed and deliver educational experiences for students. His experience of higher education was gained as a tutor for the master's programme in educational management at The Open University and as an Associate Lecturer at Leicester University for the Master of Business Administration (Education). He has been a Headteacher/Principal three times and was also an Ofsted (Office for Standards in Education) team inspector in primary, secondary and special schools. The majority of his working life in teaching has been spent in and around London, mainly in highly multi-cultural schools. He has also been a Consultant Headteacher in Thurrock and has worked on performance management/threshold training for the DCSF and is also is a trained School Improvement Partner (SIP).

Alan Dyson is Professor of Education at the University of Manchester, where he co-directs the Centre for Equity in Education (with Mel Ainscow) and leads work on education in urban contexts. He was formerly Professor of Special Needs Education and Director of the Special Needs Research Centre at the University of Newcastle. He has worked in universities since 1988. Prior to that, he spent 13 years as a teacher, mainly in urban comprehensive schools. His research and teaching interests are in the relationship between social and educational inclusion and, particularly, in the relationship between education and other areas of public policy in urban contexts. He has undertaken funded research sponsored by the Economic and Social Research Council, the Joseph Rowntree Foundation, government departments, local education authorities and other public bodies. He has recently led the National Evaluation of Full-Service Extended Schools and a study of school governing bodies in disadvantaged areas, and is currently involved in the National Evaluation of Extended Services.

John Elliott is Professorial Fellow within the Centre for Applied Research in Education, which he directed from 1996–9, at the University of East Anglia. He is well known internationally for his role in developing the theory and practice of action research in the contexts of curriculum and teacher development, and has directed a number of funded collaborative classroom research projects with teachers and schools. These include the Ford Teaching Project (1972–4) and, more recently, the Teacher Training Agency-funded Norwich Area Schools Consortium (NASC) on the 'curriculum and pedagogical dimensions of student disaffection' (1997–2001). He is currently an Advisory Professor to the Hong Kong Institute of Education and a Consultant to the Hong Kong government on the strategic development of its curriculum reform proposals. In 2000, he was appointed a Local Council member of Norfolk Learning and Skills Council.

Ron Glatter is Emeritus Professor of Educational Administration and Management at the UK's Open University, where he was a professor for many years. Before that he was Reader in Educational Administration at the Institute of Education, University of London. He was the founding Secretary of what is now called the British Educational Leadership, Management and Administration Society (BELMAS), later became its national Chair and is now Honorary Vice President. He was given the BELMAS Distinguished Service Award in 2007. He was the opening keynote speaker at the EU Presidency Conference on 'Schools facing up to new challenges', in Lisbon. His most recent work has focused on the impact of reform initiatives, new models of school headship and various aspects of inter-school collaboration. He is a member of the Council of the Institute of Education, University of London, and a Trustee of both the Advisory Centre for Education and the Research into State Education Trust.

Denis Gleeson is Professor of Education at the University of Warwick. He has published widely in the sociology of post-compulsory education, employment and the state, and has held various research grants and fellowships funded by local authorities, government agencies, unions, the Economic and Social Research Council and think tanks. His recent work is in the field of academy schools, college governance and learning and skill policy. Currently he is Chair of the *Sociological Review*'s Editorial Board and an Associate Editor of *Gender, Work and Organisation.*

Ellen Goldring is Patricia and Rodes Hart Chair and Professor of Education Policy and Leadership at Peabody College, Vanderbilt University. She is Chair of the Department of Leadership, Policy and Organizations. Her areas of expertise include improving schools with particular attention to educational leadership, school choice and parent involvement. In her research on school choice, Professor Goldring addresses questions about access and equity including how parents choose, why parents choose, parent involvement, and leadership in both magnet schools and charter schools. Professor Goldring serves on numerous editorial boards, technical panels, and policy forums. Her books include *Principals of Dynamic Schools, School Choice in Urban America, Successful Schools and the Community Relationship, Leading with Data: A Path to School Improvement, From the Courtroom to the Classroom* and *Leading with Inquiry and Action.* She has worked with school systems, universities and governments in the US and internationally, in the UK, Israel, China and Hong Kong, among others.

Stephen Gorard holds the Chair in Education Research at the University of Birmingham, UK. His research is focused on issues of equity, especially in educational opportunities and outcomes, and on the effectiveness of educational systems (*Equity in Education,* 2010, Palgrave). Other recent project topics include widening participation in learning (*Overcoming the Barriers to Higher Education,* 2007, Trentham), the role of technology in life-long learning (*Adult Learning in the Digital Age,* 2006, Routledge), informal learning, 14–19 provision, the role of targets, the impact of market forces on schools, underachievement, teacher supply and retention (*Teacher Supply: The Key Issues,* 2006, Continuum), and developing international indicators of inequality. He is also interested in the process and quality of research (*Using Everyday Numbers Effectively in Research,* 2006, Continuum).

Helen M. Gunter, PhD, MSc, BA, PGCE, is Professor of Educational Policy, Leadership and Management in the School of Education, University of Manchester. She has produced over 70 publications including books and papers on leadership theory and practice, and she Co-Edits the *Journal of Educational Administration and History.* Her work has focused on education policy and the growth of school leadership where she has used Bourdieu's thinking tools to explain the configuration and development of the field. She is particularly interested in the history of the field and developments in knowledge production. Recently she completed the Knowledge Production in Educational Leadership Project, funded by the Economic and Social Research Council (ESRC), where she studied the relationship between the state, public policy and knowledge, and she has started a project on Distributed Leadership funded by the ESRC, with her colleagues Dave Hall and Joanna Bragg.

Richard Hatcher is Professor of Education at Birmingham City University, UK. He has written widely on education policy issues with a particular emphasis on democracy and social justice. Academies represent one of the most contentious issues in the contested field of education policy. They have given rise to more popular activity, by parents and citizens as well as teachers, than any other aspect of school education under the New Labour governments of Blair and Brown. Hatcher has carried out a number of empirical studies of the local policy process of establishing academies and local campaigns of opposition to them, drawing on social movement theory and situating them in the wider context of debates about democracy and urban governance. He is also personally involved in campaigns against academies as a member of the Anti Academies Alliance.

Judy Larsen has extensive experience in education across all sectors, including teaching at primary, secondary and university levels in both the UK and Australia. She has worked as a primary and secondary teacher, school Principal of a large, innovative secondary school in Western Australia, curriculum developer, education consultant and researcher. Her PhD was on change and innovation in secondary schools. Since arriving in the UK from Australia 13 years ago, Judy has undertaken a broad range of research and consultancy with the Department for Children, Schools and Families (DCSF), local authorities and schools. Her work has ranged from undertaking high-level research projects of national significance including longitudinal reviews of the Academies Programme and Building Schools for the Future to working with schools on school improvement projects. She also works closely with the National College for Leadership of Schools and Children's Services and local authorities and schools to support the development of future school leaders.

Madeline Clark Mavrogordato is a Doctoral student in the Department of Leadership, Policy and Organizations at Peabody College, Vanderbilt University. She is a Predoctoral Fellow in the Experimental Education Research Training programme funded by the US Department of Education's

Institute for Education Sciences. Her research interests include school choice, policies that affect English-language learners, and the use of experimental designs in educational research.

Kirsten Purcell, MPhil, MA, is a Doctoral research student in the Department of Geography, University of Cambridge. Her work focuses on public sector restructuring, the changing nature of policy discourse and the importance of place in the implementation of national policies. Her thesis examines the Academies Programme, analysing the ways in which national-level discourses are constructed, contested and strategically reworked at a local level, using a comparative case study approach to explore different social, economic and political contexts. This work has been funded by the Economic and Social Research Council.

Harriet Rowley, BA, PGCE, is a PhD student in the School of Education at the University of Manchester. Her work is part of a research and development partnership between the University and an academy in the north-west of England. Harriet is interested in issues of equity in schools, particularly in relation to area-based poverty and disadvantage in UK urban contexts. She has a range of experience in schools as a researcher, secondary school teacher and support worker. Since starting her career in research, Harriet has been involved with various research projects funded by the Economic and Social Research Council, the National College for School Leadership and the Department for Children, Schools and Families. Harriet regularly speaks at and attends a variety of conferences. She has recently been selected to attend a prestigious summer workshop on inequality and social change that has been launched as part of a joint initiative between Harvard University and the University of Manchester.

David Wolfe is a Lawyer specializing in public law, including education law, since 1992. He works as a Barrister, advising, writing, training and acting in court on behalf of parents/children, schools, Local Education Authorities, non-governmental organizations (including Independent Parental Special Education Advice, the National Autistic Society and the British Humanist Association) and other bodies (such as the Equality and Human Rights Commission) around issues such as admissions, exclusions, special educational needs, equality (including in particular disability discrimination) and school reorganizations. For several years, he was also a part-time chair of the Special Educational Needs and Disability Tribunal. Over the last four years, a particular focus of his work has been academies. He has appeared in most if not all of the major cases in the High Court and Court of Appeal dealing directly with academies. He has been a member of a local education authority, and a Governor at six schools and a Further Education College. He is a Patron of the Advisory Centre for Education.

Terry Wrigley, MPhil, PhD, recently retired as Senior Lecturer at the University of Edinburgh. He has written three books (*The Power to Learn*, *Schools of Hope* and *Another School is Possible*) and numerous articles and chapters; he edits the journal *Improving Schools*. His work has focused on school change/development and the implications of pedagogy, social justice and education for citizenship. He has been a vocal critic of the school effectiveness and school improvement paradigms, and engaged in the exploration of alternatives. A major emphasis of his writings is the impact of poverty and social class on schooling and achievement. He is currently working with Bob Lingard and Pat Thomson on a new book, *Changing Schools*.

Preface

Francis Beckett

The trouble with writing about academies is that they are shape-shifters. They change shape with a speed and efficiency not normally found outside science fiction. Every time you think you've understood exactly what they are, and can form a view about it, the government shifts the goalposts. Each time you have a criticism, by the time you get it into print it's no longer any part of the concept, and government Ministers can look at you with wide-eyed innocence and tell you that your idea of an academy is *so* last week.

What we were led to expect, back in 2000 by the then Education Secretary David Blunkett, were inner-city schools in areas of great deprivation (they were called 'city academies' in those days, which is why my 2007 book about them was called *The Great City Academy Fraud*). They would replace struggling inner-city comprehensives. They were to be sponsored by big companies, which would put substantial sums of capital into them (though they would not contribute to the running costs). One of the greatest attractions was supposed to be their ability to leverage (that was a very fashionable bit of American management jargon back in 2000) large sums of corporate money into educating England's poorest children.

None of that is true any more. Academies are no longer confined to, or even concentrated in, cities, or poor areas; they are just as likely to be found in leafy suburbs. Nor do they any longer replace struggling inner-city comprehensive schools. In fact, two fee-charging schools have recently salvaged their fortunes by becoming academies, while keeping those students who currently attend, and whose parents have until now paid fees. Sponsors are not big companies that expect to give money to the school, but bespoke companies set up for the purpose of earning a living by running academies for the government as businesses; or they are fee-charging schools; or chains of fee-charging schools; or religious organizations that see the scheme as a way to increase the number of faith schools the government will pay for; or public sector organizations, like universities. Instead of being a way to leverage private sector money into state education, they have become a way of leveraging money from the state education budget into the private sector.

So what the authors of this book have had to do is concentrate on the basics. And there are some basic, unchanging features that characterize academies. Academies are independent schools. Incidentally, this has led to a dreadful confusion. Traditionally, an 'independent' school has meant a school that charges fees. Academies do not charge fees, but they are independent in every sense in which schools that do charge fees are independent; that is, they are independent of the state. It is no longer possible to use the phrase 'independent school' without sowing confusion. I suggest we all get used to referring to 'fee-charging schools' for those schools that charge fees, before educational debate becomes muddled to the point of meaninglessness.

Actually – just to make the debate even more confusing – neither fee-charging schools nor academies are really independent these days. Many fee-charging schools are part of a very centralist chain of schools like the United Church Schools Trust. All academies are controlled by a sponsor, and many of them are part of a chain of schools, all run to a formula. The sponsor is in sole charge and has an inbuilt majority on their governing body. They have less freedom from their sponsor than ordinary maintained schools have from the state. Local authorities, parents and teachers can all be safely ignored so long as the sponsor is kept happy. The word 'independent' really is an anachronism in the British education system.

The Academies Programme is built upon the idea that there is nothing the public sector can do that the private sector can't do better. Academies are, as Helen Gunter points out in the Introduction to this collection, the direct and logical educational consequence of the neoliberal values and strategies that underpin current Conservative and Labour party policies. They tell you very little about education, but a great deal about New Labour political ideology. They are, essentially, a political construct, not an educational one. There is, after all, no particular reason why a school should perform better because you have changed its governance, and tinkered with the way it gets its money. 'It's very easy to invent a new kind of school', the schools adjudicator Philip Hunter once said. 'You come up with a name, play around with the governing body, decide who owns the land and appoints the staff, and decide how funding gets to it. That's it'. Sir Philip boasted of having invented foundation schools in 20 minutes in the Tate Gallery tearoom (Wilby 2008). Improving schools requires a great many things, but changing the nature of the governing body and the way the government channels money to it isn't one of them.

So contributors to this book concentrate, as they should and must, on the eternal, unchanging features of academies. I have the privilege of writing last, when all the contributions are in, and what I think I can most usefully add is what, as a journalist, I'm best qualified to add: immediacy. What are the latest ways in which academies are changing? The new Education Secretary, Michael Gove, was fairly explicit about his plans while in opposition, and remarkably open in private meetings. Shadow Ministers seldom spell out what they want to do as exactly as Mr Gove has done on this issue.

He started by talking about parent-led schools, which sounded much more democratic than academies. If parents were to be in charge, that was surely preferable to having a company or a church making key decisions about our children's education. Alas! Those who have had private discussions with Mr Gove have found that what parents will provide under Mr Gove's scheme is nothing more than the political cover. Once parents are moved to demand something new, or can be persuaded to do so, what they will get will be a school run by the usual suspects, the academy sponsors already introduced by New Labour. Mr Gove is particularly an admirer of ARK, or Absolute Return for Kids, the academy sponsor run by a group of hedge-fund billionaires.

As to how academies are already changing as I write, what strikes me most forcibly is how far they are falling short of living up to their billing. The idea that turning a school into an academy would 'transform' it (to the sort of marketing folk who sponsor academies, no school is ever just improved, it is always 'transformed') is every day shown to be rubbish on stilts trying to walk across the Atlantic.

In January 2010, 74 academies had put pupils through at least two sets of GCSEs, allowing us to monitor their progress. A third of these had worse results than before they were academies. Darwen Aldridge Community Academy in Lancashire has just produced its first GCSE results, and they are worse than the school it replaced. It has a 23 per cent pass rate for pupils achieving five or more A*–C grades including English and maths. The previous year, pupils at the then Moorland High gained a 31 per cent pass rate. The academy's principal, Brendan Loughran, said a range of initiatives had been introduced to improve grades and he believed the academy was on track to make 'significant' improvements this year. The academy was set up to make a 'complete break with cultures of low aspiration which afflict too many communities and their schools'. They all say that.

Kent's academies are excluding twice as many pupils as their predecessor schools.

The biggest academy sponsor, the United Learning Trust (ULT), has recently guided Sheffield Park Academy into special measures. The ULT is an academy sponsor in trouble. A subsidiary of the United Church Schools Trust, which runs a chain of fee-charging schools, it is run in a highly centralized way. Its headteachers have to refer even quite small decisions to the central organization. 'I'll have to ask head office if I can talk to you', said one of its heads apologetically when I telephoned him with a journalistic question. The government has had to tell ULT to stop expanding until it can get its act together.

Amid a tale of less than unalloyed success, the government has moved to make scrutiny of academies harder. One of the less-publicized clauses in the Children, Schools and Families Act 2010, one of New Labour's last pieces of legislation, removes the scrutiny of the Charities Commission from academies, while leaving them all the rights and privileges of being charities. It was apparently becoming too much of a burden to have to show that they fulfilled all the requirements of charitable status. Although remaining charities, they will be exempt from the requirement to register with the Charity Commission. According to Schools Secretary Ed Balls, this is 'an important but sensible piece of deregulation'. If Charity Commission scrutiny is a bureaucratic waste of time, I can think of several organizations that I would free from it before I freed academies.

Altogether, I see no reason to revise the verdict I came to in that 2007 book, *The Great City Academy Fraud*:

> In a very limited sense – does it work for those pupils who attend Academies, leaving aside the rest of the community in which they live? – the answer is a pretty definite maybe. Throwing money at a problem does yield results. The improvements are modest, and certainly no more than you would have expected the extra money to buy.
>
> Had the money been spent differently, and not been handed over to private sponsors to spend as they wished, the improvement it bought might have been greater. Had the money been spent more or less evenly among those state schools that needed it, it might have bought more overall benefit. There is no real evidence that the Academy model itself has produced any benefits.
>
> (pp. 148–9)

Francis Beckett is an author, journalist, broadcaster, playwright and contemporary historian.

Introduction: Contested Educational Reform

Helen M. Gunter

Introduction

The modernization of the education system in England over the past quarter of a century is based on creating schools as small businesses regulated by a performance management regime. Such restructuring is about how successive UK governments have handled neoliberal challenges to the post-World War II welfare state in England, and how policy production has drawn on particular knowledge claims.[1] There are specific historical antecedences located in Thatcherism that continue to structure New Labour policy, with attacks on the purposes and workings of democratic institutions, the integrity of the public domain and the professionalism of the public sector workforce (Smyth and Gunter, 2009). Consequently, the Academies Programme is simultaneously radical and conservative: it is about major root and branch changes to the purposes of public education through dismantling the post-war settlement, and as such it is about restoring the dominance of private interests by bringing 'all human action into the domain of the market' (Harvey, 2007, p. 3). This book will focus on a major aspect of this reform of the state through a critical examination of the Academies Programme during the New Labour governments, 1997–2010.

Having its origins in the City Technology College (CTC) initiative under the previous Conservative administrations (1979–97),[2] the Academies Programme has official purposes that are about improving educational provision through the extension of the market and the creation of diverse provision (Ryan, 2008). However, the programme is very controversial, where Moynihan (2008) promotes privatization in the following terms:

> Private sector sponsors are sometimes criticised because they are not educationalists. This misses the point. The predecessor schools may have been run by educationalists, and yet they were unsuccessful. Sponsors do not need to be educational experts because they appoint a principal to run the schools, but they should bring high expectations and a track

record of success. And they can help in creating a 'can-do' brand that supports success.

(p. 14)

But Wrigley (2009) argues differently by stating that the 'power over children's education is being handed over to a rag-tag bunch of second-hand car dealers, carpet salesmen and tax-evading city traders' (p. 48). Consequently, the Academics Programme is an important site through which to study public policy, and so this book will not only chart the antecedence, evolution and impact of this major reform initiative but will also provide strategic understandings of the state, governance and the policy process.

The story of academies

At the time of writing there are 200 academies with a New Labour plan to open a further 100 in September 2010 (see Appendix 1). The Academies Programme was announced by the then Secretary of State for Education, David Blunkett, on 15 March 2000 (Blunkett, 2000a):

> We need all schools to achieve high standards for all pupils if we are to build a successful and inclusive economy and society in the 21st century. My vision is one of excellence and diversity, a vision of transformation. It is already starting to change the way every secondary school in England operates: those that are high performing; those that are improving fast; those that are coasting; those that are struggling or failing. But we must go further and faster.
>
> (n.p.)

There was a specific goal of raising standards in areas of social and economic disadvantage:

> For too long, too many children have been failed by poorly-performing schools which have served to reinforce inequality of opportunity and disadvantage. City Academies will create new opportunities for business, the voluntary sector and central and local government to work together to break this cycle and improve the life chances of inner city children.
>
> (Blunkett, 2000b, n.p.)

Academies were presented at the time as part of a wider strategy to improve inner-city schools that includes Education Action Zones[3] from 1998, Excellence in Cities[4] from September 1999, and from 2002 a focus on education in particular conurbations with City Challenge in London, from 2008 in Manchester and the Black Country[5] (Morris, 2002) and from 2003 the *Every Child Matters* agenda covered all children in all schools.[6] Government Ministers have remained publicly enthusiastic about academies (Clarke, 2003; Kelly, 2006; Miliband, 2002), and after visiting the US, Morris (2000)[7] stated:

> We are determined that every child, no matter which school they go to, should get a good start in life and City Academies will draw on the very best practice in schools – from both sides of the Atlantic . . . Good schools can act as engines of regeneration – raising both educational and community achievement.
>
> (n.p.)

The first three opened in 2002, with 27 open by 2006, leading to claims of rapid success:

> They are schools local people can be proud of. Academies have improved the number of pupils getting good GCSE results by almost three times the national average (nearly 8 percentage points compared to 2.6 percentage points). The evidence shows the Government was right not to accept the underachieving schools they replaced.
>
> (Kelly, 2006, n.p.)

By 2007 Alan Johnson stated that 'Academies work – and are worth it' (Johnson, 2007, n.p.), and based on performance and popularity (Hansard, 2007) the programme has now been expanded, with plans for 400 (Balls, 2007a; BBC News, 2006a).

So what is an academy? Like other state-funded schools[8] academies provide non-fee-paying secondary education for children in a local community. However, what makes academies different is: first, they are independent of local authorities and are funded directly from the centre (see Coles, 2008); and second, they are sponsored by private interests who control the curriculum and the workforce. This independence has been outlined by Adonis (2007c):

> Academy sponsors have integral control of, and responsibility for, the management of their Academies. They appoint a majority of the governors; they control the school estate; they have unambiguous responsibility for management and appointments; they instill their ethos and expectations; they develop – within broad parameters – their own curriculum; and their budget comes as a single block grant from the government to allocate as they think appropriate, with no intermediaries taking a top slice on the way. By the standards of state-funded schools at home and abroad, this is a high degree of independence.
>
> (n.p.)

The key features of the original Academies Programme are outlined in Table 0.1. As each academy is set up, a Funding Agreement is contracted between the national ministry in London and the academy that lays out the arrangements (e.g. admissions) that is the condition of funding. Each academy is a company limited by guarantee with charitable status, and must operate within company and charity laws (see Appendix 2).

The Academies Programme has seen some major changes in its first decade, as outlined in Figure 0.1. In particular, the range of sponsors has been widened, and so academies in England are currently defined as

> all-ability, state-funded schools established and managed by sponsors from a wide range of backgrounds, including high performing schools and colleges, universities, individual philanthropists, businesses, the voluntary sector, and the faith communities. Some are established educational providers, and all of them bring a record of success in other enterprises which they are able to apply to their Academies in partnership with experienced school managers.
>
> (DCSF, 2009a, n.p.)

Figure 0.1 is a product of policy watching and tracking, were changes have been incremental and often linked to political strategy to enable the programme to be sustained.

Notably there have been shifts in the location of power. Significantly, local

Table 0.1 2000 launch of city academies

Oversight and funding	National ministry (DfES, superseded from 2007 by the DCSF)
Title	City academies
Sponsors	Business, church, charity, individual
Sponsor investment	Fifth of capital costs, up to £2m
Running costs	Funded by DfES/DCSF
Parity of funding	Same as other schools in the area and an equivalent share of the LEA funds for local services, plus £123 per pupil.
Sponsor powers	Owned and run by the sponsors who would 'normally' set up a charitable company. Power to decide on: 1. composition of governing body, approved by Secretary of State 2. leadership and management structures and appointments 3. pay and conditions of staff 4. disapplication from parts of national curriculum 5. structure of the school day.
Admissions	Control of the intake by selecting up to 10% based on aptitude for school specialism. Admissions criteria should be fair and must admit pupils of different abilities. Pupils can be excluded with the agreement of the Secretary of State.

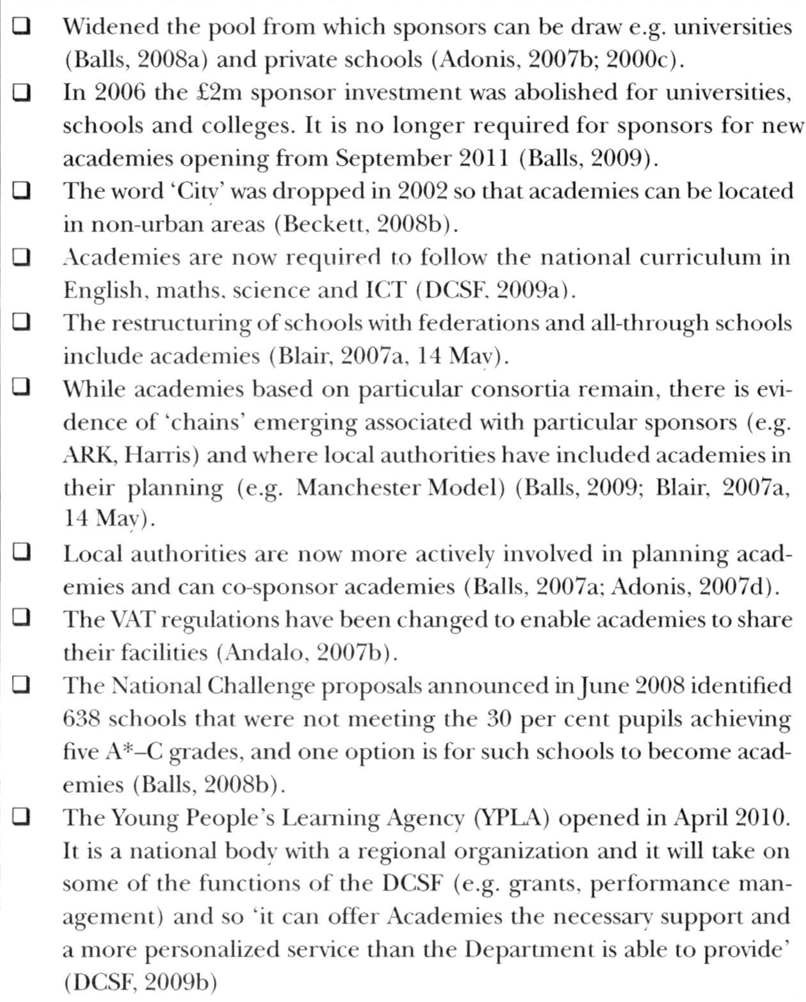

- Widened the pool from which sponsors can be draw e.g. universities (Balls, 2008a) and private schools (Adonis, 2007b; 2000c).
- In 2006 the £2m sponsor investment was abolished for universities, schools and colleges. It is no longer required for sponsors for new academies opening from September 2011 (Balls, 2009).
- The word 'City' was dropped in 2002 so that academies can be located in non-urban areas (Beckett, 2008b).
- Academies are now required to follow the national curriculum in English, maths, science and ICT (DCSF, 2009a).
- The restructuring of schools with federations and all-through schools include academies (Blair, 2007a, 14 May).
- While academies based on particular consortia remain, there is evidence of 'chains' emerging associated with particular sponsors (e.g. ARK, Harris) and where local authorities have included academies in their planning (e.g. Manchester Model) (Balls, 2009; Blair, 2007a, 14 May).
- Local authorities are now more actively involved in planning academies and can co-sponsor academies (Balls, 2007a; Adonis, 2007d).
- The VAT regulations have been changed to enable academies to share their facilities (Andalo, 2007b).
- The National Challenge proposals announced in June 2008 identified 638 schools that were not meeting the 30 per cent pupils achieving five A*–C grades, and one option is for such schools to become academies (Balls, 2008b).
- The Young People's Learning Agency (YPLA) opened in April 2010. It is a national body with a regional organization and it will take on some of the functions of the DCSF (e.g. grants, performance management) and so 'it can offer Academies the necessary support and a more personalized service than the Department is able to provide' (DCSF, 2009b)

Figure 0.1 Major changes to the Academies Programme

authorities are now involved in planning, and recently established academies must now follow core aspects of the national curriculum. However, academies still remain independent of local authorities and there is a more diverse range of academies in terms of sponsors, together with independent schools and CTCs converting to academies. It is also the case that 'chains' of academies under one sponsor or organization are developing, such as ARK, the Harris Academies and the United Learning Trust. The different origins of academies are listed in Table 0.2, where the emphasis remains on

Table 0.2 Types of academies

Type	Number (as of Sep. 2009)
An academy replaces predecessor 'failing' school(s)	172
An academy as a newly created school	15
A CTC is converted into an academy	10
An independent school is converted into an academy	3

'failing' schools becoming academies, but the opportunities for successful schools to join the programme have been opened up.

The new types of sponsor mean that not only private, wealthy philanthropists or companies are involved but also public and voluntary sector organizations such as local authorities (only as co-sponsors), universities and schools. In removing the £2 million required investment from these potential sponsors, Ed Balls (2009) argued that 'the test will now be the organisation's educational track record, their skills and leadership and their commitment to working with local parents, teachers and pupils rather than ability to contribute financially'.

So why is this a contested reform? Academies are seen as integral to the future provision of quality education in England (Adonis, 2007c; Astle and Ryan, 2008), but the argument is also made that the public are being defrauded and so academies need to be brought back into state control (Beckett, 2009). Press stories abound with concerns over ownership, the political links of sponsors and the wider issue of the destruction of successful comprehensive education (Benn, 2007). What is also emerging is the fact that the original academy investors are angry at the changes to the programme, such as the requirement to follow aspects of the national curriculum, where the Independent Academies Association has argued that their members are now dependent on the 'whims of quangos' (BBC News, 2009b; see also House of Commons, 2009). New entrants as sponsors such as universities have argued that their involvement is a means of creating aspirations for children, though Oxford and Cambridge have not signed up due to what they regard as a potential conflict of interest in regard to university admissions (Fearn, 2008). While little is known about the schools that have converted from private fees to state funding, emerging narratives do identify the challenges of state regulation for pedagogic values (Avison, 2008; Burnett, 2009). So while it seems that there are different positions emerging within the academies camp, there is a major campaign both nationally and locally by a range of people about whether academies are delivering on what was promised; serious bigger-picture issues are being raised about the impact on democratic authenticity.

Debating academies

The Academies Programme has been evaluated over a five-year period by PricewaterhouseCoopers (PwC), with positive gains being noted:

> The general picture in relation to pupil performance in Academies is one of overall improvement against a range of indicators at Key Stage 3, Key Stage 4 and post-16 levels. Furthermore, Academies' progress *in terms of pupil achievement has generally exceeded corresponding improvements at a national level and amongst other similar schools.* This means that since they opened in 2002 and 2003, for example, the early Academies have begun to significantly close the gap between their performance levels and performance in other schools.
>
> (PwC, 2007, p. vii, emphasis in original)

Accounts by academy leaders give additional evidence about how they are positively responding to their new 'independence' to make changes to teaching and learning, staffing and new structures (Gilliland, 2008; Grundy, 2008; Marshall, 2008; O'Hear, 2008; Seldon, 2008; Wilshaw, 2008). In addition Ministers have identified the positive feedback from OfSTED (e.g. Adonis, 2006), and the National Audit Office (NAO) (2007) reported that performance had improved: 'taking account of both pupils' personal circumstances and prior attainment, Academies' GCSE performance is substantially better, on average, than other schools.' (p. 6).

This emerging positive evidence on academies is being questioned in both officially commissioned and independent reports. Indeed, OfSTED has been critical of the standards in some academies (e.g. Unity Academy in Middlesborough and The Business Academy in Bexley). The House of Commons select committee commented in 2005 that 'the Government should ensure that the current programme of Academies is thoroughly evaluated, both in respect of the performance of individual Academies and the impact on neighbouring schools, before embarking on a major expansion of an untested model' (House of Commons, 2005, section 2, para. 25). Independent analysis has confirmed variation in overall performance so far:

> The government has set the National Challenge benchmark of schools having at least 30% of their pupils achieving five GCSEs at A*–C (including English and Maths) by 2011, in order not to be considered as 'underachieving'. So far, the majority of Academies are not managing to reach this target.
>
> (Curtis *et al.*, 2008, p. 73)

Evidence further suggests that both academies and mainstream schools are improving, confirming the PwC (2008) analysis that as yet there is no 'simple uniform "Academy effect"' (p. 8). Indeed Machin and Wilson (2009a) argue that, when comparing academies with 'matched schools' that had not converted,

> these changes in GCSE performance in Academies relative to matched schools are statistically indistinguishable from one another. The same pattern emerges if all state schools in the Academy's Local Authority are used as the comparator group. To control explicitly for pre-policy trends in GCSE scores for several years before Academy status . . . we make use of school-level data on GCSE performance going as far back as 1995/96. We find a pattern of no short-run effects of becoming an Academy on GCSE performance when long-run differences between the Academies' predecessors and matched schools are taken into account.
>
> (p. 8)

From Gorard's (2005) perspective it seems that 'policy is being made on the basis of little useful evidence, and is seldom allowed to fail for electoral reasons' (p. 176). By 2009 he makes the case that 'there is no clear evidence here that Academies work to produce better results than the kinds of schools they replaced but neither is the evidence as clear as in 2005 that they are completely failing to do so' (Gorard, 2009, p. 112).

So in spite of the official story of emerging success with room for improvement, a number of important critiques have been made, though researchers have found it difficult to obtain data because academies through their 'independence' are not subject to the Freedom of Information Act (de Waal, 2009).

The first area of interest is the impact on the curriculum. Wrigley (2009) argues that academies are entering students for easier examinations, because the GNVQ Intermediate pass is deemed equivalent to four A*–C grades at GCSE. Titcombe (2008), reporting on his work with Roger Davies, has shown that 'Academies have increased their use of vocational qualifications like GNVQ by a factor of fourteen times compared to their predecessor schools' (p. 56), and there is

> a tendency for GNVQ science to replace GCSE science to such an extent that in some of the most improved schools no pupils took GCSE science courses at all. We showed that 'school improvement' was also linked to poor provision and take up of European languages and history and that the 'most improved' schools tended to have the most impoverished curriculum in terms of pupil access to these subjects.
>
> (p. 50)

A second and connected area of interest is admissions, where even with the legal requirement to comply with the admissions code (Hansard, 2007) with banding systems designed to enable children from a range of abilities to make up the academy population, there is evidence that children with higher-level abilities dominate (Beckett, 2007; Wrigley, 2009). Additionally, Gillard (2008) identifies that King's Academy in Middlesborough excluded 26 students, or ten times the national rate, and there is the problem of what are regarded as unfair expulsions (Beckett, 2004; Quinn, 2008). Taylor (2006) reports on how parents of children at Trinity Academy, near Doncaster, mobilized to challenge exclusions for what they regard as spurious reasons (148 children suspended in the first six months), and to highlight a form of covert selection where less troublesome students from outside the area have been brought in to boost results. Consequently, serious claims are being made about the composition of the academy school population where Wrigley (2009) argues that academies 'are simply teaching different children from before' (p. 57).

Such evidence about what is actually happening within academies relates directly to issues about the status and role of private interests in publicly funded education. New Labour, like the previous Conservative governments, has sought to involve private sector interests and finances:

> Sponsors challenge traditional thinking on how schools are run and what they should be like for students. They seek to make a complete break with cultures of low aspiration which afflict too many communities and their schools. We want this to happen, which is why we entrust the governance of Academies to them. On establishing an Academy, the sponsor sets up an endowment fund, the proceeds of which are spent by the Academy Trust on measures to counteract the impact of deprivation on education in their local communities.
>
> (DCSF, 2009a, n.p.)

The sponsor is regarded as 'the lynchpin of the governance of each Academy' (Adonis, 2008, p. vi), which takes place through the integration of private beliefs with corporate requirements (Green, 2009; Moynihan, 2008; Pike, 2009):

> Lord Harris of Peckham, sponsor of seven Academies plus other specialist schools, keeps a very close eye on his schools. He does not interfere with the professionals on a day-to-day basis, but he does judge quality and ask searching questions. His own success has permeated the culture of his schools and he will visit them, keeping his finger on the pulse. He makes a particular point of speaking to the students, who are aware of him and his role as sponsor.
>
> (SSAT, 2007, p. 90)

What is integral to change is that 'Academy conversion is a powerful means to 'reboot' or restart a school towards rapid improvement' (Moynihan, 2008, p. 16), and in particular a sponsor can provide a 'shock to the system' in order to bring about change, not least to highly unionized schools where it is argued that there is usually resistance to change (p. 21).

While government has widened the pool from which sponsors can be drawn to include schools, universities and local authorities, it remains the case that business and faith groups who dominated originally (Woods *et al.*, 2007) continue to do so (P. Curtis, 2009). Those from the original first wave of academies persist in stressing the particular contribution of a business sponsor:

> A business sponsor brings a certain background, a certain level of expectation and a certain can-do approach. Universities have a lot to offer, but the culture can be different and it will be interesting to see how that works with some of the most challenging schools. That remains to be seen.
>
> (House of Commons, 2009, Ev4)

Concerns have been raised about the nature and role of sponsorship, particularly that the lack of business sponsors is what ended the CTC programme, and a lot of effort and public money has gone into wooing sponsors (Andalo, 2007a; BBC News, 2004a). While academies are non-profit organizations, sponsorship can be seen as market publicity, while some sponsors want anonymity in ways that prevent the public from knowing who is funding local education (Beckett and Evans, 2008). Sponsorship is not new, as maintained schools seeking specialist status (e.g. business, languages, sport) have been sponsored by business, but what is different is that sponsors of academies have the power to appoint the governing body, control the conditions of service for staff, and effectively 'own' the school assets. Opponents argue that the dominance of class prevails so that 'educational interests are subordinated to narrow capitalist economic interests' (Hatcher, 2009, p. 112).

There are reports of the imposition of business methods on schools with no break times, no staff room and no playgrounds (Shepherd, 2008). Innovation seems to be largely conservative with the use of uniforms, house systems and the reintroduction of head boy and girl roles. Titcombe (2008) outlines serious issues regarding the curriculum:

> Much bizarre and educationally doubtful experimentation is taking place based on the whims and prejudices of sponsors, ranging from the evangelical presentation of religious mythology as historical truth and the discrediting of science, to a belief in the need to rigorously train all pupils in the practices and ethics of free market capitalism so as to

> properly prepare them for employment. One Academy is installing a 'call centre' so that 'pupils' aspirations can be 'raised' by training for this type of work, and in Manchester and Birmingham a whole range of Academies are being planned, each specialising in preparing pupils for employment in specific industries or commercial activities. Manchester Airport, one such prospective sponsor, has overtly stated that the principle purpose of its Academy will be to provide employees for the airport.
>
> (p. 56)

These arguments are about the purposes of education: to train children as labour for local industries and services and/or to educate the person about science, the arts and wider culture. Some of the critiques of the Academies Programme focus on the utilitarian nature of schools as training camps, where secondary modern education is being reintroduced under the aegis of innovation and economic renewal. The ability of a private individual who has generated wealth to control the education of children in a locality is seen as highly problematic:

> 'Philanthropy' essentially involves rich men and women enhancing their self-respect and public reputation by handing back some money to the desperately poor. Whatever the motives of the individual philanthropist, it is inherently hypocritical, since philanthropists generally become rich by exploiting the poor.
>
> (Wrigley, 2009, p. 52)

Through the work of Francis Beckett (2007), highly dubious practices have been given public scrutiny regarding the use of public funds, and a police investigation took place regarding the promise of honours for sponsorship.

Underpinning this evidence and arguments about the curriculum and the role of sponsors are matters of democratic renewal and authenticity. The official line is that academies are very popular and are oversubscribed, with three applications for each academy place (Adonis, 2007a; Johnson, 2006; Knight, 2008). However, such arguments have already been dispelled by research into CTCs, where Walford (1991) showed that 'popularity' is not the same as quality, and parents can and do oppose investment in one school at the expense of all schools (Dale, 1989; Meikle, 2007). Millar (2008) argues that the statement 'they work because they are oversubscribed' needs to be challenged:

> Even if they are (and not all are . . .), that means many pupils may end up being offered places in other local schools. And these may have been diminished because they haven't had similar investment, they have had

> their more able students creamed off by the Academy, and they are taking in the excluded or special needs pupils the Academy doesn't want.
>
> (p. 4)

There are underlying assumptions about the exercise of choice built into the Academies Programme that run deeply back into the CTCs project, and the challenges made then through research are alive and well in the present. At the heart of this are the processes being used to bring about the closure of a school or schools to make way for an academy and there are claims made that the predecessor schools were not always failing, with illustrative case studies of schools that had been turned around, received national awards but then found themselves to be declared by OfSTED to be in special measures (Beckett, 2007; Gillard, 2008). Additionally, local authorities find themselves drawing up plans for academies because of the direct link with funding for new school buildings (Wrigley, 2009).

Overall, a democratic deficit has been identified with a number of features: first, the control of academies is outside of public accountability systems, particularly through their independent status, which means that they are not subjected to local elected representative scrutiny. The growth of 'chains' of academies with central management not only removes local accountability but also seems to be generating a form of organization that could have the very characteristics that have been used to criticize and marginalize local authorities (Beckett, 2008a; House of Commons, 2009). Second, concerns have been raised over parents losing control over schools through the Academies Programme (BBC News, 2006b), particularly since they do not have the same rights as parents in mainstream schools (Millar, 2006). Third, the potential impact on the community and how an academy will affect other schools, because of investment and hype around them, has been raised (NAO, 2007). Fourth, there is a lack of transparency in the discussions and deal-making that takes place regarding the decisions to set up an academy, where claims are made that the consultation process is 'flawed' (Wrigley, 2009, p. 57) or a 'sham' (*EducationGuardian*, 2008). There has been growing unease and uncertainly with the process (Mansell, 2009a) and opposition to academies (BBC News, 2009a). Campaigns in some areas have been successful (Curtis, 2006).

In 2005 the Anti Academies Alliance was formed (see www.antiacademies.org.uk) as a political campaign linking up local action as a wider campaign. It is supported by 'parents, governors, teachers, trade unions, academics and others concerned about the privatisation of education using academies, trust schools and other forms' (AAA, 2009, n.p.). Researchers have sought to report on particular campaigns: Birmingham (Hatcher, 2009); Bradford (Hatcher, 2008a); Camden (Benn, 2008; Needham *et al.*, 2006); Conisborough and Denaby (Needham *et al.*, 2006); Devon (Clinch, 2008);

Hackney (Hatcher and Jones, 2006); Islington (Muller, 2008; Hatcher and Jones, 2006); Lewisham (Powell-Davies, 2008); Merton (Needham *et al.*, 2006); Norwich (Elliott, 2008); Pimlico (Benn, 2008); Sheppey (Hatcher and Jones, 2006); Tamworth (Hatcher, 2009); Waltham Forest (Needham *et al.*, 2006), with analysis of the forms of resistance and political action taking place across England (Hatcher, 2009; Hatcher and Jones, 2006). Such accounts show that victories can be won, although some are short-term, and that in spite of large-scale public opposition an academy can be opened.

The final but important point that continues to be debated is costs. At the launch Blunkett (2000b) stated that each academy would cost about £10 million but this would vary depending on the type of building needed. While the original investment by sponsors was to be £2 million, this became up to £2 million and that gifts in kind could be given instead of cash (Beckett, 2005). This was eventually removed (see Figure 0.1) as new sponsors entered the programme (Balls, 2007b). The overall cost of the programme has come under scrutiny, where the NAO (2007) showed that the average cost of a new school is £20–22 million while the cost of an academy has been £24–27 million (p. 6). However, there have been some dramatic overspends, with the Darwen Academy costing £49 million, and The Business Academy in Bexley costing £46 million (Henry, 2007). The NAO (2007) reported that up to October 2006 the Academies Programme had cost £1.3 billion, and projected that the total capital cost for 200 academies would be £5 billion (p. 4). The overall judgement was that the Academies Programme 'is on track to deliver good value for money' (p. 8) but is very clear on the need to manage costs better.

Debating the state and education policy

The Academies Programme is an important site for examining the changes to the state and how policy is made. Specifically the aim here is to examine the interplay between the hierarchy of the state and its institutions with markets and private interests, particularly since these matters are of interest in reforms to education systems in Western-style democracies (e.g. Burch, 2009). The post-World War II welfare state settlement in England, with the emphasis on equity and social justice, was based on bureaucratic systems and professional cultures described by Marquand (1981) as 'club government'. Challenges to this control, combined with the need to maintain and enhance capital accumulation, meant that the demands of what Bobbitt (2002) calls the 'market state' required competition, consumerism and the dominance of private interests. Consequently education is a service to be 'purchased' through the exercise of preference; the service should have diverse products with different types of schools, public funding of a service requires regulation of the product and the workforce to ensure that quality delivery takes place, and private interests in relation to choice of the product are uppermost. This has been labelled as modernization, where public services have been transformed through what Ball (2008b) calls 'a *generic global policy ensemble* that rests on a set of basic and common *policy technologies* . . . *the market, management* and *performativity* [based on] . . . the increasing colonisation of education policy by economic policy imperatives' (p. 39, emphasis in original). This has created a complex, dynamic and often incoherent and contradictory policy context for all those involved, not least through the tensions involved in simultaneous delegation and control combined with the 'general "speeding up" and urgency of policy' (Ball, 2008b, p. 197).

I propose using Newman's (2001) typology of governance to help to illuminate and frame the way in which the Academies Programme can be located within this major restructuring and reculturing of public services. Newman (2001) identifies four models of governance:

- **Hierarchy**: 'towards control, standardisation, accountability, based on formal authority'.
- **Rational goal**: 'towards maximisation of output, economic rationalism, based on managerial power'.
- **Open systems**: 'towards flexibility, expansion, adaptation, based on flows of power within networks'.
- **Self-governance**: 'towards devolution, participation, sustainability, based on citizen or community power'. (p. 38)

What is helpful about the conceptualization of these four models is that, while they enable the identification of hierarchy and markets to be separated out, the emphasis is on the layering and overlaying of assumptions about the relationship between public institutions and civil society, and so 'governance comprises multiple and conflicting strands' (p. 38). Therefore New Labour's Academies Programme has: first, hierarchical elements, not least through the Funding Agreement, though the emphasis of the programme is on more autonomy through the independence from government, particularly local government; second, rational goal assumptions where managerial power to deal with problems (e.g. truancy, standards) is necessary to deliver on output data; third, open systems through which sponsor-controlled networks can be used to deliver benefits for the curriculum experience; and fourth, elements of self-governance with a philanthropic orientation to do things on behalf of the community. Overall, the Academies Programme is based on a rejection of hierarchy and the marginalization of self-governance: the independence of the academy means that it seeks to be separate from the state and through control by sponsors the local community lacks the power to remove decision-makers at elections. The form of governance that seems to be emerging is a combination of localized within-school managerial power interrelated with sponsor-approved networks. However, as this Introduction illustrates, there are challenges to this as hierarchy has imposed changes to the curriculum and the role of local authorities in planning admissions combined with the political demand for evidence to prove they are working; there remain ongoing demands for academies to be subjected to the same local 'self-governance' control as mainstream schools are. It seems that

> it is not possible to assert that Labour's approach represents a shift (or extension of earlier shifts) towards a new form of governance. The process of realigning and dispersing state power interacted with, rather than displaced, a process of concentration and the exercise of more coercive and direct forms of control. This produces particular challenges for understanding the process of change. Rather than asserting or rejecting the notion that there has been a fundamental shift, it is necessary to ask how different processes – of centralization and dispersal, of enabling and controlling, of loosening and tightening – co-existed, and what might the consequences be?
>
> (Newman, 2001, p. 163)

Hence this book seeks to examine the Academies Programme within this complex, shifting, and often unintelligible, setting. The aim is to provide the most up-to-date evidence and perspectives on the programme from a range of researchers.

The contribution of this book

There have been major reviews of the Academies Programme, such as the five-year evaluation by PwC (2005–8), one by the Sutton Trust (Curtis *et al.*, 2008), by the NAO (2007) and by the House of Commons (2009). A general synthesis of the findings so far is that there are identifiable gains in some schools but the academies have not yet proved themselves in regard to standards or value for money. As this Introduction has illustrated, positions on the Academies Programme are polarized, particularly so on the relationship between private interests and their control of public services. The government has been able to invest in a range of publicity to support the Academies Programme, where the Specialist Schools and Academies Trust has acted as the delivery arm for the department. There is some insider practitioner research and narratives (e.g. Astle and Ryan, 2008; Macaulay, 2008), and supporters continue to promote the programme (see http://conorfryan.blogspot.com). The Conservative Party are in support of the Academies Programme, not least the freedom from local authorities and with a promise that, when in government, there will be less regulation (Gove, 2008). Whereas the Liberal Democrats (2009) are in favour of extending the freedoms of academies to all schools and bringing all schools, including academies, under the strategic direction of local authorities as sponsor-managed schools.

There have been research texts that have challenged the rationale for the reform and the overall impact on the standard of education, and claims have been made about how the programme has damaged democratic development (Beckett, 2007; Chitty, 2008a). The unions have sought to inform and protect members (NAHT, 2009), have generated research and statements that find the programme wanting with the need for change (ATL, 2007) with some in direct opposition (NUT, n.d.; NUT, 2007; NASUWT, 2009; Needham *et al.*; 2006, Sinnott, 2008; Smith, 2008; UNISON 2006), and have generated a clear call from the Trades Union Congress for Academies to be converted to maintained schools (Rogers and Migniuolo, 2007). The Advisory Centre for Education (2005) is concerned, and the National Secular Society has challenged the growing dominance of faith groups in public education (Gillard, 2008). The Anti Academies Alliance is ensuring that plans are challenged and that problems with the programme continue to be made public. This is clearly troubled territory that requires a thorough and scholarly mapping of activity and conceptual critical analysis of the provision of publicly funded education.

A seminar funded by the British Educational Leadership Management and Administration Society and the British Academy was held at the University of Manchester in June 2008, with the aim of mapping research activity and emergent findings, together with constructing an agenda for ongoing research (Gunter *et al.*, 2008). This book grows out of that discussion, particularly the recognition that a range of work is taking place, with different epistemological positions and on different scales. Some researchers had found it difficult to gain access to do research (for example, difficulties in doing case study work, not being able to obtain data on GCSE results, and lack of returns on questionnaires) while others had been able to secure access to do detailed data collection. Some researchers had funding while others were developing ideas through unfunded pilot work, and some were doing doctoral studies. So an emerging field of research interest was identified with recognition that this work needed to be conceptualized and related to the bigger picture of governance and the modernization of the state.

This book seeks to make a contribution by bringing together a range of people involved in the Academies Programme. There are people actively involved in the programme from lawyers, to campaigners, to practitioners. Some seek to promote and some seek to present a critique of academies. There are researchers with empirical evidence about different aspects of the Academies Programme, together with scholarly analysis of what this means for how governance is understood and conceptualized. The aim of the book is to bring a range of people together as both a reference compendium of the New Labour policy, and to show that the Academies Programme in England is an important site for examining the growth of neoliberal ideas and practices in the framing and delivery of public services such as education.

The book opens with six chapters that examine the Academies Programme at work through examining the legal status (Chapter 1) and the local processes by which schools have been closed and academies established (Chapters 2–6). This is followed by a set of chapters that provide perspectives on the actual working of academies through analysis of evidence from the PwC team, derived from their five-year study (Chapter 7), and critical analysis on the impact of the programme on standards and outputs (Chapters 8 and 9). The final group of chapters takes forward the debates on the programme by examining governance and the education system (Chapters 10 and 11), the global nature of educational restructuring (Chapter 12) and comparison with charter schools (Chapter 13). The book ends with a summary chapter and conclusion: Chapter 14 draws together the themes and consequences presented in this collection, and the Conclusion provides a close to the book by re-examining and extending the policy framework begun in this Introduction, and making some recommendations for research and policy.

Notes

1 Unlike Scotland, Wales and Northern Ireland, England does not have a parliament/assembly and so the UK government determines education policy. The UK government public institution infrastructure has undergone restructuring. When New Labour came to power in 1997, the national ministry in London was called the Department for Education and Employment (DfEE) after reorganization had taken place in 1995 (prior to this the title was the Department for Education [DfE] and before that the Department of Education and Science [DES]). In 2001 the DfEE became the DfES, or Department for Education and Skills. In 2007 the DfES was split into two: the Department for Children, Schools and Families (DCSF) and the Department for Innovation, Universities and Skills (DIUS). The DIUS no longer exists as universities are now included in the Business, Innovation and Skills portfolio. Following a general election in May 2010 a coalition government was formed between the Conservative Party and the Liberal Democrat Party. The DCSF became the Department for Education (DfE), and in a Coda to the Conclusion of this book the policies of the new Government as pertinent to the Academies Programme have been summarized.

2 The City Technology College initiative was launched at the Conservative Party conference in 1986. The plan was to establish the colleges as 'state-independent schools' in industrial areas, sponsored by business and with an emphasis on practical and technical education. See Whitty *et al.*, 1993.

3 Education Action Zones (EAZ) were set up in 1998 and were located in inner-city areas with underperforming schools. Schools in an EAZ could change the curriculum (e.g. more vocational programmes) and the staffing structure, with higher rates of pay.

4 Excellence in Cities (EiC) was launched in 1999 with a focus on standards in inner-city/urban areas. The most successful EAZs were merged into this new programme. EiC schemes included: learning mentors, learning support units, gifted and talent programme, city learning centres and beacon schools.

5 The City Challenge is in London, Manchester and the Black Country, where the focus is on tackling underachievement in primary and secondary schools. The aim is to focus on local needs and use the learning from the London Challenge.

6 In 2003 Every Child Matters (ECM) was launched to create interagency working (local authorities, schools, health and police) focused around the child. The goals are to be healthy, stay safe; enjoy and achieve; make a positive contribution; and achieve economic well-being.

7 Following the resignation of David Blunkett in 2001 as Secretary of State for Education and Employment, Estelle Morris became Secretary of State for Education and Skills. She resigned in 2002, and was succeeded by Charles Clarke (2002–4), followed by Ruth Kelly (2004–6) and Alan Johnson (2006–7). Ed Balls was appointed in 2007 as Secretary of State for Children, Schools and Families. For changes to the structure and title of the national ministry see Note 1 above. David Miliband was schools Minister, 2002–4.

8 The phrase 'maintained mainstream or community schools' is used for schools in England that are funded by the taxpayer and are the responsibility of local authorities. This also applies to schools that are special schools. The local authority owns the land and buildings, funds the school, employs the staff, provides support services, determines and administers the admissions policy, and the pupils must follow the national curriculum. There have been policy changes that have brought diversity to the following schools.

Foundation schools: In 1988 the then Conservative government allowed secondary schools to opt out of local authority control through grant-maintained status (GMS). In 1997 New Labour brought GM schools back into local authority control as foundation schools, but the governing body retained their role as employers, admissions authority and as owners of the school's land and assets.
Specialist schools: All maintained secondary schools can apply for specialist status. The school can identify one or more curriculum specialisms with private-sector sponsors and additional government funding.
Trust schools: Are maintained (state-funded) schools supported by a charitable trust. The trust holds the school's assets on trust for the school, the governing body employs staff and sets admissions arrangements (in accordance with the *School Admissions Code*). Trust schools must adhere to the national curriculum and the 'School teachers' pay and conditions' document.
Voluntary schools: There are two types – controlled and aided. A voluntary-controlled school is a faith school where the land and buildings are owned by a charity such as a church. The local authority funds the school, employs the staff, provides support services and determines and administers the admissions policy, and the pupils must follow the national curriculum. A voluntary-aided school is a faith school where the land and buildings are owned by a charity such as a church. The school is funded by the local authority, the government body and the charity. The governing body employs the staff and the admissions policy is determined and administered by the governors. The local authority provides support services. The pupils have to follow the national curriculum.

Chapter 1

Academies and the Law

David Wolfe

Introduction

I am a lawyer who has specialized in public law, including education law, since 1992. I work as a barrister, advising, writing, training and acting in court on behalf of parents/children, schools, local education authorities and non-governmental organizations around issues such as admissions, exclusions, special educational needs (SEN) and school reorganizations. For several years, I was also a part-time chair of the Special Educational Needs and Disability Tribunal. Over the last four years, a particular focus of my work has been academies. I have appeared in most if not all of the major cases in the High Court and Court of Appeal dealing directly with academies and have noted, with great interest, the legal shifts that have taken place as the government's political approach to the academies has altered over that period.

This chapter draws on my personal experiences[1] to describe the essential legal nature of academies to summarize some[2] of the legal rights and obligations of parents/pupils at academies[3] and the law surrounding the establishment of academies. This chapter focuses on the Academies Programme as devised and developed by the New Labour governments (1997–2010) but much of the analysis is applicable to ongoing debates.

Ask the department?

The New Labour government said things like:

- 'Section 88A of the SSFA 1998 prohibits the interviewing of parents and/or children as a method for deciding whether a child is to be offered a place at a school' (*School Admissions Code 2009*).[4]
- 'Academies must have regard to the SEN code of practice and statutory guidance on inclusion' (*Academy Principals' Handbook*, 2009).[5]
- 'The admission authority for the school or Academy may refuse to admit a child who has been excluded twice, or in the case of a community or voluntary controlled school, the governing body may appeal against the

decision of the local authority as the admission authority to admit the child (see the School Admission Appeals Code for information on these appeals)' (*School Admissions Code*, 2009).[6]

That is consistent with what Ministers said to parliament when promoting those parts of the Education Act 2002 that provide for academies. For example, Stephen Timms (Schools Minister), told the Education Bill Committee on 15 January 2002:[7]

> I can give the hon. Gentleman the particular assurance that he seeks. Academies – unlike City Technology Colleges, by the way – will comply in full with the requirements on special educational needs and admissions and exclusions legislation as it applies to maintained schools.

Unfortunately, the departmental statements above are not true, or certainly not universally true.[8] Stephen Timms' assurance has only partly been fulfilled.

This chapter shows how such discrepancies arise.

Schools and the law

The starting point is the legal expressions 'maintained school' and 'independent school'.

By section 20(7) of the School Standards and Framework Act 1998, 'maintained school' means 'a community, foundation or voluntary school or a community or foundation special school'. Most publicly funded schools are maintained schools – i.e. maintained by the local authority.[9] But academies are not maintained schools. By section 463 of the Education Act 1996,

> 'independent school' means any school at which full-time education is provided for –
>
> (a) five or more pupils of compulsory school age, or
> (b) at least one pupil of that age for whom a statement is maintained under section 324, or who is looked after by a local authority . . . and which is not a school maintained by a local education authority or a special school not so maintained.

The governance arrangements for, and the rights of parents and pupils at, maintained schools are set down in Acts of parliament, regulations (also known as statutory instruments), codes of practice, statutory guidance and non-statutory guidance.

Thus, for example, Part 4 of the Education Act 1996 specifies key rules in relation to children with SEN in 'maintained schools'; regulations made under that part add detail; and maintained schools are required, by section 312 of the 1996 Act, to have regard to the SEN Code of Practice. A recent (1 September 2009) addition to that framework was that special educational needs co-ordinators (SENCOs) must now have minimum qualifications.[10] A similar approach is taken to admissions,[11] exclusions,[12] the curriculum[13] and so on at maintained schools. Compliance with those obligations can ultimately be enforced (including by a child or parent) by court action known as judicial review, by which the 'claimant' can get the court to force a maintained school to act lawfully.[14] Legal aid may well be available for such a challenge.

But none of that applies to *independent* schools.

That is not to say independent schools are uncontrolled, but the legal control (and thus the rights of parents/pupils) is very different and much more limited. Thus, by Part 10 of the Education Act 2002, independent schools must comply with 'independent school standards' as prescribed in the Education (Independent School Standards) (England) Regulations 2003.[15] They require independent schools, for example, to have regard to departmental health and safety guidance, have a first-aid policy, properly supervise pupils, keep a record of sanctions imposed on pupils and maintain an admission and attendance register; but the requirements are expressed in the most general terms.

As mentioned below, there are also some legal requirements (say around discrimination and equality) that apply to all schools, including independent schools. But the other rights and responsibilities at an independent school are defined by a contract, generally between the person placing the pupil and the independent school. In a conventional independent school, the contract will be between the child's parents and the school. Sometimes, such as where a child with a statement of SEN is placed at an independent school, it will be a public body, such as a local authority. But either way, the primary focus in establishing, for example, the process to be followed before a child is permanently excluded, is the particular contract between the school and the parent. And the provisions of the contract are enforced, not through judicial review but through the ordinary process of civil litigation that deals with breaches of contracts of whatever kind.[16]

Another term is also sometimes bandied around – 'state school'. But that term has no legal significance.

What about academies?

So how do academies fit in? Academies are, in law, *independent* schools, not *maintained* schools, let alone one of the types of maintained school, as above.

So the statutory provisions that apply to maintained schools (or particular types of maintained school) only apply to academies if they also specifically refer to academies, as a few do.[17]

Maintained schools are operated by governing bodies which are statutory corporations. An academy is operated by a private company (which the department calls the 'academy trust') created by what the department calls a 'sponsor'. That happens through a contract with the Secretary of State that, because it takes effect under section 482 of the Education Act 1996, is then known as an academy. Section 482 says this:

> 1. The Secretary of State may enter into an agreement with any person under which –
>   (a) that person undertakes to establish and maintain, and to carry on or provide for the carrying on of an independent school in England with the characteristics mentioned in subsection (2) and such other characteristics as are specified in the agreement, and
>   (b) the Secretary of State agrees to make payments to that person in consideration of those undertakings . . .
> 2. Before entering into an agreement under this section, the Secretary of State must consult the following about the establishment of the school –
>   (a) the local education authority in whose area the school is to be situated; and
>   (b) if the Secretary of State thinks that a significant proportion of the pupils at the school is likely to be resident within the area of another local education authority, that authority.
> 3. An agreement under this section shall make any payments by the Secretary of State dependent on the fulfilment of –
>   (a) conditions and requirements imposed for the purpose of securing that no charge is made in respect of admission to (or attendance at) the school or, subject to such exceptions as may be specified in the agreement, in respect of education provided at the school, and
>   (b) such other conditions and requirements in relation to the school as are specified in the agreement.
> 4. A school to which an agreement under this section relates shall be known as an Academy.

Critically, as considered further below, the Secretary of State has struck different deals with different academy sponsors.

As the department's *Academy Principals' Handbook* puts it:[18]

> Most, but not all, Education Law applying to maintained schools does not apply (through explicit mention in the statute or regulations) to Academies. A number of legislative provisions are, however, enforced in respect of Academies through equivalent provisions in the Funding Agreement.
>
> (n.p.)

In other words, academy Funding Agreements *can* (and generally *do*) require each academy to comply with the law as it applies to mainstream schools, either by specifically referring to education legislation, or by setting out equivalent requirements. But the *Handbook*'s statement simply begs questions including, first, which legislative provisions? And, second, what is the nature of the obligations under a Funding Agreement and who can enforce those obligations?

The *Handbook* also says:

> It is important to stress, however, that the exact nature of each Academy's Funding Agreement, and indeed the composition and operation of each Trust, does vary and it is necessary to understand the documents for your specific Academy. The Department would recommend, therefore, that legal advice should be sought where necessary by the Academy Trust or the Principal in order to ensure that the obligations within the agreement are complied with fully.
>
> (n.p.)

That is good advice. But unfortunately, only a page later the *Handbook* ignores its own advice when it says:

> As mentioned above, there are a number of core conditions on funding of Academies, which do not vary. These are listed at the very start of the agreement: . . .
>
> (n.p.)
>
> c) the admissions policy and arrangements for the school will be in accordance with admissions law, and the DCSF Codes of Practice, as they apply to maintained schools;
> Subject to Variation, by agreement between the Secretary of State and the Academy Trust.

That is – presumably – an oblique reference to what has latterly become known as the Model Funding Agreement (in fact there has been more than one 'model'), as considered below. But, like the New Labour government statements above, that is not a full picture, and is thus misleading.

The early Funding Agreements

It appears that when the New Labour government first started setting up academies and when the Secretary of State first started signing Funding Agreements, each one (or at least large parts of the agreement) was developed more or less from scratch. Although the agreements were, to some extent, based on the agreements that had been used for City Technology Colleges, there was wide variation, particularly when it came to the sections (generally annexes to the main agreement) dealing with matters such as admissions, exclusions, SEN, religious education (RE) and the curriculum. That, perhaps, reflected the fact that, in those early days, there was considerable stress on academies being individual and varying one to another. Not only did those early Funding Agreements vary one to another but they also generally gave pupils considerable fewer rights than those at maintained schools (regulated, as described above, by statute).

The important thing to bear in mind is that all those agreements remain in force and still apply today for those academies unless (by agreement of the sponsor and the Secretary of State) they are varied. Three examples illustrate the problem.

1. Religion

In most of the early Funding Agreements the clauses dealing with RE, and thus the parental entitlement to withdraw their child from the religious components of the school, are in a contract annex that can be amended unilaterally by the academy. Two of these Funding Agreements do not provide for the right to withdraw at all.[19] In others the Funding Agreement allows for religious elements to extend far beyond the RE and collective worship aspects of school life, such that any right to withdraw may be extremely difficult to exercise in practice. See, for example, the Bexley City Academy Funding Agreement, which while providing for the right to withdraw from RE, provides that 'there will be cross-curricular learning of Religious Education', which will be predominantly taught through English and cultural studies but also through science, geography, history, dance and drama.

2. Exclusions

As for *permanent* exclusions, some of the early Funding Agreements copy out sections of the departmental guidance (i.e. maintained school guidance) of the time on permanent exclusions (thus setting in stone for that academy rules that change regularly in the guidance itself); others merely make provision requiring the academy to have regard to the relevant guidance (so at least the academy keeps up with the rules as they change for maintained schools).

Those which replicate large sections of the departmental guidance (such as the Funding Agreement for the Peckham Academy) usually also thereby transcribe the requirements in section 52 of the Education Act 2002 and Education (Pupil Exclusions and Appeals) (Maintained Schools) (England) Regulations 2002 *as they existed at the time.*[20] However, those which merely rely on a requirement to have regard to the exclusions guidance leave the academy in a position to decide not to follow the normal procedural protections and requirements in a particular case (the courts have made it clear[21] that a decision-maker who slavishly follows guidance on matters to which it must have regard acts unlawfully). Many have few, if any, safeguards in place in relation to the process for *fixed-term* exclusions.

Most of the early Funding Agreements allow for exclusion by the principal, followed (for permanent exclusions) by a decision by the governors, followed by an appeal (similar to maintained schools). However, the detail varies enormously. Thus, for example, while most Funding Agreements provide for an appeal against permanent exclusion to an 'independent appeal panel' composed of members not associated with the academy – albeit appointed by the academy itself and thus of reduced independence – some provide only for a final right of appeal to a different group of governors to those involved in the earlier decisions.[22]

3. Special educational needs

For SEN purposes, academies are 'mainstream' schools.[23] But if a parent wants an academy named in their child's statement of SEN, the normal statutory presumption in favour of parental preference in para. 3(3) of Sch. 27 to the 1996 Act does not apply because that only applies to maintained schools. Instead, parents must rely on section 9 of the 1996 Act, which requires that regard must be had to the 'general principle that pupils are to be educated in accordance with the wishes of their parents, so far as that is compatible with the provision of efficient instruction and training and the avoidance of unreasonable public expenditure'.

Each Funding Agreement will also put in place further legal rules that vary from academy to academy.[24] If there is a dispute, parents can ask the Special Educational Needs and Disability Tribunal (now part of the First-tier Tribunal's Health and Social Care Chamber) to order that the academy be named.[25]

Once a pupil is admitted to an academy, most – but not all (as above) – Funding Agreements currently require the academy to have regard to the SEN Code of Practice and the departmental guidance on inclusion. All the current Funding Agreements require that pupils with statements of SEN receive the provision detailed in their statements, but the local authority, or LA (not a party to the Funding Agreement), remains responsible under statute for arranging such provision. It cannot, however, put in place and enforce arrangements under its financial delegation scheme[26] to ensure that an academy makes the provision in the statement of SEN (see para. 8.6, SEN Code of Practice) as it could do for a maintained school.

Thus, if an academy did not make the special educational provision specified in a child's statement of SEN, the LA's only recourse would be to invite the Secretary of State to exercise his/her powers under the Funding Agreement – a far weaker lever. The LA (and thus the child) is in the worst possible position when it comes to ensuring that the provision specified in a statement is actually made: if the child were in a maintained school, the LA could exercise control under its scheme of delegation; if the child were placed by the LA in a conventional independent school (as many with the greatest needs are), the LA would at least have powers under its contract with the independent school in question; but, at an academy, the LA has no mechanism of control other than (as above) to ask the Secretary of State to exercise his/her powers under the Funding Agreement.

Overall

The ministerial commitment to legal equivalence in SEN, admissions, exclusions and so on has simply not been fully seen through. And as above, those are not just matters of historical interest; a Funding Agreement is a contract that remains until the parties agree to change its terms (unless an Act of parliament overrules the contract position). But, as seen from the copies of Funding Agreements on the department's website, the original agreements remain in place, warts and all. I have been told that the department has proposed amendments, but academies have apparently refused (as a party to an agreement is entitled to do) to agree to changes.

One notable exception is where some structural change created a wider need to amend a particular Funding Agreement. That happened when the agreement for Haberdashers' Aske's Hatcham Academy had to be amended in 2008 when the academy expanded to absorb Monson Primary School. At that point, the department took the opportunity to improve the provisions in the contract relating to various things including appeals against permanent exclusion. However, it also – perhaps inadvertently – removed the limited ability previously enjoyed by the Haberdashers' Aske's Hatcham Academy (and enjoyed by all maintained schools[27]) to refuse to admit a pupil who had been permanently excluded from two other schools.

The emergence of a 'model'

Perhaps as a response to that variability (either variability between one Funding Agreement and another and or between the provisions made in Funding Agreements for academies and the position in maintained schools) the department then started to develop what it has called the Model Funding Agreement.

But there is not just one model.

The model has changed over time (the latest New Labour model is dated January 2010, the previous was October 2009, the one before that June 2009), sometimes shortly after (and responding to) comments made on the model of the time in the course of cases brought in court challenging the establishment of various academies,[28] or, perhaps, changes of political approach to academies, or maybe just of past problems with the previous model.

But any particular Funding Agreement will have been based on the terms of whichever model existed at the time of negotiation. Even the latest model makes clear that there is scope for negotiation on even basic provisions. See clause 13 of the January 2010 model:

> Conditions of grant
> General
>
> 13) Section 482(4) of the Education Act 1996 provides for the agreement to specify other conditions and requirements. These conditions in respect of the Academy are that:
> a) the school will be at the heart of its community, sharing facilities with other schools and the wider community;
> b) there will be assessment in the core subjects of the national curriculum at Key Stage 3, and the opportunity to study for external qualifications as defined by section 96 of the Learning and Skills Act 2000;
> c) the admissions policy and arrangements for the school will be in accordance with admissions law, and the DCSF Codes of Practice, as they apply to maintained schools;
> d) teachers will be required to have qualified teacher status; levels of pay and conditions of service for all employees will be the responsibility of the Academy Trust;
> e) there will be an emphasis on the needs of the individual pupils including pupils with special education needs (SEN), both those with and without statements of SEN;
> f) there will be no charge in respect of admission to the school and the school will only charge pupils where the law allows maintained schools to charge.

But the footnote to that entire section makes clear that it is 'Subject to Variation, by agreement between the Secretary of State and the Academy Trust'. So not much is guaranteed even when the academy is established.

But the legal requirements can change even after that. For example, the detailed model obligations in relation to pupils with SEN and disabilities are set out in Annex C of the current model and thus of academies whose Funding Agreements are based on that model (Annex 3 in older models/ agreements). But that annex is given life in the agreements by their clause 22(a), which explains that

> [t]he admission to the Academy of and support for pupils with SEN and with disabilities (for pupils who have and who do not have statements of SEN) (including the appointment of a responsible person) together with the arrangements for making changes to such arrangements, including the requirement to secure the consent of the Secretary of State, *such consent not to be unreasonably withheld or delayed*, are set out in Annex C to this Agreement. [Emphasis added.]

In other words, if an academy whose Funding Agreement had been based on that model wants to change the arrangements for pupils with SEN (including the admissions arrangements – a particularly controversial issue for many academies) they would, of course, need the Secretary of State's consent, but he could not 'unreasonably' withhold that consent. That would give very wide latitude to such an academy to insist on changing, say, the basis on which it admitted children with SEN or disabilities, or the provision it made for them. A maintained school could not do that.

In any event, it is the position under the most recent New Labour model agreement (rather than any actual agreements, let alone *all* actual agreements) that the department and politicians describe when commenting on the position at academies. Thus, they talk as if all academies operated on the basis of the latest model. But that is simply not how it works. Thus, for example, when the department says that all academies have to have regard to the SEN Code of Practice, that is the position under the later model agreements and in later academies, but – as above – it is not universal. And certainly, the position promised by Ministers – as above – has simply not come about.

So the take-home message is: check the Funding Agreement for the particular academy of interest and don't rely on any generalizations about the position in academies.

Overall on Funding Agreements

The Funding Agreements for the later academies have rules that look ever closer to those in maintained schools.[29] But even now, there are still plenty of differences. Here are some examples.

Admissions

As above, a maintained school can refuse to admit a pupil who has been permanently excluded from two schools. But para. 37 of Annex B of even the latest Model Funding Agreement (changes having been made to Annex B in the January 2010 version) says:

> The Academy Trust will consider all applications for places at the [] Academy. Where fewer than the published admission number(s) for the relevant year groups are received, the Academy Trust will offer places at the [] Academy to all those who have applied.

In other words, an academy with a Funding Agreement using those provisions would be required by that agreement to admit all applicants if it was undersubscribed. Its Funding Agreement would not allow it to refuse entry to a pupil who had been permanently excluded from two schools in the previous two years.

Discipline

The governing body of a maintained school is required to consult parents and pupils and to produce a written statement of general principles to promote good behaviour and discipline at the school.[30] The headteacher must produce a behaviour policy (including specifying disciplinary penalties) taking into account those principles.[31] The result is that parents and pupils in such a school at least know where they stand when it comes to discipline and behaviour.

But that does not apply to academies. I have seen lawyers acting for academies argue that they are not required even to provide copies of their discipline policies to parents/pupils.

Complaints

Parents of pupils in maintained schools can complain about the actions of the school's governing body to the local authority.[32] There is no equivalent for academies.

The curriculum

Maintained schools are required to provide the national curriculum.[33] The headteacher of a maintained school can temporarily exempt an individual pupil but must notify parents if they do so, and parents can appeal against 'disapplication'.[34]

None of that applies to an academy. The curriculum obligations on an academy were, in the early days, almost non-existent. Later Funding Agreements impose more detailed obligations, coming closer to the requirements of the national curriculum. But, even where the latest New Labour 'model' provisions have been adopted, pupils or groups of pupils can be exempted from the curriculum at the school on a wider basis than would be the case in a maintained school, and without any right of appeal by parents against that decision.

Enforcing the Funding Agreement

As explained above, working out the legal framework applicable in an academy is not straightforward. But even when you know what the rules require for the academy in question, what really matters is enforcing them. The Secretary of State and the Department do not seem to comment on that.

As above, the Funding Agreement for any particular academy is – in law – a contract between the Secretary of State and the sponsor. The general legal position is that only the parties to a contract can enforce that contract. So the Secretary of State could, if necessary, bring an action in the County Court or High Court for breach of contract to challenge the academy's failure to act in accordance with its Funding Agreement. If successful, the court might award damages to the Secretary of State for the breach. In an extreme case the court might make an order for 'specific performance', i.e. requiring action.

So if, for example, an academy permanently excluded a pupil without adhering to the procedures in its Funding Agreement, the Secretary of State could sue, and ask for damages or, exceptionally, ask the court to order the academy to comply with the requirements of the contract. But neither the parent nor the pupil (nor, generally, the local authority) is a party to that contract and they would struggle to use the contract claim to enforce their rights.[35]

As far as I am aware, the Department has never actually publicly explained how it intends that a parent or pupil could go about forcing an academy to do what the Funding Agreement says. In practice, a parent or pupil would be likely to contemplate a judicial review of the academy. That is, after all, what a parent/pupil would do[36] if a problem arose at a maintained school. Such problems are, thankfully, rare – it is unusual for a school not to comply with the law. But that is partly because maintained schools know (or should know) that if they do not do what the law requires of them, court action can be brought.

So what about an equivalent judicial review of an academy? The first issue is whether it is actually possible to bring a judicial review of an academy at all. The answer is probably yes. However, the test for whether any particular body is subject to judicial review is subtle (private bodies are generally not subject because judicial review is about challenging the legality of action by public bodies). We get some comfort from a case in which the Bacon City Technology College (CTC) was challenged in a judicial review action in the High Court (just as a maintained school could be).[37] CTCs are/were, in law, similar in some ways to academies. The court accepted that Bacon CTC was indeed subject to judicial review, but Bacon CTC had not disputed the point so the case does not have huge precedent value.

That said I am also aware of instances in which parents have challenged the legality of action by academies – including alleging breaches of Funding Agreements – in which lawyers for the academies in question have specifically rejected the suggestion that their client academies are subject to judicial review. The Secretary of State has reserved his position on the point. But the point has never been directly tested in court in a disputed case because those cases have been resolved without ever actually getting to court.

But even if an academy can be judicially reviewed, that still does not necessarily mean that a parent/pupil can force the academy to comply with its Funding Agreement. In particular, they would – at best – have a legally enforceable 'legitimate expectation'[38] that the academy would comply with its Funding Agreement. In other words, they would be trying to hold the academy to the promises it had made (in the Funding Agreement) to the Secretary of State. But the legal doctrine of legitimate expectation is not absolute: public bodies are allowed to break their promises if they have a legitimate and 'proportionate' reason to do so.

What about when the law changes?

As we all know, education law changes frequently. Thus, for example (as mentioned above), new rules came into force on 1 September 2009 specifying minimum qualifications for SENCOs. But only in maintained schools, because the provision of the Education Act that allowed the Secretary of State to make the regulations only applies to maintained schools. If the Secretary of State wanted to impose the same requirement on existing academies, he would have to renegotiate each existing Funding Agreement or get parliament to amend the legislation to also cover academies.

Other legal obligations

Of course schools are not just subject to *education* law, as such. There are also general legal requirements, which apply more widely and thus potentially to schools too: equality/discrimination law, the Human Rights Act, freedom of information law, and so on. How do they bite on academies?

Equality/discrimination law

The Sex Discrimination Act 1975, Race Relations Act 1976 and Disability Discrimination Act 1995 outlaw discrimination by all schools, including independent schools and, thus, academies. The Race Relations Act 1976 also imposes more promotional 'race equality duties' on a long list of public bodies which specifically includes academies. The Sex Discrimination Act 1975 and Disability Discrimination Act 1995 do not use a list, instead imposing similar obligations on 'public authorities'. It is likely that the courts would hold that academies were caught by that obligation, but I have seen academies reserve the right to argue the contrary.

The Human Rights Act

Similarly, the Human Rights Act 1998 requires 'public authorities' to 'act compatibly' with 'Convention rights'. It is likely that the courts would hold academies to be caught by that.[39] But again, I have seen academies, and even the Secretary of State, reserve their position (January 2009):

> [T]he Secretary of State accepts for the purpose of the present proceedings that the Academy and the IAP are bodies which are amendable to Judicial Review and are public authorities for the purposes of the Human Rights Act 1998. This acceptance is for the present proceedings and should not be taken as an indication of the Secretary of State's position in any other case.

Freedom of information

Academies are bound by the requirements of the Data Protection Act 1998, like any other organization. So (among other things), they are obliged to provide 'personal data'[40] to the person to whom it relates. However, the Freedom of Information Act 2000 (FOIA) provides a right (albeit subject to some qualifications) of public access to non-personal information held by listed public authorities. The list includes maintained schools, but not academies. The Ministry of Justice, the responsible government department, having consulted on whether to add academies to the list decided nothing and simply said this on 16 July 2009:

> The Ministry of Justice will work with the Department for Children, Schools and Families to ensure that the Government consults academies (or their representatives) about including academies in an initial section 5 order, so that they are subject to the Act in the same way as the governing bodies of maintained schools in England and Wales.[41]

I have seen lawyers acting for academies rely on the non-application of the FOIA, refusing even to provide copies of school policies to parents. And some academies are reported to be relying on the non-applicability of the FOIA to refuse to provide the full details of exam results that would be required to properly analyse their performance.[42]

How are academies established?

Section 7 of the Education and Inspections Act sets out the framework through which an LA can invite proposals from persons wishing to establish new schools in their area. The schools in question can be maintained schools or an academy. If an LA goes down that route, there is a 'competition' in which there is open consultation and the LA then selects from among the proposals (unless it has itself proposed to establish a community school, in which case the decision is made by an adjudicator). Such competitions are the only way in which new maintained schools can be established.[43]

But, even though academies can be promoted in that way within the competition framework, they can also come forward entirely separately from it, and thus without any of the statutory consultation and other procedures required for competitions, nor anything equivalent.[44] The only statutory process for actually creating an academy[45] is that specified in section 482(3) of the 1996 Act, namely consultation by the Secretary of State with affected local authorities.

That said, the Department publishes guidance on what are known as 'expressions of interest', or EOI (as to which, see below), which explains that once an EOI has been approved an academy project passes into a 'Feasibility Phase': 'The Feasibility Stage provides an opportunity for the LA to consult locally on the Academy proposal and a chance to explore in detail the information and ideas set out in the EOI.'[46] But none of those phrases has any statutory meaning and none of those phases has any external legal status. Nor, of course, does 'an opportunity for the LA to consult locally' necessarily translate into an obligation for an LA to do so. So an academy proposal can – in theory at least – come forward without any public consultation.[47]

In practice, however, many academies have been established to replace one or more maintained schools. In that case, the extensive statutory procedures[48] involved in the closure (known as the 'discontinuance') of the maintained school(s) in question must still be gone through. Those procedures require that where an LA proposes to discontinue a school, it must first consult, then it must publish formal proposals on which representations may be made, then it must consider whether to approve the proposals. The formal published proposals (often described as a 'statutory notice') must specify certain information including 'details' of the replacement provision that will be made for the pupils at the school.

Plainly, if a maintained school is being replaced by (i.e. discontinued in anticipation of) an academy, then the details in question will be the details of the replacement activity. It might be thought that, given the Funding Agreement for the contemplated academy is the document which (as above) defines the academy, then publication of, and thus consultation based on, the proposed Funding Agreement would follow. But the courts have said not,[49] instead accepting, at least on the facts of the particular case, that it is sufficient for the LA to publicize the EOI, particularly given that (latterly) the Model Funding Agreement was available on the DCSF website. However, as the departmental guidance explains:

> The EOI form is designed to provide all the key details about the proposed Academy project to the Department for Children, Schools and Families (the Department). It informs officials' and Ministers' decisions about whether the project should proceed to the next stage (Feasibility).[46]

The EOI form is not a contract. However, signatures from the sponsor, co-sponsor(s) and LA are required to sign off the final version of the EOI before Ministers decide whether the project continues into the Feasibility Stage to show the agreement of all parties. Academy projects cannot pass on to the Feasibility Stage until the Department has received a completed and signed EOI.[50]

In other words, the EOI has no external legal status. And certainly, there can be no guarantee that what was proposed in it will actually be the basis for the Funding Agreement, which is what matters.[51] Nor, as above, can the 'model' Funding Agreement be relied on as necessarily being what will end up in the final (and legally operative) Funding Agreement.

Conclusions

Generalizations about the academies and the law are not possible because, for example, the rights and obligations of parents/pupils at academies (as set out in statutes and, more importantly, the Funding Agreement for the particular academy) vary from one academy to the next. Sweeping statements made by the department and by politicians generally (if not invariably) describe the position as it would be if all Funding Agreements were based on the latest model, which they are not. Such statements can thus be very misleading. The department is well aware of the problem but persists in producing and allowing documents and statements which thus mislead.

The early Funding Agreements were particularly variable and gave parents/pupils very different rights (generally much weaker rights) than the equivalent position in maintained schools. As part, presumably, of the wider change of attitude by the New Labour governments to academies,[52] newer academies have Funding Agreements based on (but not necessarily identical to) the the most recent New Labour 'model'. The model has varied over time. The latest academies offer a position much closer to that in maintained schools. But there are still important differences, including the fact that the Secretary of State cannot 'unreasonably withhold' his agreement to a request to change key provisions.

Parents/pupils also have fewer rights (including of information, consultation and transparency of process) when it comes to establishing academies than would be the case for establishing maintained schools: the process is less participative, less democratic, less transparent, less consultative and offers fewer safeguards.

Given that the legal regime at any particular academy is mostly determined by the details of its Funding Agreement, any significant change to academies overall (either to bring them all into line with the latest thinking and thus closer to the position in maintained schools or to return – as the Conservatives seem to advocate in opposition – to a more relaxed regime) would either require all the existing agreements to be individually renegotiated, or legislative intervention. In taking office in May 2010 the Coalition has changed the process by which academies are created through the Academies Act 2010. The research imperative is to examine the legal framework regarding how all maintained schools can now become academies. There is a new model agreement, but the position for the academies created under New Labour remains as I have described.

Notes

1 With particular thanks to Richard Stein and Rosa Curling of Leigh Day & Co solicitors, London.

2 A chapter of this length could not possibly describe all the various rights and obligations of pupils/parents, let alone be comprehensive in describing how they vary from one academy to the next. The law described only applies, of course, in England.

3 Legal issues also, of course, arise for the employees of academies. And the

governance arrangements of academies also engage issues of company law and charity law.

4 *School Admissions Code*, 2009, para. 1.52.

5 *Academy Principals' Handbook*, Section 8. Available at: www.standards.dfes.gov.uk/academies/publications/

6 Para. 3.30.

7 Hansard, House of Commons, Standing Committee G, column 423; see also Lord McIntosh Hansard, House of Lords, 23 May 2003, column 994 and 995.

8 Section 88A of the School Standards and Framework Act 1998 only applies to maintained schools and not, as explained below, to academies. Some academies have that obligation incorporated into their Funding Agreements, but others do not. The obligation to have regard to the SEN Code of Practice and the statutory guidance on inclusion does not apply to all academies – indeed, it was notably not even applied to some of the academies set up immediately following the ministerial commitments to ensure that academies would be required to comply with the law relating to special educational needs as it applies to maintained schools (see Peckham Academy [August 2002], West London Academy [June 2003], Stockley Academy [November 2003]). While some academies could lawfully refuse to admit a pupil on the grounds that he/she had been permanently excluded from two other schools, others could not – they would have to admit.

9 School Standards and Framework Act 1998, section 22.

10 Section 317(3A), Education Act 1996, as added by section 173 of the Education and Inspections Act 2006; Education (Special Educational Needs Co-ordinators) (England) Regulations 2008, which came into force on 1 September 2009. Consultation on the draft regulations had recognized the need for such measures thus:

> Special educational needs co-ordinators (SENCOs) play a key role within schools to ensure effective provision for children with SEN and disabilities. They are also an important point of contact with parents. The importance of their role was recognised in the statutory SEN Code of Practice (November 2001) and in the (third) report of the then Education and Skills Select Committee on SEN (July 2006). In its report, the Select Committee recorded a number of concerns and recommendations in relation to the qualifications, status and training of SENCOs, which Ministers accepted.

11 School Standards and Framework Act 1998, Part III.

12 Education Act 2002, section 52; Education (Pupil Exclusion and Appeals) (Maintained Schools) (England) Regulations 2002.

13 Education Act 2002, Part 6.

14 Examples include forcing a school to admit a pupil, forcing a school to make the special educational provision specified in a statement of SEN, challenging a school's decision to ban a parent from the school, or challenging a school's uniform policy.

15 SI 2003/1910.

16 See, for example, the challenge to the exclusion of a boy from Marlborough College: *Gray* v. *Marlborough College* [2006] ELR 516, CA.

17 For example, section 43 of the Education Act 1997 (as amended) requires academies, like maintained schools, to provide careers education; the obligation on a maintained school to provide education to an excluded pupil (section 100, Education and Inspections Act 2006) also expressly applies to academies.

[18] Available at: www.standards.dfes.gov.uk/academies/publications/

[19] See Funding Agreements for Peckham Academy and St Francis of Assisi Academy.

[20] For example, in 2004 the Education (Pupil Exclusions and Appeals) (Maintained Schools) (England) Regulations 2002 were amended by SI 2004/402 to provide that the standard of proof in an exclusion to which those regulations apply was the civil standard of proof. But that amendment would not apply to an academy whose Funding Agreement was not framed to keep pace with changes to the 2002 regulations because, for example, it had encapsulated the form of the regulations as they had originally existed. In such an academy, the criminal standard of proof (beyond reasonable doubt) would apply in accordance with the decision of the Court of Appeal in *YP* [2003] EWCA Civ 1306 (cf *VG* v. *IAP for Tom Hood School* [2010] EWCA Civ 142).

[21] See, for example, *S* v. *LB Brent* [2002] ELR 566.

[22] See the Funding Agreements for Haberdashers' Aske's Knights Academy and Capital City Academy. It was also the case in the original version of the Haberdashers' Aske's Hatcham Academy Funding Agreement but that is a rare example of an agreement which has been amended and, from 5 August 2008, provision was made for *independent* appeal panels at Haberdashers' Aske's Hatcham.

[23] Education Act 1996, sections 316–316A.

[24] Many Funding Agreements require the academy to consent to a child with a statement being admitted unless admitting the child would not be incompatible with the education of other children and there are no reasonable steps which can be taken to remove the incompatibility.

[25] I have recent personal experience of Special Educational Needs and Disability Tribunal appeals in relation to two different academies where the academies (with the agreement of the local authority) were – quite unlawfully – operating admissions arrangements for children with statements of SEN which conflicted with the requirements of their Funding Agreements.

[26] School Standards and Framework Act 1998, section 48.

[27] School Standards and Framework Act 1998, sections 86–87.

[28] For example, a new 'model' was produced in the summer of 2006 following, and apparently responding to, criticisms made of the previous model by the claimant in *P* v. *Adjudicator* [2006] EWHC 1934.

[29] For example, the model now proposes that 'the Academy Trust shall act and shall ensure that the Principal shall act in accordance with the law on exclusions as if the Academy were a maintained school.'

[30] Education and Inspections Act 2006, section 88.

[31] Education and Inspections Act 2006, section 89.

[32] Education Act 1996, section 409.

[33] Education Act 2002, Part 6.

[34] Education Act 2002, sections 90–93.

[35] Section 1 of the Contracts (Rights of Third Parties) Act 1999 allows a person who is not a party to a contract to enforce a term of it which purports to confer a benefit on him. But this is likely in practice to be of little assistance to parents/pupils because legal aid is unlikely to be available to bring a claim to enforce contractual rights and, in any event, a successful claim would be likely to lead, at best, to an order for damages, rather than 'specific performance' of the obligation in question.

[36] Assuming that less aggressive measures, such as the use of complaints procedures, had failed.

[37] *W* v. *Governors of Bacon CTC* [1998] ELR 488

38 See, for example, *Nadarajah and another* v. *Secretary of State for the Home Department* [2005] EWCA Civ 1363:

> Where a public authority has issued a promise or adopted a practice which represents how it proposes to act in a given area, the law will require the promise or practice to be honoured unless there is good reason not to do so.

The argument would be that the Funding Agreement amounts to such a promise.

39 See *YL* v. *Birmingham City Council* [2007] UKHL 27, [2008] 1 AC 95; and *Weaver* v. *Quadrant Housing* [2009] EWCA Civ 587.

40 Data Protection Act 1998, section 1.

41 www.justice.gov.uk/consultations/docs/consultation-response-_section5.pdf

42 See 14 December 2009 BBC News article, 'Academies accused of dumbing down'. Available at: http://news.bbc.co.uk/1/hi/education/8408787.stm

43 Education and Inspections Act 2006, section 28(1)(a).

44 See *Chandler* v. *Camden* [2009] EWHC 219 (Admin).

45 Ignoring matters which relate purely to, say, the building, such as planning permission requirements.

46 Expressions of Interest Guidance document, available at: www.standards.dcsf.gov.uk/academiesprojectmanagement/eoi/

47 The EU public procurement regime does not apply to the process by which the Secretary of State selects a sponsor: *Chandler* v. *Secretary of State* [2009] EWCA Civ 1011, but see the Court of Justice judgement in Case C-305/08 CoNISMa of 23 December 2009.

48 Education and Inspections Act 2006, Part 2 and Sch. 2.

49 *Elphinstone* v. *Westminster* [2008] EWCA Civ 1069.

50 Expressions of Interest Guidance document, available at: www.standards.dcsf.gov.uk/academiesprojectmanagement/eoi/

51 Indeed, there have been examples where the EOI has been published with one potential sponsor being contemplated but, in the end, the Funding Agreement is entered into by another (Sheppey Academy).

52 See the Introduction to this collection for an overview of recent changes to the Academies Programme.

Chapter 2

Local Government against Local Democracy: A Case Study of a Bid for Building Schools for the Future Funding for an Academy

Richard Hatcher

Introduction

The proposal to establish an academy, contested by a local campaign of opposition and entailing, unlike any other education policy initiative, an element of local public consultation, provides an exceptionally revealing insight into the process by which education policy is translated from the national to the local level, and the role of local government in the process. This chapter is based on a case study of the progress of Staffordshire County Council's bid for £100 million of Building Schools for the Future (BSF) government funding for Tamworth, including an academy, during the period 2007–9. Tamworth is a town of some 75,000 inhabitants in Staffordshire Local Authority, with five 11–18 secondary schools. Staffordshire County Council (SCC) was Labour-led until the Conservatives won the elections in June 2009.

I have been researching developments in Tamworth since the Hands Off Tamworth Schools (HOTS) campaign began in September 2008. HOTS is a parent-led campaign which has published leaflets and policy documents, held several public meetings of up to 100 people, collected hundreds of petition signatures, and won 1,848 votes for its six candidates in all six Tamworth wards in the county council elections on 4 June 2009, which represented 10 per cent of the total vote. My data sources principally comprise SCC documentation, HOTS publications and numerous internal emails, interviews with key campaign figures and field notes from consultation events.[1] I have had some personal involvement in the campaign, including as a speaker at three of its public meetings. The analysis in this chapter builds on my two previous studies of contested academy policy processes (Hatcher and Jones, 2006; Hatcher, 2008a).

My starting point is the conception of the policy process in education as a field of contestation in which opposition and resistance to policy, actual or potential, are constituent elements. In that context I conceptualize the local policy process to set up an academy as the product of a particular governance regime. The term 'governance' encompasses a complex range of meanings in contemporary public sector discourse. In brief, it refers to governing which utilizes a repertoire of hierarchical, market and network co-ordinating mechanisms involving state and non-state actors and agencies. A specific governance regime 'is assembled from a range of specific technologies, discourses, practices, and "empowered" actors. Each is also likely to privilege particular logics of decision-making and particular forms of practice' (Newman and Clarke, 2009, p. 127).

The governance regime in question is the alliance of SCC, the Department for Children, Schools and Families (DCSF), and Landau Forte, the would-be academy sponsors, and the strategy they adopted to utilize the procedures of local government to translate the BSF proposal from formation to implementation. It is an example of what I have elsewhere called (Hatcher, 2008a) a state governance network, comprising a coalition of actors from the local state (both elected councillors and officers), national government and the private sector.

In the case of the BSF policy process I conceptualize the governance regime as comprising two elements: a policy discourse and a process of regulative framing.

The policy discourse refers to the cognitive framing of the academy proposal: how it is conceptualized, presented and justified. However, the focus of this chapter is on the process of regulative framing. I am using the term regulative framing – adapted from Bernstein's concept of framing (e.g. Bernstein, 1990) – to refer to the principle of political control of the policy process. It can range from closed framing, unilaterally imposing policy, to open framing, inviting meaningful and inclusive participation in negotiated decision-making. Regulative framing comprises both discursive and non-discursive or coercive elements.

An analysis of the Tamworth BSF process raises two interrelated issues central to the field of urban governance theory: conflict and democracy. Local democratic renewal through popular participation has been a theme of New Labour rhetoric for over a decade (DCLG, 2008). It finds an echo in what Davies (2005, p. 312) calls 'orthodox' urban governance theory, which sees it as the basis of a progressive consensus in local politics. However, the imposition of an academy in the face of widespread local opposition puts into question not only the integrity of the consultation process but the democratic credentials of local government, and poses the question of whether the policy of academies and popular opposition to them can best be explained in terms of incompatible class interests. Exploring these issues involves a double movement: analysis of the academy process is illuminated by situating it in the wider context of urban politics and in turn can make a contribution to debates within urban governance theory.

The regulative framing of the BSF proposal

The origins of the Tamworth BSF proposal lie in 2007. Woodhouse High School, one of the five Tamworth secondary schools, was in 'special measures'. In May 2007 the schools commissioner, Sir Bruce Liddington, whose remit included developing early academy proposals, recommended that Landau Forte should assist Woodhouse High School in coming out of 'special measures'. Landau Forte is a charitable trust and is the sponsor of an 11–18 academy in Derby, a nearby local authority. In July 2007 a meeting took place between Liddington, representatives of Landau Forte, Peter Traves, Staffordshire's corporate director for Children and Lifelong Learning, and Lord Adonis, at the time the government's Minister responsible for academies. Thereafter followed a series of at least six meetings of the various proponents that culminated on 11 April 2008 when SCC submitted its BSF Strategy for Change document, entitled Readiness to Deliver (SCC, 2008a), to the DCSF. By then the proposal comprised the closure of one of the five secondary schools, Queen Elizabeth's Mercian School (QEMS), the removal of the sixth forms from the remaining four schools and their replacement by a sixth-form centre, and the establishing of an academy, sponsored by Landau Forte, to run both Woodhouse High School and the sixth-form centre. The DCSF approved the proposal in June 2008.

What I am interested in is the role of the constitutional structures and procedures of local government in the formation of the bid. The first reference to it was when it was tabled at the SCC cabinet meeting, comprising five leading councillors, on 16 April 2008. There are two remarkable things about this meeting. The first is that it was the first time that any SCC body had discussed the BSF bid, and that it did so a week *after* the BSF proposal was submitted to the DCSF (and some nine months after unpublicized discussions about an academy began). In other words, the bid did not go through any council body for discussion or approval before being submitted to the DCSF: it was submitted personally by the deputy leader of the council, Robert Simpson, who was responsible for the BSF bid, under his delegated authority.

The second remarkable feature is that the proposal document itself, *Readiness to Deliver*, was not presented to cabinet. What was tabled instead was a document called Manifesto for Change (SCC, 2008b), which comprised a set of educational objectives for Staffordshire but made no mention at all of the proposals for Tamworth including the academy, even though the minutes of the cabinet meeting state that this document (not *Readiness to Deliver*) would be the basis for public consultation. Regarding the BSF bid itself, the minutes state only that the submission of the bid 'be noted'. No discussion is recorded. A consultation document containing the actual BSF proposals, including the academy, (*Consultation Proposals for Tamworth*, SCC, 2008c), was not published until November 2008.

Following the cabinet meeting in April 2008 the next council body to receive a report on the BSF bid was the Children and Young People Scrutiny and Performance Panel (hereafter referred to as Children's Scrutiny) on 17 June 2008, but there was no mention of the specific proposal for an academy and no mention in the minutes of any discussion. The first report to Children's Scrutiny that included the actual proposal was on 22 July 2008, a month after it had been approved by the DCSF and again with no discussion noted. Thereafter there was no further reference to the BSF bid at Children's Scrutiny meetings until the meetings in January, February and March 2009, where brief reports were given on the stage reached in the policy process: there was no mention of the issues that had arisen during the six-week period for consultation meetings, which had concluded in January, and no discussion was noted.

Cabinet itself had no further discussion of the BSF proposal after April 2008 until it took a report of the consultation process on 28 January 2009 and decided to approve the original proposal, in spite of strong objections by, among others, HOTS and the headteachers of the five secondary schools. This led to a 'call-in' of the cabinet decision by four Conservative councillors, perhaps prompted by a request by HOTS documenting their concerns with the consultation process, which enabled the decision to be questioned at the meeting of the Corporate Policies Scrutiny and Performance Committee on 10 February 2009. This was the only occasion on which the BSF proposal featured on the agenda of the Corporate Policies Scrutiny and Performance Committee, and the only occasion on which there was any debate or expression of dissenting views recorded in any council body.

The four councillors raised several issues, including opposition to the sixth-form centre being run as an academy, preferring two sixth-form centres run co-operatively by the schools. As Councillor Simpson pointed out at the meeting, this was the first time that Conservative councillors had raised any objections to a proposal first published nearly a year earlier. In that context the most likely explanation for the four Conservative councillors' departure from their national leadership's policy of creating more academies is that it took place four months before the county elections in June 2009 and they saw some electoral advantage in being seen to be responsive to the widespread public opposition to the BSF proposals. Prior to the election the Conservatives promised a review of the BSF proposals. Ian Parry, one of the four councillors and a member of the Children's Scrutiny and Performance Committee, stated, 'It is my Party's intention, should we win the County Council election in June, to prefer two 6th Forms for Tamworth under the shared governance of the local high schools and not the Academy' (email from Ian Parry to HOTS member, 29 March 2009). But shortly after the

Conservatives won control of the council Parry, now the new lead member for Children and Lifelong Learning, gave a BSF Programme Review report to cabinet on 15 July 2009 which accepted Labour's BSF plan with only some minor additions.

The statutory six-week representation period ended on 1 April and the BSF proposal, unaltered from the January cabinet meeting, received final approval from cabinet on 8 April 2009.

The failure of scrutiny

From the point of view of local government as a site of public deliberative democracy the regulative framing of the policy process was a particularly closed one, in two ways. First, during the period of at least nine months leading up to the formulation and submission of the academy proposal to the DCSF, while negotiations took place in secret between leading council figures, the sponsors and the government, the proposal was not discussed by any formal body of SCC: not by the council itself, not by cabinet, and not by either the Children's Scrutiny or the Corporate Policies Scrutiny and Performance Committee.

The second issue is the absence of discussion at the meetings where the proposal was reported on, even when it had become apparent, from September 2008 onwards, that there was considerable public debate and opposition. In particular it puts into question the function of the scrutiny committees within SCC. The White Paper *Local Leadership, Local Choice* (DETR, 1999) outlined the government's expectations that

> the new forms of local governance will ensure that a council's affairs are conducted openly and subject to effective scrutiny. Councillors, local media, and others interested will be helped by these new forms of governance to question those taking decisions and to hold them to account as never before. Open and accountable decision taking will become a reality.
>
> (para. 3.59)

Clearly Children's Scrutiny failed to fulfil this function with regard to the Tamworth BSF bid. It contrasts strongly with the role it played in the policy process to establish the JCB Academy at Rocester, in another part of Staffordshire, which took place during the same time period. Discussions took place on this proposal at Children's Scrutiny on numerous occasions from 2007 onwards, including a presentation by representatives of JCB at the 17 January 2008 meeting. In contrast, Landau Forte was not required to make a presentation to Children's Scrutiny or any other SCC body. The explanation for the discrepancy would seem to be that, unlike the JCB Academy, which did not affect existing schools or provoke opposition, the

Tamworth proposal entailed a fundamental change in the town's whole secondary school system, which would create widespread public opposition; the council leadership decided to avoid it by keeping the proposal secret for as long as possible, and the members of Children's Scrutiny acquiesced. According to Di Richards, Staffordshire National Union of Teachers divisional secretary at the time:

> There's been nothing in terms of opposition and I think it is because they have only been fed this '£100 million pounds investment, we would have to have an Academy, Landau Forte are wonderful, we are keen on them, we have already been working with them'.
>
> (Interview)

I asked Julie, one of the parent leaders of HOTS, what she had learned about the local council during the campaign.

> What I have learnt as time's gone on is that there are very few councillors with expertise in those particular areas so they by and large take it as read when people tell them something. They don't appear to me anyway to have dug beneath the surface in more detail.
>
> (Interview)

A significant additional contributory factor was the exclusion of teachers' union representatives, who would certainly have questioned the BSF plans, from a role with speaking rights on the scrutiny committees (unlike in some other authorities).

Overall, the Tamworth experience provides forceful confirmation of Ashworth and Snape's (2004) review of the research evidence on the effectiveness of scrutiny in local government: that 'scrutiny has not yet developed into a robust accountability mechanism and therefore the work of local executives remains relatively unchecked' (p. 553).

The regulative framing of the consultation process

If the first phase of the BSF process took place, largely in secret, from the spring of 2007 till the summer of 2008, the second phase centred on the period of public consultation meetings, which ran for six weeks, from 10 November 2008 to 15 January 2009. There were three meetings at each secondary school, one for staff, one for governors and one for parents and community. (In addition there were meetings at six primary schools, with a different format.) Here I focus on the secondary school parents and community meetings. Attendance at the five schools was as follows: 11 at Belgrave, 60 at Wilnecote, 85 at Woodhouse, 105 at Rawlett, 450 at Queen

Mary's Mercian School (the school threatened with closure). In addition, two consultation meetings for parents and others specifically about the replacement of Woodhouse High School by an academy took place on 18 March 2009, attended by approximately 180 people.

The consultation process exposed the BSF proposal and its proponents to extensive criticism by HOTS supporters and other parents, teachers, school students and community members. In consequence the consultation meetings required careful management. A standard format for the consultation process for BSF proposals is recommended by government and was followed by SCC in Tamworth. The consultation process was not conceived as a process of deliberative democracy (DCSF, 2007). Consultation only took place once the academy proposal was at an advanced stage (DCSF, n.d.a). The consultation meeting period was short: six weeks. Consultation was structured around the 'preferred option' approved by the DCSF, not a range of options. There was no provision for a formal and equal presentation of dissenting and alternative views to balance the carefully managed presentation of the proposal (DfES, 2003c).

At each school the parents and community meetings had the same format, which was also followed at the additional two consultation meetings at Woodhouse about the proposal to turn it into an academy, except that, unlike at the other meetings, the platform included representatives of Landau Forte. New institutional theory draws attention to the rules and norms that govern institutional practices and shape participation in them. It asks such questions as: who constructs the format and the agenda? How are speaking rights distributed? What is regarded as legitimate comment? (Barnes *et al.*, 2007). The rules of engagement of the meetings were designed to advantage the academy proponents. A platform of leading councillors and officers spoke to PowerPoint presentations and then responded to questions and points from the floor. The first set of meetings was chaired by Councillor Robert Simpson, the leader of the BSF bid, not by a neutral chair. The additional Woodhouse meetings, on 18 March 2009, were chaired by Louise Allanach, project director for EC Harris Built Asset Consultancy, the project managers for the proposed academy. Comments were taken in groups of three or four, enabling the platform respondents to select which to focus on. No supplementary questions were allowed, preventing continuity and dialogue. One exchange at one of the Woodhouse meetings was illustrative of how the boundaries of legitimate comment were drawn. A questioner asked why Landau Forte College in Derby had no staff representatives on its governing body. Margaret Bell, a Landau Forte trustee, answered, 'It was a decision not to have a staff governor, but there are many other ways'. The questioner demanded that she answer *why*. The chair quickly intervened to say, 'The question has been answered and the response noted' and moved on to the next question (my field notes).

School students have a statutory right to be consulted about 'any proposed changes to local school organisation that may affect them' (DCSF, 2007). SCC arranged several consultation meetings with secondary school students, separately in each school and jointly. However, according to the school students I interviewed, the rules of engagement were biased. Little information was given about the academy, especially about how it would improve standards. The consultation was structured around only one option, SCC's BSF proposal. And the time for consultation was very short. A senior student at the school complained at the QEMS public meeting: she 'was really disgusted at the fact that we hadn't been consulted thoroughly enough' (Interview).

The consultation process was reported to cabinet at its meeting on 28 January 2009. This took the form of a presentation by Robert Simpson, the deputy leader, comprising extensive documentary evidence of the various views expressed. The *Report on the Consultation Regarding BSF in Tamworth* (SCC, 2009a) summarized the written submissions by the school governing bodies, the JCC Teachers Panel, an alternative proposal, Transformation through Partnership, from the headteachers of the five schools, together with summaries of the parents' and community's responses from the consultation meetings and issues raised at a meeting of representatives of school students. There was also a report of the consultation meetings based on transcripts, the *Tamworth BSF Public Meetings Independent Report* by Step Beyond (SCC, 2009b), a market research company.

The January 2009 cabinet meeting considered three options: the 'preferred option', the 'preferred option' but without the closure of QEMS, and the headteachers' option. Its decision was to continue with the preferred option but not to close QEMS. This was testimony to the strength of the public campaign to save the school, but it does not indicate that the consultation process was in any way a decision-making one. The majority view in the consultation meetings, as the Step Beyond report acknowledged, as well as from the headteachers and governing bodies, was opposition to the establishment of the academy, but this was rejected by cabinet. The decision whether to proceed with the academy proposal did not depend on the balance of views in the consultation process. Almost invariably opposition to proposed academies, however widespread, has been overridden, and this was the case in Tamworth.

The regulative framing of consultation extended from the consultation meetings to how they were reported to cabinet. The legitimacy of public opposition to the 'preferred option' was depreciated in two ways. First, in the report by Step Beyond (SCC, 2009b) of the consultation meetings. It acknowledged '[a] desire to *defend* local schools, heads and teachers against external criticism', '[a] strong *distrust* in CC [county council] motivations', and '[a] belief that decisions have already been made and that the CC was being tokenistic in the consultation exercise'. However, it chose to explain these views in terms of 'extremely strong emotions' – the conclusion of the report is headed 'The Influence of Emotions'. The report continued: 'These emotions were unfortunately not counter-balanced by any prior rational awareness or recognition of . . . [t]he *weaknesses* of the Tamworth education system' and '[t]he *benefits* that rebuilding or modernising schools would bring'. The report concluded that, '[w]hilst these were all stressed by Peter Traves at the meeting, unfortunately by that point people's emotions had come to the fore and so they were often not willing to believe that the Council was telling them the truth' (p. 7, emphasis in original). The counter-position of the emotional to the rational served to justify the SCC policy and delegitimize opposition to it.

Second, in the exclusion of the written submission by HOTS (2008), *Putting Communities First: Education at the Heart of Tamworth*, dated 8 December, from the reports tabled at cabinet. It was not appended, summarized or referred to. Two subsequent documents submitted by HOTS in the final period for written representations were also ignored: *A Response from Parents to Staffordshire County Council's 'Report on Consultation Regarding BSF in Tamworth'* (HOTS, 2009a), a ten-page document dated 25 January, and *Objection to Staffordshire County Council's BSF Proposals for Tamworth*, dated 1 April (HOTS, 2009b), HOTS's written submission to the cabinet meeting on 18 April 2009 which made the final decision on the BSF proposal.

At stake in these two strategies by SCC is a particular construction of the public. For SCC the legitimate public were those whose identities are defined by the institutional context of the school – as the parents of pupils at a specific school – and by the constitutional context of the consultation process as the sole legitimate site for the expression of views. What was regarded as illegitimate was a collective cross-school community-wide identity with a campaigning orientation beyond the bounds of the formal consultation process.

Underlying this were two competing discourses of local democracy: representative democracy and forms of participatory democracy.

> While in theory they can coexist and complement one another, elected representatives become uneasy about the prospect of community involvement in decisions that have hitherto been seen as their prerogative. Such initiatives require councillors to share their power with others whom they may think ill informed, lacking legitimacy and scarcely representative of the communities they claim to speak for.
>
> (Rao *et al.*, 2000, pp. 3–4, quoted in Barnes *et al.*, 2007, p. 41)

The claim to representation was a key theme of regulative framing. HOTS claimed to represent the majority of parents' interests, as evidenced by the overwhelming support for their position in consultation meetings and, later, their 10 per cent vote in Tamworth in the county council elections. SCC rejected their claims: they represented sectoral interests, in contrast to the council's claim to represent the electorate as a whole. (The views of the teachers' unions were rejected on similar grounds.) One expression of this conflict was SCC's rejection of the call by HOTS supporters for a public vote on the BSF proposals.

If the purpose of the consultation process was not to engage in a process of deliberative democracy designed to develop a policy which commanded, if not consensus, the widest possible support, if the core of the BSF proposal – the academy running the sixth-form centre and Woodhouse High school – was never open to change or compromise, one might ask what was the purpose of consultation? It had three objectives. First, to claim democratic legitimacy for the policy process, in accord with government policy (DCLG, 2008). Second, as far as possible to construct support for the policy, in line with the government booklet entitled the *Academies Marketing Toolkit* (DfES, 2003c). Third, to register the strength and key themes of opposition in order to adjust subsequent policy presentation, as SCC did.

The local state against local democracy: academies and class interests

The experience of the academy policy process in Tamworth can be situated in the context of current debates about public participation and local democracy. These have been prominent themes of New Labour since it was elected in 1997 (Davies, 2008). The most recent policy statement is the White Paper *Communities in Control: Real People, Real Power*, published by the Department for Communities and Local Government (DCLG, 2008). It 'aims to pass power into the hands of local communities, to encourage vibrant local democracy in every part of the country, and to give real control over local decisions and services to a wider pool of citizens' (p. 1). Labour's discourse is an expression of 'orthodox' urban governance theory (Davies, 2005, p. 312).

> Local managers have to mobilise citizens and include local knowledge in public policies . . . The urban bureaucracy should not be a closed hierarchy, and neither should it be a hands-off enabling framework. Rather, it should be innovative, it should encourage participation and identify new partners, it should be organised horizontally and be open to interaction with community members.
>
> In governance theory, there is an understanding that rather than being at odds, efficiency and democracy are mutually reinforcing . . . Governance theory assumes that there are multiple sources of legitimacy,

> e.g. legitimacy does not only emerge from having followed democratic election procedures but also from having involved key stakeholders in the formulation or implementation of a policy. And cooperation from stakeholders ensures a higher degree of efficiency.
>
> (Kjaer, 2009, p. 141)

It is evident that the Tamworth experience does not correspond at all to the visions of popular participation and local empowerment of either Labour policy or 'orthodox' urban governance theory. I asked two of the leading activists in HOTS, both mothers of pupils at secondary schools, what they thought they had learned most from the whole BSF policy process. Carolyn's blunt answer was '[t]hat there is no democracy'. She continued, 'As a parent I am a stakeholder and we have completely been ignored and this consultation process has been so fast, so short that nobody's been listened to' (Interview). Julie said:

> Having been through it all I just don't trust the system at all, actually. You know, although I know that deals are done behind doors and with people in high places and with money who can sort of get what they want, having read about things like that in the past, you still sort of hope that when it comes to your own locality that things don't happen like that. But from what I've seen it is just like that.
>
> (Interview)

Carolyn's and Julie's views resonate with many research studies which have criticized the failure of those in power to allow meaningful popular participation in local policy-making. For example, Barnes *et al.* (2007), speaking of their case studies, conclude that 'our findings have often led us to be relatively pessimistic about the potential of new initiatives to overcome entrenched institutional or political forms of power' (p. 184). This poses a problem for 'orthodox' urban governance theorists. If local participation is in the interests of a modernizing local government, why does it not act in accordance with those interests?

The source of their dilemma lies in the consensus model of local politics that underpins orthodox urban governance theory: '[P]articipative governance is strongly oriented towards the production of consensus. The "partnership" model of participation is one which assumes that different interests can and should be subsumed by a common goal' (Newman, 2005, pp. 131–2).

If consensus is possible then failure to achieve it tends to be explained in terms of institutional inertia and bureaucratic path dependency. In contrast, critics adopting a 'sceptical' (Davies, 2005, p. 312) approach within urban governance theory argue that many of the contested issues in local politics arise from opposed and irreconcilable interests (Davies and Imbroscio, 2008). However, they often display a reluctance to identify these as predominantly conflicting *class* interests. Newman and Clarke (2009), for example, foreground the complexity and ambiguity of local politics at the expense of obscuring its dominant capitalist logic. One consequence is that the coercive, as against discursive, power of the local state is underplayed. In contrast, Marxist approaches see urban contexts as sites of the contested and crisis-prone processes of capitalist production, consumption and accumulation, including the reproduction of labour power, giving rise to struggles around not only production but reproduction (Geddes, 2008; Jessop, 2002). Governance theory has no concept of the local state as capitalist, but in a Marxist perspective the local state is subordinate to the class power of the central state and its function is primarily to promote at the local level the social, political and economic conditions for the capitalist market while also attempting to satisfy subaltern social interests provided they are compatible, and to override them when they are not. The local state has both been the principal agent of the neoliberal transformation of urban space through deregulation and privatization and had the principal responsibility for the management of the ensuing contradictions and crises at the local level. In this context there has been a policy convergence between the two main political parties in local government (Eisenschitz and Gough, 1993; Whitfield, 2006). Miliband (1982) points out that it has been argued from John Stuart Mill onwards that participation in local government promotes class harmony, and that central government in Britain has very rarely had to contend with a serious rebellion by Labour authorities.

This theoretical approach can provide an explanation of the BSF policy process in Tamworth and its centrepiece, the proposed academy. Capitalist class interests provide both the principal object of education policy – the efficient reproduction of labour power to produce the future workforce required for the competitiveness of the British economy – and one of the means to achieve it: the handover of schools which are public assets, accountable, at least to some extent, to local communities both through elected local government and through representation on governing bodies, to private owners and managers without local accountability. In the case of Landau Forte, it is a trust controlled directly by two multimillionaire capitalists (a property developer and an international hotelier) and their representatives. This act of privatization cannot be justified on the grounds that academies represent a convergence of class educational interests: there is no evidence that academies are more effective at raising the educational attainment of students from poorer backgrounds than comparable schools (Machin and Wilson, 2009b), and in fact the proportion of such students in academies has greatly declined (PwC, 2008). Class interests are also in play in Landau Forte's refusal to recognize trade unions and to allow staff governors.

The role of the local state has been to implement this element of the neo-liberal agenda by managing the privatization of part of the Tamworth school system. The Labour leadership of SCC has proved itself reliable agents of government policy, at the cost of abusing the structures and procedures of local government and abandoning any final remnants of an independent local social democratic tradition in education. The implementation of the academy policy did not require concessions to the governance agenda. While, for example, managing a housing estate may benefit from some low-level 'empowerment' of local citizens to help implement government agendas, establishing an academy entails their disempowerment, at both local authority and governing body levels, and the transfer of power to a private sponsor. While consent was sought through the consultation process, the academy proposal did not depend on it; its implementation was assured regardless by the uncompromising coercive power of the local state. That is why academies do not feature in the government agenda for 'communities in control' – there is no mention of academies in the White Paper (DCLG, 2008) – and why, as we have seen in Tamworth as elsewhere (Hatcher and Jones, 2006; Hatcher, 2008a), the process of policy formation and implementation at the local level has been tightly regulated, closed and exclusive.

Acknowledgements

I would like to thank all those who co-operated with this research, and especially Julie for the comprehensive supply of information. Named HOTS supporters are quoted with their permission. Thanks also to Ken Jones for his comments.

Note

[1] All the Staffordshire County Council documents and minutes of meetings referred to can be found on the council's website (see www.staffordshire.gov.uk/). Hands Off Tamworth Schools publications can be found on the campaign website (see www.freewebs.com/handsofftamworthschools/).

Chapter 3

The Birth of Norwich's First School Academy: A Case Study

John Elliott

Introduction

In early January 2008 Norfolk County Council voted in favour of a proposal to establish an academy school in north Norwich to replace the Heartsease High School. The sponsors were a local Christian businessman and the Bishop of Norwich. The Secretary of State ratified the decision in March and the 'Open Academy' opened as Norfolk's first academy the following September. This case study particularly focuses on the formal consultation processes that led to such an outcome and how these were experienced by many Heartsease High governors, parents and local residents. It depicts their experience of the statutory and non-statutory consultations by the Norfolk County Council and sponsors respectively as denying them any significant voice in the outcome in spite of formal procedures that appeared to the contrary. This experience is characterized in the case study as a 'democratic deficit' in the way Norwich's first school academy was established. The fact that the sponsors were the Diocesan Anglican Bishop of Norwich and a local evangelical businessman posed an issue about the extent to which the power exercised by religion in local community settings should be democratically regulated, particularly in areas such as north Norwich where formal religious allegiance is weak.

Although many teachers and members of the general public object to school academies on principle, on the grounds that they are less accountable for the use of public resources than other state-funded schools, this is not the issue that is primarily at stake in the events depicted. While some local politicians, governors and parents objected to academies in general, others specifically objected to the sponsors proposed for the academy at Heartsease, and the power it would give them in the area. What brought the two groups together was their shared experience of a 'democratic deficit' in the consultation processes.

This case study is a piece of 'insider research', inasmuch as I was a community governor of Heartsease High and an active participant in the events depicted. In undertaking it I drew on my long experience of using qualitative and action research methods in the field of education. My experiences and interpretations of events were continuously linked with and cross-checked against those of other members of what became known as the Heartsease Campaign Group, consisting of some governors, parents, local residents, a teachers' association representative, the local MP, a city councillor and two county councillors. As events 'hotted up' successive drafts of the case study were produced in response to information and feedback from members of this group. Each draft constituted documentary evidence of shared experience to date and provided a basis for 'connected actions' on the part of members of the campaign. Hence, this case study was constructed in an action context as a piece of action research.

Direct observational experience at face-to-face meetings was a primary source of information on which I based many of the interpretations contained in this case study. Wherever possible I have attempted to corroborate such a source by reference to secondary sources, such as news items in the local press or formal minutes of meetings. In the case of the Heartsease High School governors' meetings the minutes may not be easily 'open to inspection', given the fact that the school no longer exists. A great deal of the informational sources I drew on in this case study took the form of private emails, and I have made every attempt to refer to such sources when they played a major role in this account.

How the Heartsease High governors became disaffected

In January 2006 the governors met the deputy director of Children's Services about the prospect of establishing an academy on the site of the existing school.[1] The deputy director reminded the governors that the school had long been problematic because of its size (well below the minimum viability mark for secondary schools of 600). He identified the school as still belonging to a vulnerable group of schools with respect to performance (it had been in special measures from September 1997 to March 2000) although the authority had been delighted with progress made over recent years. However, inasmuch as it continued to have poor GCSE results (as determined by the 2003 figures) and was situated in an area regarded as one of social deprivation, it qualified as a candidate for academy school status.

A decision by the Secretary of State in favour of an academy, the deputy director said, would depend on a feasibility study and this could only go ahead with the agreement of the governors. A decision was needed by the end of February 2006. When asked whether it was likely that a feasibility study might go against an academy being built, the deputy director said that this would happen if the study demonstrated that it would not attract sufficient numbers of pupils (800) and there was opposition from the community.

At the next governors' meeting, on 8 February, the chair reported on a recent meeting he had had with the deputy director, who had said that if the governors voted in favour of a feasibility study they could withdraw from the process at any time, but felt that such a study would provide them with more information on which to judge the merits of the proposal.[2] On 20 February the Heartsease governors met the prospective sponsors in the presence of the deputy director of Children's Services and a DfES adviser. The former MP for Norwich North, Dr Ian Gibson, was present as an observer (he was opposed to the proposal to replace Heartsease High with an academy from the start, unlike Charles Clarke, the MP for Norwich South).

After the meeting the governors voted for a feasibility study with conditions, having been reassured by the DFES adviser that this would not be a vote in favour of an academy. Several governors had reservations but the reassurance that at this stage they would only be committing themselves to a feasibility study, plus the invitation to state 'conditions' for the study, swung the vote to thirteen in its favour 'with conditions' and three (including myself) against. At the top of the list of conditions specified for the feasibility study by the governors was '[t]hat the study provides spaces for extensive public discussion within the community and this area of the city about the desirability of the proposed Academy and the feasibility of its stated goals and purposes'. Also included was a reference to a very successful sixth-form partnership between Heartsease and two neighbouring secondary schools in North Norwich (referred to as the Kett Sixth Form Centre). The condition specified that any academy should strengthen rather than disrupt the partnership.[3]

The feasibility study was launched in January 2007 and included a questionnaire that was distributed to households in North Norwich (to be completed by 20 August) plus three public meetings in the area over the summer; people were also invited to give their views by telephone and via the internet. The promised outcome was a public consultation report as part of a feasibility report to be completed in September 2007 and submitted to the Secretary of State.

By September 2007 the governors as a whole had not received a draft copy of the feasibility report that they would have an opportunity to comment on, and had become increasingly disillusioned with the way Cambridge Education Associates (CEA) and Children's Services had handled the consultation process. The latter appeared to be more concerned with arrangements for replacing the school with an academy than with listening to concerns and anxieties being expressed at the grass roots. The governors increasingly came to feel that they had been bypassed and were now surplus to requirements.[4]

After much deliberation the governors voted by a significant majority to oppose the proposal, having learned some time previously that they had no power of veto and that their vote would carry no legal weight.[5] In the *Eastern Daily Press*[6] the deputy director of Children's Services stated that he would be disappointed if what he had heard about the vote was correct, and that the academy project was 'a great opportunity for the community around the existing school'. Two months later, in the lead-up to the county council cabinet decision, and following the county council scrutiny committee meeting in mid-October – where by a majority of one, the members voted against a proposal to refer the proposed academy back to the cabinet for further analysis – the governors of Heartsease issued a public explanation for their opposition to the academy.

The statement made the following points:

1. Governors were not fully informed at the start of the process by Children's Services.
2. The position of the governors, following the meeting with the proposed sponsors, was misrepresented by an official to the county council's scrutiny committee as a vote in favour of the academy when it was in fact a vote in favour of a feasibility study only – therefore no U-turn.
3. Governors were dismayed by the biased and unscientific nature of the questionnaire distributed by CEA.
4. During the consultation process governors became aware that the characteristics and rationale for the new academy constantly shifted when claims were countered with evidence. It was a 'no-win' situation.
5. The benefits for pupils became increasingly difficult to discern in the light of up-to-date performance data (Elliott, 2008).

The statement ended with a summary of Wrigley's report (2007)[7] on the academic success of the Academies Programme and the claim that it broadly supported the conclusion that there was little evidential basis for establishing an academy to replace the existing school. The report also pointed out what Heartsease governors had become only too aware of; namely, that there is a democratic deficit in the governance of academies and in the process of establishing them. The governors concluded that:

> the decision of the County Council to go ahead with this replacement does not even have the warrant of questionnaire findings from surveys carried out by CEA and the County Council itself. Response rates were far too low to provide valid measures of public opinion.

The statement was sent to the county council and released to the press. I think that in constructing it, we, the governing body of the school, had more or less accepted that there was little that could be done at this stage to influence the cabinet decision.[8] We simply wanted to make the reasons for our opposition clear to the local community and the general public in a coherent form and correct any impression that Children's Services had given that we had inexplicably reneged, without good reason, on our original views. Most of the points contained in the document, both about the desirability of replacing the school with an academy and about the authenticity of the consultation process, had been made by governors at various meetings and in a variety of contexts.

For example, in May 2007 I produced a critique of the questionnaire issued by Planet Public Relations for CEA and distributed across North Norwich.[9] After pinpointing specific ways in which the instrument was biased and unscientific, the critique argued that it was not in the main designed to elicit people's views about whether Heartsease High should be replaced by an academy but rather to transmit the message that there will be an academy and that answering the questions provided an opportunity to have a say in how it will shape up. I concluded that the fact that the Christian sponsors and the county council had endorsed the questionnaire by allowing their logos to be printed on the front cover raised questions about their integrity in allowing a document of such poor quality to go out in their name.

This critique summed up the feelings of many governors about the consultation process, as it seemed to be emerging. It also elicited a response from some, if not all, county councillors representing communities in North Norwich. They were disturbed to find the council endorsing such a poor-quality product,[10] and a copy of the critique found its way to its chief executive. However, in addition the council carried out its own opinion survey, as it was legally obliged to do so.

The critique was also distributed to the MP's Committee of Inquiry into Academies that met in the House of Commons on 12 June 2007. The meeting was observed by some Heartsease High governors. In spite of it getting wide circulation, and being presented verbally at a public consultation meeting and over local radio, no response to it was forthcoming from CEA and the prospective sponsors. Indeed throughout the whole consultation process CEA met the governing body as a whole on only one occasion: the last scheduled meeting of the summer term, 2007. This was the meeting at which concerns were raised that the questionnaire had not been distributed to the Plumstead Estate, probably the most 'disadvantaged' area in the neighbourhood. CEA countered by saying that they had investigated this by sampling some addresses on Plumstead Road and that those addresses had received the questionnaire. However, Plumstead Road, a road of private housing and shops, doesn't run through the Plumstead Estate, which is still mostly an area of council housing. Hence the later complaint by parents that many had not received copies of the questionnaire.[11]

Parents say, 'we have not been given a proper opportunity to voice our opinion'[12]

As the formal consultation process drew to a close a group of parents organized a petition in the Heartsease area against replacing the school with an academy. Five hundred and fifty parents and local residents signed it, stating that they will not send their children to the proposed academy. The chair of Children's Services reported response, in the news item cited above, was to express sorrow that 'this type of feeling has sprung up at the last minute' when 'there have been many opportunities for people to make their views known'. She pointed out that both the council and the CEA surveys had shown a majority in favour of an academy. What she apparently failed to grasp is that many parents and residents in the local community did not experience the consultation process and its instruments as opportunities to authentically express their views. This might explain why the response rates to both questionnaires[13] were very poor, as local MP Dr Ian Gibson pointed out.[14] The council's own consultation elicited 62 per cent of just 258 respondents in favour of the proposal.[15] This is hardly a sample size that warrants pressing confidently ahead with it. Yet on this basis councillors were pronouncing that the people had spoken; the *Eastern Daily Press*[16] declared that its position was also aligned with 'the voice of the people'. When it came down to identifying where these people came from it was discovered that the questionnaire had been distributed beyond the boundaries of the city and that many respondents were not residents of urban Norwich, let alone members of the local communities surrounding and near the school.[17] Indeed inasmuch as the questionnaire could be accessed via the internet, respondents could have resided across the country and indeed the world. Certainly some county councillors, who were opposed to the academy proposal, believed that pressure had been applied by the sponsors for church members outside as well as inside Norwich, across Norfolk as a whole, to respond in favour of an academy. Hence the referral of the process to the county council scrutiny committee where one Labour councillor was reported to argue that it 'smelt of corruption'.[18] Indeed the parents who organized the petition have advised me that the vast majority of local residents who signed the petition received neither the county council's questionnaire nor CEA's in the first place! As for the CEA questionnaire it elicited a narrower majority in favour of the proposal (49/41 per cent) than the county council's.[19]

The school staff speak out

Shortly before the governors issued their explanation for opposing the academy at their September 2007 meeting, three-quarters of the staff signed a petition saying that they were appalled by the proposal on the grounds that it placed education and public resources in the control of private individuals and failed to acknowledge the achievements of the existing school, now listed as one of the top 100 improved schools in the country for its Key Stage 3 results.[20]

The fact that governors, staff and parents/local residents declared their opposition in the final weeks leading up to the council's decision is surely indicative of their frustration with a prolonged two-year consultation process that favoured the expression of pro-academy and anti-Heartsease High attitudes on the basis of very weak evidence.

This determination to force compliance with a proposal that had little evidence to support it was criticized by the Liberal Democrat spokesman on the county council a few days before the cabinet met in the New Year. He accused the council's Conservative leaders as they stood on the brink of a decision to close Heartsease High of 'blindly chasing the government's 30 pieces of silver' (an extra £20 million). He argued that such a decision would do nothing to 'improve the bad image of consultation' that had developed in the process leading up to it.[21]

The Norwich City Council voices dissent

The Norwich City Council had bid for unitary status as a local authority, which conflicted with the county council's bid. In July Dr Ian Gibson, MP, had urged the New Labour government to put the proposal to replace Heartsease High with an academy on hold until the unitary status issue had been settled. With the impending possibility of becoming responsible for Norwich schools the city council referred the academy issue to its scrutiny committee who took evidence from a range of interested parties, including the sponsors and CEA, at a meeting in early August 2007.[22]

In the light of this evidence the scrutiny committee recommended that the city council should oppose replacing Heartsease High with an academy. The full council backed the recommendation on the grounds that the money to be invested in an academy would be better spent improving schools across the city. Many interpreted the decision as largely 'political', given the tension between the county and city council on the unitary status issue. However, a systematic list of reasons for opposing an academy was published on the city council's website.[23] The *Eastern Daily Press*[24] pronounced that the city council opposition was a 'Big Setback' for the long-term prospects of the academy proposal, given it is likely to acquire unitary status shortly. However, arrangements had been made to put the academy into effect in the existing school buildings for September 2008. It seems that neither the city council nor the local member of parliament was able to halt the birth of Norwich's first academy.

The authenticity of formal consultation

What appears to characterize the 'consultation processes' depicted above is the absence of debate and discussion, and the disregard for reasons and evidence. These are all features of what I have called the 'democratic deficit' in the consultations themselves. Good arguments about the 'accountability deficit' in school academies as publicly funded institutions, and the morality of placing a substantial and continuing amount of public money in the control of one or two private individuals, or about the lack of evidence that establishing academies significantly overcomes the achievement gap between pupils from socially deprived neighbourhoods and the rest, all appear to have fallen on deaf ears. It does not appear to worry those who are promoting academies that there is no strong evidential basis for them, or that they pose an 'accountability deficit'. In their eyes academies are so self-evidently a good thing that the idea that they may not in themselves bring educational benefits to the socially deprived is unthinkable. Hence, the most frequent response to the dissenting voices depicted in this case study is one of being appalled by such opposition when the case for an academy is regarded as so self-evidently of benefit to the children in the area. When local politicians, officials and prospective sponsors are allowed to get away with this kind of response in the face of good arguments and evidence we truly know where the power to shape decisions lies. Certainly not in the local communities that academies are supposed to benefit.

A delegation meets Ministers in the House of Commons

I circulated a draft of this case study to a broad cross-section of people known to oppose the proposed academy.[25] The intention was to cross-check for factual accuracy and the extent to which my interpretations of situations and events chimed with those of other peoples'. Among the comments received was the following from a county councillor who had been outspoken on behalf of his political party in opposing the proposal:

> There is a postscript to your case study. The sponsors for the Academy have now advertised for a Principal at a salary of £100,000 pa. This is before the Minister has given the go-ahead. It is before the board of the Academy has been established so other governors such as parents and staff will have no say in this. It is also before the number on roll is known. The salary level for heads in state schools is determined by the number on roll. It is also, I believe significantly above the salary for the current head, and thus, as [a county councillor] has pointed out it means less money to be spent on the kids.[26]

The process of establishing an academy to replace Heartsease High reached the stage where the 'democratic deficit' that lay at the core of the opposition's case became clear for all to see.

However, New Labour Ministers remained blind. On 30 January 2008 a delegation from the Heartsease Campaign Group, consisting of a local county councillor, two governors (including myself), two parents and a teachers' representative met with the Secretary of State for Children, Schools and Families (Ed Balls) and the Minister of State (Lord Adonis) in the House of Commons. Dr Ian Gibson, MP for North Norwich, had requested the meeting on behalf of the Campaign Group.[27] However, 'the wind was rather taken out of the sails' of the delegation by the then Secretary of State's announcement at the meeting that the current headteacher, an atheist, had been appointed principal-designate of the proposed academy. Such continuity of leadership is a rare event to date in the Academies Programme as it had unfolded, and appears to contradict the rhetoric that accompanied it about the need for a radical change of leadership. Evidently the sponsors felt that there was no problem about appointing an atheist to promote a Christian ethos in the proposed academy. The delegation understandably interpreted the appointment as at least partly aimed at disarming objections to the academy, particularly those surrounding the sponsors' intention that as an organization it would have a distinctive Christian ethos.[28] Politics, it seems, is no longer limited by language that possesses stable meanings.

This case study was part of the documentation submitted at the meeting with New Labour Ministers Balls and Adonis, which also included a petition signed by over 500 local residents saying they would refuse to send their children to an academy controlled by one of the sponsors. The parents who organized the petition made it very clear that the local residents felt they had not been properly consulted about the proposed academy, and they challenged the Secretary of State to say how many additional signatures would make him change his mind. Not surprisingly he refused to commit himself. The parent delegates subsequently gathered 1,000 additional signatures to the petition, which Ian Gibson presented to Ed Balls on their behalf. The local councillor in the delegation critiqued the county council's handling of the consultation process, and I explained the governors' decision not to support the proposal on the grounds of inadequate consultation with governors and local residents. It was explained that the governors had been led to believe they would be able to comment on the feasibility report before it was sent to the Secretary of State, but they never received a copy. When I challenged Ministers to say whether they had received this report (due the previous autumn) they admitted that they had not.[29]

On 4 February Ed Balls wrote to Ian Gibson. In his letter he referred to the delegation and expressed the hope that it had found the meeting 'helpful and constructive' and 'felt they had a proper chance to express their views'.

He also adopted the 'official view' of the county council and CEA about the adequacy of the consultation processes, but addressed none of the delegation's specific criticisms of that process.[30] However, he was at this point clearly aware of the level of opposition, which was then substantiated by continuing local press coverage. His final decision was expected on 11 March. It was announced, in favour of the proposed academy, over a week in advance of this date – reportedly to prevent any further destabilization in the situation.[31] Lord Adonis had already informed Ian Gibson of certain concessions that the government was prepared to make, concerning the provision of religious education (will follow the Agreed Syllabus for Norfolk Schools), membership of the group of trustees (to include the principal of Norwich City Further Education College), and policies regarding exclusions and the admission of pupils with special educational needs. The delegation did not experience these as 'concessions' since they did not significantly depart from intentions that had been previously stated by the sponsors themselves.

One member of the Campaign Group expressed the view that the group had won some battles before finally losing the war.

Subsequent events at the open academy

On 3 July 2009, almost a year after the new Open Academy had been launched (but with the new building as yet incomplete) the *Norwich Evening News*, carried the front-page headline, 'Mystery as new Academy head quits'.[32] The announcement was, according to the newspaper, made by one of the sponsors, the Christian businessman, at a hastily convened school assembly. On the previous day I had been alerted to the situation by private sources and was told that the sponsor had personally escorted the head from the premises, suggesting that she had been reluctant to quit her post. The *Evening News* referred to a letter, signed by the chairman of governors and that was sent out to all parents, announcing the changes with 'immediate effect', with the two vice principals taking over the leadership responsibility in the short term. No explanation was given in the letter for the sudden departure of the head. Nor was it clear whether she might return at some point. In the event she did not. To my knowledge the explanation for her departure, in spite of parents reportedly wanting answers, was still not forthcoming at the beginning of the September 2009 term. According to my sources, that were cross-checked, the head had run into conflict with a recently appointed member of staff. The *Evening News* invited comment from readers on the situation and published a letter from me on 6 July, which read:

> No surprise at head's departure
> For some of us, her appointment was a cynical political decision on the

> part of its sponsors to overcome resistance from parents and the local community to the transformation of Heartsease High into Norwich's first academy.
>
> How else might one explain the appointment of an unbeliever to be head of a school supposedly aimed at promoting a Christian ethos? Her 'shelf life', whatever the circumstances of her exit, would have inevitably been a short one.
>
> The mystery surrounding [her] departure also comes as no surprise given that Academies, in contrast to other state-funded schools, can easily escape normal democratic accountability.

Later I learned that the head's departure was followed by one of the assistant heads leaving shortly afterwards. He had not returned by the start of the next term. It certainly appears that the development of a distinctive Christian ethos in the school had got off to a rather shaky start with a leadership crisis that came to a head only shortly before the summer recess – it was clearly so severe that it could not be contained until then.

On 18 July the *Eastern Daily Press* announced a 'New leader for Open Academy'. It reported that the permanent exit of the previous head had now been confirmed and that she had been temporarily replaced, while the governors looked for a permanent replacement, by a headteacher from an 'outstanding' OfSTED school in a neighbouring county who is a member of the National Leaders of Education programme (NLE).[33]

Just over a month later, on 27 August, the *Eastern Daily Press* carried the headline 'Open Academy posts record GCSE results'. Its education correspondent announced, 'Pupils at Norwich's only Academy have shattered all their targets by doubling the school's GCSE results in a year', pointing out that the percentage of pupils gaining five or more A*–C grades including English and maths 'surged from 16 per cent to 31.25 per cent, while the proportion getting five A*–C's in any subjects improved from 38–47 per cent.' The article refers to the academy being given the go-ahead 'despite fierce local opposition' and allegations of 'ineffective local consultation'. Its message is that the results show that the government was right to face down the opposition. They are likely, it claims, 'to ease any pressure on the Academy's leaders and could convince more members of the community to support it and send their children there to study'. The article mentions the additional money provided to the school as a result of it acquiring academy status, for the purposes of enriching the curriculum and appointing more 'specialist' and 'advanced' teachers and the new 'spectacular eco-friendly building' taking shape on site. It all suggested the emergence of a very special and privileged facility that will deliver unparalleled results, neglecting to point out that the results reflected well on the work of the old Heartsease High that it replaced only one year previously.

A summary analysis

Simon Jenkins (2008) claims that 'Ed Ball's embrace of Academies forms part of a cull of communities in Britain.' This case study supports such a claim inasmuch as it tells a story about how a local school community was rendered powerless, over a period of twelve months (2007) to influence a decision that will now shape its future and that of its children. It shows how a consultation process that included a feasibility study commissioned by the New Labour government enabled 'structures of domination'[34] to come into play to effectively stifle local voices. These structures distanced local government from local people by aligning it to central government as an implementer of national initiatives rather than as a creator of spaces for local initiatives. They created a 'hierarchy of credibility' (Becker, 1998)[35] that rendered the oppositional voices in the community nonsensical. The true picture of the situation was assumed to reside only with those aligned to the small cabal of county councillors that made up the county council's cabinet (composed entirely of members of the Conservative Party and none of them representing areas in urban Norwich), those executive officers in charge of Children's Services, and the prospective sponsors. The most widely read local newspaper in Norfolk – the *Eastern Daily Press* – eventually declared a barely concealed alignment with those in favour of an academy. By the autumn of 2007 the campaign to stop the academy realized that it was now probably powerless to resist what now appeared to be a forgone conclusion from the start. However, in the process it had some influence on the kind of school that emerged and how it related to other schools in North Norwich, at least in the short term.

Acknowledgements

The author would like to acknowledge helpful comments on drafts of his case study from members of the Heartsease Campaign Group, particularly Robert Wordsworth, Peter Harwood, Mervyn Scutter and Christine O'Hanlon and to thank the editorial board of *FORUM* for agreeing to publish an earlier version of this case study in its fiftieth anniversary edition (2008, 50, [3], 353–66).

Notes

1 Minutes of extra governors' meeting, Heartsease High School, 19 January 2006.

2 Minutes of governors' meeting to support this, Heartsease High School, 8 February 2006.

3 Although governors were invited to suggest conditions the final list was compiled by the chair, in discussion with the headteacher, and submitted to the county

council without further consultation. I was informed via email of this list by a fellow governor who managed to obtain a copy from the chair.

4 As a community governor this was a feeling I increasingly experienced as shared with the majority of governors.

5 The lack of legal entitlement to object or appeal was confirmed in section 2.3 of a report by the director of Children's Services for Norfolk to the county council cabinet meeting on 7 January 2008 (Item 12), entitled *The Outcome of Public Notice Procedure*. Available at: www.norfolk/gov/uk/consumption/groups/publicdocuments,committeereport/cabinet070108item12pdf.pdf

6 *Eastern Daily Press*, 13 Sep 2007, available at: www.EDP24.co.uk

7 This research into the impact and effectiveness of school academies was carried out at Edinburgh University and takes into account the report of the National Audit Office (February 2007).

8 However, section 3.4.2 of the *Outcome of Public Notice Procedure* report (see above, n. 5) to the critical Norfolk County Council cabinet meeting on 7 January 2008 gives a brief summary of the Heartsease governors' objections to the proposal and consultation procedures.

9 The critique was circulated via email to the local MP, Dr Ian Gibson, and some local city and county councillors. It can be made available on request.

10 Information about how people reacted to and made use of the critique was conveyed to me privately, either face-to-face or via email.

11 This complaint about lack of consultation was expressed through a petition organized by a group of parents and signed by 550 local community members, as reported in section 3.4.5 of the *Outcome of Public Notice Procedure* report (see above, n. 5).

12 *Eastern Daily Press*, 4 Oct 2007, available at: www.EDP24.co.uk

13 One questionnaire formed part of the county council's statutory consultation procedures while the second questionnaire formed part of the non-statutory feasibility study carried out by Cambridge Education on behalf of the sponsors.

14 *Eastern Daily Press*, 2 Oct 2007, available at: www.EDP24.co.uk

15 This information is given in section 5.15 of the *Outcome of Public Notice Procedure* report (see above, n. 5).

16 *Eastern Daily Press*, 2 Oct 2007, available at: www.EDP24.co.uk

17 Some county councillors' concerns about the consultation process resulted in an Item (4a) for consideration at the county council cabinet scrutiny committee meeting on 23 October 2007, entitled 'Posting a closure notice for Heartsease High School to replace it with The Open Academy'. The minutes of the meeting indicate that concerns were expressed about the lack of weighting given in the consultation process to the views of local residents in the area surrounding Heartsease High School. The minutes record that a motion to refer back the concerns expressed about the consultation process to the full cabinet, for reconsideration and further analysis of consultation responses, was narrowly defeated by one vote. Meeting minutes available at: www.norfolk.gov.uk/consumption/groups/—/cabscrut2310007minspdf.pdf

18 This information was conveyed to me in private by a county councillor who attended the meeting, and I was led to believe that the expression referred to the role of the sponsors in manipulating responses from outside the local area. The minutes of the Norfolk County Council Cabinet Scrutiny Committee refer to one councillor's suggestion that a disproportionate number of responses came from the village of Attlebridge, where one of the sponsors lived. They also refer to another councillor's claim that responses came from as far away as Thetford.

The Suffragan Bishop of Thetford at that time was the chair of the Diocesan Education Committee.

19 See report by the director of Children's Services to the Norfolk County Council cabinet meeting, 8 October 2007 (Item 13) on 'Posting a closure notice for Heartsease High School to be replaced by the Open Academy' (p. 5). Available at: www.norfolk/gov/uk/consumption/groups/publicdocuments,committee_report/cabinet081007item13.pdf

20 Cited in section 3.4.4 of the *Outcome of Public Notice Procedure* report (see above, n. 5) to the critical Norfolk County Council cabinet meeting on 7 January 2008.

21 *Eastern Daily Press*, 5 Jan 2008, available at: www.EDP24.co.uk

22 See minutes of Norwich City Council scrutiny committee, 30 July 2007. The contribution recorded of the chair of Heartsease governors is evidence of the extent to which the governing body was mislead by the Department for Children, Schools and Familes and Norfolk County Council regarding its powers. Available at: www.norwich.gov.uk

23 See www.norwich.gov.uk

24 *Eastern Daily Press*, 9 Aug 2007, available at: www.EDP24.co.uk

25 This version varies little from Elliott (2008). The main variation consists of the addition of a postscript.

26 Private email correspondence.

27 Following this meeting on 4 February 2008, the Secretary of State sent a formal letter to Dr Ian Gibson, MP, setting out his response to the issues raised by the Heartsease delegation. The latter did not keep any formal minutes of the meeting.

28 This concern was raised in one of the documents submitted to the Secretary of State in preparation for his meeting with the Heartsease delegation. Authored by two of the parents in the delegation, on behalf of others living in the area, it unequivocally stated that 'whilst not totally against academies the parents do not want this school run by a religious group'. Available on request.

29 The local county councillor in the delegation had already submitted in writing the views he expressed at the meeting, as part of the documentation sent in preparation for the meeting. Available on request.

30 A copy of the letter can be made available on request.

31 See article 'Heartsease academy gets the green light', available at: http://network norwich.co.uk/Mobile/default.aspx?group_id=45835&article_id=107778

32 *Norwich Evening News*, 3 July 2009, available at: www.eveningnews.24.co.uk

33 The following definition is from www.nationalcollege.org.uk/—/national-leaders-of-education.htm

> National leaders of education (NLEs) are outstanding school leaders who, together with the staff in their schools, use their knowledge and experience of teaching to provide additional leadership capacity to schools in challenging circumstances. Many NLEs will have previously worked to support schools in challenging circumstances and all have worked beyond their own school.

34 A term coined by Habermas to refer to external and internal power constraints that distort human communication and which can only be overcome by critical theorizing. See Bullock and Woodings (1982), pp. 297–8.

35 See Becker (1998), pp. 90–3. In any system of ranked groups those in the higher ranks are given greater rights to define the way things are than those in the lower ranks.

Chapter 4

Academy Consultation Meetings: Local Discourse on a National Policy

Kirsten Purcell

Introduction

This chapter focuses on the Discourses[1] that were articulated at consultation meetings regarding three proposed academies in different locations in England. Under the New Labour government consultation with key stakeholders was one of the primary objectives of the 'Feasibility Stage' in setting up an academy, a period that lasted on average six to nine months which began when the Expression of Interest received ministerial approval and ended with the signing of a legally binding Funding Agreement to establish the academy (DCSF, n.d.b, p. 3). This consultation was a combination of that undertaken by the local authority as part of the statutory process to close the predecessor school and that conducted by the proposed sponsors to 'consult widely to develop plans for the organisation, management, and operation of the Academy' (p. 11). The data for this research was collected during consultation meetings for members of staff, school governors, parents, students and community representatives in three contrasting case study sites: Penchester, Bromton and Hetherby.[2]

Based upon this data and an analysis of national policy documents, I argue that national Discourses about choice and diversity, public–private partnerships, independence and innovation were replicated, reworked and contested at a local level in discussions about specific proposed academies. However, I warn that focusing only on the presence of national Discourses conceals the very real and practical concerns of those who were affected locally by the academy proposals, concerns which did not relate to the ideological principles of academies but instead bear considerable resemblance to many of the concerns expressed with regard to school closure and school reorganization more generally. Thus, the focus of this chapter differs from previous research that critiques the handling of the consultation process from the perspective of those campaigning against the academy (Bailey, 2005; Elliot, 2008; Hatcher, 2008a; Muller, 2008), as I do not seek to evaluate the process of establishing academies and the management of the consultation meetings, but rather the content of these meetings, the issues that were raised and the Discourses that were drawn upon.

Researchers studying proposed academies have shown particular interest in campaigns against the establishment of these schools, with scholars analysing the membership, strategies, successes and limitations of specific campaigns (e.g. Benn, 2008; Hatcher and Jones, 2006; Pennell and West, 2007; Regan, 2007). In so doing, they touch upon the concerns of the campaigners, their objections to the privatization of state education and to the proposed sponsor of the school, and their concerns about accountability, admissions, curriculum and the potential impact of the academy on wider educational provision. Although these accounts provide valuable insights into the activities and thoughts of campaigners, in this research I analyse the perspectives of a broader range of actors – local authority officials, sponsors and their representatives, and members of staff, governors, parents and students of the existing schools – emphasizing the importance of considering the perspectives of those situated on both sides of the debate. The three case studies presented here also provide the opportunity for comparative analysis and shed light on the discussions in localities where there are not strong anti-academy campaigns, highlighting that the cases which usually attract attention in the press and in academia are not representative of the situation experienced in many places where academies are being established.

The chapter begins with a brief explanation of my approach to this research, followed by three substantive sections. First, I demonstrate that under New Labour the Discourses drawn upon in national policy documents about academies shifted over time. Second, I analyse the Discourses articulated during the consultation meetings in my case study sites, highlighting instances where the national Discourses were repeated, reworked or contested at the local scale. Finally, I discuss the localized concerns expressed in these meetings that did not relate to national policy Discourses or the distinctive features of the Academies Programme. I argue that these are similar concerns to those documented in the existing literature about school closure and school reorganization more generally, and that this focus on practical concerns was reinforced by the way in which the consultation meetings were managed by the proponents of the academies.[3]

The research approach: a discourse analysis of academy consultation meetings

The data for this research was collected during consultation meetings conducted by the local authority and proposed academy sponsors in Penchester, Bromton and Hetherby. These case studies were chosen to provide contrasting examples of proposed academies, each in the Feasibility Stage at the time of data collection. In Penchester, an academy was proposed to bring together two 11–16 secondary schools, one in an economically disadvantaged suburb and the other in a more affluent adjoining area. It was the first academy proposed for the city, and the sponsor was an individual philanthropist with business interests in the area. In Bromton, the predecessor school for the academy was a faith voluntary-aided 11–16 secondary school in a multi-ethnic, inner-city location. Several academies were planned for the city as part of a broader BSF (Building Schools for the Future) programme, and the proposed sponsor for this academy was an international children's charity that already had academies operating in other areas in England. In Hetherby, a faith organization and a prominent local person were the proposed sponsors for an all-age academy, created through the combination of several first schools, two middle schools and one high school, enabling the transition from a three-tier to two-tier (primary and secondary) school system. The predecessor schools were located in former coalmining villages where there are high levels of unemployment.

I attended public consultation meetings in each of these case studies, including private meetings with members of staff, governors and students where access was granted. The presentations were audio-recorded when consent was given by the speakers, and written notes were made during the question and answer sessions that followed.[4] This chapter is based upon the notes and transcripts from the consultation meetings for the secondary schools in Penchester and Bromton, and for those with students of a broadly comparable age range in Hetherby: the middle and high schools. The data were examined using discourse analysis.

My approach to discourse analysis is informed by Foucauldian theories of Discourse, with methodological guidance drawn from scholars working within a broadly Foucauldian framework (e.g. Duncan, 1990; Rose, 2001), combined with analytical techniques taken from interactional sociolinguistics (e.g. Tannen and Wallet, 1987). Consequently, I bring together two different conceptions of discourse, drawing upon Gee's (1999, pp. 6–7) distinction between Discourse with a 'big D' and discourse with a 'little d'.[5] In interactional sociolinguistics, the term 'discourse' is used to refer to language-in-use, to 'actual instances of communicative action in the medium of language' (Johnstone, 2008, p. 2); while the Foucauldian concept of 'Discourse' embodies beliefs, values and categories which constitute a way of looking at the world (Mills, 1997, p. 6), a 'social framework of intelligibility within which all practices are communicated, negotiated or challenged' (Duncan, 1990, p. 16). These Discourses, therefore, enable and constrain the statements that can be made and how they are understood in specific contexts, with Discourses thus revealed as and produced through recurring themes in the language of individuals, that is, the 'little d' discourse of individuals. Discourses were identified in my data set through a process of coding using the computer software package ATLAS.ti.

National academy Discourses: a shifting discursive landscape

In 2000, the Academies Programme was launched as 'a more radical approach . . . to raise standards by breaking the cycle of underperformance and low expectations', with academies designed to be 'part of a wider programme to extend diversity within the publicly-provided sector' (Blunkett, 2000c). City academies were promoted as publicly funded independent schools, led by private sponsors from 'business, the churches, and the voluntary sector' who would 'bring a new focus and sharpness to the running of schools' (DfEE, 2000, p. 4). City academies were encouraged to develop their own distinctive ethos and were granted 'greater freedom than currently available to maintained schools' (p. 4). They were given flexibility with regard to their management, teaching and admissions arrangements and were 'expected to devise innovative ways of delivering and developing the curriculum' (p. 9). Indeed, innovation has been repeatedly recognized as a key rationale for the programme (Ball, 2005, p. 218; Benn, 2008, p. 33; Hatcher and Jones, 2006, p. 334).

So, as summarized by Woods *et al.* (2007),

> the policy discourse from which academies emerge reflects the 'third way' commitment to combining private principles, values and ways of working with those of the public sector, with the aim of making the traditional public sector more innovative and entrepreneurial.
>
> (p. 238)

The Discourses articulated at the national policy level in 2000, therefore, were about public–private partnerships, diversity and parental choice, freedoms and flexibilities, radical change and innovation.

However, as I have explored in more depth elsewhere (Purcell, 2008) and as other academics have recognized (e.g. Ball, 2009b; Beckett, 2007; Pennell and West, 2007; Rogers and Migniuolo, 2007), the Academies Programme evolved over the duration of the New Labour Government. These developments included changes to the kinds of schools that became academies, the type of sponsors and the form of their financial contributions, the details of the academy Funding Agreements, the role of local authorities and the procurement and delivery of the new buildings. This was accompanied by a discursive shift in the presentation of the programme.

In the final Academies Prospectus published by the New Labour government, academies continued to be described as 'independent state schools', with their independent status seen as 'crucial in enabling Academies to succeed' (DfES, 2007, p. 3). However, there was no mention of freedoms and flexibilities, academies were no longer promoted as bringing radical change and there were only infrequent references to innovation. The range of sponsors had broadened to include 'educational foundations, universities, philanthropists, businesses, private school trusts and the faith communities' (p. 3). Notably, on the DCSF Standards website the relevant experience of these sponsors was emphasized: 'Some are established educational providers, and all of them bring a record of success in other enterprises which they are able to apply to their Academies in partnership with experienced school managers' (DCSF, 2009a). Increasing importance was placed on partnership, not only with these 'experienced school managers', but with other schools, with local authorities and with local stakeholders, 'fitting each Academy to its community and circumstances' (DfES, 2007, p. 3). Thus, although 'Academies are not maintained by the local authority . . . they collaborate closely with it, and with other schools in the area' (DCSF, 2009a), an attempt to bring together the Discourses of independence and partnership.

The Discourses articulated at the national level in more recent policy documents, therefore, were about the involvement of experienced sponsors, partnerships with other educational providers and with the local community, and independence combined with an increasing role for local authorities. The next section seeks to analyse to what extent and in what ways these changing national Discourses were replicated, reworked or contested at a local scale.

Local academy Discourses: repeating, reworking and contesting national Discourses at a local scale

National policy Discourses were referred to in the articulations of individuals speaking at the consultation meetings in my case study sites; both those proposing the academy and those participating in the meetings as members of staff, school governors, parents, students and community representatives. What follows is not an exhaustive analysis of all the national Discourses mentioned in these local discussions; rather I highlight instances in which the national Discourses of choice and diversity, the involvement of private sponsors, independence, partnership and innovation were replicated, reworked, exploited[6] or reversed. I demonstrate that the discursive tensions which developed due to the changing nature of the Academies Programme were reflected in local discourse, alongside tensions which were produced locally through the blending of conflicting national and local Discourses.

Choice and diversity: exploiting and reversing a national Discourse

In Penchester, the local authority explicitly made reference to the national Discourse of choice and diversity, arguing that an academy will 'increase diversity in the district'. However, promoting diversity in school provision was presented as a new duty placed upon local authorities, with the county council making it clear that this was a national, not necessarily local, agenda.

The proponents of the academies in Bromton and Hetherby did not make this link between academies and increased diversity. Instead they exploited the Discourse, using the vocabulary of choice in terms of providing students with curriculum choices and equipping them with the 'skills and qualifications to have choices' when they leave school. However, participants at the governors' and public meetings in Hetherby were aware of the notion of parental choice, but reversed the Discourse, arguing that the academy would actually remove choice. The proposed faith academy would replace ten schools, becoming 'the only school available', 'the only free state school', echoing the concerns of campaigners in Hatcher and Jones's (2006, p. 337) Sheppey case study where 'there'd only be one Academy on the island so there's no choice from 11 onwards'.

The experience of sponsors: mirroring a change in national discourse

As discussed earlier, the range of academy sponsors broadened and in national policy documents their experience and skills were emphasized. Similarly, the sponsors in my case studies were eager to highlight their experience. In Hetherby and Bromton, the sponsors described their educational backgrounds, having 'been in education for 37 years' and as 'former teachers'. In Penchester, meanwhile, although the sponsor explicitly stated that he didn't 'claim to be any, any expert on education', he sought to establish his legitimacy in explaining his work with a children's charity. The sponsors in Penchester and Bromton were also quick to recount their experience with other academies, and emphasized their connection with the locality, either in terms of their business activity or personal stories about being brought up in the area.

Despite these attempts to present themselves as appropriate sponsors, objections were still raised. In particular, there was great suspicion about the motives of the sponsors in all three cases. Questions were asked about what the sponsors would get out of it, and why they had not previously offered their support to the school. Concerns were voiced about the sponsor having a majority on the governing body, with participants questioning the accountability of the sponsors to the community, echoing the fears described by Elliot (2008, p. 358) in Norwich. In Bromton and Hetherby, there were also worries about the religious ethos of the proposed academies with one parent asking, 'will the Academy respect different ethnics . . . and different religions?' while a governor questioned the use of the phrase 'Christian values', arguing that 'they shouldn't be touted as only Christian', especially given that 'there are all sorts of people here'.

Independent but working together: replicating conflicting national Discourses

The tension at the national scale between academies as independent schools while working in partnership with the local authority and other educational providers was replicated at the local level. In Hetherby, academies were described as independent schools within the maintained sector, while in Bromton, the sponsor declared that academies were 'free from some local authority restraints, but work with them', a statement which closely replicates that on the DCSF Standards website cited earlier. The sponsors also emphasized that they would work with other schools: feeder primaries in Bromton, other sixth forms in Penchester and neighbouring 14–19 educational providers in Bromton and Hetherby, with the sponsors in Hetherby repeatedly making reference to being 'part of the local family of schools, and not independent from them'.

However, this did not prevent staff and members of the public from raising concerns about the democratic accountability of the academy in question, asking, for example, 'if the local authority thought things weren't going how they should be, what clout have they got to change the school?' and pointing out that, 'it's not the same as ultimately I have a councillor to go to [at the moment]'. Furthermore, the sponsors' Discourse of partnership did not prevent the new academies from being perceived as a threat to neighbouring schools, with regard to pupil numbers, educational standards and city-level partnerships, concerns similar to those expressed by campaigners in Islington (Muller, 2008, p. 78). In raising these objections, however, individuals demonstrated an unusual capability to take a strategic overview, to consider the implications not just for themselves or their children but collectively, contrasting to the individual concerns discussed below.

Innovation while building on what already exists: blending conflicting national and local Discourses

While local proponents of the academies inherited the tension between independence and partnership from national discourse, they also produced their own contradiction by taking the national innovation Discourse and tempering it with a local Discourse about continuity and building on what already exists. So, one of the sponsor's representatives in Bromton argued that new staff contracts would be introduced to enable greater flexibility: 'it is about innovative new approaches, breaking out of existing norms to improve the quality of life for students and staff'. In Hetherby, the structure of the all-age, partnership-wide academy was described as 'innovative and new', with the sponsor promising 'a broad, balanced, innovative curriculum that inspires them'. However, although the sponsors explained that there would be change and, particularly in Penchester, detailed what would be different and new, they also chose to emphasize continuities, presenting the academy as the 'next step' in Bromton, 'building on existing good practice' in Hetherby, and as 'evolution rather than revolution' in Penchester. Blending these conflicting Discourses, I argue, is a reflection of the complex role that local authority representatives and sponsors had to play, traversing between discourse at different scales, playing a mediatory role, translating national Discourses into a form that tried to avoid criticizing and alienating the people who worked in, studied at or sent their children to the predecessor school.

Local academy Discourses: practical concerns about school reorganization

Focusing only on the presence of national academy Discourses, however, conceals the very real and practical concerns expressed by many of those individuals affected locally by the proposals. These kinds of concerns about the practicalities of establishing a school are touched upon by other writers, with the site of the new school being an issue for some campaigners in Pennell and West's (2007, p. 15) study, and the impact of building work on children's safety expressed as a concern by school staff in Islington (Muller, 2008, pp. 80–1). Hatcher and Jones (2006, p. 334) explicitly recognize that 'general sentiments – responses to the Academies project – were combined with support for more localised causes', and I would echo their observation that 'what stands out . . . is the diversity of issues' (p. 338). Here, I provide details about some of the concerns that were frequently voiced in my case studies in order to demonstrate that the discussions at the consultation meetings were not predominantly ideological debates about the principles of the Academies Programme, but rather the expression of localized and often individual concerns that relate to school closure and school reorganization more broadly and which are firmly rooted in place.

Localized concerns

The particular geographies of my case study sites brought about specific concerns. For example, in the dispersed village communities in Hetherby, there were worries about transportation, especially the cost of public transport, the likely increase in traffic, and the length and safety of the walking route to the new schools. The concern was particularly that students would start making this journey at age 11 rather than age 13, a concern that resulted not from the academy but from the school reorganization from a three- to two-tier system made possible by the academy funding. While in Bromton, members of the community feared that the new buildings would restrict their access to the green space that currently surrounds the school, which is valued by this inner-city community for dog walking and playing football. They were keen to see the environmental quality of the site improved, with 'allotments where kids grow things', trees to 'fence off pollution from [the main road]' and reassurance that there was no contamination of the site from the industry across the road.

There were also concerns about changes to the structure of the schools, concerns which, again, are not specific to academies. There was particular unease in Hetherby, where discussions were as much about the transition to a two-tier system and the creation of an all-through school as about the unique features of an academy. For example, proponents argued that a two-tier system would reduce the number of transfers between schools, and that an all-through school would bring consistency and continuity in policies, practices and personnel. However, despite assurances that the age groups would be kept separate where appropriate, concerns were still raised by governors that it would be 'intimidating and daunting for four-year-olds', and by parents that it was 'really unrealistic' to think that 'a group of 16-year-old boys will look after the little ones'. There was similar scepticism in Penchester to the sponsor's suggestion that the 'older ones' in the new sixth form would 'help the younger ones', acting as 'mentors and role models'. The size of the school, class sizes and staff–pupil ratios, the internal structure of the school and changes to the catchment areas were also subjects raised in the consultation meetings.

Finally, there was immense concern about the disruption and uncertainty that the proposals would bring. Parents worried about the 'hassle' and 'upheaval' for their own children, about the effect on 'one of my boys [who] has only one year until his GCSEs'. The building works invoked particular concerns about the loss of space and facilities during the construction process, that the children would have to move schools again once the new buildings were ready, and the impact of the buildings on residents living near to the school. Staff, parents and students were anxious about the uncertainty that surrounded the proposals, noticing that in the meetings the sponsors kept 'saying "might do" and "may do" . . . We don't know what'll happen'. As one participant in Hetherby highlighted, 'you said increasing staff–pupil ratios if we can afford it, what if you can't?'

Therefore, for many individuals in my case studies their concerns were not objections to the principle of an academy but very localized concerns about themselves and/or their children and the practical impact that the academy would have on their well-being. So while Hatcher and Jones (2006, p. 336) warn, 'it would be wrong, though, to overestimate the localism of the campaigns', I would argue that when a broader range of individuals is considered, individuals perhaps without the national networks and ideological motivations of anti-academy campaigners, local specificities are crucial.

Concerns about school reorganization

I contend that these localized Discourses bear considerable resemblance to many of the themes expressed in school closure and school reorganization consultation meetings more generally. For example, Basu (2007, pp. 113, 116) identifies similar fears in her case study of school closures in Ontario, including fears about the safety of younger children, walking long distances to school, and the impact on community programmes and facilities. The latter two concerns were also raised in Bondi's (1987, p. 212) Manchester case study, while children's safety and transportation to school were among the concerns voiced by the parents of a primary school closed in Invercargill, New Zealand (Witten *et al.*, 2003, pp. 214, 217).

The focus on localized practical concerns was reinforced by the way in which the consultation meetings were managed by the proponents of the academies. First, what an academy is was explained to varying degrees of accuracy and depth in the consultation meetings and so it is possible that many of the participants did not fully comprehend how the situation was different from any other school closure and the establishment of any other new state school. As my interview data suggest, there was not always a full understanding even among the most involved parents and governors, with academies described as 'ordinary schools with bells on', the only perceived difference being 'how the schools feed into it'. Second, the proponents of the academies generally presented the consultation meetings as spaces to discuss what the academy might be like, rather than the more fundamental question of whether there should be an academy. For example, in Bromton, the principal designate said to staff, 'now we have the opportunity to work together on what the [Bromton] Academy will be like'. This mirrors Hatcher's (2008a, p. 24) and Elliott's (2008, p. 360) findings that the consultations were not designed to elicit people's views about whether the predecessor school should be replaced by an academy but rather asked participants what they would like to happen at the academy. Hetherby was an exception in this regard, with the local authority explicitly asking people to contribute alternative models. However, it was made quite clear and was keenly felt by the consultees that any alternative model was unlikely to succeed, especially since the funding was only available through the Academies Programme.

Summary and conclusions

Under the New Labour government the Academies Programme evolved, with changes that were accompanied by a notable discursive shift: the strong statements about choice and diversity, freedoms and flexibilities, radical change and innovation were replaced by a more cautious discourse of private sponsors but with relevant experience, and independence from but also partnerships with local authorities and other schools. Based upon data collected during consultation meetings in three case study sites, I argue that these national policy Discourses were repeated, reworked and contested at the local scale. For example, although the national Discourse of choice and diversity was repeated by proponents of the academy in Penchester, the sponsors and their representatives in Hetherby and Bromton exploited the Discourse, using the term 'choice' for a different purpose than was intended, while the consultees in Hetherby reversed the Discourse, arguing that in replacing ten schools with one faith academy, choice would be removed.

Furthermore, the changes to the Academies Programme produced discursive tensions at the national level, tensions that were in turn reflected in local discourse. The tension in national policy documents between academies being independent schools yet encouraged to work in partnership with other educational providers, local stakeholders and the local authority was replicated at the local scale. However, while local proponents of the academies inherited this tension, they also produced their own contradiction by blending the national Discourse of innovation with a local Discourse about continuity and building on what already exists. I contend that this is a product of the complex role that local authority representatives and sponsors had to play, mediating between discourse at different scales, tempering national Discourses to avoid criticizing the people who worked in, studied at or sent their children to the predecessor school.

Focusing only on the presence of national academy Discourses, however, precludes recognition of the localized concerns of members of staff, governors, parents and students affected by specific proposals. Indeed, much of the discussion in the consultation meetings was about practical concerns with regard to the school site, transportation, traffic and children's safety, changes to the structure of the school, catchment areas and class sizes, and the disruption and uncertainty that the changes would bring. Consequently, I argue that for many individuals their concerns were not ideological objections to the principle of an academy, but personal concerns about its practical impact. Thus, there are parallels with, and I would suggest significant value in learning from, the existing work by scholars on school closure consultations more broadly.

To conclude, I would like to emphasize the presence of and the relationships between the three dialectics that underlie my argument in this chapter: national and local Discourses, ideological and practical debates, and collective and individual concerns about the Academies Programme. First, at the local scale, national Discourses and the tensions between them were reproduced and reworked, at times brought together in uneasy combination with local Discourses. Second, in the absence of strong anti-academy campaigns, ideological debates about the principles of the Academies Programme were scarce, and instead consultees expressed localized concerns about the practical impacts of the proposed new school. Third, at the local level, while collective concerns were occasionally voiced, more often they were overshadowed by the frequent expression of individuals' concerns about themselves and/or their children and the impact of the academy on their well-being.

These findings have important implications for the quality of democracy and the potential for collective action. Under the New Labour government academy proposals did not always result in high-profile campaigns; instead, the process of consultation often involved a reworking of national policy Discourses and the articulation of localized and individual concerns. During these consultations, local authority representatives, including those directly elected, found themselves in a mediating position between central government and local people, delivering a policy that may have conflicted with their own ideological perspectives. However, the financial ramifications of not doing so were such that there was little scope for open discussion about the principles of academies, leaving participants able to influence, at best, what the academy would be like when it was opened, rather than whether it should be opened at all. Thus, as my research has shown, consultation meetings at the local level are more likely to focus on practical and individual concerns rather than encouraging deeper democratic participation through a broad discussion of the issues.

Acknowledgements

This chapter is based on doctoral research funded by the Economic and Social Research Council. I am grateful to Molly Warrington and Helen Gunter for their comments on a draft of this chapter. I would also like to thank all the participants in each of my case studies.

Notes

1 I use Discourse with a capital 'D' throughout this chapter to refer to Foucauldian Discourses, and discourse with a lowercase 'd' to refer to the linguistic understanding of discourse as communication in the medium of language.

2 Pseudonyms are used in this chapter to protect the identity of those speaking at the consultation meetings.

3 I use the term 'proponents' throughout this chapter to refer to local authority officers and to the sponsors and their representatives. However, I must highlight that there was considerable variability in the extent to which the local authority supported and actively promoted the academy.

4 Extracts from these notes are presented as quotations in this chapter, although I appreciate the problems in doing so.

5 Following Gee (1999, pp. 9–10), the term 'discourse analysis' is used to collectively refer to analytical approaches to 'big D' Discourse and 'little d' discourse.

[6] This is a term taken from interactional sociolinguistics where it is used in relation to frames rather than Discourses. Frames are the interpretive schemata that enable participants to understand 'what it is that is going on' (Goffman, 1974, p. 10), and they entail expectations about how an individual will participate in an interaction (Kendall, 2008, p. 543). For example, a speech activity may be categorized as taking place within a 'narrative frame', 'teasing frame', 'caregiving frame' or 'examination frame'. Exploiting a frame involves using a frame for a different purpose than was intended. The terms 'blending' (i.e. combining two or more frames) and 'conflicting', used later in this chapter, similarly derive from interactional sociolinguistics. While I recognize that a frame is not equivalent to a Discourse, I have found it helpful to borrow this vocabulary to describe the ways in which participants refer to, manage and contest different Discourses.

Chapter 5

Academies in the Public Interest: A Contradiction in Terms?

Harriet Rowley and Alan Dyson

Introduction

The Academies Programme was one of the most contentious policies of the post-1997 Labour governments. For good reasons, critics were suspicious of sponsors' motives for their involvement and concerned that, in the absence of full democratic accountability, they would act in ways that did not reflect the public interest. Although we recognize this danger, in this chapter we wish to argue that it was not inevitable that it would materialize. We do so by presenting an example of an academy sponsored by an organization from beyond the world of education and educational governance as usually defined, yet working in the interests of local people. Weston Academy is one of a small number of schools sponsored by social housing landlords (Thornhill and Kent-Smith, 2009), in this case, the sponsor is Weston Housing Trust, whose responsibility is to provide affordable housing in the areas served by the academy and beyond. In line with the trust's overall mission, the aim of the academy is not only to improve pupils' attainment, but also to provide a range of services for children and their families in an effort to build a sustainable community. Although this one example cannot legitimize the Academies Programme as a whole (if it needs such legitimation), we wish to argue that it nonetheless shows how this programme has been able to bring new resources and perspectives to bear on problems with which school systems have struggled for generations – notably, the link between deprived areas and poor educational outcomes.

The evidence on which these arguments are based stems from a development and research partnership between Weston Housing Trust and the Centre for Equity in Education in the University of Manchester. Under the aegis of this partnership, a team of researchers from the Centre gathers evidence in relation to the aims, strategies, implementation processes and impacts of the academy initiative. This evidence is then used to inform a 'critical friend' relationship between researchers and trust and academy leaders, in which the strategies and practices of the academy are interrogated with a view to their further development. Through this process, trust and academy leaders have the opportunity for evidence-based reflection on their work. In return, researchers have the opportunity to work closely with housing and education practitioners and to understand the challenges and opportunities with which the current policy context presents them. In this way, they are able to pursue the core agenda of the Centre, which is to identify the potential for more equitable structures, policies and practices to be developed in the English education system. A key element of the partnership is the sponsorship by the trust of a doctoral studentship, held by the lead author of this chapter.

Using the evidence generated by the partnership's activities, we examine in this chapter the rationale behind the trust's involvement with the academy, and by using a theory of change framework we analyse how it hopes to achieve its vision. We then discuss the main tensions that the partnership has encountered, in an effort to further explore how those working on the ground are interpreting the current policy context. This discussion leads us to recognize that the impact that Weston is able to have at this stage is limited due to contradictions within policy. We argue that policies that encourage competition between schools and the pursuit of narrow targets are at odds with those that encourage schools to form partnerships with other services and meet the needs of children and their families holistically. Reflecting on our work with Weston Academy, we argue that its efforts to embark upon ambitious plans to transform the community that it serves are inhibited due to policy pressures to improve standards and lack of guidance on how to develop a coherent community strategy. We also suggest, however, that the distinctive nature of the Weston initiative raises questions about how we understand the governance of the school system and the role of schools in wider social strategies.

An unusual partnership?

Weston Academy is located in the suburbs of a manufacturing town which itself forms part of a large industrial and post-industrial conurbation. It opened some two years ago, bringing together two previously separate schools facing 'challenging circumstances'. Weston is typical of many other schools within the Academies Programme in that it is intended to improve education in an area where schools had previously struggled to perform. Informants in the academy and the housing trust report that local people experience significant levels of social exclusion, high unemployment, low adult literacy levels and low levels of aspiration – problems which have partly caused and have certainly been compounded by schools which consistently achieve below national average results. However, what makes Weston Academy different from many is the core business of its sponsor as a provider of social housing. As part of a long-term national policy of reducing the role of local authorities as direct providers of social housing, Weston Housing Trust was set up to manage a large stock of social housing transferred from the local authority in 2000, taking over many of the duties (and some of the staff) previously discharged by the local authority itself. There is a significant overlap (though not perfect congruence) between the areas where the trust provides housing and the areas from which the academy recruits its students. Around one-third of the academy's intake live in trust-managed housing. Managing housing in this sense extends beyond allocations, rent collection and repairs, and extends to the creation of sustainable communities where people want to live and social problems are minimized. In many ways, therefore, the sponsorship of the academy was seen as extension to the regeneration work the trust had already begun. As one board member explained:

> As a housing trust, we made promises to our tenants. We have improved the houses themselves, updating kitchens, bathrooms and so on; then we turned our attention to the physical environment – improving lighting and security, regenerating the "no-go" areas. We promised our tenants lots, and we delivered (recent survey suggests 90% satisfaction level amongst tenants). Now we are promising them an Academy that will work for them too – they expect us to deliver.

To this extent, the academy has a role in a wider strategy, and its core task of offering 'good schooling' to local children is set within the context of the trust's overarching vision of a sustainable community.

At a time when partnership working between schools and other services has been actively encouraged by government, the relationship between the trust and the academy can be seen as in many ways an 'ideal partnership'. Both the predecessor schools and the housing trust were working in the same localities and were, in their different ways, seeking to reduce the effects of deprivation. The housing trust prides itself on its distinctive ethic, working in the public interest yet free of the bureaucratic constraints of many public services. Its strap-line – 'great homes, great neighbourhoods, great people' – recognizes its commitment not only to managing 'bricks and mortar', but also to developing neighbourhoods that people want to live in and of which they are proud. It is, therefore, an example of a sponsor capable of bringing a perspective to bear on schools from outside the traditional educational world. However, that perspective is rooted recognizably in a concern for the public good rather than in the potentially more idiosyncratic interests of wealthy individuals and businesses. In this respect, it is significant that both the academy and the sponsoring housing trust have followed similar trajectories in terms of governance. Both have their origins in local authority-managed services. Both retain a distinct public service ethos and work with the grain of local policy – the academy aligning itself with the local authority's direction of travel in education, and the trust contributing to the local strategic partnership. Yet both do this while remaining outside the formal mechanisms of local authority control. Moreover, although the connections between housing and education may not be immediately obvious, they are, in fact, inextricably linked. We now turn, therefore, to exploring this relationship further.

Unpacking the relationship between housing and education

Typically, regeneration efforts in areas of concentrated deprivation have tried to create sustainable communities by providing suitable housing, diversifying tenure and improving other services such as schools, health centres and leisure facilities. In this way, they seek to retain (or even attract) more 'aspirational' and better-off families in order to create more of a mixed-income community (Silverman *et al.*, 2006). However, in reality this has been difficult to achieve and, due to a variety of political, social and economic factors, many social housing providers and schools working in deprived areas have found themselves dealing with an increasingly challenged and disadvantaged population. Once caught in this spiral of decline, service providers such as schools find themselves trapped in a vicious circle where the decline of the area and the decline of the school reinforce one another (Power and Mumford, 1999). As this happens, those living in the area often face increasing challenges and, in some cases, present increasing challenges to service providers. Housing estates become subject to high levels of antisocial behaviour, unemployment and crime, with the consequence that social housing providers struggle to make the houses on the estates that they mange desirable places to live. These problems also manifest themselves in the schools that serve these areas and consequently standards of achievement are low, which in turn adds to the difficulties different types of families face.

A range of critics (see Crowther *et al.*, 2003; Woods *et al.*, 1998) have argued that the marketization of schooling and housing has exacerbated the situation by contributing to the further concentration of social and economic poverty within certain areas. When the Conservative governments applied market theories to the public sector in the 1980s and 1990s it was claimed that by increasing choice such organizations would have to be more responsive to consumers and, by creating a climate of competition, schools and housing would improve as they strove to meet the high demands of the customer (Woods *et al.*, 1998). However, choice also allows better-resourced people in deprived neighbourhoods to opt out of local provision or to move entirely, thus reinforcing patterns of area segregation. The spatial concentration of poverty has also been exacerbated by the trajectory of housing policy over the last 50 years. During this time, the country has witnessed a process of 'residualization of public housing' where social housing has become increasingly targeted at the ever smaller group labelled as 'the poor' and has become increasingly concentrated in particular geographic areas (Gregory, 2009, p. 12). In this way, a situation has arisen in which residential areas are increasingly polarized in terms of the wealth and poverty of their residents, and where the residents of different areas have very different experiences (Dorling *et al.*, 2007; Lupton, 2001). Affluent parents are more likely to have the informal knowledge and financial resources to ensure they live in favourable conditions where there is good housing, schools, health services and other life-enhancing opportunities. Poorer families are more likely to end up living in poor housing, attend schools which struggle to maintain standards and use public services which are increasingly unable to meet the volume of challenges that are presented to them.

In many deprived areas both housing and education providers have been trying to tackle the problems associated with concentrated disadvantage. In the past, their efforts have tended to be uncoordinated and they have failed to work together as partners and consider the implications of their policies for one another (Evans, 1998). There has also been a lack of co-ordination at policy level between the two sectors, which in turn has been echoed on the ground level. Whatever the merits or otherwise of the Academies Programme, therefore, it is arguable that it has created a situation, in the Weston case at least, where the traditional disconnection of housing and education can be overcome and a coherent strategy for addressing shared issues can be developed across the two sectors.

Promising developments

In an effort to track and inform the development of Weston Academy's approach, the research team has adopted a theory of change framework (Anderson, 2005; Connell and Kubisch, 1998; Dyson and Todd, 2010). Put simply, this means working with stakeholders in the academy initiative to elicit and co-construct a 'theory' of how that initiative will work – that is, a set of linked assumptions about how the actions embodied in the initiative will lead to the outcomes to which it aims in the situation within which it is located. By tracking how those actions unfold and the short- and medium-term impacts they have, researchers are then able to substantiate or disconfirm this theory, without necessarily waiting for end-point outcomes to emerge. This tracking process also acts as a useful developmental tool by giving stakeholders early feedback as to how far the impacts they expect to have are actually materializing.

At this stage, the research team has concentrated on the process of theory elicitation and on tracking the early stages of its implementation. Data have been collected through a series of interviews with key stakeholders in which they were invited to outline what they saw as the aims of the academy initiatives, what they saw as its principal action components or strands, and how they thought the strands of action would lead to the intended outcomes. In an iterative process, a theory of change was modelled diagrammatically (see Figure 5.1) and refined through further discussion with the stakeholders. In contrast to the action planning with which leaders of initiatives are typically familiar, such modelling deliberately simplifies complex actions and causal pathways in order to emphasize strategic goals and inform the strategic development of the initiative.

Figure 5.1 therefore groups the multiple aspects of the work of the academy into a number of strands. In brief, these strands of actions (rectangles) consist of:

- a teaching- and learning-oriented strand concerned with enhancing student engagement with learning, creating diverse pathways to success, and thereby improving student achievement
- a vocational strand, concerned with building on the academy's business and enterprise specialism to develop young people's entrepreneurial and vocational skills
- an Every Child Matters strand, concerned with offering student support and developing active citizenship
- a community strand, concerned with maximizing the involvement of families and communities with the academy, acting as a hub for community and community development activities, and providing a base for family and community support work.

The end-point outcomes (hexagons) that the stakeholders hope that these strands of actions will eventually produce are also pictured. The lines of direction (arrows) indicate the ways in which the stakeholders theorized how their plans will contribute to achieving their objectives. The diagram also indicates two distinct but overlapping aspects of Weston Academy's approach: actions and outcomes which are broadly concerned with school improvement, and those which are intended to impact the wider community.

Weston Academy: a product of its time

Since the development and research partnership began, the research team has been cognizant of the fact that, in many ways, Weston Academy reflects an important strand of the policy agenda pursued by New Labour during its period of office. The Green Paper *Every Child Matters* (2003) and the

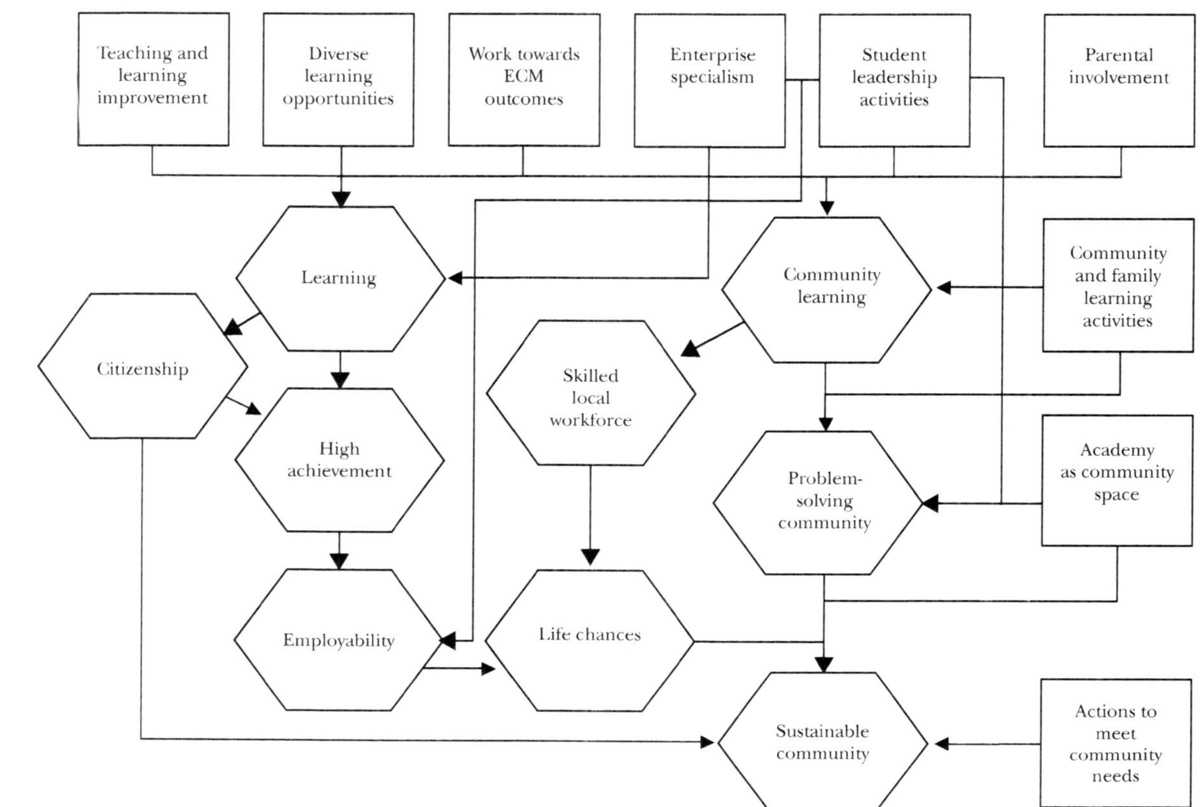

FIGURE 5.1 Weston Academy theory of change diagram

ensuing legislation (Children's Act 2004; Education and Inspections Act 2006), together with policies which sought to target deprivation at area level (Education Action Zones, 1998; Excellence in Cities, 1999; National Challenge programmes, 2008) and the increased provision of child, family and community services (in the current extended services agenda), all signified a distinctive positioning of schools and schooling. In different ways and to different extents, they emphasized the role of schools in combating the effects of social disadvantage, and the consequent need for schools to work with each other and, particularly, with partners from other organizations and services who might be able to enhance their efforts in this respect. Viewed in this light, Weston Academy is a prime example of two sectors which share a set of similar values and goals coming together and recognizing how working together can enable them to have a greater impact upon reducing the effects of deprivation upon community members' lives.

However, by no means all educational policy that New Labour governments pursued was consistent with this pattern and Weston Academy reflects some of the tensions and contradictions that this has generated. As is widely acknowledged, New Labour's efforts at combating the effects of educational disadvantage were set in a wider policy context in which the market-driven policies of the 1980s and 1990s were retained. The 'third way' (Giddens, 1998) approach to policy in practice meant a continued extension of the role of competition, choice and high-stakes accountability which called into question the real meaning of the welfarist language in which policy was sometimes cloaked. The emphasis on school autonomy vis-à-vis local control continued to weaken both the ties between schools and local areas and the capacity of local authorities to engage schools in their 'place-shaping' strategies. At the same time, the 'standards agenda' required schools to pay high levels of attention to the business of ensuring that their students do well in tests and examinations, and made the development of a community-oriented role problematic. In many ways, the Academies Programme was the logical conclusion to this pattern; schools largely divorced from local democratic control and (in some cases) distanced from the local family of schools, on the assumption that this increased independence would somehow pay dividends in increased innovation and higher standards of attainment.

There seems, therefore, to have been a contradiction emerging in policy that continues to be echoed at the ground level. On the one hand, the government persisted in introducing market-driven policies that increase competition, accountability and give greater independence to single institutions. On the other hand, they also encouraged collaborative practice and placed greater emphasis on public services working holistically on an area-wide level (Ranson, 2008). These two sets of policies are arguably based on fundamentally different value systems, reflecting a lack of confidence and indecision by the Labour governments as to how far they were really committed to creating conditions for all to achieve (Ranson, 2008).

Weston Academy could perhaps be said to embody this contradiction. Operating as an academy, the school has independence from the local authority, and greater freedom and investment than other schools in the area, but has come under increasing pressure to improve standards quickly. However, the sponsor has goals that certainly include, but also extend well beyond, the internal performance of the school and the standards of attainment achieved by its students. The housing trust needs to tackle deprivation on an area-wide scale, working with a range of partners including public, private and third sector organizations to create a more sustainable community. While, therefore, a high-performing academy is crucial to the realization of these aims, it would be a wasted opportunity if the academy was not using its considerable resources and unparalleled access to children and families to make a wider contribution to the trust's area agenda. It would, of course, be a disaster if the 'success' of the academy were ever to be bought at the expense of this wider agenda – if, for instance, it were to raise standards following the path of some other schools by engaging in large-scale exclusions of local children and young people, or seeking to recruit its students from other, more advantaged, areas.

Establishing a new school is challenging in any circumstances; doing so in a situation where educational outcomes have historically been low is doubly challenging. However, finding a way to transform these outcomes under intense scrutiny and pressure for short-term gains, and at the same time to play a key part in a wider area strategy is considerably more challenging yet. Not surprisingly, these challenges have been reflected in tensions in the academy initiative. In the next section, therefore, we explore three tensions that have arisen during the initial stages of the academy's development.

Initial tensions

The first tension was between the broad strategic aims of the academy initiative and the detailed actions needed to realize those aims. As Figure 5.1 indicates, stakeholders were able to identify how they expected broad strands of actions to contribute to end-point outcomes. However, breaking down these connections into more intermediate stages and translating the broad strategies into concrete plans has proved a major challenge. Furthermore, when stakeholders did strategically plan actions, such as a particular intervention, they often found it difficult to link this back to their original motivations or what intermediate steps would be involved in order to produce their intended outcomes. For example, many members of the academy's executive board felt that parental engagement was a high priority not only to improve the children's academic results and attitude to learning but also to ensure that parents are given the opportunity to develop new skills to equip them to improve their own lives. However, developing strategies that actually improve parental engagement in an area where many are disillusioned with education has been a real challenge for the school. Another challenge related to this tension that the stakeholders have faced is choosing which broad categories they should prioritize first and how to decide which courses of action they should take. As one stakeholder commented:

> Most of the time we are fire fighting–dealing with whatever comes through the door so trying to act strategically can be a real challenge. It's difficult to coordinate everything that is going on in the school and ensure that it relates to our original goals. (Interview)

Tensions of this kind are not unique to the Weston initiative. As we suggested earlier, over the last decade there has been an increase in policies that encourage schools to be more community-oriented and provide services above and beyond the standard curriculum. However, research which has evaluated schools' efforts in these areas has identified similar challenges to those experienced by Weston Academy (Cummings *et al.*, 2005; Cummings *et al.*, 2007; Crowther *et al.*, 2003; Dyson *et al.*, 2006). This evidence suggests that, while governments have provided detailed guidance (some would say, prescription) in respect of the standards agenda, there has been no equivalent guidance as to how schools are to engage in the wider family and community agenda. Quite how a school is to develop 'extended' provision and wider partnerships, how it is to prioritize among a wide range of possible actions and outcomes, and how it is to reconcile all of this with its 'core business' of teaching and learning has been left largely unspecified. Rather than answer these fundamental questions governments have either provided a list of activities that schools might choose to offer or shied away from providing any specific advice and relied on local developments. This has meant that many schools have worked in a rather *ad hoc* or uncoordinated approach that does not necessarily match the specific needs of the community but works on the basis of practitioners' hunches or is tailored towards particular funding grants. Although, therefore, the policy context has provided encouragement for schools to engage with ambitious area agendas, there has been no supportive framework that helps them achieve their goals.

The second significant tension reflects a contradiction that exists within policy. We argued earlier that the Academies Programme reflects the continuation of market-driven and standards-oriented approaches within education, placing schools under significant pressure to improve academic attainment quickly. On the other hand, it is set within a context where schools are also expected to develop partnership approaches, become increasingly community-oriented, and embrace the wider Every Child

Matters agenda. Weston Academy is a good example of a school that has tried to make progress in both these policy areas. However, balancing these fundamentally different concerns has been a real challenge for the stakeholders. As we might expect, the focus in the early period of the academy's development has been largely upon within-school development strategies aimed at improving results. In focusing on these strategies, the academy's leadership has been able to draw on extensive prior experience of 'what works' in driving up standards. However, the development of a viable community strategy has proved more problematic. The development of such a strategy takes the academy into largely uncharted waters. It has taken the bold step of appointing a senior professional with community development expertise to its senior leadership team – but this expertise is not shared by other members of the team whose background is in schools, while the community manager has only limited prior experience of schools. Moreover, the challenges in this field are fundamentally more complex and intertwined than those in school 'improvement', the intended outcomes are broader, and the most effective lines of action are less certain. A longer-term, more exploratory approach is necessary, but this sits ill with demands for short-term gains and with the planning cycles that follow from such demands. The problem is compounded by the fact that the basic structures and resources of the academy, from its buildings (it continues to occupy the buildings of its predecessor schools) to its staffing structures and inherited relationships with families and with other agencies, are based on traditional school models.

The consequence of all this is that it has proved easier in the short term for the academy to put in place its clearly defined and high-priority strategy for generating high standards of attainment than to develop an effective community strategy. There is evidence that this situation is beginning to change and that such a strategy will emerge in due course, accelerated, no doubt, by the eventual move into purpose-built accommodation. The danger, of course, is that the two aspects of the academy's work will have become sufficiently disconnected that they fail to inform each other in the ways that were originally envisaged.

Finally, there are tensions around how and how far the academy can challenge existing governance and accountability arrangements. The academy embodies a relationship between two social agencies – a school and a housing trust – that is fundamentally different from those to which we have become accustomed in this country. Strictly speaking the academy is not in partnership with the trust in the way that schools historically have developed partnership arrangements with many other organizations. Nor are the academy and trust governed by a 'third party' such as the local authority, which might have similar powers over each. Rather, within the frameworks and accountabilities of the state education system, a non-educational but publicly oriented organization – the trust – takes responsibility for the school. This raises issues which go way beyond the technical guidance that is available on academy governance – issues particularly around the degree of control over 'purely' educational matters which the trust should exercise, the legitimacy of such control given the non-educational orientation of the trust, and the balance that is to be struck between the government-mandated agenda for all schools, and the trust-driven agenda which sees the academy as a resource for community sustainability. There are also issues around accountability. The narrowly focused accountability mechanisms of Ofsted (Office for Standards in Education) and the publication of results hardly address the agenda for which the trust needs (at least in part) to hold the academy's leadership to account. Moreover, the trust itself is accountable for the use of public monies and, less formally, to its residents for the quality of service it provides for them. These are forms of accountability that are quite different both from the traditional accountabilities imposed on schools and from the electoral accountabilities of local councils. Quite how they extend to its stewardship of the academy is unclear.

None of these issues is irresolvable, but, in the absence of clear guidance, they have created some uncertainty in the academy initiative. It is entirely possible that arrangements will emerge which will reconcile the multiple governance and accountability demands to which it is subject, and which might see it forging a new kind of democratic accountability by drawing on the trust's links with local people. On the other hand, the worst-case scenario is that these multiple demands will never adequately be reconciled, that the academy will find itself pulled in different directions, and that the trust will find itself responsible for an institution which it cannot entirely control.

Some final thoughts

It is far too early in the life of Weston Academy to say whether and how the tensions identified above will be resolved, or whether and how the academy initiative will achieve its ambitious aims. The strong impression at this early stage is of a bold initiative beset by tensions and uncertainties that are largely not of its own making. It is certainly the case that this situation arises to a significant extent out of the contradictions and indeterminacies of government policy. A greater coherence in national policy, a clearer steer as to where policy is heading, and more authoritative guidance where guidance is needed would all make the task of the Weston Academy and Trust considerably easier. Whether any of these is likely to emerge in the post-New Labour era is, of course, a moot point.

However, it is also important to recognize that some of the tensions and uncertainties arise because the Weston initiative – and other analogous initiatives elsewhere in the country – are genuinely moving into uncharted waters. In particular, the academy initiative challenges some assumptions about how the school system in England should function, and does so in two fundamental respects. First, the school system has operated historically as a hermetically sealed world. Schools have operated in more or less splendid isolation from other agencies and organizations involved with the children, families and communities they supposedly serve, and have accordingly been managed through largely self-contained structures originating (increasingly) in Sanctuary Buildings and (decreasingly) in civic centres and county halls across the country. The Weston initiative suggests that this need not be so. Schools might actually be governed from outside the education system and, moreover, might be so in a way that does not necessarily fatally compromise their social responsibility, or even their democratic accountability. This external perspective might turn out to offer little more than the flawed inputs of governing bodies or 'old-style' local education authorities. Just possibly, however, it might turn out to be enriching, enlivening and democratically engaging.

Second, and related to this, the Weston initiative questions the assumption that we know what schools are for, and that they are primarily for teaching things to children. Weston Academy, by contrast, draws on an English tradition which goes back at least as far as Henry Morris's village colleges in Cambridgeshire (Morris, 1924), and which sees the school not simply as a producer of more or less 'educated' individuals but as a social institution, integrated into a network of local resources and services, and contributing to the sustainability of local communities. This tradition has spluttered into life somewhat fitfully from time to time, and is arguably enjoying something of a revival within the current extended services agenda (DfES, 2005c). However, Weston challenges us to think what it might mean, not just in the current policy context, but in a context where flexibilities have (in some respects at least) been increased, and innovation is being positively encouraged.

As we stated at the outset, the Weston case is not enough by itself either to condemn or to justify the New Labour academies initiative as a whole. However, academies have happened, and are happening. While it may be important to identify and critique their problematic aspects, it may also be advisable to learn from the unique experiments they offer. That is what our ongoing work with the Weston initiative seeks to do.

Chapter 6

From Reality to Vision: The 'Birth' of the Petchey Academy in Hackney

David Daniels

Introduction

> It is the 1st September 2005 and I am sitting with the only other employee of the Petchey Academy, an administrator, in a borrowed office loaned by the Learning Trust in Hackney.[1] The room is devoid of any normal office accoutrements with the exception of two desks. No telephone, no computer: only seemingly a very large blank sheet of paper! Where do we start and what do we do next?

This extract from my diary provides an insight into the start of the Petchey Academy. From the outset I was aware that I was not just opening a new secondary school: I was opening an 'academy' secondary school. What could, should and would be the difference between opening this academy and a typical secondary school? From such humble beginnings in September 2005, the Petchey Academy opened in September 2006 with 180 students and has risen to be an academy which Ofsted (Office for Standards in Education) declared in January 2009 to be a 'good school with many outstanding features, some of which are unique'. Without externally validated results, we could not claim the accolade of outstanding overall at that point in time.

The question I have frequently asked myself is: what knowledge, experience, support, academic training and professional expertise did I possess to achieve considerable success in such a short time? In addition, what other factors have, in hindsight, contributed to our current success? Crawford (2007) also reflects how daunting setting up a new school is: 'Sitting on a tiny primary school chair I thought "£29 million and a school opening in a year's time – where do I start?"' (p. 15).

The purpose of this chapter is to reflect on the resources, activities and practices I have used, together with the patron (Jack Petchey), sponsor (the Petchey Foundation) and chair of governors (Andrew Billington – chief executive of the Petchey Foundation), to 'give birth' to the Petchey Academy. It is principally a self-reflective piece in which I call on aspects of theory that supported my thinking about the development of the Petchey

Academy. At the time of writing, the Petchey Academy has just commenced its fourth year of operation, with a student body of 720 students – ultimately to number 1,250. The chapter will involve reflections on entrepreneurial leadership and in particular how this is facilitated by the Funding Agreement of the Petchey Academy (DCSF, 2005)[2] and what makes the opening of this academy different to that of any other new secondary school.

As a 'pioneer' principal of an early academy, I also gave considerable time to reflecting on my headship experiences in two previous schools and the development of a leadership and management style appropriate for this new venture, which I describe as 'pragmatic, instructional and authentic' (PIA).

Secondary education in Hackney

In 2002 the benchmark of five A*–C grades at GCSE stood at 32 per cent for the Borough of Hackney, which was well below national average. In addition, Hackney possessed some of the highest deprivation indices in the UK, with over 40 per cent of secondary age students and their parents deserting education within the borough, preferring to take places at secondary schools in contiguous local authorities.

Following an unsatisfactory outcome for the local authority's inspection, the DfES (Department for Education and Skills, now the DCSF, Department for Children, Schools and Families) removed the responsibility for education from the local authority and awarded the contract to The Learning Trust in 2002. The reason for adopting the academy solution is evident from the 2006 commissioned report into academies in Hackney (Hackney Council, 2006) in which The Learning Trust reminded the commission that:

> It was clear to the Trust and the Authority that a large improvement in and a rapid expansion of secondary education was needed. The question was how that could be provided in a Borough that had no spare resources. The Trust told the Commission that the Government's Academies Programme was seized on, not because of enthusiasm for the thinking behind the programme, but because it offered the only way of rapidly providing Hackney children with more and better secondary schools.
>
> (p. 5)

The Learning Trust commenced a massive drive to raise standards in existing maintained schools by embarking on a major change programme as described in the joint London Challenge[3] and the Learning Trust's publication *A Vision for Hackney Secondary Schools* (DfES, 2003b). In brief, the vision focused on the introduction of four academies to replace closed schools to increase capacity and broaden choice. This was to be set within a drive to raise standards universally in the secondary sector, through increased collaborative work that would provide a curriculum design to match the needs of Hackney students, together with improved professional development opportunities and support.

The Petchey Academy

The Petchey Academy is a brand new academy that did not have a direct predecessor school and is sponsored by the Jack Petchey Foundation. The Foundation was established some ten years ago, with the aim of supporting young people in London to maximize educational and personal developmental opportunities through the provision of grants. To date, the Foundation has donated nearly £60 million to such causes, and over 1,600 secondary schools in London and South East Essex participate in the monthly Petchey Student Awards. The Foundation is the brainchild of Jack Petchey, OBE, a well-known London East End philanthropist, who from humble beginnings achieved financial success through commercial ventures in a variety of spheres.

The new Petchey Academy building stands on the site of the former Kingsland School, which, having had an excellent reputation in the past, fell on difficult times. Suffering from poor recruitment, falling rolls, low achievement standards and a significant period spent in the Ofsted (Office for Standards in Education) category 'special measures', it was closed in 2003; the school was demolished and plans were made to use the site to build the Petchey Academy.

It was the Foundation's wish to create an academy with distinctive features and specialisms[4] utilizing the greater freedoms of early academy Funding Agreements to explore in depth how the provision could be different from that of a maintained secondary school. The ethos of the academy was to embrace the multi-cultural profile of students in which approximately 50 per cent are of African/African Caribbean heritage. Of the remaining 50 per cent approximately 10 per cent can trace their East End ancestry beyond two generations, with the final 40 per cent being made up of students from the South Americas, Eastern and Western Europe and Asia.

Following government policy dating from the mid 1990s for all secondary schools to have a specialism, the Petchey Academy adopted a unique specialism, drawing together the areas of medical science, health and social care. The Specialist Schools programme (SSP)[5] helps schools, in partnership with private sector sponsors and supported by additional government funding, to establish distinctive identities and develop an enriched curriculum through the specialism. Following consultation with the Learning Trust, and the City and Hackney national health trusts, it was recognized that Hackney had a lack of the ethnic minorities residing in Hackney working in the higher echelons of the medical and caring professions. Hence the specialism of medical science, health and social care was created, which at the time was unique. The Expression of Interest (DfES, 2003a) defined the intentions of the academy in a broad-brush style. However, this was to be followed by a rude awakening on 1 September 2005 when I started work at the academy; I needed to translate these generalized statements into the *reality* of planning, culminating in a *vision* for the new academy, in time for its opening on 1 September 2006.

'Growing' an organization: leadership dimensions

In my previous leadership roles as a headteacher of both GMS (grant-maintained status) and LEA (Local Education Authority maintained) schools, I arrived to find well-established schools, albeit at different stages of development and challenge. On this occasion, however, the embryonic Petchey Academy, with its gleaming blank sheet of white paper, posed many questions that, as an experienced headteacher, I did not always have immediate solutions for.

At the start of the Academy in September 2005, I was the sole employee with educational experience. At the time, I reflected carefully on my previous leadership experiences, to unpick what might be relevant to this very different scenario. Getting leadership 'right' with no antecedents would be vital to the culmination of a successful opening and establishing a potentially high-achieving academy.

In my first headship (1996–2001), my style could generally be described as transformational. Leading a school established some 450 years ago required a high level of understanding of its history and the ability to understand sensitively what changes were needed in a rapidly changing and challenging environment. As Stewart (2006) remarks, 'transformational leaders focus on restructuring the school by improving school conditions' (p. 4).

Taking on my second headship (2001–5), of a school in the Ofsted category of 'serious weaknesses', was a situation which called for drastic positive action to rebuild a leadership team, with the return of Ofsted but a year away. My learning process and leadership style in this case is better described by an environment in which Bush and Glover (2003) quote the work of Miller and Miller (2001), wherein transactional leadership 'is leadership in which relationships with teachers are based upon an exchange for some valued resource. To the teacher, interaction between administrators and teachers is usually episodic, short-lived and limited to the exchange transaction' (Miller and Miller, p. 13).

The issue with identifying too closely with any one set of definitions is that, as Hopkins (2001) states, 'the debate over educational leadership has been dominated by a contrast between the (so-called) transactional and transformational approaches' (p. 1). While I have located the first two 'learning' headships in the context of which, to some writers, almost implies extremities of style, the challenge for me was to gain clarity as to what leadership-style models or characteristics would be needed to open a new academy. One thing I was very clear about as a leader was that I have always held a personal and professional belief in the need for leadership to be authentic. As Duignan (2004) writes, 'the focus of authentic leadership is on "elevating leaders' moral reasoning" (Terry, 1993 [p. 46]) which is central to Burns' (1978) seminal distinction between leadership that is *transactional* and that which is *transformational*' (p. 1).

While I was entering a role in which the pressure would be on me from the outset to succeed, any need for pragmatism would need to be balanced by raising the leadership of the academy to a level where, as Hodgkinson (1991, p. 1) says, 'such leadership elevates the actions of the leader above mere pragmatics or expediency'. During the preparative year before opening the academy, I also came across the writings of Bhindi and Duignan (1997) and, in particular, one quote from this article caught my attention. Referring to the work of Bass and Stodgill (1990), they comment that 'leadership made a critical difference or otherwise in the success of organisations across the whole spectrum of life: church, military, politics and the government' (p. 117). Furthermore, Bhindi and Duignan (1997) quote Ramnarayan and Rao (1994), which clarified the enormity of the leadership task facing me at the time: '[T]he lasting tribute to leaders is that the culture, institutions and practices set in motion by them persists long after their departures from the organisation scene. Whereas the organisation moves, *the imprints of these leaders continue to inspire them*' (p. 3, original emphasis).

I was acutely conscious of the responsibility vested in me in creating something which would long outlive my professional input and had to be 'fit for purpose' for years to come. So what and who would be the focus of my leadership and how would I approach it?

Given the embryonic state of the Academy, there was a need for leadership, as Duignan (2004) explains, to 'challenge others to participate in a visionary dialogue of identifying in curriculum, teaching and learning (especially pedagogy) what is worthwhile, what is worth doing (moral purpose) and preferred ways of doing and acting together' (p. 3).

Who were to be these 'others'? During the preparatory year 2005–6, there was some opportunity to identify future staff, who arrived from a wide range of educational backgrounds and experiences, or indeed none at all! While the desirable emphasis in leadership was to be located in 'authenticity', the question uppermost in my mind was how to induct the potentially disparate staff into a non-existent organization in which possibly the only 'given' was the personal life motto of our patron, Jack Petchey: 'If I think I can . . . I can!'

One might argue that the focus of leadership models might well have called for a combination of both a transactional and transformational approach, although the latter would hardly be transforming what was, but rather 'forming' what would be. Commencing with staff who in general were unknown to me and had not been present during the preparative year, I identified a need to pass on quickly and effectively the desired ethos and expectations of the Academy. For these reasons, I was attracted to the construct of instructional leadership, which Leithwood *et al.* (1999) define 'as an approach to leadership that emphasizes the behaviours of teachers as they engage in activities directly affecting the growth of students' (p. 8).

I consequently positively embarked along a pathway that might be generally expressed as 'instructional' leadership within a motivational environment which was essentially 'authentic': an approach which I describe as 'pragmatic, instructional and authentic (PIA) leadership'.

Why pragmatic? Although I argue that authenticity is important to leadership of a new academy, I was acutely aware that since their inception academies have been expected to do remarkable things, especially in the realms of raising achievement of some of the most troubled and underperforming inner-city areas. The Petchey Academy, along with other new academies with no direct predecessor school, faced a somewhat different task. They would be under pressure to persuade a variety of individual and professional organizations and government that, from the day of opening, they would have the sustainability to be successful, especially given that the first measure of their success (at that time) would not appear until three years later, i.e. Key Stage 3 SATs (Statutory Attainment Test) results.

Why instructional leadership within the 'pragmatic, instructional and authentic' model descriptor? There are two reasons in particular. First, Hopkins (2001) and others provide strong arguments as to why they consider

> the (*transformational*) approach a necessary but not sufficient condition for school improvement, for the simple reason that it lacks a specific orientation towards student learning. In line with many other educational reforms, transformational leadership simply focuses on the wrong variables.
> (p. 3)

Second, drawing on Hallinger (1992) and Sheppard (1996), he goes on to present the case that 'there is considerable empirical support for this [instructional] model, particularly as it relates to student outcomes' (Hopkins, 2001, p. 3). However, he suggests that there is not the same degree of evidence on student outcomes for either the transformational or transactional models.

Thus, if the sponsor and I wanted our students to become successful learners, I felt it was important to consider the relevance of authentic learning to the establishment of the Petchey Academy. In adopting the influence of authentic leadership I wished to ensure that the student learning, as Duignan (2004) suggests, adapted from Starratt (2004), would bring personal meaning through learning within a context which links learning with growing personal confidence. These principles have become enshrined in what is known by many as 'the Petchey Way'. In striving to promote students' personal discipline and good behaviour, rather than telling them that they have broken a rule we pose the question, 'is this the Petchey Way'?

Only one 'head'!: leadership theory into practice and staff recruitment

The appointment cycle for the opening in 2006 began in October 2005. Having examined a number of short- and long-term staffing models of new academies and 'new start' schools, I, together with the governing body, made a conscious decision to appoint a strong, experienced senior leadership group who would initially lead in the major learning areas, together with having whole academy responsibilities. In fact the terms 'leaders' or 'lead in' are now accepted as the styling for staff who take a leadership role. The use of terms such as 'head of department', were jettisoned from the start. I argued that if there was to be strong instructional leadership, which would be directed as Hopkins (2001), drawing on Hallinger's work (1992), suggests, it must define the academy's mission and effectively manage the instructional programme to promote the academy's climate. Then the emphasis should be on leading rather than balkanizing the academy into distinct areas.

If the key aim was to create the desired leadership model of PIA, then I needed staff at a high level who could themselves operate as exponents of it. Furthermore, they should also be able to take the lead from me, cascading the elements of the specific functions under three main headings:

1. defining the school mission
2. managing the instructional programme
3. promoting the school climate.

Initial cascading took place with senior leaders meeting at weekends before the opening of the academy while still undertaking their regular work. More recently specific training days (of which we have ten per year rather than five) focus on defining and transmitting 'the Petchey Way', with an emphasis on PIA to new staff.

The essential importance of vice principals within the PIA framework at the academy provoked a discussion between myself and the chair of governors, whose own experience of recruitment was different to that of the traditional educational approach – typically, advertisement, application and interview, including possibly a presentation and assessment task(s).

He questioned how we would know we were about to appoint someone who could share in defining the academy's mission, practices and climate. He proposed a method that initially surprised me as, in my experience, it was unusual in educational recruitment practice: he suggested asking permission of short-listed applicants' current headteachers for me to spend a day shadowing the applicant both teaching and performing managerial and leadership activities. Surprisingly very few headteachers objected and some were very interested in the idea. This took me as far north as Preston and down to the south coast, covering some 28 long-listed applicants. By approximately March 2006 all senior leaders positions (two vice principals and four assistant vice principals) had been filled by staff in whom we had the confidence that they would take us along the route of PIA. The academy was divided into four learning areas: the natural world; the controlled world; communications; and the human spirit. Each learning area had an assistant vice principal in charge, who together with academy-wide responsibilities also directed one of the pastoral houses. The academy was designed to be a vertically grouped organization in which the house system would play a fundamental role in supporting students; there is no 'Year' system.

Collaboration: establishing relationships, breaking down preconceptions

'If it is legal, affordable and has clear benefits for students, let's look at the proposal'. This has become an established part of the PIA leadership environment at the Petchey Academy, which is constantly undergoing review. One of the major issues confronting a new school, and in particular a new academy, is related to the perceptions about it both locally and in the wider educational context. The Petchey Academy collaborates on a number of fronts and differing levels, and not just in ways specified in the Funding Agreement. As an extended-hours academy we provide a wide range of resources to the locality, local primary schools, and we are member of the Central Hackney Schools Consortium of primary, secondary and special schools. Within the Consortium we play a significant role in terms of curriculum development and will be taking the lead in one of the new diplomas.

Entrepreneurial opportunities at the Petchey Academy

The differences between opening this academy and a new maintained school are manifested through the entrepreneurial attitude it has to a range of organizational, curricular and human resource issues and to the almost total absence of restrictions. Brush *et al.* (2008), in quoting Aldrich

(1979), provides a commentary that locates academies within an entrepreneurial framework: 'A central activity in entrepreneurship is the creation of new organizations. Organizations are defined as goal directed boundary-maintaining systems that emerge when entrepreneurs take the initiative to engage in founding activities' (p. 547).

In a paper written for the NCSL (National College for School Leadership), Macaulay (2008) comments on the existence of entrepreneurial activity in academies: 'Examples of individual Academy sponsors engaging in social entrepreneurialism are evident in the Academies Programme' (p. 13). She goes on to quote Busson, founder of ARK (Absolute Return for Kids), which sponsors a number of academies: 'If we can apply the entrepreneurial principles we have brought to business to charity, we have a shot at having a really strong impact, to be able to transform the lives of children' (p. 13). Evidence is still limited to support this statement as a number of ARK academies are still in infancy and will require some years to provide evidence of Busson's assertions that there will be no 'excuses' (Ark Academies, 2009).

From its inception as a non-profit organization, the governing body of the Petchey Academy asked some very basic but essential questions about the ways schools operate with respect to curricular provision, the management and leadership, and what will be needed to challenge the historically low attainment of students in Hackney. In addition, they were concerned with understanding what we needed to do to ensure the success and well-being of all our students and staff. In brief they wanted to underpin the existence of the academy with the five outcomes of *Every Child Matters* (DCSF, 2009c).

If 'every child matters' and every child is different, then the personalization of education, which is very much a part of the current DCSF agenda, is of significant priority. From the beginning, the Academy wished to develop a timetabling structure in which students could progress through the system at a rate appropriate to their own achievement and needs. The concept of a centralized timetabler constructing a timetable for the whole Academy annually has been replaced by timetabling being performed by learning centre leaders who, within their own time block, are at liberty to plan, change and amend temporarily the teaching within their area. Thus if more Sanskrit is needed in the communication learning area, this can be organized within the framework on a negotiated basis without creating a major timetable change. Thus setting on the basis of attainment can be either horizontal (in age) or vertical (out of age).

The marginal influence that schools have on the lives of some students was clearly established many years ago in the publication *Fifteen Thousand Hours* (Rutter *et al.*, 1979). This is of particular relevance to students in Hackney, a significant number of whom come from challenging backgrounds. While Rutter did not advocate a longer working week, the governing body of the academy accepted the need to increase the contact with students to offset external social influences. Thus, the working week (and hence year) is longer, providing approximately six weeks additional academy–student contact over the course of the year. The academy has its own conditions of service, which are commercially based and enhance activities and experiences well beyond those of an *extended school.* The curriculum is delivered through themes and harnesses the competencies of the Royal Society for Arts 'Curriculum for the 21st Century'[6] and allows greater flexibility in teaching cross-curricular themes. However, perhaps one of our most significant departures is linked to the way we respond to the government's rhetoric and guidelines concerning healthy eating.

All students take lunch at the Academy. Students are provided with a single-item menu on a daily basis (vegetarian and religious options are available) and no snacks, with the exception of water and fruit, may be brought into the Academy. This, together with an individual learning plan for every student, which covers academic, social and health targets, is the basis upon which the Academy is founded. In terms of the workforce, almost every adult is a 'tutor' and belongs to a house group (site staff, administrative staff, teaching assistants and trained teachers). Our belief is that every adult, with appropriate training support, can offer experiences of life to the benefit of students. Every adult member of the Academy is therefore considered to be an educator, we try to avoid the separation of teachers and support staff.

Admission to the Academy is based on a banding system. All academies in Hackney (soon to be five in number), plus one Catholic secondary school, require primary pupils to sit a nationally validated test, the NFER (National Foundation For Educational Research) Cognitive Ability Tests. This is taken in the primary school and serves to place them in five bands based on attainment in the tests. The nearest 20 per cent in each band, taken on distance from home to the academy and not ability, are offered places.

Conclusion

Could a new secondary school have achieved and put in place what has become 'the Petchey Academy' now? Largely I believe they could, as indeed can be seen by such prime examples as the Chafford Hundred School in Thurrock.[7] However, I would argue that there are significant differences that earmark the potential ability of academies to go beyond and above the potential for new maintained schools to be successful in the long term. In making this statement I am aware that not all academies share similar Funding Agreements or historical provenances. However, among these are:

1. the significant amount of independence which, although some aspects are shared with maintained schools, does provide a greater potential for entrepreneurial activity freed from local control

2. the increased ability to be creative in recruiting the all-important leaders and in the longer term a reduction of central regulation
3. the ability to reflect on and, as appropriate, apply some of the positive aspects of the grant-maintained experience and that of the independent sector; and most importantly to generate a critical mass to bring a whole range of initiatives and clear direction to a confluence appropriate to the needs of each and every academy within the context of its local needs and challenges.

Such advantages for the Petchey Academy (and Hackney) have provided the potential for becoming one of the highest attaining secondary schools in the UK and contributing to one of the fastest improving local authorities in England at Key Stage 4.

Establishing an academy *per se* does not provide the recipe for a successful new school. In the case of the Petchey Academy, I believe it was, and still is, the degree of and opportunity for risk-taking which enables its success – opportunities which do exist in the maintained sector but, in my personal experience as a headteacher, are more difficult to harness. The bringing together of architectural innovation and a staff who are required to be 'pioneers' with a governing body, sponsor and patron for whom failure is not an option inspires our students to want to succeed against the odds. Gorard (2009), commenting on the effectiveness of academies, states that 'it is not immediately clear that they are doing a better job overall than their colleagues in non-Academy schools in similar circumstances, for whom I have similar admiration' (p. 112).

I can only comment on one academy, the one I lead on behalf of the governing body. The popularity of the academy has risen, from approximately 900 plus applications for entry in September 2006 to over 1,300 applications for 180 places in September 2009, because parents are now opting for Hackney schools rather then sending children to schools in other local authorities.

Our prediction for the first cohort of GCSE candidates to take the full GCSE examinations in June 2011 against the national benchmark of five A*–C including English and mathematics is a conservative 75 per cent, with a reasonable expectation of being able to exceed 80 per cent, and an aspirational target of 86 per cent, based on a normal distribution of average point scores on entry.

In creating a PIA leadership model for the senior leadership team, the style of leadership was recently highly commended. In particular, the executive management group was described as 'formidable' during the Ofsted 2009 inspection. I would submit that to date PIA has provided 'fitness for purpose'; however, time will tell whether PIA will need to be amended or radically overhauled as the academy moves from infancy through to maturity.

In reflecting on the establishment of a new academy, as opposed to a new maintained school, I have arrived at some very clear conclusions. While new maintained schools have significant potential for innovation and entrepreneurism, they are still subject to an overarching national framework. This is not the case universally with academies and hence the need to accept 'ordained' norms does not always exist. This is the great enabler for academies!

It is also a human issue. What makes the Petchey Academy different is that we are working to convert the *reality* of one man's own struggle in life against significant odds, into a *vision* for the future for young people in West Hackney. Trite perhaps, but it is in the best traditions of the philanthropists throughout history who have wanted directly to make a difference to the opportunities for young people in London and other cities in the UK. At least for this generation Jack Petchey is real, credible and lifelike when he visits the academy. Perhaps, in generations to come, he may become one of a number of people such as Dame Alice Owen[8] who will have impacted positively on the future of young people in Inner London.

Notes

1 The Learning Trust in Hackney was contracted by the Department for Children, Schools and Families (DCSF) in 2003 to lead and manage education in Hackney. It is independent from the local authority and is mandated to deal with all statutory and non-statutory activities pertaining to the efficient management and leadership of all activities related to the needs of Children's Services. See: www.learningtrust.co.uk/(accessed 20 December 2009).

2 The Funding Agreement for each academy is part of the legal agreement between the academy trust and the DCSF. It defines the terms of reference for the academy and lays down the principles to be followed by the governing body and the leadership of the academy.

3 The London Challenge is a partnership between all those who seek more for London's young people. London's strength depends more than ever on its education system. Just as London is determined to be a world leader in other areas, so, through a unified effort, London can be established as a leader in education, a world class city for learning and creativity. See the 'London Challenge' at http://ibtl.londongt.org/index.php?page=TheLondonChallenge (accessed 20 December 2009).

4 Any maintained secondary school and any maintained or non-maintained special school in England can apply for specialist status in one of ten curriculum specialisms: arts, business and enterprise, engineering, humanities, languages, mathematics and computing, music, science, sports and technology. See 'specialist schools' at www.standards.dfes.gov.uk/specialistschools/what_are/(accessed 20 December 2009).

5 See Note 4 above; 'Specialist schools' at: www.specialistschools.org.uk/schools/specialistschoolsprogramme/default.aspa (accessed 20 December 2009).

6 The Royal Society of Arts Opening Minds project was launched in 1999. In conjunction with Creative Partnerships they challenge us to question the validity

of subjects. They advocate a competency-led approach with negotiated learning targets. RSA Curriculum for the 21st Century-Opening Minds framework at www.thersa.org/projects/education/opening-minds/opening-minds-framework (accessed 20 December 2009).

7 The Chafford Hundred Business and Enterprise College opened in 2001 as a locally maintained new secondary school. In 2009 it was within the top 5 per cent of schools in England and Wales based on measurement (CVA – contextual value added) of the progress its pupils had achieved. Chafford Hundred School at www.chaffordhundredcampus.thurrock.sch.uk/home.php?catid=1&subcat (accessed 20 December 2009).

8 Dame Alice Owen's School has a long and distinguished history dating back to the foundation in 1613. It was established in Islington to educate 30 boys. The school has now moved to Hertfordshire, and is one of many instances in which private benefactors have been involved in educational provision through the centuries in the UK. Dame Alice Owen's School at www.damealiceowens.herts.sch.uk/about_us/dame_alice_owen.html (accessed 20 December 2009).

Chapter 7

What Works? An Empirical Assessment of Strengths, Weaknesses and Next Steps for the Academies Initiative

Judy Larsen, Valerie Bunting and David Armstrong

Introduction

This chapter provides an overview of the findings from the Pricewaterhouse-Coopers (PwC) five-year evaluation of the Academies Programme, undertaken for the then Department for Children, Schools and Families (DCSF) between 2002 and 2008. The chapter will focus on the following key research questions. First, performance – to what extent do the data indicate that the initiative has impacted positively on pupil performance? Second, drivers – to the extent that standards in some academies have improved, which specific aspects of the initiative have contributed most to the improvement, for example, independence, sponsorship, new buildings, classroom teaching and assessment? Third, recommendations – what does the research evidence suggest in terms of how the initiative can most effectively be taken forward?

Background to the PwC evaluation

PwC was commissioned by the predecessor of the DCSF in February 2003 to conduct an independent longitudinal evaluation of the academies initiative over a five-year period (see PwC, 2003; 2005; 2006; 2007; 2008). The overall aim of the evaluation was to assess the programme's contribution to raising educational standards, particularly in schools with high numbers of pupils with disadvantaged backgrounds, and to examine the impact of the unique features of academies, including independence, sponsorship, governance, leadership, teaching and learning, and buildings.

The approach consisted of the following key elements:

- **Annual qualitative stakeholder interviews** – with principals, governors, sponsors or their representatives, headteachers from neighbouring schools, and others as appropriate, including local authority representatives and DCSF officials (over 400 were undertaken over the course of five years).

- **Annual surveys of staff, pupils and parents** – for example, the final year of the evaluation included responses from more than 3,500 academy pupils, nearly 1,000 parents and around 750 staff.
- **Annual quantitative analysis of pupil data** – administrative records on pupil profile and performance were examined for more than 20,000 academy pupils over the period 2002–7. These data were compared with similar data for pupils in the academies' predecessor schools and two comparison groups of schools as well as data for schools in England as a whole.
- **Documentary evidence** – a wide range of documentary evidence was reviewed, including academies' annual financial reports and accounts provided to Companies House and the Charities Commission, Funding Agreements,[1] Ofsted (Office for Standards in Educations) inspection reports and evaluation reports by the National Audit Office and others.

The evaluation was undertaken in the first 27 academies with data collected in the year immediately prior to opening[2] and subsequent years. Because of the staggered phasing of their opening the sample size for the evaluation grew each year, as set out in the table below.

These first 27 academies were located in London and in other large urban cities such as Manchester and Middlesborough. The majority had completely new buildings and two had substantial refurbishments. Two were all-age academies (primary through to secondary). Sponsorship models ranged from individual philanthropists, partnerships between individuals and organizations (e.g. a private sponsor and a university), City Technology Colleges (which were offered incentives in the form of capital upgrades in return for supporting a failing school) and faith organizations (which had already opened and managed independent schools). Some of these earlier sponsors had previous educational experience, while others did not.

Table 7.1 Sample of 27 academies: year of opening

Phase	Year of opening	Number of academies
1	2002	3
2	2003	9
3	2004	5
4	2005	10
All phases	**2002–5**	**27**

Source: PricewaterhouseCoopers (2008), *Academies Evaluation: Fifth Annual Report*, p. 29.

Furthermore, some sponsors were responsible for more than one academy in the sample.

Academies within the local and wider policy contexts

Academies were launched in March 2000, with the first three academies opening in 2003. By 2007 (four years into the evaluation) there were nearly 23,000 pupils in the 24 academies for which quantitative data were analysed.[3]

While each of the academies in our sample was established in a different community and location around England, a range of contextual factors are notable: some academies were transitioned as whole schools from a predecessor to an academy, almost overnight; others had a long lead time to their transition; and in some academies there was a phased intake, starting with one year group and expanding each year. In addition, a small number of academies were City Technology Colleges. These were highly successful schools that were transitioning to academies in order to expand their intake to include pupils from neighbouring failing schools. In this way, these already successful schools were extending their influence to an expanded group of pupils.

Sponsorship variations were also significant across academies. The first three academies were sponsored by high-profile business people with local interests in the community. For example, some had grown up in the area, or had business links to the local community. In general, business people who were sponsors did not have previous educational experience. On the other hand, some sponsors had considerable previous educational experience and were already managing and leading very successful consortia of private schools. These sponsors also brought the added value of economies of scale, curriculum knowledge and school infrastructure support, such as human resource and school financial management experience.

Alongside these differences in sponsorship were variations in the structures and operational aspects of governance. Sponsors of multiple academies typically had a central trust which oversaw the management, strategic planning and accountability for all of the academies within their group. This model provided the benefits of belonging to a 'family' of schools, while allowing for local variation and representation. In the early stages of the evaluation there was a lack of clarity around individual local school and community input into governance in some of the academies that belonged to a group. However, over the course of the evaluation there was greater clarity and inclusion of staff, parents and community representatives on the governing body became more usual.

In addition to the above factors, all of the early academies were opening in a dynamic policy context with a high level of political and public scrutiny.

Changes to the 14–19 curriculum, the introduction of Every Child Matters (ECM) with the requirement for schools to collaborate to deliver extended services, and the launch of the parallel schools upgrading programming under Building Schools for the Future (BSF), were all relevant and important in the context of the academies' policy.

The final significant factor is that whereas in the past new schools were commissioned through their local authority, in the case of academies, the DCSF became both a policy development and a delivery arm. Notably, in the early stages of the programme, the independent nature of academies and their freedoms outside the local authority contributed to an uncertainty about how academies were to operate within their local family of schools in delivering the above policies, which were predicated on the basis of collaboration within and across schools.

Pupil profile

Three key aspects of the pupil profile in academies are worth highlighting: first, the evidence showed a very strong demand for academy places. There was a clear growth in the total number of places (a 44 per cent increase in pupil numbers since the first academies opened), and generally high demand for academy places (on average 2.6 applications for every place). Second, there was a mixed picture in relation to the social profile of pupils. There were almost 8,000 pupils from socially deprived backgrounds[4] attending academies in 2007 – just under a third of the total. The *absolute number* of pupils from such backgrounds grew significantly since the first academies opened but the *proportion* declined at a faster rate than other schools, with a fall of nearly 6 percentage points (pp) in academies compared with 2pp in comparator schools and 1pp across all English schools. Third, the average level of prior achievement of pupils entering academies at Year 7 was below the England average in 2007 (26 compared with 27.4), though it was a point higher than the figure for the predecessor schools in 2002. This would suggest that academies were not 'cherry-picking' the brightest pupils, although they had a 'more balanced' intake compared with their predecessor schools.

Pupil performance

Figure 7.1 shows the average annual improvement achieved by all academies at GCSE by 2007.

The figures show that the average academy improvement (7pp) exceeded that of the comparison groups (4pp) and England as a whole (2pp). However, there was considerable diversity across individual academies in the levels and improvements achieved against many performance measures.

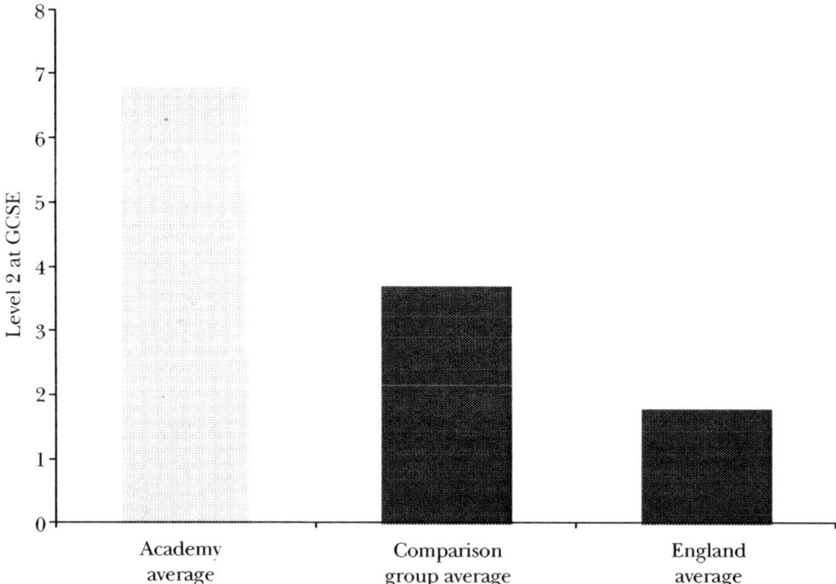

Figure 7.1 Average annual percentage point (pp) change in pupils achieving Level 2 (attainment at grades A*–C) at GCSE

Source: PricewaterhouseCoopers (2008), *Academies Evaluation: Fifth Annual Report*, p. 211.

For example, improvement in some of the earlier academies appears to have taken longer – perhaps due to the very low baselines from which they started. Linked to this, for the earlier academies, the DCSF's academies project team was in its infancy and many of the systems and support structures were not sufficiently established. It is also worth noting that some academies used vocational courses to secure higher and faster improvements in attainment. When English and maths were taken into account, rates of progress were generally less substantial (though still ahead of comparator schools and the England average).

One of our key findings was that aggregating across all academies, although useful, can mask some of the important differences that exist between and within academies. To illustrate this, Figure 7.2 summarizes the improvements in performance at Key Stage 3 for the Phase 4 academies that opened in 2005.

The figures show considerable diversity between academies; in most academies the results are generally improving, but in some (F and G) they are declining. And the figures also show that within academies there is considerable diversity; in Academy A, for example, the English results deteriorate over the period whereas those for maths and science improve.

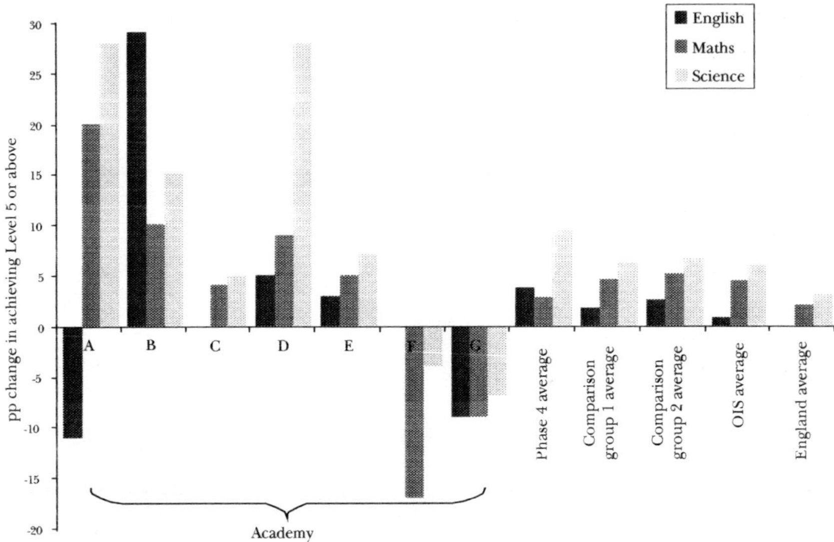

FIGURE 7.2 Change in percentage of pupils in Phase 4 academies achieving Key Stage 3, Level 5 (i.e. the level of achievement expected of most pupils at end of Key Stage 3): 2005–7

Note: Phase 4 academies opened in 2005 (England average and comparison groups 1 and 2).

Source: PricewaterhouseCoopers (2008), *Academies Evaluation: Fifth Annual Report*, p. 210.

This diversity across individual academies suggests that, rather than a simple uniform 'academy effect', there has been a more complex and varied process of change taking place.

Towards an understanding of the variable rates of progress

We have seen above that academies opened in different contexts and with different pupil profiles; they also experienced different rates of improvements. In order to examine more closely evidence of contextual factors and their impact on achievement, we undertook case studies of two different academies, both of which opened in 2002 (see Table 7.2).

At the time of their opening the Academies Programme was just being established and these earlier academies were navigating an evolving policy context; in many ways they were trailblazing. A broad range of variables were examined, such as pupil profile data including the number of pupils in receipt of free school meals (FSM), pupils with English as an additional language (EAL) and pupils with special educational needs (SEN). In order to ensure comparability primary school data were disregarded from the all-age academy, and we utilized data related to pupils at Key Stage 3 and Key Stage 4 only. In addition to pupil profile data, contextual variables such as leadership and school buildings were taken into account alongside pupil prior attainment scores for Key Stage 3. Table 7.2 summarizes the variables examined for these two academies.

Academy 1 entered the programme with the second-lowest performance of all the academies. Furthermore, the percentages of pupils with FSM, EAL and SEN (without a statement) were also substantially above the national averages, which at the time were 14.9 per cent, 8.6 per cent and 15.9 per

Table 7.2 Contextual variables for case studies

	Opened 2002			
	Academy 1		Academy 2	
	2002	2006	2002	2006
Total number of pupils (headcount)	615	1,415	859	753
15-year-olds achieving Key Stage 4, five A*–C (%)	6.0**	32.0	26.0**	59.0
FSM (%) (national average 14.9%)	45.9	38.2	39.3	38.6
EAL (%) (national average 8.6%)	11.1	13.0	56.6	47.9
SEN with statement (%) (national average 2.4%)	3.9	5.0	1.3	1.2
SEN without statement (%) (national average 15.9%)	40.7	45.8	24.7	26.7
Prior attainment at Key Stage 2 average point score for Year 7 intake (note 21.0% is considered a low individual score)	24.0	25.7	24.5	25.4
Opened in new building	Y		N	
Stable leadership in first two years of opening	Y		N	
Sponsors with previous experience in education	N		Y	
Multiple academy sponsor	N		N	
Phased intake	N		N	
Changes to admissions	N		N	

** last validated performance
Source: PricewaterhouseCoopers case study analysis.

Table 7.3 Pupil performance in academies 1 and 2 – Key Stage 4, 2002–6 (five or more GCSEs A*–C)

	2002	2003	2004	2005	2006
Academy 1	6%	21%	34%	29%	32%
Academy 2	26%	35%	26%	54%	59%

Source: PricewaterhouseCoopers case study analysis.

cent respectively. The academy opened in a completed new building, located in a catchment area with high socio-economic deprivation, and with all of the associated social problems. Within four years this academy had increased its performance at Key Stage 4 from 6.0 per cent to 32.0 per cent. Leadership was initially stable, and the foundation principal was in the post for four years. In addition, the academy had a staff made up of both new and TUPEd[5] staff. The academy had also made significant changes in its middle management in the first two years, and faced an additional set of challenges associated with becoming an all-age (primary and secondary) academy. Consequently, the pupil population almost doubled between 2002 and 2006, and at the time of the research was in excess of 1,400 from reception to Year 13, making it one of the largest academies in the programme. Sponsorship of this academy was provided by a single sponsor with no previous educational experience.

Academy 2 came to the programme with pupil performance at Key Stage 4 of 26 per cent: 20pp above Academy 1. The baseline percentages of pupils with FSM and SEN were also above the national average, and more than half the pupils in Academy 2 had EAL. As with Academy 1, this academy was also located in an area with high socio-economic deprivation. In contrast to Academy 1, Academy 2 had a refurbishment, rather than a complete new build. Furthermore, the refurbishment of the buildings was ongoing when the academy opened, resulting in much disruption in the first year. Academy 2 also experienced high levels of turbulence associated with leadership changes due to the ill health of the principal. Sponsorship was provided by a joint sponsor with previous experience in education.

Despite both academies' GCSE results declining at certain points over their first four years, both made significant progress while at the same time maintaining their commitment to young people within the categories of FSM, EAL and SEN.

The case studies illustrate that these two academies shared some common features such as high percentages of FSM, EAL and SEN, and both were located in areas of high socio-economic deprivation. These academies utilized enablers, such as new buildings, strong leadership, and an uncompromising commitment to success from the sponsors, governors and staff. They re-engaged pupils and were also working to engage their local communities. As first-phase academies they demonstrated that with strong commitment from all stakeholders, additional resources provided through the sponsor and the programme, and through the utilization of a range of enablers, significant and rapid improvement is possible.

The above case studies highlight the contextual variations that are linked to the variable achievement of academies in the sample over time. Notwithstanding the variations, the evaluation identified particular features of the academies model that were impacting positively on pupil achievement.

Independence

Principals and sponsors were unequivocal and unanimous in their view that independence offered both real and symbolic flexibilities and freedoms that contributed to school improvement. In some areas, the DCSF sought to modify the earlier Funding Agreements to ensure access by all pupils to core subjects, closer alignment with the maintained sector and greater accountability. This reining back of the flexibilities originally granted to academies was an important policy shift in terms of ensuring that academies offered a broad and balanced curriculum, including English, mathematics, science and ICT.

Sponsorship

The evidence suggests that sponsorship contributed significantly to school improvement, and Ofsted data confirmed this view. Sponsors provided academies with a broad range of expertise and resources both directly from the sponsor(s) and from their business and personal associations. Some sponsors provided significant additional funding (in some cases more than £2 million) both towards the capital build of the academy and to other areas, such as uniforms and additional facilities.

By 2008 the range of sponsors had been diversified and the requirement to commit £2 million had been removed for some sponsorship categories.

However, our study highlighted a number of challenges associated with an expanding programme. These included securing sufficient numbers of high-quality sponsors as well as increasing the representation from female sponsors and sponsors from black and minority ethnic groups.

Leadership

The quality of leadership in academies was generally very good, with leadership in a fifth to a third of academies rated by Ofsted as *outstanding* and the number in the *good* category substantially above the average for England as a whole.

The main challenges facing academy principals included: building coherent teams; establishing a full set of policies, including an effective discipline policy; and responding to the wider pressures of the communities in which they were located. The demanding nature of the task may explain why principal attrition was high, with 11 of the 27 academies within our sample experiencing a change in leadership, often within the first 12 months of opening. In addition, there were no academy principals from black and minority ethnic (BME) backgrounds in our sample, and just under a quarter of principal appointments were female (compared with 36 per cent of secondary heads in England).

Buildings

We found some evidence that academy buildings were contributing to school improvement through, for example, providing opportunities to extend the curriculum and teaching hours. Flexible designs challenged traditional pedagogy, with some academies exploring alternative pupil groupings and innovative use of ICT in order to raise attainment. Notwithstanding the fact that some staff reported that the building processes needed to be carefully managed in order to minimize disruptions, in the final year of the evaluation 83 per cent of staff agreed that new school buildings had contributed significantly to the positive experience of the pupils.

There were, however, some concerns. Buildings and facilities were the second most frequent 'worst academy feature' identified by pupils and the third most frequently identified by parents and staff. Pupils were chiefly concerned about toilets and insufficient space to socialize during break and lunch times; parents most frequently specified inadequate design features and the length of time it had taken to complete the building; staff highlighted design faults, particularly inadequate teaching space and lack of storage.

Teaching and learning

Survey responses confirmed that academies put considerable effort into working in partnership with parents and pupils: attendance, behaviour and a consistent focus on improving teaching were emphasized as essential to improving attainment. In addition, most academies had exercised their independence by extending the school day and at the same time had introduced a broad range of extended school opportunities. Some academies had changed their curriculum to better reflect diverse learning pathways, introducing General National Vocational Qualifications (GNVQs) and other vocational courses. In some cases this was, initially at least, at the expense of ensuring a broad and balanced curriculum, particularly in relation to core subjects such as English, maths, and science. Over the course of the evaluation there was evidence of a pulling back of innovation in academies which opened in the early phases and a continued focus on getting the basics right.

Ofsted inspection reports suggested that teaching and learning was variable in academies. Inexperienced middle management and a relatively high percentage of teachers without qualified teacher status were identified as potential factors. Ofsted reports concurred with our findings that performance at sixth form required continued focus in collaboration with 14–19 curriculum delivery partners. Some sixth forms had very small numbers of pupils, raising concerns about their financial viability and their ability to provide a responsive curriculum for all pupils.

Academies moving forward: contribution and challenges

The evaluation reviewed and evaluated the distinctive features of academies, set them in their wider context and examined them beside local and national comparators. Unsurprisingly, our conclusion was that there is no simple uniform 'academy effect', since there was a complex range of variables interacting within each academy. There was, for example, evidence that sponsorship, governance, strong leadership, buildings, teaching and learning were all impacting positively upon school improvement, but it was not possible to disaggregate any one variable as uniquely significant, in terms of its impact on pupil achievement. When we examined the rate of individual progress we found that it is also important to take account of the changing individual contexts and the changing profile of academy pupils.

Academies are one of six types of schools within the English state sector,[6] i.e. schools primarily funded by the state. They are also independent schools, and as such identify themselves as part of the independent sector. As such academies provide a new school type, in that they are both state funded and independent. As the policy has expanded to encourage closer links between the independent and state sectors through the emergence of new partnerships,[7] academies have the potential to extend opportunities to pupils from all social classes to be educated in the same environment, without being based on the ability to pay.

It is important to note, however, that in some contexts, we noted a diminution of the role of the local authority in relation to school accountability, challenge and support, since academies are technically and legally outside the local authority jurisdiction. This is amplified in authorities where there are now large numbers of academies. Changes in the policy context throughout the course of the evaluation, resulted in a reassessment of the academies model, including their strategic relationships between the local family of schools and local authority. The drivers for these changes were the requirement to collaborate on 14–19 curriculum delivery, and other areas requiring collaboration and partnerships, e.g. joint solutions for the reintegration of excluded pupils. Linked to this, academies have changed the roles and relationships between central and local bureaucracies and schools. We observed over the course of the evaluation the emergence of new central structures to support academies, and in April 2010 the management of the funding of academies was moved away from the Department to a newly created agency, the Young People's Learning Agency (YPLA).

What are the future challenges associated with the Academies programme?

With the proposed expansion of the programme there are a number of challenges. A key concern is ensuring fair and equitable access for all pupils, and particularly those from disadvantaged backgrounds, for whom the programme was originally intended. The potential difficulty of navigating an additional set of systems associated with areas such as admissions appeals is also particularly pertinent in relation to this group. Alongside this concern is the need to ensure that the profile and attainment of schools which are not academies is equally high on the policy agenda, and that these schools are not adversely affected by any lack of resources or privileges associated with academies' independence.

Our study identified a number of challenges associated with the programme including concerns relating to how some academies maintain the upward pattern of improvement as they mature beyond their infancy while at the same time continuing to support the most vulnerable and disadvantaged pupils. Attrition of enthusiasm and tiredness among staff and leaders create risks for continuing improvement as the newness of the school wears off. There are similar issues with sponsors, particularly those who may have become disillusioned. Further challenges for some academies included continuing to involve and engage parents (in particular) in the life of the academy, as well as engaging with the local community of schools and the wider community. Academies in our sample saw this as critical to improving pupils' achievement and many had introduced a wide range of programmes and opportunities for parents and local communities to be actively engaged with their schools. Notwithstanding the positive outcomes, some reported that engaging parents continued to be a significant challenge.

Many of the academies in our evaluation reported that they continue to experience close scrutiny and attention from unions, politicians, the wider community and neighbouring schools, including in some cases a strong and persistent disapproval of academies as a policy initiative. This had impacted on staff morale and, to a greater or lesser extent, on recruitment. This finding corroborates the findings in literature on new schools (Fink, 1997; Larsen, 2001).

Despite good working relationships with individual officials, some interviewees, including sponsors, reported the institutional process of negotiating with DCSF to be frustrating at times. Across the spectrum of academies in our evaluation, questions emerged relating to the capacity of DCSF to drive the policy while at the same time working as a delivery and support and challenge agent for such a diverse range of academies across the country. The implications and impact of the shift of management of opened academies away from the DCSF to the YPLA together with with the change of government in 2010 were not understood at the time of our research but raise further questions in terms of the management of academies in relation to local community schools.

Finally, for parents and pupils who did not secure a place in an academy, concerns were raised about the different admissions appeal protocols for academies. Unlike the LA-maintained sector where admissions appeals are directed to the admissions' adjudicator, at the time of our research, the policy position required parents appealing admissions for academies to direct their appeal to the Secretary of State.

What are the areas requiring further investigation?

We know from other international school improvement models, such as the charter schools, that longitudinal evaluations beyond five years have been necessary to capture the longer-term impacts of structural reform. A number of the issues and questions raised throughout the evaluation require further investigation. These include:

- how academies fit and operate within the structural, educational and compositional diversity of provision across the full spectrum of school types[8]
- the extent to which academies extend parental choice and whether or not parents recognize and value the distinctive features of academies
- the longer-term contribution of academies to improving the educational

attainment and life chances of pupils in disadvantaged categories, including FSM, EAL and other vulnerable groups, such as looked-after children and those with social, emotional and behavioural issues
- the extent to which academies are offering a broad and balanced curriculum that extends post-16 and post-19 education and training opportunities for pupils
- with the expansion of the number of academies, the implications for the role of central government in relation to policy development, delivery and support and challenge of a significant number of academies
- how the first 27 academies, which enjoy higher levels of independence, operate within the broader policy context, which includes a focus on stronger collaboration with local authorities, and closer alignment with broader educational policy in relation to curriculum, admissions and exclusions
- the impact of the changing nature of independence and sponsorship, given the changes including sponsorship by universities and local authorities and the removal of the requirement for the £2 million donation from sponsors, and the impact of a deregulated workforce on teachers' pay and conditions and most importantly on the quality of teaching and learning and pupil attainment.

As the research community continues to gather quantitative and qualitative evidence in relation to the impact of academies it is important, in our view, that such issues are fully examined and reported on.

Notes

1 The Funding Agreement is the contract between the Secretary of State for Education and Skills and the academy. It sets out the terms under which the academy is funded and defines the framework for accountability. It also references to existing legislation and policy. More information is available at: www.dcsf.gov.uk/foischeme/subPage.cfm?action=disclosures.display&i_subcategoryID=34&i_collectionID=190, accessed August 2010

2 Not all academies in the sample had predecessor schools as some opened as new schools with a phased intake.

3 Comparable data were not available for schools with a phased intake (i.e. those schools that opened with a year cohort and added an additional year group).

4 Used as a proxy for disadvantage.

5 The Transfer of Undertakings (Protection of Employment) (TUPE) Regulations. These regulations are designed to protect the rights of employees in a transfer situation, enabling them to enjoy the same terms and conditions with continuity of employment offers.

6 Community- and voluntary-controlled, foundation, voluntary-aided, City Technology Colleges, trust schools and academies.

[7] Particularly under the new sponsorship arrangements, whereby independent schools can sponsor an academy without any financial contribution.

[8] Coldron (2007) suggests there are features of diversity – namely structural, educational and compositional.

Chapter 8

Are Academies Working?[1]

Stephen Gorard

Introduction

This chapter considers each of the annual cohorts of new academies in England, from 2002 to 2006, and shows that their level of success in comparison to their predecessors, national averages, their changing compositions and their changing exam entry practices are insubstantial. There is no clear evidence that academies produce better results than local authority schools with equivalent intakes. The Academies Programme therefore presents an opportunity cost for no apparent gain on this limited measure of success.

The background

A programme of city academies was announced by the Secretary of State for Education for England in 2000, to complement the Specialist Schools programme. Schools running at-risk, in special measures, or with poor examination results had not previously been allowed to become specialist schools. This meant that the extra initial and recurrent funding given to specialist schools exacerbated the existing competitive disadvantages for so-called 'failing schools'. The Academies Programme was meant to change that.

> Academies *will* break the cycle of underachievement in areas of social and economic deprivation.
>
> (DfES, 2004a, emphasis added)

> We expect that all Academies will make steady upward progress . . . Good teaching, excellent facilities and motivated pupils *will* deliver real improvements in educational standards.
>
> (DfES, 2004b, emphasis added)

Academies were originally intended to replace schools in areas of high socio-economic disadvantage with falling intakes and poor results, and which were increasingly spurned by local parents able to find an alternative school for their child. These new schools are mostly relaunched versions of one or two existing secondary schools, independent of local government control, have voluntary or private sector sponsors, are allowed to have a specialist curriculum, and can select 10 per cent of their intake by aptitude. They have received substantial public investment, new buildings, state-of-the-art facilities, and changes in leadership. Have they worked?

The first three academies opened in 2002, and success for these schools was claimed almost immediately by their sponsors (BBC, 2004b). On examination, this success was illusory. Originally happy to accept short-term indicators of success, when these were shown to be false the advocates of academies suddenly rejected any short-term indicators of failure. Academy sponsors, the then DfES and government minsters began to change their claims of immediate success into demands that we wait until a whole cohort of students had been through the academy system. The 2007 results were the first for the students in the age 15 cohort who almost all joined their academies as academies, as opposed to previous cohorts who had the school(s) change around them. Thus, we are now able to expand considerably on the snapshot of only three schools published in 2005 (Gorard, 2005).

Data for all academies includes their Key Stage 4 results (or KS4), the terminal qualification level for pupils aged 15 starting their final year of compulsory school, their composition in terms of pupils eligible for free school meals (FSM, an indicator of family poverty), their rates of exclusion (from the pupil level annual schools census, or PLASC, a database of all school pupil characteristics held by DCSF), and the equivalent results for their predecessor schools. The DCSF website and the PLASC (along with the National Pupil Database, or NPD) has details of a further eight academies opened in 2003, three in 2004, seven in 2005, and fourteen in 2006. There are other more recent academies and some others named academies but with no available student achievement data at time of writing. Only simple descriptions and comparisons are used, along with a correlation computed between the school-level values for Key Stage 4 results and eligibility for FSM.

Overall picture

Are academies a solution to the perennial problem for school improvers? Do they deliver superior educational outcomes without changing the nature of their student intake? Which ones have improved their results other than in a trend from before they were academies, and which of these has done so without a substantial change in FSM intake?

The academies that were open in 2005/06 took a considerably higher proportion (36 per cent) of children eligible for FSM than the remaining educational institutions in England (13 per cent). This is not surprising, given that they were to have been selected as some of the most challenged schools in the most deprived areas. It also goes some way towards explaining the generally lower level of raw-score results in academies for students aged 15/16. Over the period covered, national school-level results at Key Stage 4 and the percentage of students eligible for FSM correlated at around –0.5 (Pearson's R). Schools with more FSM students tended to have a considerably lower percentage of students reaching Level 2 at Key Stage 4 (five good GCSEs at grade A*–C, or equivalent, often needed for entry to sixth form).

Students in the open academies generally entered fewer full GCSEs than in the other institutions (the General Certificate of Secondary Education is, at the time of writing, the most prevalent qualification taken at Key Stage 4), although their GCSE equivalent entry (including other qualifications deemed by DCSF to be at the same level as GCSE) was identical (see Table 8.1). This is largely because academies are more likely to enter their students for dual (and higher) award subjects and qualifications, and other recent alternatives to single full GCSEs. Fewer students in academies reach Level 1 (any GCSE or equivalent) and markedly fewer reach Level 2. The achievement gap between academies and other schools in the proportion reaching Level 2, including English and maths, is around 20 per cent (the difference between the two scores, divided by their sum, see Gorard, 2006).

It is not fair to compare academies with all other institutions in terms of results because of their markedly different intakes (Gorard, 2000). Traditional value-added analyses do not do justice to the real difference in intakes between schools (Gorard, 2010). So, a simple way of looking at and judging the performance of academies in relation to their stated aims is over time, and especially in comparison with the schools they replaced.

Table 8.1 Selected examination results, all schools in England, 2005/06

	Non-academies	Academies
Percentage gaining Level 2	58	46
Percentage gaining Level 2 with functional English and maths	46	31
Percentage gaining Level 1	89	81
Mean full GCSE entries per student	7.6	6.3
Mean GCSE A*–C per student	4.8	2.9
GCSE equivalent entries	9.5	9.5

Source: PLASC/NPD KS4 2005/06.

School-level analysis

The first three academies opening in 2002 did not outperform the schools that they replaced, despite the annual national increase in GCSE scores across the board (Gorard, 2005). In general, by 2004 they had reduced their

FSM intake, increased their rate of exclusion, and had declining scores in GCSE terms. What they have all done, both in absolute terms and relative to their surrounding schools, is to substantially reduce the percentage of students eligible for FSM since becoming academies (see Table 8.2). Given the objectives of the programme, this was and is success of a kind in stemming the apparent spiral of decline. All still have high levels of student poverty, but they are now closer to their local authority average. However, given the strong correlation between deprivation of intakes and examination outcomes, this success in changing the intake means that we would expect, *ceteris paribus* – examination outcomes to rise irrespective of anything that the academies have done in addition. And this is what we find.

By 2007 (see Table 8.3) the Business Academy had an even lower Level 2 percentage (31 per cent of students) than in 2004 (34 per cent). Not surprisingly, this was associated with a slight increase in FSM, from 37 per cent in 2004 to 39 per cent in 2007 (see Table 8.2). The other two 2002 academies had considerable increases in Level 2 results – Unity from 17 per cent to 45 per cent and Greig City from 26 per cent to 65 per cent. Again, this is associated negatively with a shift in FSM, from 50 per cent to 45 per cent for Unity and 47 per cent to 39 per cent for Greig City.

Nevertheless, the gains at Level 2 are impressive until we look at Level 2 including English and maths, the new DCSF standard threshold. Here there is no clear gain for either school (Greig City has 19 per cent in 2003 and 21 per cent in 2007, for example, while Unity declines from 14 per cent in 2006 to 12 per cent in 2007). This suggests that the shift in the more general Level 2 figures, above and beyond what might be expected by the reduction in

Table 8.2 FSM percentages for 2002 cohort of academies, 1997–2007

	1997	**1998**	**1999**	**2000**	**2001**	**2002**	**2003**	**2004**	**2005**	**2006**	**2007**
Business	53	49	52	50	49	46	42	37	38	39	39
Greig	48	56	42	43	31	39	43	47	44	38	39
Unity	60	62	51	46	57	47	49	50	49	44	45

Note: The figures 1997–2002 are before the academies.

Table 8.3 Level 2 percentages for 2002 cohort of academies, 1997–2007

	1997	**1998**	**1999**	**2000**	**2001**	**2002**	**2003**	**2004**	**2005**	**2006**	**2007**
Business	13	24	14	10	17	–	21	34	29	32	31
Greig	14	11	15	25	30	–	35	26	54	59	65
Unity	13	2	13	4	17	–	16	17	16	34	45

Note: The figures 1997–2001 are before the academies. Results are not publicly available for the first year of each academy.

FSM, is due to changes in exam entry policy (see above). On this measure, the Business Academy is doing somewhat better than its two peers (with 27 per cent gaining Level 2 including English and maths in 2006). The picture is confusing, because the exams have changed, their prevalence in the wider population has changed substantially since 1997, school intakes change and so on. Perhaps the later academies can make the situation clearer.

Of those eight schools becoming academies in 2003, the attainment figures for the Walsall Academy in 2007 are not available. The school has not shown a clear improvement since becoming an academy in the previous years, moving from 50 per cent in 2003 to 57 per cent in 2006 (only 24 per cent with English and maths), while its FSM intake has decreased sharply every year from 26 per cent in 2003 to 11 per cent in 2007 (see Table 8.5). Thus, any changes in its Level 2 scores over time are easily explicable in terms of changes in student intake. There is no great improvement to be attributed to the other changes associated with academization. Other than Walsall, the 2003 cohort of academies are all clearly schools with highly deprived intakes, with the academy at Peckham taking nearly two-thirds of its students from families living in poverty. In terms of the original aims of the Academies Programme these look like the right kinds of schools (which cannot be said for all subsequent cohorts).

Of the academies other than Walsall, Manchester and Peckham have, like two of the 2002 academies, had a recent run of increases at Level 2

Table 8.4 Level 2 percentages, including English and maths, for 2002 cohort of academies, 2003–7

	2003	2004	2005	2006	2007
Business	15	13	15	27	19
Greig	19	10	10	15	21
Unity	7	7	6	14	12

Table 8.5 FSM percentages for 2003 cohort of academies, 2004–7

	2004	2005	2006	2007
Walsall	26	16	14	11
Manchester	51	62	61	50
Academy at Peckham	60	65	64	53
Capital City	39	34	34	35
City Academy	36	37	46	45
Kings	38	32	30	25
West London	41	42	43	41
Djanogly City	35	36	29	38

(see Table 8.6). Unlike them, these increases (while lower) also occur when English and maths are included, suggesting that exam entry policy has not changed that much and so does not account for most of the increase in scores (see Table 8.7). But like the 2002 academies, FSM has also fallen – from 62 per cent in 2005 to 50 per cent in 2007 for Manchester and from 65 per cent in 2005 to 53 per cent in 2007 for Peckham. Thus, the combination of parallel increases in Level 2 scores nationally, some changes in exam entries and substantial decreases in FSM students are sufficient to explain rises in Level 2 scores here. Again there is no need to search for further factors such as leadership, building or independence from local authority control. Most of the other 2003 academies show no clear improvement. Indeed, City and West London both had lower Level 2 scores in 2007 than 2006, while Capital City had a lower Level 2 score in 2005 than its predecessor school had in 2000, three years before academization. In addition, some of these schools experienced substantial reductions in FSM that might have

Table 8.6 Level 2 percentages for 2003 cohort of academies, 2000–7

	2000	**2001**	**2002**		**2004**	**2005**	**2006**	**2007**
Walsall	12	13	22	–	50	67	57	–
Manchester	8	14	12	–	8	25	28	33
Academy at Peckham	21	21	22	–	12	22	30	38
Capital City	23	13	14	–	29	17	29	48
City Academy	17	22	25	–	33	52	50	48
Kings	20	19	21	–	34	43	35	47
West London	17	20	13	–	35	28	47	37
Djanogly City	44	52	55	–	51	57	56	67

Note: The figures 2000–2 are from before the academies. Results are not publicly available for the first year of each academy.

Table 8.7 Level 2 percentages, including English and maths, for 2003 cohort of academies, 2004–7

	2004	**2005**	**2006**	**2007**
Walsall	5	21	24	–
Manchester	6	12	22	20
Academy at Peckham	10	18	23	24
Capital City	17	11	17	22
City Academy	16	19	18	21
Kings	26	23	23	34
West London	8	11	25	24
Djanogly City	19	18	25	35

been expected to show up in higher Level 2 scores. Kings, for example, moved from 38 per cent in 2004 to 25 per cent in 2007.

Taken as a whole, the 2003 academies do not portray the 'steady upward' progress proposed by the DfES in 2004 (see above). Djanogly is the only academy here to have a higher Level 2 score in 2007 than previous years, a growth in Level 2 including English and maths *and* no reduction in FSM intake. And even Djanogly had years before academization with higher FSM but still high Level 2 scores – the percentage in 2002 when the predecessor school was closed was the same as the academy achieved in 2006. As yet, there is no clear evidence that academies perform any better than their predecessor schools once changes in national Level 2, FSM and exam entry policy are accounted for.

There were only three new academies in 2004, of which one (Northampton) had markedly lower levels of deprivation, suggesting that it might not have been the most deserving local choice for the investment (see Table 8.8). Northampton (like Walsall before it, and others including Harefield, Trinity, Salford and Landau Forte after it) has a lower than national average FSM intake, and so should probably not have been considered for the programme in the first place. All three academies show a slight drop in FSM intake since 2005.

Of the 2004 cohort, the London Academy has not made much improvement in the general Level 2 indicator (see Table 8.9) but has moved from 24 per cent with English and maths in 2005 to 39 per cent in 2007 (see Table 8.10), while mostly retaining its FSM intake. Northampton's Level 2 score for 2007 is no better than for 2005, and not much better than in 2002 despite a decline in FSM from 20 per cent in 2004. Stockley has made some

Table 8.8 FSM percentages for 2004 cohort of academies, 2005–7

	2005	2006	2007
Stockley	44	44	40
Northampton	19	18	16
London Academy	43	44	41

Table 8.9 Level 2 percentages for 2004 cohort of academies, 2000–7

	2000	2001	2002	2003	2004	2005	2006	2007
Stockley	21	17	8	14	–	19	31	44
Northampton	19	21	29	19	–	34	40	33
London Academy	24	21	30	40	–	48	48	55

Note: The figures 2000–3 are from before the academies. Results are not publicly available for the first year of each academy.

Table 8.10 Level 2 percentages, including English and maths, for 2004 cohort of academies, 2005–7

	2005	2006	2007
Stockley	9	16	25
Northampton	18	24	22
London Academy	24	31	39

gains at Level 2 on both indicators, with a small drop in FSM (44 per cent 2005 to 40 per cent 2007). In general, and over a short haul, the small 2004 cohort appears to have done rather better than previous cohorts. However, there are only two that should be academies and too much should not be read into this pattern. If both the Level 2 indicator and FSM level were actually random and each school could go up or down annually, then one in four schools would have an increase in Level 2 without a decrease in FSM every year. One or two academies out of fourteen with one or two years of success does not therefore suggest any kind of positive pattern for the programme as a whole.

Of the 2005 cohort, Salford, like Northampton above, does not really fit the profile of academies as originally envisaged. It was scoring 44 per cent at Level 2 when it was still the Canon Williamson School in 2004, with a relatively low FSM score of 29 per cent (see Table 8.11). Despite this, it has further reduced its FSM intake to 18 per cent in 2007, meaning that other local schools that were more worthy of academization initially now have to take an even larger share of students from families living in poverty. Harefield, with 16 per cent FSM in 2007, and Trinity, with 15 per cent FSM in 2007, are similar to Salford in these two respects. They were not the right schools to become academies in their areas (according to the programme aims) and their further decrease in FSM intake since academization has led to other local schools increasing their FSM intake further. Rather than

Table 8.11 FSM percentages for 2005 cohort of academies, 2005–7

	2005	2006	2007
The Marlowe Academy	36	35	29
Haberdashers' Aske's Knights Academy	54	45	44
The Harefield Academy	21	20	16
Trinity Academy	21	22	15
The Academy of St Francis of Assisi	55	47	47
Salford City Academy	30	29	18
St Pauls Academy	–	25	26

reducing segregation by poverty these academies have worsened it.

If we leave these three aside the picture for the remainder of the 2005 cohort is again mixed (see Table 8.12). Marlowe has increased its score at Level 2, but decreased its FSM intake from 54 per cent to 44 per cent over the two years available, and only manages to get around 5 per cent of students to Level 2 with English and maths, suggesting that its new Level 2 scores are not really comparable with those before 2005.

Haberdashers' is similar (but with slightly better English and maths). St Francis has shown some progress on the overall Level 2 indicator since academization, while changing from 55 per cent to 47 per cent FSM and showing no progress at all on the Level 2 indicator including English and maths (see Table 8.13). St Pauls has one impressive year in 2007 (the figures for 2006 are not substantially better than its predecessor). It will be interesting to see what happens to this 82 per cent figure, achieved without decline in FSM and echoed in English and maths. It is perhaps notable that an FSM intake of 25 per cent, while marginally higher than the national average, puts St Pauls in a very different position to many academies struggling on 40–60 per cent FSM intake. So again, the evidence is far from conclusive but gives no indication that the programme as a whole is being effective in its own terms.

The most recent cohort of academies, at time of writing, to have available results was created/converted in 2006 (see Table 8.14). Landau Forte is a rebadged City Technology College (CTC) with high scores and low FSM, making little upward progress over time, and which does not fit the profile of an academy as originally envisaged.

On the first, and only, set of Level 2 figures we have so far, Westminster is doing worse than the school it replaced despite a drop in FSM intake from 45 per cent in 2005 to 41 per cent in 2007 (see Table 8.15). North

Table 8.12 Level 2 percentages for 2005 cohort of academies, 2001–7

	2001	2002	2003	2004	2005	2006	2007
The Marlowe Academy	4	4	4	15	–	27	37
Haberdashers' Aske's Knights Academy	9	18	11	15	–	29	42
The Harefield Academy	23	17	13	22	–	31	38
Trinity Academy	33	22	26	21	–	34	64
The Academy of St Francis of Assisi	15	24	24	22	–	40	43
Salford City Academy	22	24	39	44	–	50	62
St Pauls Academy	52	46	52	54	–	59	82

Note: The figures 2001–4 are from before the academies. Results are not publicly available for the first year of each academy.

Table 8.13 Level 2 percentages, including English and maths, for 2005 cohort of academies, 2006–7

	2006	2007
The Marlowe Academy	5	7
Haberdashers' Aske's Knights Academy	14	20
The Harefield Academy	31	35
Trinity Academy	19	40
The Academy of St Francis of Assisi	16	16
Salford City Academy	27	41
St Pauls Academy	39	51

Table 8.14 FSM percentages for 2006 cohort of academies, 2005–7

	2005	2006	2007
David Young Community Academy	44 & 39	49 & 42	42
The Barnsley Academy	50	53	37
John Madejski Academy	35	31	29
Sheffield Park Academy	41	40	36
North Liverpool Academy	59 & 39	61 & 38	39
Sheffield Springs Academy	32	35	35
Harris Academy Merton	22	24	30
Burlington Danes Academy	37	37	21
Westminster Academy	45	41	41
Harris Academy Bermondsey	66	63	61
Grace Academy	27	29	28
St Marks Church of England Academy	27	27	27
The Gateway Academy	31	35	36
Landau Forte College	8	9	10

Note: David Young and North Liverpool academies had two predecessor schools. Their FSM intake after becoming academies is clearly lower than the weighted average of their predecessors.

Liverpool, Grace and St Marks are not clearly doing any better than the schools they replaced to become academies. In 2003, 25 per cent of student at the St Marks predecessor attained Level 2, and in 2007 after a general increase in GCSE scores and the money and impact of an academy and an intake remaining at 27 per cent FSM, 25 per cent of St Marks students again attained Level 2. In 2007, after a huge decrease in FSM intake from the two predecessor schools, North Liverpool attained 37 per cent at Level 2 but had already attained an average score of 35 per cent in 2004 long before becoming an academy, and when one of the predecessors had a staggering 61 per

Table 8.15 Level 2 percentages for 2006 cohort of academies, 2002–7

	2002	2003	2004	2005	2006	2007
David Young Community Academy	9	12	12	16	–	41
The Barnsley Academy	11	9	29	43	–	61
John Madejski Academy	15	12	15	10	–	26
Sheffield Park Academy	22	20	27	28	–	39
North Liverpool Academy	23	28	35	17	–	37
Sheffield Springs Academy	24	19	25	19	–	31
Harris Academy Merton	25	19	21	31	–	40
Burlington Danes Academy	26	32	28	34	–	44
Westminster Academy	27	26	27	27	–	23
Harris Academy Bermondsey	30	27	33	41	–	58
Grace Academy	30	22	16	22	–	33
St Marks Church of England Academy		25	18	19	–	25
The Gateway Academy			13	12	–	41
Landau Forte College	71	82	80	77	86	

Note: The figures 2002–5 are from before the academies. Results are not publicly available for the first year of each academy.

cent FSM intake. Grace has gone from 30 per cent at Level 2 in 2002 when not an academy to 33 per cent in 2007 after a larger rise in average national scores. So these five academies are, if anything, evidence of the failure (over this very short time period) of the Academies Programme.

John Madejski has a clearly higher Level 2 score in 2007 than in any previous year for which data is available, but only managed 5 per cent of students with Level 2 including English and maths, despite a decrease in FSM from 35 per cent to 29 per cent. The picture for the other academies is more mixed. David Young, Sheffield Park, Burlington Danes and Harris Merton portray an increase at Level 2 (both indicators) but an equivalent drop in FSM over the same period. Barnsley shows a similar increase from a higher base, but with a huge drop in FSM from 53 per cent in 2006 to 37 per cent in 2007. This is an amazing change in intake over one year, and it would be interesting to find out how this occurred. In addition, the growth in Level 2 at Barnsley obviously predates academization, and the gradient of improvement declines somewhat after 2005. In this situation, we cannot attribute the 2007 improvement to the Academies Programme. Sheffield Springs, Harris Bermondsey and Gateway retain or even increase their share of FSM students and yet show an increase in the general Level 2 indicator for one year. But as before, three schools out of 14, or indeed four or five schools in total out of 35 academies, with a year or two of good scores is not sufficient to argue that academies as a whole have been differentially effective.

Discussion

This sceptical consideration of the advances made by schools converted to academies between 2002 and 2006 is necessary. Claims to success of the programme must be able to survive such a consideration if it is to be continued ethically in terms of its public funding and especially in terms of the potential opportunity costs for students facing their one chance of education. The claims to success of the programme by the DfES as early as 2004 were based partly on the misleading comparison with the prior results of the very different CTCs (DfES, 2005a). These claims to success were repeated in the Associated Academy Portfolios sent in a pack to potential sponsors by Christine Horner, Office of the Schools Commissioner, DfES (12 October 2006) following a meeting between Adonis and potential sponsors, and by DfES (2005a, p. 2): 'In 2003, their first year, the average 5+ A*–C results in the three open Academies was 24%, compared to an average of 16% in their predecessor schools in the previous year'.

As Table 8.2 shows, neither of these figures is correct, and one academy actually had lower results in 2003 than its predecessor.

Of the 24 or so academies discussed above, only around five appear to be gaining appreciably higher results for their students than in previous years (including those when not an academy). Is this enough to declare the Academies Programme a success? Not really. None of the five is in the earliest cohort. The earliest example is, as explained, no more than would be expected by chance and the later examples have very few years of data to examine. The response by Adonis and others to Gorard (2005) was that one or two years of data is not enough (despite their prior recorded claims of success for the programme). If a couple of years' data were not enough in 2005 then they are not enough for the 2005 and 2006 cohorts now. However, the picture is mixed and a few schools do appear to be bucking the usual pattern by gaining higher scores with the same intake (as assessed by FSM at least) and without sacrificing English and maths. If we note these schools now and see that this form can be reproduced annually then this would be much more impressive than simple *post hoc* identification via dredging. In summary, there is no clear evidence here that academies work to produce better results than the kinds of schools they replaced but neither is the evidence as clear as in 2005 that they are completely failing to do so.

It is a concern that with the expansion of the programme an increasing proportion of the 'wrong' schools are being selected to receive the money and attention involved. Walsall Academy has only around 11 per cent FSM intake, for example, and in 2005 nearly 70 per cent of students got to Level 2. If this is a school in urgent need of government intervention then nearly all schools in England are in the same position. This situation is likely to worsen with private schools and universities entering the fold as sponsors (Hatcher, 2006).

To say that struggling academies are doing no better than their non-academy peers is not to denigrate them; but it does suggest that the programme is a waste of time, effort and energy, at least in terms of this rather narrow measure of Key Stage 4 outcomes. There are also opportunity costs. The students passing through the school while it experiments have only that one shot at initial education. The money involved could have been used differently – spent on refurbishing the most deprived schools or used to follow the most deprived students to whichever school they attend.

Note

1. This chapter is a shortened version of Gorard, S. (2009), 'What are academies the answer to?' *Journal of Education Policy*. 24, (1), 101–13. I am grateful to the editors for giving permission to reprint it here.

Chapter 9

'Rapidly Improving Results': Penetrating the Hype of Policy-Based Evidence

Terry Wrigley

Introduction

The Academies Programme was introduced in March 2000 as a means of rescuing 'seriously failing schools' and with the aim of 'breaking the cycle of underperformance and low expectations' (Blunkett, 2000c). The decision was made by ministerial pronouncement, with no significant parliamentary debate, and hidden within the 'Fresh Start' initiative. The first three academies were announced by September 2000 and opened in September 2002. The programme has been in trouble ever since.

Having committed to what was, in many ways, a relaunch of the abandoned City Technology College (CTC) initiative by the Thatcher government (see Beckett, 2007; Chitty, 2008b), New Labour Ministers have felt compelled to construct positive evidence ever since. To draw upon a phrase previously used about the launching of war on Iraq (see Glees, 2005, among others), this was policy-based evidence rather than evidence-based policy.

Only 12 academies had been opened (three in September 2002, nine in September 2003) when the government announced a target of 200 by the year 2010. There were at the time no meaningful GCSE results with which to justify this, unless one counts the June 2003 sitting at the first three academies, whose candidates had spent only nine months in the academy.

It can only have been based, as Clyde Chitty argues (2008b, pp. 27–8), on New Labour's 'enormous faith in the expertise and integrity of private business' – again, scarcely a belief that is well supported by evidence! As Francis Beckett (2007, p. 12) pointed out, Education Secretary David Blunkett was 'setting a breakneck pace, so fast that most people did not see what was going on'.

Already in November 2004, the schools minister David Miliband was facing challenges from investigative journalists for *File on 4* (2004) about the lack of evidence. The first government-commissioned PricewaterhouseCoopers (PwC, 2003) report had been dispatched but Miliband had not yet seen it. Miliband found himself arguing that converting 200 out of the 450 schools situated in disadvantaged areas was 'judicious' and 'common sense' (*File on 4*, 2004, p. 6). The *File on 4* (2004) radio programme then highlighted adverse inspection reports, mass expulsions, a declining proportion of pupils in poverty, and some academies whose GCSE results stubbornly fail to improve.

In March 2005, a parliamentary select committee concurred with these criticisms concerning the rashness of government decision-making on academies. MPs pointed out that the current Education Secretary, Charles Clarke, was intent on citing evidence of improved GCSE results at only three academies, while five out of eleven had not improved and some had declined: 'We fail to understand why the DfES is putting such substantial resources into academies when it has not produced the evidence' (House of Commons, 2005, p. 53).

In fact, the 2004 results of the first three academies showed that only one had improved its GCSE results. Significantly, this was the Bexley Business Academy; it had replaced a secondary modern school so this was hardly comparing like with like.

A newspaper report by Matthew Taylor (2005), focusing on the first three academies, pointed out that one had failed its Ofsted (Office for Standards in Education) inspection, another had 'serious weaknesses' (though the report was then buried), and the third received a 'hit squad' after six months. Once able to access the first PwC (2003) report using the Freedom of Information Act, this journalist discovered the report had commented that US 'Charter Schools', the nearest parallel to England's academies, had only enjoyed a 'modest' improvement (Taylor, 2005).

The remainder of this chapter reviews the accumulating data on academic attainment in the academies, and demonstrates the paucity of evidence to underpin the government's continuing optimism and hype.

Early GCSE results: trumpeting a miracle

Confirmation of 2004 GCSE results in January 2005 gave Ministers their first real opportunity to argue the proven merits of the academies. Shortly afterwards, they were also able to draw upon the publication of the second PwC (2005) evaluation report which they had commissioned.

In its official response to this report (PwC, 2005), the government department (DfES, 2005b, p. 9) pointed out that 40 per cent of the predecessor schools (i.e. schools closed to make way for academies) were in 'special measures'. This raises the question, of course, as to why the other 60 per cent were considered in need of closure. Despite a consistent ministerial insistence that GCSE had dramatically improved, the evaluation report stated that 'six brought about increases and five did not' (the remaining school only had Year 7 pupils).

At this time, the PwC reports and Ministers were still able to speak of 'five or more A*–C grades' without more ado. It was becoming apparent that this was problematic. Towards the end of the year, the term 'or equivalent' began to appear, albeit inconsistently and without explanation, the consequence of a wider challenge to government claims of rapidly rising results nationally.

The phrase 'or equivalent' refers to an official decision to assign a GCSE equivalence for vocational qualifications.[1] Though sometimes for elitist reasons independent schools were challenging the new-found 'equivalence' between a distinction in cake decorating and an A* in physics. However, the immediate concern in evaluating academies is with the GNVQ Intermediate award,[2] which was now officially 'equivalent' to four A*–C passes.

Beyond the academies, Roger Titcombe and Roger Davies (2006) were challenging government claims of rapid improvement in some secondary schools, including the official list of the '100 most improved schools'. These schools were being held up as an exemplar of what other schools could achieve if they really tried. This research highlighted the extensive adoption of the GNVQ Intermediate because of its inflated 'equivalence'. They pointed to the adverse impact on the curriculum, including the loss of languages, science, history and geography.

Growing pressures forced the DfES to switch from using 'five or more A*–Cs or equivalent' as its main indicator of success to 'five or more A*–Cs or equivalent but including *English and mathematics*' (to be abbreviated from here onwards in this chapter as '5ACeq' and '5ACEM' respectively). However it retained the former indicator, renamed 'Level 2 *threshold*', and Ministers continued to use it extensively to hype the Academies Programme and confuse the public.

My own analysis of the 2005 results showed that although seven of the eligible eleven schools had apparently improved (5ACeq), in almost every case this was because of a substantial switch to GNVQ. The 'improvement' was not matched in terms of 5ACEM, which had barely moved; in the most extreme case only one in nine pupils with 5ACeq achieved 5ACEM (nationally four out of five). Although this varied between academies, similar curriculum damage to that identified by Titcombe and Davies (2006) was apparent.

I should emphasize that I am not espousing a traditionalist rejection of vocational qualifications. Ironically, Titcombe and Davies (2006) discovered that the GNVQ device was not leading to the introduction of new subjects such as construction or engineering, but predominantly to a replacement of well-established GCSEs in science and ICT by easier GNVQs in those subjects. My point is to challenge spurious comparisons between academies and other schools on the basis of false equivalences, namely the substitution of easier qualifications. It is also important to raise the question of the 'street value' of these replacement qualifications: were employers likely to regard, let us say, a GNVQ in computing and a C in art as the equivalent of five A*–C grades in a broad range of subjects? This phoney equivalence was setting young people up for disappointment and failure.

It is notoriously difficult to make a qualitative comparison between two different qualifications. However, one fair start for such a comparison can be found by establishing that pupils achieving a particular level in one examination tend to achieve a specific level in another. Based on the academies data, I was able to show that nine out of ten pupils gaining a C or above in GCSE sciences also gained a C or above in GCSE maths. By comparison, only half of pupils passing GNVQ Intermediate in science gained a C or above in GCSE maths, with the other half gaining Ds or Es. Similar results emerge when ICT is compared with maths. Further comparisons supported the argument that a GCVQ (Intermediate) equates at its lower threshold with an E grade rather than a C. For example, nobody with an E or above in English or maths appeared to fail GNVQ Intermediate.

It emerged, following correspondence with OfSTED and the Qualifications and Curriculum Authority (QCA), that there had not been a rigorous evaluation of the supposed equivalence, either in terms of quality (why a simple GNVQ Intermediate pass, rather than merit or distinction, was deemed to be worth a GCSE C grade) or quantity (why a GNVQ in one subject was worth four GCSEs). The fallacious quantitative equivalence is highlighted by academies that had entered their highest attainers for two GNVQ Intermediates (each 'equal' to four GCSEs), two vocational GCSEs (each worth two academic GCSEs), and a full range of standard GCSE. Officially these pupils had been successful in the 'equivalent' of 20 subjects!

Drawing on data from published DfES performance tables (available at www.dcsf.gov.uk/performancetables) supplemented by the DfES National Pupil Database, I began a series of annual comparisons beginning with results from 2005 (academies) and 2002 (the predecessor schools). The first analysis involved academies opened in 2002 and 2003 but not the 2004 starters, i.e. it covered all candidates who had completed Key Stage 4 (their two-year examination courses) at the academy. I set out to examine how much substance there was to official claims of rapid improvement (based on 5ACeq) by asking the questions:

1. What proportion of pupils reaching that level had qualified in five or more different subjects?
2. What proportion had achieved 5ACEM?

Table 9.1 below shows these proportions (percentages (i) and (ii) were recalculated using pupil numbers, for greater accuracy). The ratios shown in columns (i) and (ii) demonstrate the increasing gap between data based on 'equivalences' and more substantive qualification levels. It illustrates how many of the pupils claimed by government statistics as successful had not

Table 9.1 Analysis of GCSE results

	5ACeq	5 subjects	(i)	5ACEM	(ii)
2002	24%	20%	84%	14%	62%
2005	37%	22%	60%	15%	40%

achieved either a C or above in five subjects, or a C or above in English and mathematics. The 2005 data for the academies indicates a significant change in examination policy rather than a genuine educational improvement, including a dramatic increase in GNVQ entries.

A further concern arising from the 2005 results was the large numbers of academy pupils finishing compulsory schooling without five or more A–G grades. Around 90 per cent in all schools nationally achieve five A–G grades, and failure to do so can seriously disadvantage a pupil in terms of employability. Only one of the academies reached this level in 2005; results in the others stretched down to 66 per cent with a mean of 79 per cent. These are levels that in normal circumstances would probably trigger 'special measures' (commonly referred to as 'failing school') in inspections. This suggests a possible neglect of lower-attaining pupils, and raises questions about the purported mission of the Academy programme.

The third PwC (2006) evaluation report, appearing in early summer 2006, also attempted to come to terms with the 2005 results. PwC (2006) emphasized the low attainment of the predecessor schools (all except one within the lowest decile of average point scores for their pupil intake, based on Key Stage 2). However, when comparing current attainment in the academies with similar schools, they could only claim that 'the absolute differences are generally small' (p. ii). They identified great unevenness in improving attainment, excusing the weaker ones because of building delays or too little 'lead-in time'.

The report attempted to develop an evaluation based on three comparator sets (also used in PwC, 2007 and 2008).

1. Schools with the lowest 10 per cent of Key Stage 2 attainment on entry.
2. Schools with the lowest 15 per cent of Key Stage 2 attainment on entry.
3. 'Overlapping intake schools' defined as schools with a least ten pupils coming from the same primary school.[3]

There are clear tensions within the text between more and less optimistic interpretations, with uncertainties showing through in phrases such as 'were, in general, quite strong' (p. 19), but the statistics themselves should have raised politicians' anxieties. For example, the improvement on 5ACeq between 2002 and 2004 was little different from comparator schools, and between 2004 and 2005 only 2 percentage points (pp) better than improvement nationally.

Most seriously, however, the PwC analysts seemed unaware of the growing controversy about 'equivalence'. Indeed, the report makes no mention of the GNVQ factor or the new official Level 2 criterion involving English and maths.

My own analysis was resumed when 2006 results were confirmed. This now included the academies opened in 2004 as well as 2002 and 2003. The 2005 starters were not included, in line with previous decisions, because their pupils had only studied nine months of their Key Stage 4 examination courses at the academy. This time there was a significant improvement in 5ACEM results, mostly between 2005 and 2006, after little improvement from 2002 to 2005. This might suggest a sudden push from the Specialist Schools and Academies Trust on its academies in terms of this indicator. Overall, on 5ACEM from 2002 to 2006, the academies had improved by almost 8pp, compared with a national gain of 4pp. There was still a serious disproportion between 5ACeq and 5ACEM figures (42 per cent and 22 per cent respectively) and little improvement in 5AG (now at 81 per cent). The net improvement of 5ACEM over the national improvement – in other words an 'academy effect' – averaged around 1pp per year, completely out of proportion to the additional cost of academics; even this figure took no account of the changing nature of the pupil population in the academies.

A curriculum analysis based on the 2006 examination statistics from the DfES data (National Pupil Database) also confirmed earlier concerns. Even for the 42 per cent of pupils who were relatively successful (i.e. 5ACeq), the curriculum was becoming limited:

- Two-thirds of them gained a C in English, with similar figures for mathematics.
- Two-thirds of them had achieved a C or above in science, but after adjusting for the false equivalence of GNVQ, this reduced to just over half.[4]
- Only a quarter of these relatively successful pupils gained A*–C in either geography or history. Even taking account of some entries for sociology or (half-GCSE) citizenship, it was still well below half.
- Only a quarter obtained a C or above in any European or Asian language; indeed, two-thirds of these 5ACeq pupils did not study a foreign language at Key Stage 4.
- A quarter did not follow any course in a creative or performance art. Only two-thirds were entered for a design and technology GCSE and only a third obtained a C or above.
- However, almost all passed a vocational qualification. Indeed, there had been a massive increase in entries for GNVQ Intermediate: thirteen

entries for every ten pupils, compared with one in ten at the predecessor schools.

It is doubtful whether many of these pupils would count as well educated in most European countries. Certainly, a Level 2 'threshold' based on a GNVQ and one other subject would be viewed as a derisory standard elsewhere.

In February 2007 the National Audit Office (NAO, 2007) reported to parliament on the Academies Programme. This was an interesting document, with a text that inclined strongly towards the positive and a visual appearance clearly intended to impress. The document still made unquestioning use of the 5ACeq statistic, with no critique of the 'GNVQ=4' factor or attempt to question the 'street value' of GNVQ. Despite its positive spin, the report concluded that academies were not doing as well as Excellence in Cities schools, with a high proportion of free school meals (FSM). Ironically, the report included a chart which showed that the academies improved no faster in their first three years than the predecessor schools had been doing in the three years before closure. The report's analysis of attainment took no account of the impact of population change.

The House of Commons Committee of Public Accounts (2007) sitting a month later were not slow to see problems. Building on this report, they pointed out that seven out of eleven inspections had shown academies to be inadequate or just satisfactory, with only four being good, including concerns about the quality of teaching and pupil behaviour. They were critical of the high costs, and raised the important question as to whether any improvement was because they were academies or because of the free start or new buildings, for example.

Nevertheless, Ministers remained committed to the programme, continuing to make prominent use of the 5ACeq statistics alongside selective use of other data. In a letter to Roger Titcombe, schools Minister Andrew Adonis (2007e) simply sweeps aside the argument that GNVQs are easier: 'I cannot agree with the assertions that GNVQs are easier. However, this is something of a sterile debate, as GNVQs will be replaced by new diplomas from 2008.' He failed to say that a BTEC[5] would still be available to play the same role as GNVQs had, and that a 'key skills' qualification in literacy and numeracy was being introduced as a substitute for GCSE English and maths.

MPs were right to be sceptical, as both evidence and the opposition movement co-ordinated by the Anti Academies Alliance (see www.anti-academies.org.uk) built up. In a report on specialist schools, for the very organization now responsible for academies, the Specialist Schools and Academies Trust (Jesson and Crossley, 2007), it became clear that there were other ways to success than becoming academies. Appendix 4 shows 45 specialist schools with over 50 per cent FSM and 40 per cent or above 5ACeq; of these, 27 showed over 32 per cent 5ACEM, i.e. 10pp higher than the average attainment for academies (range 18–23 per cent). The average (unweighted) FSM for academies was 38 per cent, with only a quarter over 50 per cent FSM.

Government Ministers made much of the need to replace 'failing schools' with academies. This aligned with New Labour 'inclusion' rhetoric in terms of saving the inner-city poor. This is clearly an oversimplification, and an increasing proportion of schools converted into academies were by no means failing. Campaigners at Islington Green School had been able to refute arguments that their school was 'failing' when it appeared on a poster from the London Challenge highlighting very successful schools in the form of a London Underground map. This did not ultimately prevent its closure. Indeed, an analysis by the Association of Teachers and Lecturers discovered that the government was actually targeting more and more successful schools. Less than 20 per cent of pupils in predecessor schools of the first batch of academies (the 2002 starters) achieved 5ACeq; the average for predecessors of 2005 and 2006 starters was around 28 per cent and 44 per cent. Schools now being targeted for conversion to academies were generally performing better than those that had already become academies.

PwC's report (2007) published in July gave little comfort to government. Attainment was similar to the comparison groups; it was improving a little faster (but no account was taken overall of the changing pupil population in the academies); and some dubious practices were evident in the selection of pupils. Furthermore, the evaluation gave the lie to claims that the academies were educationally innovative, indicating that pressure to drive up results was reversing earlier development. The report included two case studies showing how a changing pupil profile was reflected in changing attainment, and called upon the government department to review admission processes to 'ensure that there are no overt or covert barriers preventing the most disadvantaged pupils from accessing Academies' (p. xiii).

Nevertheless the government's privatization juggernaut rolled on, targeting increasing numbers of schools. In the autumn of 2007, the new Prime Minister, Gordon Brown, announced that schools with fewer than 30 per cent 5ACEM were now in line for closure, regardless of socioeconomic composition. Not surprisingly, this affected a high proportion of schools in the poorest areas: indeed two-thirds of schools with more than 35 per cent FSM. Half the secondary schools in Sunderland, Newcastle or Liverpool were on the hit list, as were half of Birmingham's once its grammar schools were removed. In the face of a growing campaign, the government was also keen to avoid adverse publicity on academies, including resorting to a special protocol for the inspection of academies and a dedicated OfSTED team.

The final official evaluation by PwC (2008) revealed great pressure for places (2.6 applications for each place) and a decline of 6pp in the proportion of pupils on FSM. It reiterated the recommendation that pupil intake and profile in academies should be formally monitored (p. 7). It issued many warnings: exclusion rates were above average, there was 'considerable diversity' in attainment and progress, and 'performance at sixth form requires continued focus' (p. 6). Most interesting perhaps is the statement that 'The diversity across individual Academies suggests that, rather than a simple uniform 'Academy effect', there has been a more complex and varied process of change taking place' (p. 8). Significantly it also proposed that 'Academies should report attainment for sub-groups of pupils (e.g. those on FSM, SEN [special educational needs], EAL [English as an additional language]) in order to ensure that achievement for these pupils continues to receive appropriate attention' (p. 8). There was a 'mixed picture on teaching and learning' relationships: surveys showed large numbers of pupils citing teaching staff as one of the best features but equally large numbers citing relationships with teachers as one of the worst things about their school.

The report has revealing statistics about population characteristics as the programme continued. The proportion of FSM was 35 per cent in 2007 (average across 2002–5 starters) compared with 42 per cent at their predecessor schools. In 2007, FSM pupils formed 41 per cent, 37 per cent, 34 per cent and 27 per cent of the population for academies opened in 2002–5 respectively (pp. 37–43). The attainment on arrival (Key Stage 2 average point score) was also much closer to the national average: 26 for academies (2007 intake) compared with 27.4 for all schools – compared with 25 and 27.2 in 2002. In other words, the gap had halved.

The report seeks to analyse improved attainment in the first four sets of academies only, i.e. those opening from 2002 to 2005. It provides a set of figures limited to the years during which each school was an academy, compared with the summer immediately before conversion (i.e. the point of closure of the predecessor school). This in itself is a questionable procedure, since the summer of closure may well be a low point due to disruption or demoralization. The finding of an average annual improvement of 5pp compared with one for all schools nationally is therefore unsound. However, what is most surprising is a failure to connect analysis of a changing population with changing results.

My own analyses for 2007 and 2008 focused precisely on this issue, and raised challenges for methodology.

1. Account had to be taken of any rise in attainment across all schools nationally, in order to separate out a net 'academy effect'.[6]
2. An appropriate allowance has to be made for the reduced proportion of FSM pupils as a factor in attainment.
3. Beyond this, the academies had significantly increased in size compared with their predecessor schools, with most of the additional numbers not

on FSM (i.e. not specifically marked as suffering poverty or disadvantage). This would be a further factor in evaluating attainment. Without these adjustments one would not be comparing like with like.

The key national data is that (2007) 49 per cent of non-FSM pupils achieve 5ACEM but only 21 per cent of FSM pupils. This has the implication that additional non-FSM pupils could be benchmarked against the expectation that around half could be expected to achieve 5ACEM.

I eventually settled on the following method (amending the above sequence).

1. First subtract from the pp increase in the academies the pp increase for all schools nationally (column labelled 'extra').
2. For academies with additional pupils without FSM, divide this additional pp by two (because half of pupils without FSM nationally achieve 5ACEM). It is important to emphasize that these are additional pupils, so it is more appropriate to benchmark against national norms than against predecessor schools. It is conceivable that some will come from deprived urban homes, but it is quite probable that most are enrolled by the positive choice of concerned and supportive parents (column labelled 'adjusted', most schools).
3. For the remaining academies, the reduced percentage of FSM pupils was divided by three, in line with the different national expectations of pupils with and without FSM, as above (the approximate gap between 49 per cent and 21 per cent) (column labeled 'adjusted', remaining schools).

The data is presented in Table 9.2. Consistently in the above, FSM data on the GCSE year has been used, since this may be out of line with FSM proportions for the school as a whole. The analysis was applied to academies opening in 2002, 2003, 2004 and 2005. (This aligns with recent PwC evaluations, based on a judgement that more recent additions should be allowed some time to settle, and that the earlier cohorts provide a more reliable indicator.) Totals for 'extra' and 'adjusted' are weighted averages, i.e. they take account of the different sizes of schools.

The raw gain on 5ACEM of 2002–5 starters, from 2002 (predecessors) to 2008 (academies), is 17pp. This apparently represents a net gain ('extra') over other schools of 12pp.

There has been a reduction in the percentage of FSM pupils over this period in the academies from 40 per cent to 32 per cent. Adjusting simply for this reduces the net gain to 7.5pp. However, adjusting for the recruitment of additional non-FSM pupils, as described above (2.), wipes out this gain entirely. The improved attainment is not due to academy governance

Table 9.2 Attainment gains adjusted for national gains and school population change

Academy	Raw gain	Extra	Adjusted
A	23	18	–9
B	12	7	2
C	8	3	–16
D	9	4	3
E	19	14	–2
F	21	16	8
G	27	22	–1
H	12	7	–2
I	22	17	9
J	10	5	–4
K	43	38	3
L	17	12	14
M	16	11	10
N	12	7	–12
O	28	23	14
P	4	–1	–15
Q	16	11	–8
R	0	–5	–27
S	19	14	14
T	25	20	19
U	9	4	0
Total	17	12	0

per se, but the consequence of *academies' populations being substantially different from those of their predecessor schools.*

Clearly, as PwC (2007 and 2008) concludes, there are enormous differences between academies, to an extent that it is difficult to see a general 'Academy effect' (PwC, 2007, p. viii; 2008, p. 8). However, what is also apparent from the above is that some of the cases used as 'success stories' by Ministers for the media are more apparent than real. Thus Academy G's raw gain of 27pp entirely disappears when one takes account of the recruitment of new pupils: its Year 11 is 70 per cent larger than the predecessor school's, but with a smaller percentage of FSM pupils. Indeed, it has nearly four times as many non-FSM pupils as its predecessor school. It should be emphasized that it is overwhelmingly from the non-FSM pupils that 5ACEM achievers emerge.

The success or otherwise of academies cannot simply be evaluated in terms of higher-level examination results. As PwC reports show, it has proved very difficult to reduce the proportion of pupils leaving with less than five A*–G grades. The curriculum distortion resulting from pressure to rapidly improve GCSE results remains an issue; the GNVQ has disappeared but could be replaced by BTEC, and there is potential for massaging examination statistics by using a new 'equivalence' between key tests in literacy and GCSE English, similarly numeracy replacing GCSE mathematics. Of course, this also applies to other schools under duress, but the political pressure on academies is extreme. These are schools in the spotlight, intended to demonstrate the superiority of privately managed schools and the benefits of a business takeover of education on a much wider scale.

Conclusion and wider implications

Exposing the spurious 'improvement' of the academies should not allow any of us to be complacent. In recent years evidence has mounted on the extreme levels of poverty in England (as elsewhere in Britain) compared with other developed countries, and of the impact of material and social deprivation on school achievement and life chances. The difference in average attainment levels between FSM and non-FSM pupils is a crude but undeniable indicator of the weight of disadvantage. The obstacles in the way of success accumulate and reinforce each other as pupils proceed from early childhood through primary school and secondary school. A recent study sponsored by the Sutton Trust (2008) focused on those FSM pupils who, against the odds, are in the top fifth of performers at age 11. The attrition rate is such that only a quarter are still in the top fifth at GCSE, and only around a sixth reach university.

Academies are not the only failure. There have been few successes for the New Labour governments with regard to school attainment and poverty. The Academies Programme is the action of a government which is built on unquestioning faith in the private sector (see Ball 2007; 2008b), but which has also single-mindedly sponsored a paradigm of school change that is saturated in neoliberalism (see Wrigley 2006a; 2006b; 2008). Underlying this, the New Labour governments had a very slow pace for reducing the extremely high levels of child poverty, and within several years had begun to backslide on that – even before the devastating impact of the present financial crisis.

Though there is ongoing debate about the mediating mechanisms, poverty remains the prime cause of school failure. It is not difficult to imagine how its cultural/psychological manifestations, such as a sense of shame and futility, impact upon school participation and achievement. These emotions are often reinforced by traditional school discipline, which can sap the self-respect of more disadvantaged students; by learning as alienated labour:

- you are told what to do
- you are told how long to do it for
- you hand over the product, not to a real user or audience but to the teacher
- in exchange, the teacher gives back a mark – a kind of surrogate wage.

For pupils, learning seems to have an exchange value, never a use value; there is limited evidence of school learning involving real products or audiences (see Wrigley, 2006a, p. 105). New thinking well beyond the limited imagination of the school improvement and school effectiveness paradigm (Wrigley, 2003) is needed if we are to find our way out of this cul-de-sac.

Notes

1 Given that the prime benchmark of a secondary school's 'effectiveness' in England is expressed in terms of the percentage of its pupils gaining five or more A*–C grades at GCSE, a means had to be found of expressing other qualifications as an equivalence of one or more A*–C grades.

2 The General National Vocational Qualification or GNVQ can be awarded at various levels. GNVQ Intermediate has been deemed to be equal to four GCSE A*–C grades. In other words, qualitatively it is judged equal to at least a C at GCSE, and quantitatively GNVQ in a single subject is judged as equal to four separate GCSE passes. No evidence is available to underpin either of these claims.

3 Of these, the third set seems dubious: in local authorities that retain selection at 11 years of age, a same primary school's pupils will divide between grammar schools and secondary moderns, and there will be a similar division wherever two nearby secondary schools are differently perceived in terms of status and academic success by parents.

4 It is worth noting Titcombe and Davies' (2006) point that the GNVQ in science does not provide a sufficient curriculum basis for studying a science A-level.

5 BTEC is an acronym for the Business and Technology Education Council. The majority of its qualifications are designed to certify work-related skills.

6 This is appropriate regardless of whether one agrees with arguments about examination grades becoming easier.

Chapter 10

Academies, Policy Networks and Governance

Stephen J. Ball

One of the strategies which we will be using is seeking to engage philanthropists who have funded Academies or Trust schools on the grounds that one of the key problems with Academies is the nature of its intake, the fact that over half the children often come in with almost no numeracy or literacy skills. And I think there is a reason therefore why Academy business sponsors, philanthropists might wish to consider putting a little bit of an investment into the primary schools that feed into the Academy so that they are tackling the intake at source and tackling some of the problems before they become much more expensive to remedy when the children are eleven/twelve/thirteen.

(*Jean Gross, director of Every Child A Chance Trust* [*ECAC*])[1]

Introduction

The argument of this chapter is very simple: that is, academies are important and significant in themselves but they are but one small part of a set of much broader changes in public sector education and the 'modernization' of the public sector as a whole. Indeed, they are indicative of what is a significant shift in the organizing principles of state services and public sector governance and in the form and modalities of the state itself. I will illustrate the argument by showing some of the ways in which one academy sponsor, KPMG, is involved in a set of other educational initiatives within state education and indeed is a participant in the processes of education policy. My point is that the focus of interest on academies should not divert attention away from the bigger picture.

Academies are, as I have argued elsewhere, a 'policy condensate' (Ball, 2007), they are, among other things, an experiment in and a symbol of education policy beyond the welfare state and an example and indicator of more general turbulence taking place in public sector governance and regulatory structures. Indeed, it may be that the programme signals a discursive-strategic shift towards a new kind of regulatory regime although at the same time the extent of change should not be overstated. Thus, in what follows I shall try not to overemphasize or underemphasize the overall significance of academies (or of other 'sponsored' policies).

Nonetheless, academies (and other 'sponsored' policies) involve a self-conscious attempt to promote new policy narratives, entrepreneurism and competitiveness in particular. Through these narratives new values and modes of action are installed and legitimated and new forms of moral authority established, and others are diminished or derided.

Academies drastically blur the welfare state demarcations between state and market, public and private, government and business. Indeed, they are one part of a set of evolutionary policy 'moves' (which also include other policies like trust schools, school competitions and the contracting out of school management) which contribute to the ongoing de-construction of the welfare state education system and the reculturing and re-invention of public sector institutions. That is, a reformation of the overall institutional architecture of the state and its scales of operation – a process of 'destatization' wherein tasks and services previously undertaken by the state are now being done by various 'others' in various kinds of relationships among themselves and to the state and to the remaining more traditional organizations of the public sector. In many cases the working methods of these public sector organizations have also been fundamentally reworked, typically by the deployment of market forms (competition, choice and performance-related funding). That is to say, academies are one small part of a more general shift towards a new form of 'polycentric' and 'strategic' governance that is based upon network relations within and across new policy communities designed to generate new governing capacity and enhance legitimacy. Or more accurately and modestly they signal a subtle and not necessarily wholehearted reworking of the judicious mix of hierarchy, markets and networks (Jessop, 2002) within the structures and processes of government.

Heterarchies

Within all of this then some academy sponsors like KPMG are involved in a range of aspects of education policy, and other policy conversations, and occupy a range of roles and relationships within the state and the educational state in particular, as sponsors and benefactors, as well as working as contractors, consultants, advisers, service providers, etc. (see Ball, 2007 and 2009a). Thus, in terms of the bigger picture they are contributing to the reworking of state institutions in both ways – sponsoring innovations and selling policy solutions. Both social responsibility and profit motives are engaged.

The example below is intended to illustrate some of the work of and the variety in the kinds of relationships that are involved within policy *heterarchies*. Heterarchy is an organizational form somewhere between hierarchy and network that draws upon diverse horizontal and vertical links that permit different elements of the policy process to co-operate (and/or compete). *Heterarchical relationships* replace some bureaucratic and administrative structures and relationships with a system of organization replete with overlap, multiplicity, mixed ascendancy and/or divergent-but-coexistent patterns of relation.

Heterarchies have many of the characteristics of 'assemblages' of and for policy and governance, inasmuch as they are made up of heterogeneous elements placed in diverse relations to one another with unstable membership. They are sets of 'functions', and are co-functioning, symbiotic elements that are unalike but perhaps also converging. They are temporary, compared with what they replace, and operate differently according to local circumstances, and may be relatively loose and opportunistic, contested and precarious. They are made up of processes (exchanges) and relationships rather than constituting a structure. They are, to an extent, self-organizing, imaginative and experimental, polyvalent and often involve considerable stumbling and blundering. They may thus be 'more likely to give bad decisions a second chance to be rectified' (Thrift, 2005, p. 25), but equally bad decisions may lead to the demise of elements or sections of a heterarchy. Heterarchies are examples of what Kickert *et al.* (1997) refer to as 'loosely-coupled weakly-tied multi-organisational sets'. They are a policy device, a way of trying things out, getting things done, changing things and an attempt to 'routinise innovation' and incubate creative possibilities (Thrift, 2005, p. 7). Innovation has been a key component of the academies condensate.

These new policy communities bring new kinds of actors into the policy process, validate new policy discourses – discourses flow through them – and enable new forms of policy influence and enactment and in some respects disable or disenfranchise or circumvent some of established policy actors and agencies. Currently in England they colonize the spaces opened up by the critique of existing state organizations, actions and actors and drastically blur the already fuzzy divide between the public and the private sector. New linkage devices and lead organizations (like the Specialist Schools and Academies Trust, or SSAT, and the National College for Leadership of Schools and Children's Services, or NCSL) are being created over and against existing ones, excluding or circumventing but not always obliterating more traditional sites and voices. In England the move from hierarchies to heterarchies at the school level has also been in part a tactic in the flexibilization of professional labour in schools (see Ball, 2009b). Initiatives like academies have provided capillaries through which new forms of management (see below) and its metaphors are able to flow through educational organizations, and are attempts to *embody* those metaphors in the public sector workforce, in the creation of new kinds of 'willing' subjects.

These reworkings are also part of and contribute to other related features of the changing English state – they contribute to what Skelcher (1998) calls 'the appointed state' and what he also (Skelcher, 2000) calls the 'congested state'. Between them these descriptors seek to capture both the proliferation and fragmented array of agencies and actors involved in local and regional governance, and in the provision of public services (Sullivan and Skelcher, 2004) and give some indication of the 'democratic deficit' which results from the increasing participation of quangos and other non-elected agencies and organizations in the governance of 'public' institutions and their 'weaker accountability, audit and governance standards' (Skelcher, 1998, p. 181). Heterarchies also work to disperse and re-spatialize policy, creating new sites of influence, decision-making and policy action. That is, the 'territory of influence' (Mackenzie and Lucio, 2005) over policy is expanded and at the same time the spaces of policy are diversified and dissociated and therefore potentially policy processes are made more opaque.[2]

The Academies Programme is a good example of the complexity and instability and the experimental nature of these governance reforms, the programme has gone through at least three iterations, in response to lack of sponsors, rising costs, inefficiencies and opposition. This is not, I would suggest, a careful and pre-planned process of reform – rather, within the general logic of reform there is a great deal of muddling through and trial and error and, as a result, different and changing interpretations of policy by key policy actors. Some of these generic characteristics of heterarchy are evident in the example that follows.

A heterarchy?

The particular heterarchy to be discussed here is as represented (see Figure 10.1), both partial and very schematic (see Ball, 2009b, for a different example). Indeed it could be configured in a number of different ways. It selects out and highlights a set of relationships that serve to illustrate some more general processes and moves and relationships within New Labour's education policies. It identifies a limited set of actors and forms of relationships within a dense, complex and fast-changing field of relationships – some of the elements are out of date as I write; that is the nature of heterarchies. Not all of the elements and relationships can be fully explained in this text within the limits of space available. The material used here is one small part of an Economic and Social Research Council-funded study (RES-062-23-1484) of 'Philanthropy and Education Policy'. I will draw in particular upon interviews with Jean Gross (director of the ECAC) and Jo Clunie (consultant to the KPMG Foundation). I also interviewed Mike Amato, the head of the KPMG Corporate Social Responsibility Division.

KPMG is one of the world's 'Big Four' professional services firms; it employs over 136,500 people in a global network spanning over 140 countries.

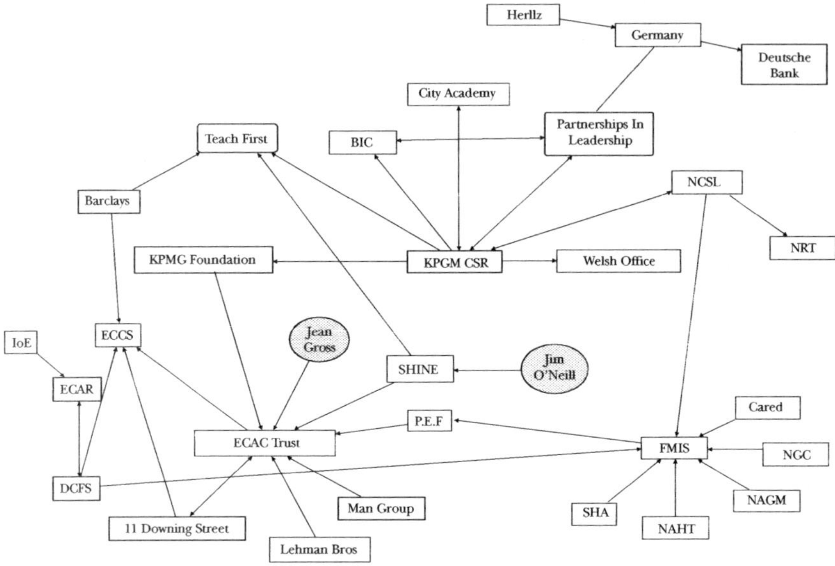

Figure 10.1 A heterarchy

Composite revenues of KPMG's member firms in 2008 were US$22.7 billion (14.5 per cent growth from 2007). KPMG mainly works in three areas: audit services, tax services and advisory services. This includes financial advice, performance improvement and programme management to the UK Home Office, the Department of Health and the National Health Service. For example, in 1998, the School Teachers' Review Body (STRB) commissioned KPMG Consulting to 'explore the key factors differentiating the roles of headteachers, deputies and other teachers with similar senior management responsibilities, and how jobs should be ranked, in a variety of school sizes, types and structures.[3] The German, Spanish, Swiss and UK practices of the firm were recently merged into a single entity – KPMG Europe.

KPMG is a sponsor of the London City Academy, Hackney, jointly with the City of London Corporation. The school specializes in business and financial services and opened in September 2009. This sponsorship operates through the Corporate Social Responsibility Division of the firm, which has other educational involvements. For example, KPMG was also a founder of the Partners in Leadership national programme supported by government, the then NCSL (now the National College for Leadership of Schools and Children's Services) and Business in the Community (BiC). This pairs a headteacher with a business leader, working together on the headteacher's agenda to discuss matters related to management and leadership. The programme was developed from a London pilot in 1996 initiated by KPMG. Since its launch, 5,000 headteachers have been matched with a business leader and 1,200 companies throughout the United Kingdom have been involved. KPMG also participates in the extension of this programme in Germany, providing mentoring support to headteachers in Berlin, Brandenburg and Frankfurt. Since 2005 altogether 86 schools have registered for the German scheme. A similar programme in Wales is backed by the CBI, Welsh Training and Enterprise Councils, the Education Business Partnership and the Welsh Office. According to the project website it 'is having a positive impact on improving the skills of headteachers, raising standards in schools and increasing business involvement in schools'.[4] KPMG have also worked with the National Workforce Remodelling (NWR) team to develop the Financial Management in Schools programme (FMiS) and contributed a Financial Recovery Planning Checklist to NCSL's FMiS work. The FMiS programme was put together by a partnership of organizations – DfES (Department for Education and Skills), NCSL, KPMG, SHA (Secondary Headteachers Association), NAHT (National Association of Headteachers), NAGM (National Association of Governors and Managers), NGC (National Governors Council), Confed (Confederation of Education and Childrens' Services Managers). KPMG has also worked with NCSL on a strategy to enhance the capacity of school leaders 'including developing further the role of highly skilled school business managers that could save up to a third of headteachers' time'.[5] This work has explored the potential of two new roles in primary schools – advanced school business managers (ASBM) and school business directors (SBD) – through demonstration projects in a range of scenarios. Business in the Community, working with PricewaterhouseCoopers, KPMG and N. M. Rothschild and Sons, has delivered two of the demonstration projects focusing on secondary schools. KPMG is also a supporter of Teach First in England. Variously through such schemes and initiatives, from different points of articulation, some of the methods and sensibilities of business and the narrative of enterprise are imported into education. KPMG is also the NCSL auditor.

Like many other large companies KPMG also runs a volunteering scheme for employees to work with children in schools; '[A[lmost all the big City firms do either one or both of Reading Partners, Number Partners' (Jean Gross). Sir Mike Rake, ex-chairman of KPMG International and of KPMG Europe, was also chairman of Business in the Community and now chairs the government's Commission for Employment and Skills.

KPMG also funds a foundation, which was established in October 2001. The Foundation has a capital sum of £10 million. The Foundation is a completely separate entity to KPMG LLP (UK), although it is totally funded by KPMG in the UK. 'The focus of the KPMG Foundation is on education and social projects for the disadvantaged and underprivileged, with particular emphasis on unlocking the potential of children and young people'.[6] Most significantly the Foundation was responsible for the launch of the ECAC.

The Trust was established in 2007 and grew out of the Every Child a Reader project (ECAR), a three-year, £10 million scheme, now being rolled out nationally, which was funded by a partnership of businesses and charitable trusts (including the KPMG Foundation, SHINE, the JJ Charitable Trust and the Man Group plc Charitable Trust with matched funding from government). The project was initially based at the Institute of Education, University of London, and the involvement of the KPMG Foundation came about as a result of a long period of research that began with a concern with the issue of dyslexia:

> Our starting point was dyslexia but it led us to the larger issue of illiteracy. Learning that 35,000 children leave primary school unable to read and write was unacceptable to our Trustees. Our research led us to Reading Recovery and from there we launched Every Child a Reader.
>
> (Jo Clunie)

The ECAC also runs The Every Child Counts programme (ECC), which is aimed at Year 2 primary pupils who have fallen behind their peers and is again jointly funded by the DCSF.

The Every Child Counts programme is aimed at Year 2 primary pupils who have fallen behind their peers. The programme aims to enable the lowest attaining children to make sufficient progress to reach expected levels of attainment at Key Stage 1 and beyond. It provides training and support for teachers so they can work with pupils in one-to-one and/or small group intervention sessions. Pupils receive daily intervention sessions for approximately a term.[7]

Barclays has signed on to be a national sponsor of ECC, pledging £1.2 million. This will provide a co-ordinating structure to encourage local business support for at least 150 schools to help over 6,000 children aged 7 years who have the greatest difficulties with maths. It will also establish sponsorship relationships between 20 Barclay's branches in England and their local primary schools. Businesses across the country are to be encouraged to contribute up to £12,000 a year each, over three years.

> We are very conscious that every child needs basic numeracy skills for survival. That is why Barclays have committed to this national campaign in support of Every Child Counts. In the current complex financial climate, it makes economic sense to intervene early with youngsters to help them develop core numeracy skills which will help them manage their finances one day successfully, which in turn helps to drastically reduce the costs to society as detailed in this report.
>
> (Mike Amato, head of Distribution and Product at Barclays)

In January 2009 the ECAC published a report, *The Long Term Costs of Numeracy Difficulties* (ECAC, 2009), which estimates these costs to be £2.4 billion a year. Apart from Amato, the trustees of ECAC include John Griffith-Jones (KPMG chairman), Paul Marshall (co-founder of Marshall Wace Asset Management, a European equity hedge fund group with circa US$2 billion under management), Jim O'Neill (head of global economic research for Goldman Sachs, co-founder of the charity SHINE), Dwight Poler (managing director of Bain Capital), Andrew Scott (trustee and deputy chairman of the Man Group plc Charitable Trust) and Corinne Vigreux (also chair of trustees of the Sofronie Foundation).

New forms of policy?

I want to emphasize and indicate four things here.

One, that through their senior executives companies like KPMG can provide fast and direct access to 'policy conversations' inside government. 'We got that report onto Gordon Brown's desk a few days before the pre-budget when he was chancellor and that was the turning point. He saw that and I think he understood the numbers' (Jo Clunie).

Such people provide a very powerful profile for initiatives like ECAR and ECC, as well as delivering to philanthropic organizations established relationships with and within the state, and thus specific points of potential influence and access.

> We have a great trustee who works for KPMG and understands how Government works. We recognised that we had to build a coalition of funders to encourage Government to support the programme at almost 50 per cent of the cost. The total cost was £10m.
>
> (Jo Clunie)

Two, that these business-based philanthropic interventions can offer novel and joined-up responses to 'wicked' problems (van Beuren *et al.*, 2003, p. 193) which the public sector has 'failed' to solve, and which are also politically attractive:

> When we were running Every Child A Reader we thought about Every Child Counts and indeed came up with the title and vaguely talked about it to various politicians and officials. We'd hoped, this might be something we do next. But then there was a quite quick announcement by Downing Street; I think it was when Gordon Brown had just come into Downing Street at Number 10. We'd worked with him in Number 11 before. There was an announcement that there would be a program called Every Child Counts, it was a political announcement and I think nobody was quite

> certain then, including Downing Street, of who would run this or how it would happen.
>
> (Jean Gross)

In this case, these problems are viewed from and to an extent constructed within a business perspective. Numeracy and literacy are seen as both educational problems and problems *for* business.

Three, such initiatives work through new sorts of *ad hoc* and temporary policy networks, which are established through a variety of forms of participation and exchange, like consortia, trusts, partnerships and volunteering, and of funding, like matched-funding and sponsorship. '[W]e pulled together four core funders and suggested that Government match fund the programme. If Government had not match funded the programme would not have happened' (Jo Clunie).

These kinds of modes of working and relationships offer the state various flexibilities (such programmes are tightly targeted, have specified outcomes and time-limited and shared-funding commitments) alongside the possibility of innovation and experimentation, the outcomes may or may not be scaled up and rolled out.

> [T]hat partnership model of doing, piloting, trialling something together allows everybody a get-out clause. If it doesn't work the government can back off, they're not committed to it . . . what a charity can do, particularly a business charity, is in seeing something that's not happening that needs to be national policy but probably has a long-term effect. So politicians are unlikely to pick it up on their own; front-loading the funding, so putting some initial investment into that, that comes from outside, from philanthropists, for a time-limited period that is purely there to prove the case. And to do that kind of lobbying that goes along with having connections, business connections, and then get government, either local or national government, to pick it up.
>
> (Jean Gross)

Four, the philanthropists themselves want to see clear and measurable impacts and outcomes from their 'investments' of time and money. A business perspective is brought to bear upon educational issues and problems. This is indicative of a generic shift within business philanthropy towards forms of strategic and development philanthropy based on the methods of private equity investment (see Ball, 2008c) – a mix of caring and calculation:

> So they are business oriented and not just gently philanthropic and we'll give money to people. They want results and they want measured results but they will wait for those results. And I'm trying to persuade PEF

> (Private Equity Foundation), for example, that although they've put a lot of their money into – quite rightly – into stuff that will help NEET (Not in Education, Employment or Training) young people now I also want them to be thinking about how they help the nought to eight-year-olds who will be the NEETs of the future as a parallel strategy.
>
> (Jean Gross)

Based on very direct points of access and relationships with state actors from which 'partnerships' are established, various kinds of flows between the sectors – of people, information and ideas, language, methods, values and culture – are opened up; as Jessop (2002) suggests, 'states have a key role in promoting innovative capacities, technical competence and technology transfer . . . often involving extensive collaboration' (p. 121). Existing networks based on business and social and political relationships with their 'embedded ties', are used and extended here – trust and reciprocity are important. There are opportunities to speak to and establish relationships with Ministers and officials at meetings and events. Such contacts can be exploited for different purposes:

> When you do work in the semi-business sector you have tentacles there; through that to connections . . . one of the things I've learned is the business world operates to a much greater extent than the public sector on who you know and who your contacts are . . . Network, network, network. That was new to me, totally new.
>
> (Jean Gross)

The director of ECAC plays a key role in mediating and facilitating relationships here. Jean Gross is, as Williams (2002) puts it, a 'competent boundary spanner' (p. 103), someone 'especially sensitive to and skilled in bridging interests, professions and organisations' (Webb, 1991, p. 231). She is a *heterarchical actor*, with experience across a range of fields and sectors, who can 'speak' different sectorial languages, and who has accumulated a significant fund of trust. Her background includes work with local authorities, in consultancy and with the DCSF as part of Capita's National Strategies team:

> I just got into dialogue with officials who I'd worked with in the department and I think they thought about, well, who could do this and we could do it, the National Strategies could do it. And so we ended up as a partnership and we all do it, the National Strategies do it and we do it and officials do it, but I chair the delivery group. I try not to say that we run this program. But we are regarded as the lead agency but not the lead funder, the government are putting more money in.
>
> (Jean Gross)

In a sense the business charities are seeking to 'sell' their policy ideas to government and outcomes evidence is used to make the case for wider take-up and funding. Reports like that on the costs of innumeracy also play a part in reframing the policy debate in ways that speak to the concerns of government and its policy agenda.

The general point of the KPMG example is to offer a glimpse into the complexity and inter-relatedness of current participation in state education, education discourses and education policy processes and conversations by philanthropic, voluntary and private interests (both organizations and individuals), as well as to indicate the blurring between the sectors and their interests, a blurring within which relationships and values are hybridized. There is a variety of asymmetrical and diverse power relations involved in this complex of reciprocal, multi-level, interdependencies, 'some happening spontaneously, others created deliberately through public policy and institutional engineering' (Davies, 2005, p. 313). There are no obvious primary nodes or 'hegemons' (Goodwin, 2009) within the example used here, although KPMG plays a key role, and indeed is engaged in a wide variety of corporate social responsibility activities. It is also extremely difficult to be specific about the forms and relativities of power involved in such complex and fluid heterarchies or to map all of the relationships involved. The strategies deployed here are essentially those identified in the entrepreneurship literature as social mechanisms of entrepreneurship (see Stuart and Sorenson, 2007).

Discussion

> [W]hen we started ECAR our objective was just to get government to pick it up and run with it at the end of the pilot. I don't think we really had onboard how much of a policy shift there would be.
>
> (Jo Clunie)

Heterarchies 'enlarge the range of actors involved in shaping and delivering policy' (Newman, 2001, p. 125). Such a mode of governance involves a 'catalyzing of all sectors – public, private and voluntary – into action to solve their community's problems' (Osborne and Gaebler, 1992), and in this example and in many others one consequence is to bring about changes to the 'boundary between state and civil society' (Bevir and Rhodes, 2003, p. 42) and between state and the economy. In general terms this is the move towards a 'polycentric state' and 'a shift in the centre of gravity around which policy cycles move' (Jessop, 1998 p. 32).

As noted in the example, to achieve coherence and functionality these heterarchies rely on particular forms of trust and reciprocity and 'the strength of weak ties' and in some of their aspects they draw upon social relations established elsewhere, in business for example (see Ball, 2008a) or between charities, voluntary organizations and their lead and link organizations (Charities Aid Foundation, National Council of Voluntary Organisations, New Philanthropy Capital, etc.) or social relations between sponsors, officials, politicians and other policy actors. A good deal of this activity by definition takes place 'elsewhere' or behind the scenes in the day-to-day business of the DCSF, SSAT, the Cabinet Office, Prime Minister's Office, etc. The boundaries and spatial horizons and flows of influence and engagement around education are being stretched and reconfigured in a whole variety of ways.

There are now various manifestations of new policy heterarchies at local and national and international levels in education, which include academies and their sponsors, which are working on and changing the policy process and policy relations. Business is integrated in a number of ways through these heterarchies in the governance and provision of state education, in driving educational innovations and introducing new ways of doing education policy. Within and through these heterarchies new organizational sensibilities, values, perspectives, interests and policy narratives are brought into play and given legitimacy. Academies are important but are just one example of these changes in the modes of state activity (see Ball, 2008b) and the participation of philanthropists, business and the voluntary sector in the solution of state problems.

All of this involves changes both in the form and modalities of the state – some forms of 'direct' control are being foregone (where they existed) in favour of 'effective' control through calibration and other steering mechanisms. Some parts of the state have less control than before, other parts have more – for example, where direct relations are established between the DCSF and schools and school providers, e.g. academies or school programmes (National Strategies, ECAR, etc.). At the same time, local government, professional organizations and trades unions are increasingly marginalized.

In effect the current state of governance, at national and local levels, is a specific and unstable mix of hierarchy, heterarchy and market. It is not that heterarchical modalities of governance involve a giving up by the state of its capacity to steer policy. This is not a 'hollowing out' of the state; rather, it is a new modality of state power, agency and social action – 'metagovernance' (Jessop, 2002, p. 242) – and in some ways a new form of state. The 'methods' and relations of heterarchy do not totally displace other forms of policy formation and policy action, but 'the state, although not impotent, is now dependent upon a vast array of state and non-state policy actors' (Marinetto, 2005, p. 599). This might be best understood through the appropriation of a term used by Tikly (2003), that is what might be called here 'governance-in-the-making', which is comprised 'of complex and sometimes contradictory elements that provide both continuity and discontinuity [with] what went before' (p. 166). I do not in any way want to suggest that older, more direct methods of government and governing have been totally displaced (Dean, 2008) but there is great liquidity, intertwining, blurring and instability in the processes of governance. The task here, as in relation to other contemporary social arenas, is to theorize continuity and change together.

Notes

1 Both Jean Gross and Jo Clunie read the chapter and made minor changes, which I incorporated. I am very grateful to them and my other interviewees for their time and help.
2 see www.antiacademies.org.uk/for more information.
3 See www.ncsl.org.uk/media-901-e2-leading-from-the-classroom.pdf (accessed 24 June 2009).
4 See www.ourfutureplanet.org/newsletters/resources/Welsh%20Assembly%20 Government%20Social%20Enterprise%20Strategy%20for%20Wales%202005. pdf (accessed 13 August 2010)
5 NCSL announcement available at: www.teachingexpertise.com/articles/the-ncsl-and-you-3213 (accessed 29 October 2009).
6 See www.kpmgfoundation.org/index.asp (accessed 6 July 2009).
7 www.everychildachancetrust.or/index.cfm (accessed 13 August 2010).

Chapter 11

Joining Up the Dots: Academies and System Coherence

Ron Glatter

Introduction

In this chapter I will look at the policy on academies through the lens of governance, in particular examining the tension between school autonomy and system coherence and arguing that the policy must be considered holistically. We should focus not on an academy or academies in isolation but on their relationship with the rest of the school system, given that academies are and will remain for the foreseeable future a small minority of all publicly funded schools. In my view this approach has been seriously neglected as the policy has developed and the small amount of research that has been done has not taken it seriously either.

The context: democratic quality and reform strategies

I will mention briefly some aspects of the wider context. Scholars have recently attempted to measure how democratic various democracies are. The data relates to the UK as a whole rather than England although academies are currently confined to England. The UK comes low down in a league table of 'democratic quality' constructed by Ringen (2007) who has called Britain 'the most concentrated political system in Europe'.[1] In another survey, using a different methodology, the Everyday Democracy Index was constructed. One aspect of this focused on public services and again the UK's position is disappointingly low, partly, according to the authors, because of the limited power now accorded to local government which means that 'power has been taken much further away from citizens than in some other countries' (Skidmore and Bound, 2008, p. 95). The veteran education commentator Peter Wilby (2009) suggests the relevance of this to academies: 'The point of Academies is political, not educational. They are part of central government's long campaign to marginalise Local Authorities'.

Another important aspect of the context in which academies were introduced has been referred to by Pollitt (2007) as 'serial restructuring' (p. 531).

According to him, comparative studies have shown the UK to have the most activist, hard-driving government in relation to public sector reform. He argues that organizational reform is exceptionally easy for politicians, partly because of the lack of constitutional restraints such as federal structures or a proportional voting system and partly because of the multiplicity of consultants and ministry special units dedicated to promoting reform. As a consequence there have been so many interlocking changes that rigorous evaluation has hardly been possible, but there is no convincing evidence, either in Britain or elsewhere, of the effectiveness of the kinds of reform strategies that have been pursued. Also these strategies have incurred very large costs in terms of distraction, dislocation and loss of organizational memory, the effects of which are generally impossible to estimate. It will be interesting to see whether the economic recession of the late 2000s changes the approach to reform and if so in what direction.

School autonomy and the private sector

A central doctrine in recent schools policy has been the importance of 'self-government'. So, near the end of the last period of office the Conservative government said that 'more self-government for all schools is central to raising standards and extending diversity' (DfEE/Welsh Office, 1996, p. 1). This is echoed in Labour's identification of school success with 'self-governing . . . status' (DCSF, 2008a, p. 8). This strong emphasis may well be related to the pivotal role that elite private (i.e. 'independent') schools play in English culture and society, and the consequent pressure on politicians to be thought to deliver at least some of their supposed features for free to users of the public system. A review conducted for the association representing these schools (the Headmasters' and Headmistresses' Conference, HMC) concluded that the main reason for their superior performance was their independence rather than other factors such as intensive exam preparation or the background of the intake. 'Headteacher and teacher freedom seem intrinsic to their success. A major issue for the present and future governments will be to find an optimum national shape for education which fully harnesses the power and effectiveness of school autonomy' (Smithers and Robinson, 2008, para. 8.10). Leading articles and comment pieces in the 'quality' press frequently reflect this position.[2]

However, this view leaves out of account the exceptional advantages and privileges which private schools students in England tend to enjoy (Glatter, 2009a). This is illustrated in Table 11.1, based on OECD data.

What is striking here is not the difference with other countries in terms of average class sizes in state schools – the UK is closely in line with the international average (though it falls short in the primary sector, 25.8 against the average of 21.5) – but the huge difference between our state and private

Table 11.1 Average class size: lower secondary education (adapted from OECD, 2008, table D2.1)

State schools		Private schools	
UK	23.7	UK	12.0
OECD average	23.8	OECD average	22.6

school averages. Class sizes in UK private schools are on average little more than half the size of those in state schools. By contrast with the UK situation, there is only a small difference overall in class sizes between state and private schools across OECD countries, and at least some of this difference must be attributable to the large UK discrepancy.

There are disputes about the role of class size in school effectiveness (though small classes are undoubtedly part of the appeal of private schools to many parents who send their children to them). However, in this context these disputes are irrelevant. Differences in class size stand here as a proxy for differential resourcing on a very significant scale, a gap which has serious implications for social mobility given the continued domination of the UK's top jobs and professions by the 7 per cent of the population who have attended private schools (Panel on Fair Access to the Professions, 2009).

I would suggest that the private school sector is a major influence, and a largely unspoken one, on the whole debate about school structure in England. It is the elephant in the room. The gap in resources appears unbridgeable on any realistic scenario, although when he was chancellor Gordon Brown set bridging it as an aspiration. As suggested above this is a real dilemma for policy-makers in England and perhaps explains why they often put emphasis on issues of branding rather than resources – on 'independence', uniforms and house systems for example. Some of the brands, notably 'academy', 'foundation' and 'trust', evoke a sense of traditionalism, solidity and individuality and imply, like private schools, control by the owners or trustees and the market rather than by the public and their elected representatives.

School autonomy: a magic bullet?

It is doubtful whether school self-government is the elixir that policy appears to imply. This has been questioned in a study of the long-term effects of the Conservative government's Grant Maintained schools programme of 1988–97 on pupil achievement in those schools (Allen, 2007). International evidence suggests that, while greater school autonomy is positively correlated with student performance, certain conditions are required. For example, the core responsibilities of school leaders need to be focused explicitly on educational matters to avoid the role overload that autonomy tends to generate. Also, effective school autonomy requires adequate support, including appropriate models of distributed leadership and relevant forms of training and development (Punt *et al.*, 2008). Autonomy is not the magic bullet that is often implied and its full implications need to be thoroughly understood and taken into account.

A key consideration in my view is the impact of policies emphasizing school autonomy on the wider system. In England this is not entirely an issue about autonomy *per se.* In the English system politicians have tended to confer special privileges on certain categories of publicly funded school – in particular, enhanced autonomy and special funding – and this process has accelerated recently with the increase in numbers of foundation schools[3] and the creation of academies and trust schools. The danger with the conferment of this kind of privileged status is that the 'tiering' that is already a sharp feature of the system will be reinforced and that this will accentuate stratification based on social factors and academic ability. The rationale for differences in levels of autonomy over areas such as admissions and the curriculum is hard to discern. The differences often appear to be due to adventitious historical or political factors, for example that a particular category of school is currently a political 'favourite' whose success must be engineered.

The result is a highly fragmented system whose disjointed character has recently come under criticism from a variety of directions. A study for a right-leaning think tank concluded that '[t]he English education system is built on a web of contradictions . . . Coherence is something the current system is conspicuously lacking' (Davies and Lim, 2008, pp. 9, 74). The former government adviser Robert Hill has argued that '[f]or too long education policy has been about trying to create successful institutions rather than an effective school system' (Hill, 2008), while an eminent policy analyst has criticized 'the current trend within policy to a fragmentation and differentiation of school types' (Ball, 2008b, p. 197) instead of a common system.

These criticisms have particular force because international research, notably the OECD's (Organisation for Economic Co-operation and Development) studies in their Programme for International Student Assessment (PISA), shows that the countries that do best in terms both of overall performance and relative equity have comprehensive, integrated systems of schooling (see, for example, OECD, 2007). Those countries with selective systems or which, like England, put emphasis on choice and diversity, do markedly less well on both these crucial dimensions.

Towards a holistic approach

For these reasons I regret that the focus of most research, analysis and commentary on new school models is on the individual institutions as though they were islands. This was a feature of the work done on grant-maintained schools in the 1990s and the pattern is being repeated with academies. Following this approach simply reflects and arguably reinforces the fragmentation that the policy builds into the system. I believe we need a more systemic, holistic approach based on local areas that examines the impact that an academy has on the local offer as a whole. The then House of Commons Education and Skills Committee recommended in 2005 that the impact of academies on neighbouring schools should be monitored (House of Commons, 2005, p. 16) but a recent review indicates that we still have little evidence about this very important aspect (Curtis *et al.*, 2008).

A central theme in the conclusions of the five-year national evaluation of a sample of academies undertaken for the Department for Children, Schools and Families (DCSF) (PwC, 2008) was the variability of the academies studied in both character and performance, which meant that no distinctive uniform 'academy effect' could be observed. Arguably this is a characteristic that academies share with other types of schools in the English system. There is no such thing as a 'bog standard'[4] school and when comprehensive schools were first becoming widespread in the 1970s observers noted their great variability (e.g. Richardson, 1975). Perhaps ironically, the policy emphases of the past 20 years have focused on two features, school autonomy and diversity, which were already pervasive in the system and have created an even more complex patchwork of provision (moderated to some extent by the national curriculum and assessment frameworks). In this context the need to take a systemic view rather than focusing heavily on individual unique institutions appears even more pressing, and the recommendation by a team from the London Institute of Education that the 'role [of academies] in the overall system needs to be clarified' (Curtis *et al.*, 2008, p. 77) seems extremely pertinent.

Models of educational governance

In this section I will look at such issues of governance in a more focused and analytical way. Structures of governance vary widely from country to country, and they are often in flux. Even so, the changing governance of school systems usually displays a number of tensions, for example tensions between:

- the coherence of the system and its fragmentation
- the autonomy of individual schools and the wider community and public interest
- diversity of provision and social equity
- competition and collaboration
- central and local decision-making.

These are subtle and delicate processes and the balance that is struck between them at any point in time in any country will have an impact on the kind of schooling that students receive. In other words, governance matters.

In this connection it is relevant to refer to a framework I have proposed elsewhere of models of educational governance (see Glatter, 2003). The models are ideal types that are separated purely for the purposes of analysis. In practice every country works on the basis of some mixture of these models. Sometimes the models will complement or reinforce each other as they impact on the real work of education in schools and communities. At other times the interaction of the models is likely to cause conflict, which those affected must try to resolve.

The models are competitive market (CM), school empowerment (SE), local empowerment (LE) and quality control (QC). It is not possible to explore their characteristics in any detail here but I can identify the main focus or 'centre of gravity' of each (see Table 11.2).

Of these four models, the dominant ones in relation to freestanding academies (that is, those that are not part of a 'chain') appear to be SE and QC. In SE most powers are vested in the school and ultimate responsibility is located with the governing body and/or board of trustees, as with independent schools.[5] This model is analytically distinct from CM in that the focus is more on the institution itself and the way it is governed than on its competitive activities 'against' other institutions. However, since academies are largely funded by the taxpayer, this governance model is not deemed sufficient and is supplemented by QC, which involves laid-down rules and requirements and operates through set procedures, controls and monitoring arrangements. In contrast to SE, where the main focus or 'centre of gravity' is the school itself, in QC the main focus is located within, or closely connected to, the central state.

All governance models have strengths and weaknesses. Under SE, with its emphasis on the school as an individual unit, there may be substantial innovation, but if so it is likely to be confined to the school itself rather than generalized to the wider system. Considerable variation from school to school is likely to result from this model, as indeed was found in the five-year national evaluation of academies referred to above. In this respect the model

Table 11.2 Four models of governance and their centres of gravity (adapted from Glatter, 2002, p. 229)

Model	Centre of gravity
Competitive market (CM)	Arena of competition
School empowerment (SE)	Individual school
Local empowerment (LE)	Local 'family of schools'
Quality control (QC)	Central state or equivalent

reflects some of the weaknesses of the fragmentation of governance sometimes found in contemporary society, whereby 'each organisation pursues its "core business" more or less single-mindedly, with wider perceptions of the public realm or public good disappearing into the spaces between them' (Clarke and Newman, 1997, p. 155).

The QC model operates through a range of technical-rational, performance-based processes such as target-setting, performance reviews, audit and inspection. The processes in use in English publicly funded education have come under sharp criticism. For example, Keep (2004, p. 3), writing within the context of 14–19 education, points to 'the large, elaborate and complex system(s) of performance management' as being highly unusual in the developed world. One aspect of this distinctiveness is the governance set-up, specifically in relation to the high degree of control which the central state wields over policy and practice in relation to the setting of targets: '[I]n England local government and social partners – major players in other European national systems of accountability – are more or less completely absent' (p. 3).

Academies thus operate within two contrasting governance models. Also, the next level of governance above the individual school is the central state. Not surprisingly this presents major logistical problems of supervision and the relevant central department (at the time of writing the DCSF) does not have the capacity to undertake 'the policy development, delivery, and support and challenge of a significant number of Academies' (PwC, 2008, para. 10.8). In a country the size of England this is always likely to be a problem in relation to the 'independent state school' model. The solution attempted in this instance has been to transfer these functions to a new government agency, the Young Peoples' Learning Agency (YPLA), whose original and central remit is quite different (Dunton, 2009). Whether this arrangement is sustainable remains to be seen.

'Academy chains': a way forward?

One variant of the academy model needs to be considered because it modifies substantially the previous analysis in relation to governance. This is the 'academy chain', in which one organization sponsors a number of academies. Curtis *et al.* (2008) identified five organizations that were sponsors of at least five academies each – fourteen in one case (the Christian charity United Learning Trust). They all had plans for further expansion and there was, in addition, at least one new entrant with ambitious intentions.

This model appears to have a growing attraction to policy-makers and those advising them. For example, the right-leaning think tank Policy Exchange has recommended that the Academies Programme should be reformed to allow any organization, whether large or small, for-profit or charitable, to bid to become a sponsor, but it has also suggested that preference should be 'given to groups who are successfully running other Academies, which would encourage federations, and those who have prior educational experience' (Meyland-Smith and Evans, 2009, p. 59). This proposal is based on a study of the current Academies Programme and relevant examples in Sweden and the United States. The authors argue that this approach provides 'the potential for developing a coherent brand which conveys information about quality to parents and the ability to set up multi-school teacher training programmes' (p. 56). They claim that it is more 'scalable' than the oft-mooted notion of individual schools established by parents, teachers or community organizations, which they see as a fragile idea. Such groups, as well as freestanding academies, would be overseen by multiple 'authorizers' appointed by the DCSF and inspected by OfSTED (Office for Standards in Education). They could include local authorities but also other bodies such as universities and educational charities.

The 'school chain' notion also appealed to the Labour government. In the White Paper issued in its thirteenth year of office it stated that it would 'develop and promote an accreditation system for education providers wishing to operate groups of schools – Accredited Schools Groups' (DCSF, 2009d, para. 3.19). Criteria within the accreditation system that was to be developed relate to demonstrated capacity in governance, leadership, management, school improvement and achieving transformational change. This was seen 'as a mechanism for overcoming underperformance and spreading excellence in the system' (para. 3.18).

It is interesting that the 'school chain' concept has support from different points on the political spectrum. Were a considerable number of non-state organizations to come forward to sponsor groups of schools – an unknown factor at this stage – the implications for the governance of schools could be highly significant. Even the present level of support provides an acknowledgement of the limitations of the SE model and of the related notion of school autonomy, most famously expressed in Tony Blair's advocacy of freestanding 'independent non-fee paying state schools' (Blair, 2005, p. 4) modelled on the elite English private school. The development could be argued to have the potential to lead to a reduction in the fragmentation of governance that the SE model promotes and thereby to enhance system coherence. The emphasis in the proposals referred to above on sponsors' educational experience and on capacity, quality and accreditation implies a potential strengthening of the QC model at the expense of SE, with implications for improving educational performance.

However, the school chain concept raises acute questions of governance. If this structural form were to become widespread and some sponsors maintained substantial numbers of schools it would prompt questions about the distribution of power in the school system. Ideological questions, such as have already arisen in relation to academy sponsors with religious affiliations, would come to the fore. These along with other questions relating to commercial interest would need to be considered if, as the Policy Exchange document referred to above proposes, for-profit providers were allowed to enter the system. This set of developments would enhance – or exacerbate – what Ball (2009b, p. 102) has described as 'the complexity and interrelatedness of participation in state education, education discourses and education policy conversations by philanthropic, voluntary and private interests'. Harris (2009) has referred to 'the prospect of an expanding shadow state' soaking up the government's traditional responsibilities.

Perhaps the most significant issue would concern local accountability. The head offices of chains would be likely to be distant from the social, economic and geographical communities in which the schools were located. The notion of, in the words of the Policy Exchange document, 'developing a coherent brand' implies substantial control being exercised remotely, well beyond the level both of the school and of the locality. The consequence of the development of chains seems likely to be the further dilution of the local empowerment (LE) model of governance, in which the school is viewed explicitly as a one of a 'family' of schools, as part of a local educational system and as a member of a broader community in which there are reciprocal rights and obligations. Recent pronouncements have stressed the importance of this perspective for the achievement of national policy objectives[6] but in the technocratic and corporatist approach implied by chains, there seems little scope for notions of local democratic and strategic co-ordination or community governance. The potential significance of this will be touched on below, but it seems clear that school chains, and in particular their impact on the governance of the wider system both locally and nationally, should be an urgent priority for research.

Taking a 'family' perspective

I suggested earlier that taking a systemic view would mean focusing on local areas and looking at the local offer as a whole. An important perspective here is that of the family. Most discussion of and research into new structures of schooling looks at them through the eyes of policy-makers, commentators and professional educators. Very rarely is the viewpoint of the family central to the analysis. A particularly puzzling feature of the school diversity policy, of which academies have become an important part, is the lack of evidence of public or parental demand for it.

It has been suggested that, given the substantial proportion of academies whose sponsors have religious affiliations, Christian ethos schools are becoming the only option in some areas, even ones with very low proportions of believers or church attenders – Norwich and West Sussex have been mentioned (Marley, 2007). There is a rich irony in an apparently market-based initiative restricting rather than enhancing parental choice, but arguably the Specialist Schools programme has had a similar effect. In most areas of the country, for logistical reasons, only a very small range of specialisms can be available to parents, and when these are combined with other aspects of diversity such as faith or being single- or mixed-sex the choice presented is likely to seem even more restricted than previously.

Such issues come more clearly into focus when the perspective is that of the family and the unit of analysis is the 'locality' rather than the individual institution. In their recent study of school governance Ranson and Crouch (2009) use the term 'locality' to refer to a natural space that in many local authorities would equate to around a third or a quarter of the authority, perhaps 100,000 people. This might often be the appropriate unit for the kind of 'strongly collaborative local learning system' that the Nuffield Review (2009) of 14–19 Education and Training sees as essential to building coherent provision for this age group, which has hitherto generally faced a highly disjointed offer at local level.

Another example of the importance of taking a student and family viewpoint concerns some of the newer categories of sponsor of academies, particularly universities and elite private schools. Even in an era of widening participation, the distinctive expertise of universities relates to the most academically able students in the population and this is also to a large extent true of the more prestigious private schools. We do relatively well in educating such pupils at school. By contrast our performance is poor in relation to pupils of lesser academic ability – the so-called 'long tail'. For example, the OECD's PISA 2006 study of 57 countries identified the UK as having a comparatively large gap between higher- and lower-performing students (OECD, 2007, p. 35). University and private school sponsorship is likely to exacerbate rather than help to solve this longstanding problem.

In addition, linking the names of universities with particular academies might be expected to give families the false impression that admission provides a preferential pathway to higher education, thus pushing up demand for these academies. This will probably lead to more dissatisfied parents, because more children will fail to gain admission, and also to a widening of the gap between these academies and their neighbouring schools.

A question of legitimacy

The issue of democratic quality discussed earlier is very relevant to academies. An organization representing some of them has protested about a perceived erosion of their independence through increasing government regulation and requirements (Frean, 2009). As mentioned previously, the funding, challenge and support of academies is being placed under a new government agency, the Young People's Learning Agency (Dunton, 2009). These appear to be indications of the upward accountability to central government that is a pervasive feature of public sector governance in England today.

There is much less evidence of downward accountability to the local community and stakeholders. Sponsors, even when not operating 'chains', often have little or no connection with their academy's localities and yet for a small, and increasingly nonexistent, financial contribution (Mansell, 2009b) they formally control the governing body, premises, staffing and curriculum. West and Currie (2008) compared various existing frameworks for involving private sector actors in publicly funded schooling in England, including specialist schools, contracting-out and the Private Finance Initiative (PFI) as well as academies. They concluded that the Academies Programme was distinctive in that the only appeal is to central government, including OfSTED, and the courts. 'There is a loss of political control and legitimacy. The democratic deficit is clear' (p. 203). Wilby (2009) considers that the public debate on academies has been wrongly focused. 'If democratic institutions are failing, the answer is to improve them . . . not to create privately controlled, non-accountable institutions. That, and not exam results, is what the Academies argument should be about'.

The search for alternatives

There appears to be an inherent contradiction between a publicly funded schooling system and the notion of an 'independent' school in the sense envisaged by the originators and supporters of the Academies Programme. As Curtis *et al.* (2008) point out, many of the features of academies, such as significant autonomy, external partners and a new management regime can be achieved through other models – for example, federations, trust schools, extended schools and training schools. These do not challenge the integrity of the public system or its democratic basis to the degree that academies do.

A particularly promising example, which in principle contrasts strongly with the academy model, is the co-operative trust school. This is a model of governance based on the involvement of stakeholder groups including parents, learners, staff and the wider community, with an underlying philosophy emphasizing co-operation rather than competition (DCSF, 2008b). Funding is being made available to pilot up to 100 trusts with co-operative governance models and the concept is said to be supported by the Conservatives as well as Labour (Bawden, 2008). Co-operative schools are common in Spain, Sweden and elsewhere. Such a model, if successfully implemented, could provide a pathway towards a more democratically based schooling system with a significant element of downward and lateral accountability.

Conclusions

This chapter has argued that academies should be seen in context rather than in isolation. Policy-makers, teachers and researchers should consider the impact of academies on the schooling system as a whole both locally and nationally. The academy model should be compared with other frameworks, both new and existing ones, in an open-minded way and using a broad and inclusive set of criteria. If academies (or any other types of school) are privileged, for example in terms of governance or funding, because they are political 'favourites' whose success must be engineered it becomes hard if not impossible to compare the merits of different school types objectively and to learn from experiments such as the Academies Programme.

Much closer attention should be paid to the perspectives of families – students and their parents or guardians – and this implies far more 'downward' accountability to citizens and their localities than has been evident over the past 20 years or so. The further development of school 'chains' and its implications for the character of the national education system should be monitored closely. Finally, for schools largely or wholly funded from the public purse we should not try to mimic the governance set-up of private schools since their context and their accountabilities are entirely different.

Notes

1 At a Royal Society of Arts seminar in London on 31 January 2008.

2 For example: Green, D. (2008), 'Think tank: let every school be independent', *Sunday Times*, 10 August; Seldon, A. (2008), 'Goodbye Mr. Chips of Whitehall', *Sunday Times*, 5 October; and leading articles 'Keep faith with academy schools', *Independent*, 16 January 2009, and 'Independent schools', *The Times*, 25 February 2009.

3 A category of state school that owns its own land and buildings, employs its staff directly and administers its admission arrangements within the national system of regulation.

4 A phrase that former Prime Minister Tony Blair's director of communications, Alastair Campbell, is reputed to have used in describing comprehensive schools.

5 Except, of course, when these are privately owned rather than registered charities.

6 See, for example, DCSF, 2009d, chapter 3.

Chapter 12

The New Enterprise Logic of the Academy Programme

Brian J. Caldwell

Introduction

From an international point of view, the Academies Programme in England is best seen as one of many innovative approaches to the governance and delivery of education in the public sector that are intended to meet demanding expectations for schools in the twenty-first century.

Stephens Ball's (2007) description of academies as a 'policy condensate' is as accurate as any, with several 'policy imperatives' embedded in the programme: innovating; partnering; challenging the culture of under-achievement; introducing new social and policy actors; combining the narratives of enterprise and responsibility; changing roles, responsibilities, structures and accountabilities in state education; offering more choice and greater diversity; and providing an opportunity for transformational leadership (pp. 171–9). The involvement of a business sponsor makes it at first sight an extension of the City Technology Colleges in England but, from an international standpoint, the programme is also closely related to the charter school movement in Canada and the United States, which shares most of the imperatives in Ball's list. It also shares some of the characteristics of Sweden's Kunskkappsskolan ('knowledge schools'), a type of school advocated by England's then shadow Secretary of State for Children, Schools and Families, Michael Gove (2008, also reported in Nelson, 2008).

Leaving aside its apparent foundation in City Technology Colleges from the mid 1980s, the Academies Programme is largely a creation of the twenty-first century, and is therefore approaching its tenth anniversary. Academies still constitute a very small minority of secondary schools in England, numbering about 200 of about 3,000 secondary schools in September 2009. The Brown government decided to accelerate the programme to 300 schools by September 2010, and 400 beyond that.

This chapter does not offer a critique of the programme or debate the merits of the way that programme is or should be delivered. Instead, the purpose is to locate the programme in a framework that accounts for efforts around the world to meet expectations for schools in the public sector. The concept of 'new enterprise logic' proposed by Zuboff and Maxmin (2004) is adopted as a starting point. A framework that emerged from a recent international study is then employed to locate the programme in the wider international setting.

A central theme in this chapter and its major conclusion is that the Academies Programme and other innovations in the governance of public (state) education around the world are best seen as a largely pragmatic response to real or perceived failures in approaches to delivery that prevailed in the twentieth century. The programme is often cast as one of many neoliberal projects but it is argued that this is, to a large extent, a retroactive judgement or an attempt to place an ideological frame around a fairly pragmatic policy.

New enterprise logic

As far as meeting expectations is concerned, the Academies Programme appears to fall in the intersection of three inter-related movements. The first is that governments and others are increasingly aware of the standing of their countries in the international pecking order as far as schools are concerned. For example, the White Paper of June 2009 drew attention to England's improved performance in the Trends in International Mathematics and Science Study (TIMSS) and the relatively high proportion of top-performing students in the Programme for International Student Assessment (PISA), but noted with concern the relatively wide spread of performance of its highest and lowest achievers (DCSF, 2009d). Participating countries are sensitive to their TIMSS and PISA rankings.

The second movement is the effort in all countries to ensure a new alignment of education, economy and society. There have been different alignments in the course of the last hundred years or from one country to another at a particular point in time. The alignment may have been strong in the industrial and post-industrial eras. There appears to be considerable disjunction during the information age in a time of globalization.

The third movement reflects a phenomenon explored by Zuboff and Maxmin (2004) who coined the concept of 'new enterprise logic'. They proposed that the way an organization should work should be turned on its head so that the starting point of organizational form and function is the needs and aspirations of clients, customers and consumers, or, in the case of schools, students and parents. This contrasts with the traditional approach where these actors are seen as the end points in a delivery chain, and operations from start to finish are configured accordingly.

Shoshana Zuboff is the former Charles Edward Wilson Professor of Business Administration at Harvard University. She has challenged many of the views traditionally held in business schools around the world, including her own views from earlier times. She questioned the impersonal, market-oriented, highly competitive approaches to governance in the public and private sectors, pointing to their failings in a commentary on the global financial crisis. She is a liberal in the US sense, and was a powerful advocate for Barack Obama in the 2008 presidential election campaign. She is not a neoliberal in the way that label is applied to those on the Right. She reflected on traditional approaches: 'We weren't stupid and we weren't evil. Nevertheless we managed to produce a generation of managers and business professionals that is deeply mistrusted and despised by a majority of people in our society and around the world' (Zuboff, 2009).

Zuboff and Maxmin contend that individuals are now giving voice to their desire for 'self-determination' (Zuboff and Maxmin, 2004, p. 93), a phenomenon that is manifested in several ways in education, including personalizing the learning experience: 'parents want their children to be recognized and treated as individuals' (p. 152). They suggest that the 'old enterprise logic' persists and that its rules are 'woefully inadequate when it comes to responding to the realities of life in the new society of individuals'. Moreover:

> The old organizations have become sufficiently insulated and self-congratulatory to ignore the chasm that has formed between their practices, invented for a mass society, and the new society it has spawned. This insularity has afflicted political and civic organizations and is an important explanation for their loss of membership and declining level of active participation . . . We conclude that the new individuals are being blamed for the problems of the old organizations, when the facts suggest the opposite. It is not the new individuals who have failed the old organizations, but rather the old organizations that have failed the new individuals . . . When the old clothes no longer fit, make new ones.
>
> (Zuboff and Maxmin, 2004, pp. 116–17)

The Academies Programme is an illustration of what is proposed by Zuboff and Maxmin. There are other illustrations in England and elsewhere. Other schools in the state sector in England and elsewhere are arguably more responsive to community expectations and student needs. The priority for personalizing learning pervades the school reform movement in England and in many other countries. It is not limited to academies. The proposals in the White Paper for the so-called pupil and parent 'guarantees' are consistent with expectations implied in the Zuboff and Maxmin call for 'new enterprise logic'.

It was noted earlier in this summary of 'new enterprise logic' that traditional approaches tended to see students as the end points in a delivery chain, and operations from start to finish are configured accordingly. It is not the idea of 'delivery chains' that is of concern but how they are configured. Michael Barber, the first head of the Standards and Effectiveness Unit and then head of the Prime Minister's Delivery Unit, considered the delivery chain as a 'crucial concept', illustrated thus:

> The best way to think about it is to imagine what is implicit when a Minister makes a promise. Supposing that a Minister promises, as David Blunkett did, to improve standards of reading and writing among eleven-year-olds. Implicit in this commitment is that, one way or another, the Minister can influence what happens inside the head of an eleven-year-old in, for example, Widnes.
>
> (Barber, 2007, p. 85)

Barber recognized the complexity of delivery chains and that there are many delivery chains in which the student is the end point. Zuboff and Maxmin would contend that the student is both the starting point and the end point.

Michael Keating, who headed a number of government departments at the national (Commonwealth) level in Australia, takes a similar view to Zuboff and Maxmin. In a comprehensive study of changes in public sector delivery over several decades he concluded that

> [t]he reforms of public administration affecting service delivery stemmed fundamentally from public dissatisfaction with many of the services provided. The major problems were their lack of responsiveness to the particular needs of the individual client or customer . . . society has become more educated and wealthy and its individual members have developed greater independence and become more individualistic . . . This individualistic society is both more demanding and more critical of service provision.
>
> (Keating, 2004, p. 77)

This focus on the individual does not mean that concern for the common good is abandoned. It is the proper role of government to be concerned with the common good but, as Keating observed, 'there has to be a reinterpretation of the notion of equity as a guiding principle for the delivery of public services', away from uniformity and towards the differentiation of services, 'with the assistance provided varying according to each recipient's particular needs' (p. 78).

One reading of trends in some countries is the passing of highly centralized approaches to governance in education that dominated the twentieth century. Michael Barber recorded this passing in the following terms:

> The era of the large, slow moving, steady, respected, bureaucratic public services, however good by earlier standards, is over. In the new era, public services will need to be capable of rapid change, involved in partnerships with the business sector, publicly accountable for the services they deliver, open to diversity, seeking out world class benchmarks, and constantly learning.
>
> (Barber, 2003, p. 115)

Another reading of trends is that centralized control through a complex array of accountability requirements for schools is increasing, even though the phenomenon is not new: there has been a national curriculum since 1988 at the same time that there has been a weakening of the role of the local authority.

Flexibility of a kind that Barber has in mind was reinforced by Bentley and Wilsdon (2004), who suggested that an 'adaptive state' is required if the best approaches to service delivery are to be achieved at a particular point in time:

> We need new systems capable of continuously reconfiguring themselves to create new sources of public value. This means interactively linking the different layers and functions of governance, not searching for a static blueprint that predefines their relative weight. The central question is not how we can achieve precisely the right balance between different layers – central, regional and local – or between different sectors – public, private and voluntary. Instead, we need to ask *How can the system as a whole become more than the sum of its parts?*
>
> (p. 16, emphasis in original)

Tom Bentley was writing for Demos at the time and it is interesting to note that he is now deputy chief of staff to Australia's Prime Minister Julia Gillard, who was former deputy Prime Minister and Minister for education under Kevin Rudd, whom she replaced as Prime Minister in June 2010. He is therefore in the thick of things as a so-called 'new federalism' is constructed in Australia, re-balancing the relationship between federal and state governments, seeking a response to the question he posed with Wilsdon.

Zuboff and Maxmin (2004) illustrated 'new enterprise logic' in different ways. For example, they selected the idea of a federation to describe the new arrangements for support of an enterprise. A federation may involve one or more networks. Writing in a general sense, they contend that

> [f]ederations are not defined by what they make, what they sell, or what services they perform. Federations are defined by the constituencies that select them for support and by the ways they invent to provide that

> support. Some federations may specialise in supporting certain constituencies, others may specialise in providing only levels of deep support, and still others might specialise in their ability to aggregate support through various levels.
>
> (p. 338)

Zuboff and Maxmin describe federations in a variety of ways including 'flexible, agile and operationally excellent', distinguished by 'style, creativity, imagination, authenticity, and consistency' (pp. 338–9).

England is one of a small but increasing number of countries that have established federations of schools along the lines described by Zuboff and Maxmin, and more were proposed in the White Paper of June 2009. These federations include academies in some instances. Federations are established when it makes good sense among the partner schools to do so. They are neither an extension of nor a replacement for arrangements with local authorities. They are illustrations of the reconfiguration that Bentley and Wilsdon wrote about.

From 2004 to 2006 I was engaged through Educational Transformations in a series of seminars, workshops and consultancies in several countries. The focus was on efforts at the school and system levels to achieve transformation, which was defined as significant, systematic and sustained change that secured success for all students in all settings. The findings of this three-year research and consultancy project were summarized in Caldwell (2006). The Zuboff and Maxmin idea of 'new enterprise logic' was the most helpful descriptor of what was emerging with the new enterprise logic of schools taking the following form:

1. The student is the most important unit of organization – not the classroom, not the school and not the school system – and there are consequent changes in approaches to learning and teaching and the support of learning and teaching.
2. Schools cannot achieve expectations for transformation by acting alone or operating in a line of support from the centre of a school system to the level of the school, classroom or student. Horizontal approaches are more important than vertical approaches although the latter will continue to have an important role to play. The success of a school depends on its capacity to join networks or federations to share knowledge, address problems and pool resources.
3. Leadership is distributed across schools in networks and federations as well as within schools, across programmes of learning and teaching and the support of learning and teaching.
4. Networks and federations involve a range of individuals, agencies, institutions and organizations across public and private sectors in

educational and non-educational settings. Leaders and managers in these sectors and settings share a responsibility to identify and then effectively and efficiently deploy the kinds of support that are needed in schools. Synergies do not just happen of their own accord. Personnel and other resources are allocated to energize and sustain them.

5. New approaches to resource allocation are required under these conditions. A simple formula allocation to schools based on the size and nature of the school, with sub-allocations based on equity considerations, is not sufficient. New allocations take account of developments in the personalizing of learning and the networking of expertise and support.

Schools in the Academies Programme have these characteristics but so do many other schools in the state sector, in England and in other countries where new organizational forms are taking shape. Specialist schools in the secondary sector, for example, have partners in the public or private sectors who provide cash or in-kind support. There has been an increase in the number of networks and federations. Distributed leadership is or should be commonplace.

There are differences in the extent to which each of these five characteristics is evident, among the academies themselves and among other schools, and between both kinds of schools. No one organizational form is necessarily good or bad, right or wrong, but is simply a different configuration that will have its ups and downs, benefits and shortcomings. The *Academies Evaluation: Fifth Annual Report* by PricewaterhouseCoopers (PwC, 2008) illustrates this point with its review of strengths and weaknesses and its recommendations for change. The report noted that 'Academies are generally operating in similar ways to improving schools in the LA [local authority] maintained sector' (p. 17) and concluded that 'there is insufficient evidence to make a definitive judgement about the Academies as a model for school improvement' (p. 19). There is evidence of a degree of convergence between academies and schools in the jurisdiction of local authorities and more will occur if the recommendations in the report are taken up. Indeed, in time this convergence may mean that the distinction will disappear in a manner that suggests a high level of pragmatism rather than ideology (a point taken up towards the end of the chapter).

International project to frame the transformation of schools

The three-year project described above that led to the identification of 'new enterprise logic' was extended in 2007 and 2008 through the International Project to Frame the Transformation of Schools. Its purpose was to explore how schools that had been transformed or had sustained high performance had built strength in each of four kinds of capital (intellectual, social, spiritual, financial) and aligned them through effective governance to secure success for their students.

There were two stages in the project. The first drew on work in the first three years to identify ten indicators for each form of capital and governance. The second called for case studies in five secondary schools in each of six countries: Australia, China, England, Finland, the United States and Wales (the Australian component also included a primary school and a network of primary and secondary schools). The project was carried out by Melbourne-based Educational Transformations, with different components conducted by international partners supported by funding from the Australian government and the Welsh Assembly government. Findings are reported in Caldwell and Harris (2008). There are six separate country reports, with the England component reported in Goodfellow and Walton (2008) based on case studies at Beauchamp College, Birchwood Community High School, Pershore High School, Plumstead Manor School and Ringmer Community College. Each was a second-phase specialist school that had achieved the status of a high-performing school. The final report of the project also drew on experience over several years in the Haberdashers' Aske's Federation that included Knights Academy (formerly the Malory School). One charter school was included in the five schools studied in the United States.

Intellectual capital refers to the level of knowledge and skill of those who work in or for the school. Social capital refers to the strength of formal and informal partnerships and networks involving the school and all individuals, agencies, organizations and institutions that have the potential to support and be supported by the school. Spiritual capital refers to the strength of moral purpose and the degree of coherence among values, beliefs and attitudes about life and learning (for some schools, spiritual capital has a foundation in religion; in other schools, spiritual capital may refer to ethics and values shared by members of the school and its community). Financial capital refers to the money available to support the school. Governance is the process through which the school builds its intellectual, social, financial and spiritual capital and aligns them to achieve its goals.

This view of governance was seen as a breakthrough to the extent that the practice is traditionally conceived in terms of roles, authorities, responsibilities and accountabilities. These were accepted as pre-conditions while the processes of capital formation were seen as requirements for sustained success. Effective leadership is a prerequisite of effective governance.

The ten indicators of social capital are particularly relevant in framing key aspects of the Academies Programme.

1. There is a high level of alignment between the expectations of parents

and other key stakeholders and the mission, vision, goals, policies, plans and programmes of the school.

2. There is extensive and active engagement of parents and others in the community in the educational programme of the school.
3. Parents and others in the community serve on the governing body of the school or contribute in other ways to the decision-making process.
4. Parents and others in the community are advocates of the school and are prepared to take up its cause in challenging circumstances.
5. The school draws cash or in-kind support from individuals, organizations, agencies and institutions in the public and private sectors, in education and other fields, including business and industry, philanthropists and social entrepreneurs.
6. The school accepts that support from the community has a reciprocal obligation for the school to contribute to the building of community.
7. The school draws from and contributes to networks to share knowledge, address problems and pool resources.
8. Partnerships have been developed and sustained to the extent that each partner gains from the arrangement.
9. Resources, both financial and human, have been allocated by the school to building partnerships that provide mutual support.
10. The school is co-located with or located near other services in the community and these services are utilized in support of the school.

Schools in the Academies Programme generally satisfy some of these indicators, especially indicators 3, 5 and 9, as do local authority schools, especially at the secondary level. However, as one would expect, the pattern is not uniform, and this was noted in the report of PwC (2008). Indeed PwC recommended greater attention to indicator 3 ('to ensure that all Academies have representative participation that reflects their school and local community') and indicator 8 ('delivering joint solutions in partnership with the Local Authority and the wider family of schools'). It should be noted that six of the ten indicators were satisfied in all schools in the second phase of the International Project to Frame the Transformation of Schools (indicators 2, 5, 6, 7, 8 and 10) while the other four were illustrated in the majority of schools. Similar analysis could be undertaken for indicators of the other forms of capital and of governance (see Caldwell and Harris, 2008, for a listing of all indicators and an instrument to guide a school self-audit).

Charter schools and scenarios for the future of schools in the United States

The same framework may be used to describe charter schools in Canada and the United States. Charter schools are publicly funded no-fee schools that have a high degree of operational independence. They are established by states/provinces/districts. Private and sometimes public enterprises are granted a charter to operate them. There are some similarities with schools in the Academies Programme in England. They are described and analysed in more detail in Chapter 13. Reference is made in this section to their popularity among parents, especially when they are located in disadvantaged settings, and to plans by the Obama administration to extend them.

The popularity of charter schools is illustrated in the following account of a lottery in Harlem, which has the most charter schools per square mile in any jurisdiction in the United States:

> T[illegible]l their fists. The disap- p[illegible]he April 17th Harlem S[illegible]t ever held in the his- to[illegible] available places, and 9[illegible]e. The desperation of th[illegible]hool district, not one pu[illegible] of its pupils reading at[illegible]
>
> ([illegible]nomist, 2008a, p. 44)

At H[illegible]cent of six-year-olds were [illegible]2006–7 school year, wher[illegible]art of the year. The chan[illegible]n, wishes to 'charter- ize' t[illegible]

De[illegible]d, efforts to reform the pu[illegible]kthrough in highly disad[illegible]harter initiative. As repor[illegible]'s mayor, Richard Daley, [illegible]an aimed to open 100 ne[illegible]ough Renaissance 2010. [illegible]naissance Schools Fund [illegible] new schools had been c[illegible]on in the Obama admini[illegible]4.35 billion will be made a[illegible]ucational innova- tion. Du[illegible]ublic charter laws or put a[illegible]l jeopardize their applica[illegible]009).

The [illegible]s, as illustrated in the lottery experience in New York, and the level of business support, as illustrated in Renaissance 2010 in Chicago, suggests a strong alignment of the charter initiative with indicators of social capital in the framework constructed in the International Project to Frame the Transformation of Schools. One of the five case study schools in the [illegible] ter school (see Zhao *et al.* [illegible]

Serious prop [illegible] States well beyond organi [illegible] ted in the charter school [illegible] mmission on the Skills of [illegible] k in 2006. The project wa [illegible] n and the Economy, a nc [illegible] m liberal tradition in th [illegible] ators and policy-makers s [illegible] its search for ideas. Visits [illegible] the Czech Republic, Engla [illegible] land, Italy and New Zealar [illegible] o governance that were [illegible] lowing.

What is the International project to frame the transformation of Schools?

- Schools woul [illegible] d, schools would be op [illegible] n limited-liability orga [illegible] ry role of school distri [illegible] contracts with the ope [illegible] cancel or decide not to [illegible] perform well, and find [illegible]
- The contract [illegible] he safety, curriculum, [illegible] of public schools. The [illegible] he state.
- The schools [illegible] a pupil-weighted forr [illegible]
- The schools [illegible] funds are spent, the sta [illegible] nt, their schedule and [illegible] lum and met the testing and other accountability requirements imposed by the state.
- Districts could provide support services to the schools, but the schools would be free to obtain the services they needed wherever they wished (these excerpts from the National Centre on Education and the Economy, 2007, p. xxvii).

Charter schools and academies are relatively modest innovations compared with the elements in this scenario, the merits of which are not considered here (see Hodge, 2007, for a critique).

The importance of trust

[illegible] a loss of trust in traditional organiza- [illegible] s loss is likely a factor in the creation [illegible] in the United States. Indicators are [illegible] reate them (the major parties sup- [illegible] nts for places (waiting lists and the [illegible] o observe that there is a lack of trust [illegible] tion and effectiveness of each of the [illegible] he strategies that have created these [illegible]

[illegible] or aspiring leaders declare a passion [illegible] rdon Brown is a case in point. He set [illegible] ch at the University of Greenwich in [illegible] clared that 'education is my passion' [illegible] ding a school 'that aimed high [and] [illegible] k and achievement'.

[illegible] thing more than a demonstration of [illegible] y moving. The leader must be trusted [illegible] driven by a compelling vision that has [illegible]

[illegible] in discourse on leadership in recent [illegible] cal leaders, although some writers [illegible] kuyama (1995) used this position in [illegible] high-trust societies, contending that [illegible] . imposes a kind of tax on all forms of economic activity; a tax that high-trust societies do not have to pay' (pp. 28–9). Covey (2006) suggests that 'this low-trust tax is not only on economic activity, but on all activity – in every relationship, in every interaction, in every communication, in every decision, in every dimension of life' (p. 19).

No amount of passion or trust will suffice if well-thought-out strategies are not designed and delivered. Returning to the passion of Gordon Brown, his vision for education was replete with strategies for its realization, building on those of his predecessor Tony Blair, emphasizing parental engagement, 'real-time' feedback on pupil progress, strengthening early childhood education, personalizing learning, expanding programs for the gifted and talented, and raising the standards of teaching.

Finland is a 'high-trust' country as far as schools are concerned: there is a high level of trust to the extent that there are no national tests of student achievement and teachers and those who support them are free to use their professional judgement in approaches to learning and teaching. There are few private schools and no counterpart to academies and charters.

Expressed another way, in a 'high trust' country like Finland, there has been little or no demand for alternatives to traditional state-run comprehensive schools; in 'low trust' countries like England and the United States, there is moderate to strong demand.

Neoliberalism as a *post hoc* explanation

Campbell, Proctor and Sherington (2009) reported a study of school choice in Australia and analysed the findings in terms of the neoliberal agenda:

> New regimes of 'school choice' are part of a wider set of practices and discourses across the Western world and beyond that transform citizens into consumers who make choices. The origin of the new approaches to markets and consumption are found in the rise of neoliberalism as the dominant set of beliefs that govern both economic and public policy.
> (p. 4)

They described neoliberalism in terms of a re-definition of the good 'parent-citizen', a return to nineteenth-century liberalism that trusts markets as efficient regulators of activity, and the rise of globalization (pp. 4–6). They acknowledge that the neoliberal label has supplanted 'economic rationalism' as a descriptor of these developments, at least in Australia.

While a neoliberal frame may be a convenient, if not entirely legitimate, way to describe what has occurred, it is another thing to claim the ideology as a cause of what has transpired. School choice between public and private sectors, with government support for private schools, has been a feature of the Australian scene for nearly half a century, and a recent history of the phenomenon (Wilkinson *et al.*, 2006) suggests that the funding mechanism has been a pragmatic political response to parental demand.

In his preface to *Who Rules? How Government Retains Control of a Privatised Economy*, Michael Keating (2004), cited earlier in the chapter in the context of public sector reform in Australia that 'stemmed fundamentally from public dissatisfaction', stated that 'I have personally felt for some time that the critics of what they describe as "economic rationalism" or "neoliberalism" have ignored the evidence and too often misunderstood the changes that have occurred and their rationale' (p. vii).

Conclusion

Initiatives such as the Academies Programme may be cast in a new light given the framework of the four forms of capital and the new view of governance that emerged from the International Project to Frame the Transformation of Schools. The programme can be located in a continuum of strategies that are suggested in the different sets of indicators, especially those in the list for social capital. The programme emerges as a highly pragmatic response rather than a sustained ideological press to overturn public education. It is a complex response, to be sure, and Ball's list of elements in a 'policy condensate' describes it well. More effort than seems warranted has been invested in searching for an ideology of the Academies Programme. The *Economist* offered the following perceptive commentary on the legacy of Margaret Thatcher and Tony Blair:

> In opposition Mr Blair's team developed the concept of the 'stakeholder society' and the grandiose 'third way', which avowedly reconciled market economics with social democracy. Mrs Thatcher harvested ideas from radical think-tanks and continental intellectuals. But, for both leaders, theory served mostly to rationalise their instincts. The 'third way' was as much a description of the political realities of the 1990s as a manifesto. Mrs Thatcher started with a notion of Britain and only retroactively found it validated by Hayek and Bastiat.
>
> (2009, p. 46)

There may have been elements of a philosophy or an ideological bent of one kind or another in the City Technology Colleges or the Academies Programme in England, or the charter movement in the United States, but they are essentially pragmatic responses to concerns expressed across the community about schools. Effort should be invested in making the programme work well or replacing it with one that works better rather than searching for an underlying theory or fitting it up as a neoliberal project.

Chapter 13

International Perspectives on Academies: Lessons Learned from Charter Schools and Choice Options around the Globe

Ellen Goldring and Madeline Mavrogordato

Introduction

Academies, like charter schools in the United States and other market-based reforms around the world, have been developed to provide innovative opportunities and choices to better meet the needs of disadvantaged students and their families (Curtis *et al.*, 2008; DCSF, 2009). The purpose of this chapter is to review the lessons learned from research on charter schooling in the US and market-based educational reforms in other countries and their implications for understanding the possible promises and pitfalls of academies in England. This review focuses on practices, common barriers and challenges, and the empirical evidence in regard to the main arguments for school choice.

New public management: charter schools in the United States

Throughout the world the boundaries between public and private entities and firms have become more blurred and porous (Henig *et al.*, 2003). It is no longer the case that public organizations are exclusively managed, financed and governed by public entities, nor is it true that private entities have no forms of public engagement or oversight. Some refer to this as the 'mixed economy', while others refer to these hybrid models as the 'new public management' (Hood, 1991). In the public sector, the new public management includes a new focus on standards and measures of performance, private sector style of management and hiring, efficient and effective allocation of resources, competition, autonomy and decentralization, and rewards linked to outcomes (Hood, 1991). Changes in public and private firms occur in the provision of social services, including education.

In the US, charter schools are part of the new public management in education. Charter schools are publicly funded schools that have an independent board of overseers or directors that receives a contract or 'charter' from an authorizer to operate the school. The most prevalent authorizers of charter schools are states, local school districts, universities or colleges, special-purpose boards and municipal bodies. Authorizers review and approve new charters (contracts), monitor performance and accountability and make contract renewal decisions. In exchange for a charter, the charter school receives considerable autonomy from traditional public school[1] regulations. Charter schools can recruit and enrol students without the confinement of an encatchment zone, thus providing parent choice; they can hire and fire their personnel independent from the school district where they are located, and they can innovate and develop their own instructional focus and curriculum.

While the US Department of Education monitors the academic progress of students, most decisions regarding education, including those about curricula, assessments and graduation requirements, are left up to states. Charter school laws vary from state to state, and thus there are different charter school authorizers. Nine states do not even permit charter schools, and some states have extremely restrictive charter school laws that limit the number of charter schools that can open. Other states have much more liberal laws regarding charter schools. Arizona, for example, has one of the most far-reaching and open laws regarding charter schools in the US. In this state, local school districts even have the power to authorize a charter school located outside of their own geographic boundaries (Dee and Fu, 2004).

Charter schools, like all other traditional public schools, must follow state standards and state graduation requirements; thus teachers and their schools are held accountable for the learning outcomes of their students. Students must participate in annual state standardized testing programs and their schools are subject to federal accountability standards under No Child Left Behind (NCLB) legislation.[2]

Charter schools typically employ a mix of public and private resources and monies to deliver educational services.[3] Charter schools cannot charge tuition fees. Funding for these schools comes from public monies, including federal, state and local allocations. However, charter schools tend to receive less funding from public sources than traditional public schools. 'Charter Schools were underfunded by a weighted student average of $1,801 when compared to similarly weighted state per-pupil funding for districts. A complementary analysis of charter and district funding in 27 urban cities produced an even greater disparity: charter-weighted funding shortfall of $2,256 or 23.5%' (Speakman, 2008, p. 87). In addition, charter schools typically do not have access to funding for facilities or transportation. There are a number of public–private initiatives and partnerships to provide funding for charter school facilities. For instance, the Credit Enhancement for Charter School Facilities programme 'awards funds to public and nonprofit entities that help leverage other funds from the private sector for the purchase, construction, lease or renovation of facilities by increasing the creditworthiness of charter schools' (US Department of Education, 2008, p. 2). Other schools open non-profit foundations so they can raise monies from private donors and corporations to supplement their public monies. For example, the KIPP Foundation, a non-profit organization associated with the Knowledge is Power Program, a network that now comprises 82 charter schools across 19 states that focuses on serving low-income students, received more than US$38.5 million between 2000 and 2006 from Doris and Don Fisher, the founders of Gap, Inc. This amounted to 62 per cent of the funding that the KIPP Foundation had received from donors (Doxbury, 2006).

Furthermore, some charter schools are managed by for-profit organizations termed 'education management organizations' (EMOs), such as Edison Learning, an organization that has partnerships with 120 schools in the US and the UK. While most charter schools are run by non-profit organizations, there are a considerable number of charter schools affiliated with for-profit organizations. Referred to as market-oriented charter schools, charters run by EMOs 'can be characterized as profit driven, desiring to draw large student populations in order to maximize net profits from per-pupil funding formulas relative to the costs of operating a school through achieving economies of scale' (Lacireno-Paquet *et al.*, 2002, p. 149). Bulkley (2004) reported 21 companies managing more than 300 charter schools in the US. EMOs differ in the types of services they provide and in the models they use with schools from providing administrative back-office services to providing full company-developed, highly specified curricula and assessments (Bulkley, 2005).

In terms of the demand side, charter schools are open to parent choice, and their leaders have leeway as to where to locate their schools. Charter schools are often located in areas with lower rent costs (Lubienski *et al.*, 2009). This may be because charter schools often do not receive public funds to finance their facilities. While facility costs are important for charter schools to consider, charter school boards also weigh whether or not they want to serve the students in areas where it is least expensive to rent a facility. Proximity to a school is an important factor when parents are determining where to enrol their children in school (Neal, 2009; Smrekar, 2009), and therefore students who attend a given charter school often live in the surrounding neighbourhood. Research shows that some charter schools, particularly for-profit charters, are inclined to locate in neighbourhoods that contain some disadvantaged students, but they 'ring' or encircle areas of concentrated poverty without being located in the poorest neighbourhoods (Lubienski *et al.*, 2009). This trend may be an effort to avoid having to serve the most disadvantaged students. It appears that 'competitive incentives . . . have encouraged schools to sort themselves based largely on their preferred clientele, with different groups of schools asserting their advantageous position to serve more affluent students' (p. 641).

Arguments for charter schools and findings from the US and abroad

The main arguments for school choice and other mixed economies in the provision of schooling pertain to four key areas.

1. Access, equity and diversity.
2. Student achievement.
3. Innovation and professional autonomy.
4. Parent engagement and involvement.

1. Access, equity and diversity

A key rationale behind charter schools is that they will improve access, equity and diversity for all students. Theoretically, school choice provides a mechanism whereby low-income students and their families can gain access to higher-quality schools, without moving their place of residence. Most neighbourhoods are, to a greater or lesser extent, segregated by socioeconomic status, ethnicity and race (Jencks and Mayer, 1990; Orfield and Lee, 2006; Rawlings *et al.*, 2004). Poor, minority neighbourhoods tend to have schools that are of low quality.

Residential segregation is associated with a lack of diversity in many, if not most, public schools because school attendance is linked to residential zones. When schools are anchored to residential areas, school choice is available to those who can afford to choose their place of residence or pay for private schools; those who face a very constrained set of housing choices also face limited school choices when traditional public schools are the only option (Carnoy, 2000; Hoxby, 2003).

Researchers have been anxious to determine if school choice options 'cream off' the most elite students and if they provide lower-social-class families an alternative to inferior neighbourhood schools (Yu and Taylor, 1997). Choice could contribute to 'cream skimming' if families have limited information and knowledge about how to access choice schools. Furthermore, given accountability pressures, schools may have incentives to try to attract those students and families who are easier or less costly to educate (Lacireno-Paquet *et al.*, 2002). However, since funding is tied to enrolments in the US, there are also incentives to maintain higher levels of enrolments as well as receive federal funds that target at-risk students such as special education and English-language learners.

Several studies of charter schools have reported that, on average, charter schools do not appear to inordinately enrol larger proportions of minorities or economically disadvantaged students than do the public school districts in which they are located (Frankenberg and Lee, 2003; Gill *et al.*, 2007; Miron and Nelson, 2002). In a study of California and Texas charter schools, Booker *et al.* (2005) found that in both states it appears that charter schools are not cream-skimming the best students as many opponents of charters fear; rather, they appear to be targeting lower-achieving or more at-risk students. Lacireno-Paquet *et al.* (2002) had a similar conclusion when studying charter schools in Washington, DC, finding that charter schools 'do not appear to be cream skimming the pool of potential students' (p. 155).

There is also evidence that some parents consider the racial composition of charter schools and that they choose to enrol their children in schools where there is a large concentration of students of their race. Booker *et al.* (2005) found that charter schools in Texas and California are having an effect on the racial-ethnic sorting of students; specifically, black students 'tend to move to Charter Schools that have a higher percentage of black students and are more racially concentrated than the public schools they leave' (p. 22). In a similar investigation Bifulco and Ladd (2006) also found evidence of student-sorting along racial/ethnic lines and concluded, 'Charter Schools in North Carolina clearly increase the extent to which students are racially segregated' (p. 40). Segregation is a concern in the United States because history has shown that segregated schools generally result in inherently unequal educational opportunities and resources.

Interestingly, other countries have also experienced increased segregation after implementing policies of new public management in education. As a result of the New Zealand's Tomorrow's Schools reforms that instituted local school control and gave parents the right to enrol their children in any public school, there is 'an even greater concentration of difficult-to-teach students – those from poverty-stricken homes, those whose English [i]s weak, and those with learning difficulties – in schools at the bottom' (Fiske and Ladd, 2003, p. 62). A similar trend towards segregation is evident in Sweden as well (Daun, 2003).

2. Student achievement

The primary arguments for school choice pertain to the effects of competition on outcomes for students. It is assumed that competition will spur traditional public schools to change and innovate, leading to improved student achievement (Chubb and Moe, 1990). However, researching the effects of charter schooling on student outcomes is methodologically very complex (Berends, *et al.*, 2008; Hoxby and Murarka, 2008). Experimental studies that would allow researchers to look at the causal effects of attending a charter school are extremely difficult to implement because randomly assigning children to attend a charter school or a traditional public school is impractical.[4]

Despite these complexities, the results regarding the impact of charter schools on student achievement are mixed. In the early years of charter school implementation, many claimed that it was too early to assess impact on student outcomes (Goldhaber, 1999). Years later a substantial amount of research has been conducted, but the findings do not paint a clear picture. A review of 41 studies found that the difference in student achievement outcomes between charter and public schools is null or mixed (although some studies report positive effects and others indicate negative effects) (Hill *et al.*, 2006). Similarly, Carnoy *et al.* (2005) found that charter school students tend to perform similarly or slightly lower than traditional public school peers on the National Assessment of Education Progress (NAEP).

In contrast, Hoxby and colleagues (Hoxby and Murarka, 2008; Hoxby and Rockoff, 2004; Hoxby *et al.*, 2009) found that charter schools positively affected the academic achievement of elementary students in Chicago and in New York City. Bohte (2004) found that competition from charter schools contributed to 'modest, overall performance improvements for students enrolled in traditional public schools' (p. 501) in Texas.

More recent research, using longitudinal data, has begun to document a trend whereby initial achievement in charter schools is lower than in traditional public schools, but over time, charter school students outperform their traditional public school peers or catch up to them in mathematics (Sass, 2006). Berends *et al.* (2008) found a similar pattern whereby over the course of more than one school year the achievement growth of charter students in the lower grade levels was more than their peers in traditional public schools.

Schools in other countries have similarly inconclusive results regarding student achievement for a variety of reasons. For example, in some countries research has been unable to disentangle the effects of choice from simultaneous education reforms (Ladd, 2003). In other countries, such as New Zealand, there are no national test data available to be able to compare student achievement in different types of schools (Fiske and Ladd, 2003; Ladd, 2003).

3. Innovation and professional autonomy

A key argument for charter schools pertains to the notion that school choice will spur innovation and differentiation among schools. Malloy and Wohlstetter (2003) report that most charter school laws include the desire to 'facilitate innovative teaching' (p. 220). Lubienski (2003) notes that 'choice, competition, and innovation are cast as the necessary vehicles for advancing academic outcomes' (p. 397). Schools of choice are designed to be more organizationally independent and more decentralized in terms of their mechanisms of control compared to traditional public schools (e.g. Chubb and Moe, 1990; Raywid, 1985). Charter schools are exempt from many rules that generally govern other public schools, allowing for greater autonomy from both teachers and principals. Bifulco and Ladd (2005) found higher levels of school autonomy in areas such as influence over school programmes and policies in charter schools. Teachers in charter schools report greater influence over academic standards and curriculum compared to their counterparts in traditional public schools (Christensen and Lake, 2007; Podgursky, 2008).

There is little agreement as to what is considered innovative in the school choice debates. Lubienski (2003) conceptualizes innovation in terms of '*educational* changes (practices regarding curricular content and instructional strategies with immediate impact at the classroom-level), and administrative changes (organizational-level practices and structural designs that do not directly affect classroom techniques or content)' (pp. 404–5, emphasis in original). The research findings are mixed. Berends *et al.* (2009) found that charter schools tend to place additional requirements on students and parents, such as requiring school uniforms or parent volunteering in the school, or having students participate in community service. The magnitude of differences between charter and traditional public schools for these items ranged from 36 to 50 percentage points. Furthermore, when they examined teacher reports of innovative instructional strategies (e.g. long-term student investigations, students setting the pace of instruction, tightly structured lessons, student projects focused on complex and real-life investigations) or innovative student evaluation (portfolios), they found that teachers in choice schools differed from traditional public school teachers in statistically meaningful ways, but that differences were not large (five percentage points or less).

Perhaps where there is more widespread innovation is in terms of the administration of charter schools, especially in terms of personnel policies. Podgursky (2008) reports that teachers at charter schools are more likely to have incentive pay and bonuses to recruit and retain teachers than traditional public school teachers and are less likely to have their salaries determined by a single salary schedule. In addition, dismissal rates are higher in charter schools, although this could be because so many charter schools are relatively new. Charter schools also have great leeway in hiring practices. Teachers at charter schools are much less likely to be union members, and therefore are not part of collective bargaining agreements and tend to be hired directly by the individual charter schools, rather than a centralized agency like a school district. The implication of these hiring practices is that charter schools have more flexibility in their working (contractual) relationships with teachers. Charter school teachers tend to work more hours and a longer school year, for example (Malloy and Wohlstetter, 2003).

Interestingly, Cannata (2008) found that charter school teachers are less qualified in terms of years of experience and level of degree compared with traditional public school teachers. However, in terms of the most important reasons for choosing to teach at their particular school, charter school teachers are more likely than their peers at traditional public schools to indicate the ability to teach without certification, agreement with the school mission, involvement in school governance and ability to influence school policies.

Schools that exhibit new public management in other countries display some innovative practices, but because countries often require all schools that receive public funding be measured by performance on a national exam based on national standards, innovation is often limited.[5] The schools that are afforded the room to truly innovate are those that serve advantaged students because these students tend to be successful on national exams. Schools that serve more disadvantaged students 'do not have that luxury' (Ladd, 2003).[6]

4. Parent engagement and involvement

One of the main arguments in support of charter schools pertains to increased parent engagement (Stein *et al.*, 2008). Charter school research reveals higher levels of parent satisfaction and parent involvement compared with traditional public schools (Bifulco and Ladd, 2005; Bulkley and Fisler, 2003). These conclusions are consistent with the theory that charter schools would be more responsive to parents because they are accountable to the 'consumers'.

There are two main arguments pertaining to why charter schools may support higher levels of parent engagement. First, parents normally make a conscious decision to enrol their child in a charter school. The act of choice itself may bring schools and families closer together through the choice and information-gathering process. Charter schools must enrol students to be viable, and therefore teachers may be more open to working with students and their families and families more open to working with the school.

Second, the focused programme, purpose, or mission of many charter schools may increase the possibility of greater engagement between families and their schools, developing a 'good fit' between home and school. Earlier literature on effective schools (e.g. Brookover and Lezotte, 1979; Goldring and Shapira, 1993) and research on restructuring emphasize the need for goal consensus (e.g. Elmore, 1990). School choice attempts to resolve conflicts over goals through choice (Bryk *et al.*, 1993; Metz, 1990; Raywid, 1985). Bifulco and Ladd (2005) talk about the 'parent-school match' in charter schools where parents could feel a heightened comfort level and willingness to be involved.

Research on parent involvement in charters schools compares charter schools to traditional public schools. Zimmer *et al.* (2003) report that charter schools are more likely to use a variety of traditional parent involvement strategies than conventional public schools, such as back-to-school nights and open houses. Teske and Schneider (2001) conclude that parents who make choices tend to be more involved in their children's schools. Many charter schools also require parent involvement through formal contracts. Bifulco and Ladd (2005) found some evidence to support the hypothesis that charter school parents are more likely to participate in schooling than traditional public school parents due to particular organizational characteristics of charters such as their smaller size and lower student-to-teacher ratios.

Interestingly, the literature on choice schools in other countries focuses much more on the act of choosing as a means of spurring competition and improving schooling rather than drawing parents into schools to be active participants in their children's education. With regard to the literature on school choice, other countries tend to define parent participation as a phenomenon that occurs outside of the school as parents select which schools their children will attend, which puts pressure on schools (both traditional public schools and choice schools) to improve academic achievement outcomes. This participation is inherently external; parents are putting pressure on schools from outside, to which school faculty and staff inside must respond. However, also important in the US is direct parent involvement inside schools. The hope is that parents will do more than apply external pressure for school improvement: that they will also be more inclined to be internal participants actively engaged in their children's education. This type of direct, internal parent involvement is largely absent from the discussion surrounding school choice in other countries, with a few exceptions. One of the reasons Qatari government officials found the charter schools model attractive was because they thought the act of parents choosing schools would 'enable key constituents in society to become actively engaged in the school system' (Brewer *et al.*, 2006, p. 54). Independent schools in Qatar have designed plans for parent involvement that include more opportunities for parents to communicate with teachers and participate in school decisions as part of their contract with the government (Brewer *et al.*, 2006).[7]

Lessons for academies

The influence of new public management in education appears to be here to stay. Academies are a relatively recent manifestation of new public management, and, as such, it is worth turning to similar initiatives such as charter schools and other examples from across the globe for lessons regarding new public management in education.

Access, equity and diversity

One of the goals of charter schools and independent schools in other countries is to promote educational equity by giving low-income parents the ability to select high-performing schools for their children. Contrary to what was expected by proponents of new public management, research from various contexts shows that allowing parents to choose where to send their children to school does not automatically create equitable schools, and in some instances, can lead to schools that are more homogenous in terms of race and socioeconomic status.

Not all parents choose to participate in school choice, but rather it tends to be parents with higher levels of economic and social capital who self-select out of their home schools in favour of schools that are more homogenous schools. There are examples of this in the US, where some schools are more segregated by race, and in New Zealand, where enrolments have become 'polarize[d] . . . along ethnic and socioeconomic grounds' (Fiske and Ladd, 2003). This is also evident in Australia, Sweden and, to some extent, England (Ladd, 2003). The consequence is that school choice may not benefit the students that these policies set out to target. However, there is an important exception to this trend in some charter schools in the US. Some charter management organizations (CMOs) that actively recruit and serve disadvantaged students have replicated their original school model in order to establish multiple schools. These schools are often located in urban cores where there is a dense concentration of at-risk students. Because of their explicit targeting and sophisticated recruitment strategies, they serve large groups of minority and low-income students. Arguably, these models are the most commonly replicated charter schools in the US, because they are fulfilling one of the original expectations of charter schools: providing attractive public education options to parents who otherwise would have likely had no other alternatives.

It will be important to carefully monitor segregation as academies grow in number. This is particularly true when one considers that there has been a shift away from placing academies in areas of high disadvantage since the required free school meals (FSM) eligibility rate for academies has declined (Curtis *et al.*, 2008; PwC, 2008) and the percentage of students eligible for FSM in academies continues to decline (Curtis *et al.*, 2008). With careful planning surrounding geographic placement of academies, school mission and leadership, as well as making a concerted effort to inform low-income parents of their options, educational policy-makers in London should be able to significantly reduce the extent to which academies promote segregation and polarization.

Increased student achievement

Capturing the effects of school choice on student achievement is a difficult task in the US and abroad. Running experiments is often infeasible for several reasons. First, randomly assigning students to schools is impractical, and rarely is there an occasion for a natural experiment that involves an educational lottery. Second, several countries, such as Australia and Belgium, have universal school choice systems, and this does not allow for comparison to students not participating in school choice. Third, several countries, such as Australia and New Zealand, do not have national exams that measure student achievement. Fourth, it is difficult to disentangle the effects of school choice from other reforms. These problems prevent us from drawing definitive conclusions regarding the effect of school choice on student achievement.

It is also important to consider that, by definition, schools of choice are given the freedom to be different. They are afforded flexibility to deviate from regulations that apply to traditional public schools in the same district, and they are encouraged to innovate. Thus, it only makes sense that there is a tremendous amount of variance in terms of student achievement outcomes. Some charter schools have exhibited clear academic success when compared to traditional public schools in the same area, whereas others have proven to be a disappointment. This variability is evident in academies as well, and there is not a uniform 'academy effect' (PwC, 2008).

However, in the US there are examples of some charter schools, particularly CMOs that have founded multiple school sites, that have a reputation for consistently increasing student achievement. Aspire Public Schools in California currently has 25 schools located throughout the state in areas that target disadvantaged students. In the 2007–8 school year, the 15 Aspire schools that had been open at least two years grew an average of 25 points on California's Academic Performance Index,[8] which is approximately nine times the state's average growth (Aspire Public Schools, 2009). The results are similarly impressive for the schools that are managed by the YES Prep CMO in Houston, Texas, and the IDEA Academy CMO in the Rio Grande Valley, Texas. All of these CMOs are known for having an intense focus on academic achievement, strict discipline codes and emphasizing a college preparation. These CMOs have essentially become recognized and revered school 'brands'. Because of their success, they have become extremely popular and have been able to proliferate with relative ease. However, because these CMOs have become large, some argue that they are at risk of becoming somewhat unwieldy and bureaucratic, like traditional public school districts. KIPP schools have avoided this by essentially creating school 'franchises' that have the KIPP label and are expected to implement core aspects of the KIPP model, but control remains at the individual school level.

One lesson for academies is that if specific sponsors implement innovative models that have been found to improve academic achievement for traditionally low-performing groups, it is imperative to investigate why they are effective and identify ways to successfully replicate them. In addition, policy-makers may consider creating opportunities for excellent academies to share their innovative practices with traditional public schools.

Heightened innovation and professional autonomy

Both charter schools in the US and other examples of school choice abroad have revealed that the amount of innovation is often dictated by how much freedom is afforded to schools. Freedom to innovate varies both between and within countries. Some states have more restrictive laws for charter schools in the US, and in France autonomy is determined at the school level as administrators at private schools determine how much autonomy they want to relinquish in exchange for public funding. Freedom to innovate is limited by state or national tests that dictate desired educational outcomes. In most cases, students at choice schools around the globe are required to take an exam that tests mastery of state (in the case of the US) or national (in most other countries) standards. Some argue that mandating such measures restricts autonomy because everyone has the same end goal to strive for. Thus, schools tend to coalesce around the same curricula, instructional techniques and subject areas (Lubienski, 2006). Charter schools have been found to innovate in areas such as staff recruitment and hiring, school calendars and disciplinary policies, which are areas that skirt around instruction. Much less innovation is seen in pedagogy and curricula (Lubienski, 2006).

Innovation may also be limited by being a member of an education management organization (EMO), CMO or other management organization. While being a member of one of these management organizations can lead to more prestige, increased funding through private foundations and a reduction in administrative duties, they may also curtail the ability to innovate because they provide an educational model that has aspects that members must adhere to. Some argue that despite the academic successes that some management organizations have experienced, they are beginning to resemble traditional public school districts. Along with membership to a management organization comes a reduction in local control and an increase in bureaucracy. While there are many advantages, some schools of choice pay handsomely for this membership in the form of reduced freedom and autonomy. Policy-makers in England should take note of this trend and remember it when approving sponsors of new academies.

More parent engagement and involvement

Many of the charter school models in the US have instituted formal mechanisms that encourage or even mandate parental involvement through contracts (Becker *et al.*, 1997; Hoxby *et al.*, 2009). This is one innovation that has emerged out of the charter school movement. Headteachers at academies should note that it is important to provide parents with a wide array of opportunities to participate in since parental involvement can contribute to student achievement (Epstein, 1984; Marjoribanks, 1979; Lareau, 1987), and that parents from low-income backgrounds are less likely to be involved than their more affluent peers (Chavkin and Williams, 1993; Abrams and Gibbs, 2002). Many respected CMOs provide specific opportunities for parents to volunteer and participate in their children's education (e.g. KIPP, Aspire Public Schools, IDEA Academies). It is particularly important for academies to encourage parent involvement as a means of establishing and strengthening the school community as a whole, particularly since many academies were so-called failing schools that have been reconstituted as academies and are trying to cultivate new school cultures that reflect their individual models.

Conclusion

There are a multitude of examples of new public management in education across the globe. Each country, and sometimes even states or provinces within a country, have their own policies for implementing school choice. Some countries such as England and the US only have small percentages of schools that are publicly funded and independently managed, whereas other nations such as New Zealand have universal systems of school choice. Despite the vast array of examples, not one case has proven to be an educational panacea. However, there are examples of schools, particularly certain charter schools with a very clear and focused mission, that are documented to be both effective and replicable. These schools have been able to reach the goals of increasing access to high-quality schooling, improving academic achievement, spurring innovation and getting parents more involved in their children's education. Policy-makers in England can learn from these schools to discover what is inside the 'black box' of successful schools that employ new public management to improve the educational outcomes of students who attend academies as well as their peers who attend traditional public schools.

Notes

1 In the United States, traditional public schools are taxpayer-funded and publicly run. So the term 'public' school is used differently than in England, where it is used for independent or private institutions that have fees. Typically, students are assigned to attend a specific public school based on the geographic location of their residence.

2 The No Child Left Behind Act of 2001 is federal legislation that focuses on standards-based education reform. It requires that all states annually assess student learning in core subject areas such as maths and reading in order to receive federal funding. Students' scores are used to determine if schools have met adequate yearly progress.

3 In the United States there is strict separation of church and state. Consequently, no schools that are taxpayer-funded may have a religious affiliation. Because charter schools are primarily funded by public sources, they are not permitted to have religious affiliations, which is one key distinction between academies and charter schools.

4 Merely matching students who attend a charter school to a peer at a traditional public school based on a variety of student-level characteristics such as race, gender and socio-economic status is not enough, because the act of choosing to attend a charter school is not at all random. In certain situations, charter schools are oversubscribed and schools utilize a lottery to randomly select students for attendance. This allows for a natural experiment, but only at a small scale. In addition, it is generally the high-performing charter schools with excellent reputations that are oversubscribed, and this sample would not be representative of most charter schools.

5 New Zealand and Australia are exceptions. These countries do not employ national exams; however, all schools are required to follow national standards.

6 It should be noted that there is extremely limited empirical research surrounding school choice in countries other than the US and the UK.

7 It is important to remember that the Qatari independent schools model is based on the American charter schools model, so the parallels in the emphasis on parent involvement are not surprising.

8 California's Academic Performance Index (API) is a scale that runs from 200 to 1,000 that serves as a means of comparing schools based on student performance on state standardized tests. For more information see www.cde.ca.gov/ta/ac/ap/documents/infoguide08.pdf (accessed 1 September 2009).

Chapter 14

Academies and the Myth of Evidence-Based Policy: Limits and Possibilities

Denis Gleeson

Introduction

In the decade following their inception this chapter seeks to gain a picture of academy schools as a New Labour project and what the future holds for them. This is not a straightforward task given that academy development remains experimental, averse to freedom of information and external research. Despite a decade of reform involving over 200 schools opened and more planned by the Conservative Liberal Democrat Coalition, there exist no major independently funded research projects addressing academy development, save for those evaluations undertaken by preferred government consultants. A distinctive feature of this volume is that it brings together a diverse range of research evidence drawn mainly from independent research sustained through individual and collective endeavour. With few exceptions research access to academies, compared with mainstream schools, has been something of a no-go area, reflecting the political sensitivity associated with the 'goldfish-bowl' effect of early academy development (Needham *et al.*, 2006). An unintended consequence of such gatekeeping is that much valuable research into academy schools has been undertaken outside the conventional parameters of school-based research, through community, campaign, professional and trade union routes. As a near-concluding chapter, this contribution reflects on some of the recurring themes arising from such research and how it informs future thinking about education and schooling. It addresses the paradox that while academies do not appear to be that significant in the wider context of school provision, the controversy surrounding them reveals more about the state of education policy than it does about the institutional characteristics of academies themselves.

Schools like any other?

Academy schools, previously known as 'city academies', are a distinctly English phenomena. What is distinctive about them is, however, contested and unclear. Within England they are best understood in a broader context of the history of English education, associated with paternalism, patronage and philanthropic traditions. As independent state-funded institutions, academies do not follow a set pattern and are highly diverse, both individually and in terms of their antecedents, ethos, specialism, location, phase and stage of development. Equally, their forms of governance and accountability vary through trusts, business consortia, local authorities (LAs), Higher Education (HE), foundation, faith, diocese and individual sponsors. While some academies project their distinctive curricula and specialism through these means, others emphasize their ethos and mission in raising levels of achievement and attainment. Despite claims of breaking the mould of comprehensive education, academies have similarities with mainstream schools, as well as City Technology Colleges (CTCs) and US charter schools.

Historically, academies have their roots in earlier incarnations of foundation, faith, Masonic, military, charitable, trust and independent schools, that find expression in the development of pre-government-run schooling in the eighteenth and nineteenth centuries. Their independent rights of existence, moreover, predate the inception of universal secondary education in the 1944 Education Act, including the later onset of market reform. The main policy difference today is the way academies have been separated off from LA governance and accountability, and rebranded as independent state secondary schools, funded directly by government. Despite the democratic deficit associated with academy developments, academies do not represent a break with history but rather an extension of voluntaristic and nonconformist traditions, epitomized in the English public school. It is this heritage and heterogeneity which in part explains the rival narratives and tensions that constitute New Labour's 'third way' thinking, aimed at reconciling the interests of the market with those of civic society (Blair, 1999).

If academies appear to have become schools like any other, there are significant differences between them and maintained schools (Glatter, 2009b). While the funding models and legal shifts relating to academy developments have changed, bringing them closer in line with maintained schools (e.g. admissions, special needs), there remain significant differences at two levels. First, parents and pupils have fewer rights when academies are being established, in terms of access to information, consultation and representation. Compared with setting up maintained schools the process is, according to Wolfe (Chapter 1 in this volume), less participative, less democratic, less transparent, less consultative and offers fewer safeguards. Second, he argues that 'the devil is in the detail' of the Funding Agreement for each academy, that can either facilitate or restrict changes that can bring them closer to maintained schools, or reinforce their status as independent state schools. This situation may improve or worsen with private schools, universities, church and other sponsors entering the market (Hatcher, 2006).

Although academy heads often cite the innovative potential of being freed from restrictive and overarching national frameworks that constrain maintained schools, there is no clear evidence that this translates into more innovative teaching and learning practices, or raised standards of achievement and attainment (Ofsted, 2009). Yet academies, like charter schools, are officially recognized as providing new opportunities and choices for those learners in disadvantaged areas where options are restricted by poor socioeconomic conditions, residence and access to good schooling (DFES, 2004a). Recent comparative evidence suggests that US charter schools and English academies provide only a limited alternative to locally maintained schools and that their scope is smaller and more ideologically driven (see Chapter 13 in this volume).

According to Hatcher (2008a) the apparent freedoms that academies and charter schools enjoy have, in overriding traditional community and local authority controls, been replaced by far stronger regulatory interventions by government and sponsors in the everyday running of schools. Concerns remain, for example, about the suitability of the ethos brought into the education system by self-appointed sponsors, whether or not their motivation is commercial, religious or entrepreneurial (Chitty, 2008a). By definition, sponsors bring their own values to bear in the schools they run. This has controversial implications in areas of belief, equality and diversity, including trade union recognition and workforce reform – which apply to a lesser extent in academies than maintained schools. In his evidence to the Committee of Enquiry into Academy Schools (House of Commons, 2007), Chitty cites a particular example, among others, of the danger of sponsor interest in the school curriculum:

> Because Sir Peter Vardy is a prominent evangelical Christian who believes in the theory of creationism, his academies are often quoted when we talk about 'manipulation' or 'distortion' of the curriculum. And there does seem to be cause for concern here. In July 2004, it was reported in *The Times* that Sir Peter had arranged for a document entitled "Christianity and Curriculum" to be available on the website of Emmanuel College in Gateshead. This suggested, among other things, that Britain was saved from an invasion by Adolf Hitler in 1940 by an act of God!
>
> (Chitty, 2007, p. 346)

Alongside such concerns, academies operate in broader political contexts that encourage deregulation of established and standard policy practices (Ball, 2009b). As an 'experiment' or policy condensate, the Academies Programme represents the extension of a broader public service philosophy that underpins New Labour's 'third way', that develops from the prior Conservative government's policies of privatization and cuts in public services. These policy contexts involve different levels of analysis. As Beckett

(2007) argues, academies are symbolic of a wider policy shift that blurs distinctions between welfare state and market, public and private, government and business. In this respect academies occupy one part of a subtle reworking of a mix of private and public networks within the processes of government. Drawing on urban governance theory, Hatcher, in Chapter 2 of this volume, goes further in considering the neoliberal implications of such shifts at local level. He argues that many of the contested issues surrounding academy development arise from a convergence of class interests in urban contexts that involve conflicts over the 'ownership' of education. An example of this is the handover of schools as public assets, accountable to elected local authorities – through governing bodies – to private companies, chains and sponsors (Geddes, 2008; Davies and Imbrosio, 2008). The primarily commercial and business interests associated with such change of ownership are often associated with anti-union sentiments and non-negotiable changes in teachers' working practices (Needham *et al.*, 2006).

Thus, for those sceptical about the academy initiative, which such cross-cutting themes imply, it is unlikely to reduce anxiety about experimentation with a model that takes away public accountability without clear evidence of a return. The presumption that schools will flourish through more independence from the state derives from the government's belief in independent providers of education, as in health, housing and social care, in facilitating more innovative, responsive and dynamic services than the state can provide directly. In essence it is a policy based on a mistrust of the welfare state to deliver differentiated services for the disadvantaged through uniform education and welfare provision (Pollitt, 2007). More than once 'the bog standard comprehensive school' has been held up as an example of such 'one model fits all' failure. The Academies Programme should therefore be understood in the context of a reworking of the broader public service philosophy, initiated by the Conservatives from 1979 and extended by successive New Labour governments (Le Grand, 2006). What initially started out as a means of decreasing public expenditure has, in the transformation into neoliberal policy, proved costly and socially divisive in siphoning resources away from public to private provision. The concern is that the heterogeneity of academies, and the presumptions of autonomy that underpin it, make measures of their performance and contribution to education in the wider society difficult to measure (Keep, 2004).

What works

Alongside New Labour's mantra of 'Education, education, education' runs the methodology of 'what works', a term that denotes how education policy should be guided by evidence of 'best practice' (Gorard, 2005). However, almost from the start of Labour's first term of office frustration was being expressed about the failure of educational research to help guide new Labour policies (Blunkett, 2000d). Yet despite Labour's attachment to evidence-based policy, and its faith in the power and efficiency of business, David Blunkett set such a breakneck pace in implementing academies that, according to Beckett (2007, p. 12), 'most people didn't see what was going on'. Even before completion of the PricewaterhouseCoopers (PwC) five-year evaluation study, sponsored by the government, the House of Commons Education and Skills Select Committee Report (House of Commons, 2005) argued: 'We cannot wait five years for the study. These children only get one life chance and we can't afford to wait that long before we make the radical break with the past, which academies represent'(p. 37).

The same report also went on to express concern about why the then DFES had invested substantial resources into academies 'when it had not produced the evidence' (p. 37). This assessment both served to create a climate of doubt about the full range of indicators in play, including the impact of academies on local schools, and the status of evidence-based practice being promoted by government. Lack of reliable data not only frustrated critics and supporters of academies alike, many of whom welcomed the government's desire to invest in schools serving their communities, it also made academies suspicious of established educational research, which in turn reinforced suspicion that academies had something to hide. In this climate of doubt and suspicion a mixed picture of academy development has emerged in the wider context of schooling and educational policy. This climate has been further reinforced by contradictory policies of government that embrace, on the one hand, school partnership and community participation in urban regeneration and, on the other, pressure placed on academies to demonstrate their distinctiveness from other schools, through meeting enhanced performance targets (Machin and Wilson, 2009b). The case studies cited in this volume indicate clear examples of schools trying to make progress in both areas of policy, but finding it difficult to pursue the community agenda with the same degree of vigour.

The recurring theme of tension and defensiveness has characterized academy developments since their inception. Being singled out as politically favoured institutions, with privileged funding, governance and accountability, did academies no favours. At the same time reports of academies selecting their intakes and bolstering their results in order to meet targets served only to generate further suspicion (Gorard, 2009). Such tension reflects both the stress academy schools were under to perform in the market, and the pressure on government to prove that academies were working. One consequence of this is the 'damned if they do and damned if they don't' scenario that academies confronted. If they improve results it is seen as a manipulation of intake; if they perform better than local schools they are seen to be spiriting away teachers and resources; if they innovate it is seen as locally unaccountable. If they do none of these things they are seen to be a waste of public money' (Needham *et al.*, 2006).

Whether academies work or not depends on what is meant by 'working', in terms of how they measure up to their defined roles, which are constantly changing. One approach focuses on results and performance that relate to the official *raison d'etre* of academies, in improving levels of student achievement and attainment in deprived areas (DfES, 2004a). Another involves assessment of the ideological and political impact of academies in repositioning schools in the market, in setting new ground rules for the funding, accountability and governance of schooling. The interface between the two is complex and requires understanding the contexts in which academies operate, including the competing policy assumptions which frame their diverse practices (Woods *et al.*, 2007). While the policy ground keeps shifting, evaluating academies at various stages of development, from inception to completion, stakeholder engagement, their impact on other schools and as pilots, need to be taken into account. Recent empirical research shows that since 2002 academies have produced no significantly better results than local authority schools with equivalent intakes (Gorard, 2006). Moreover there is evidence that the proportion of students from deprived backgrounds attending academies has dropped (PwC, 2008; Machin and Wilson, 2009b).

In this context, it is hardly surprising that so many commentators on academies have reached the same conclusion. Yet despite the government's proclaimed attachment to evidence-based policy, New Labour's subsequent funding and development of academies since 2005 failed to take notice of the select committee's recommendations that

> the government should ensure that the current programme of academies is thoroughly evaluated, both in respect of the performance of individual academies and the impact on neighbouring schools, before embarking on a major expansion of an untested model [and] . . . expensive schemes seem to be rolled out before being adequately tested and evaluated compared to other less expensive alternatives.
>
> (House of Commons, 2005, p. 25)

Though a concern that such 'official warnings' were not heeded by government, it is equally the case that the weight of evidence emanating from community campaigns failed to shake New Labour's faith in academy schools as they unfolded. More problematic has been the climate of secrecy that has surrounded academy development and involves not just the lack of available information but equally the promotion of selectively available data. While some of the reluctance of the DfES at the time to release information stemmed from a desire to minimize the 'goldfish-bowl' effect on some schools that had become heavily scrutinized and, in some cases, destabilized by hype and pressure. However, emerging evidence that academies were performing poorly on all of the available accountability measures increased polarization over a failing experiment that was still deemed rescuable, on grounds recommended by the House of Commons Select Committee Report (House of Commons, 2005). Somewhat paradoxically OfSTED (Office for Standards in Education) reports were making the same recommendations for academies to improve areas of practice (selection, special needs, governance) that government had previously exempted from academy provision (OfSTED, 2009). Missing in the debate, however, has been the lack of attention paid to successful comprehensive schools in deprived areas that had not gone down the academy route – and the lessons that could be learned from their experience. Such an evaluation of comprehensive schools has, according to Brighouse and Woods (2006), a significant part to play in identifying local circumstances that can inform school improvement.

While important, such measurements and contrasts between academies and maintained schools need to be understood in the broader context of public policy. According to Wilby (2009) the point of academies is political, not educational, and requires a more critical policy perspective. Part of this involves the role of academies in promoting new narratives of competitiveness and entrepreneurism; another involves their status as beacons of new rules, values and strategies, for running public services on business principles. Ball (2009b) argues that services previously undertaken by the state, increasingly replaced by private, sponsored, trust and contracted-out services, are part of a set of policy 'moves' that represent the blurring of distinctions between public and private provision. This is achieved through new rules of governance and accountability that bring together different stakeholder networks, working in diverse partnership arrangements. Yet beneath the surface run tensions within and between such networks that do not necessarily operate on an equal footing – where power and conflict over competing interests are thinly disguised (Jesson and Crossley, 2007). Such is the case with academy schools, where consensus underpinning their everyday functions are scrutinized closely in relation to their 'maintained' school partners. At one level the intended curriculum conveys powerful ambitions for creating new models of enterprise, faith and entrepreneurial learning required by the competitiveness of the British economy. At another, the means of achieving such ambitions through decommissioning local authority powers, community governance and parental participation contradict the freedoms that academies claim to uphold in improving schools in deprived areas (Beckett, 2007)

Alternative futures?

Critics of academy schools are often viewed as having no viable alternatives. However, the issue is not one of alternatives but the weak social foundations on which academy schools are built. The problem is not with academy schools *per se* but with the ideological and neoliberal underpinnings that reinforce rather than challenge deep divisions in society. There is evidence to suggest that many of the features of academies, associated with autonomy, external stakeholder participation and workforce reform are already being achieved through other models, including federations, trust schools, extended schools and training schools (Brighouse and Woods, 2006). As Glatter notes in Chapter 11, such schools do not challenge the integrity of the public system or its democratic basis in the same way that academies do. This suggests that academies are, if not a distraction, a product of their time.

Had the New Labour governments, for example, better paved the way for academy provision in deprived areas through consultation with parents, heads, teachers, unions and local authorities – as they did with the business and enterprise communities – the reception to academies may have been different (Needham *et al.*, 2006). Instead, by adopting a command and business-led approach the New Labour governments created a backlash against its policies at both structural and local levels. This was exacerbated by the government promoting rhetoric about parent power, choice and community participation while, at the same time, deconstructing democratically established procedures when setting up academies at local level. While the paradigm of school improvement through performance and independence remains dominant, little attention has been given to the building blocks of school improvement – the curriculum; pedagogy; parent, pupil, professional and community involvement – that promote learning and improved performance. Moreover, the fascination with leadership and unfettered institutional autonomy, without checks and balances, runs the risk of relegating school governance and accountability to a subsidiary function detached from school improvement, thereby reinforcing rather than alleviating deprivation and underachievement (Glatter, 2009b).

While there is evidence that schools welcome a greater degree of independence and autonomy over their affairs and benefit from it, there is no widespread evidence that heads of academies or partner schools are seeking unilateral independence from local or central government. As the findings in this volume and related research suggest (Needham *et al.*, 2006), there are important gains to be made in improving education through school, community, parent, work-based learning and government partnership, which operate on the basis of sharing resources and expertise in a high-trust environment. However, the narrow emphasis on independence, performance and results alone, without addressing ways of building new cultures of pedagogy and professionalism, is a missed opportunity. Simply rebranding primary and secondary schools as academies (Wintour and Watt, 2009), or introducing 'free' schools, will not of themselves overcome issues of competition over partnership development, shared resources or how to deal with restricted or surplus school places. Free schools, though imprecise in definition (at least in an English context), are loosely based on recent US and Swedish models that have close similarities with academies. While free schools sound progressive and inclusive, on lines associated with Summerhill and Steiner in the UK, they are anything but free. According to Anders Hultin, the chief executive of Kunskkappsskolan, a system of private Swedish schools, 75 per cent of Swedish free schools were profit-making:

> Only the profit motive will drive the level of expansion and innovation that education services require . . . most free schools were profit making, (and) been able to raise investments from the private sector and form rental agreements with private developers.[1]

In contrast with New Labour policy that remains committed to promoting academies as independent state schools, outside the maintained sector, the Conservatives have taken a step further in backing for-profit schooling (Gove, 2009, cited by Wintour, 2010). Both approaches, however, advocate models of governance and accountability that are primarily led by private sponsors, chains and providers. Recent talk of an alternative approach, designed to overcome such stark contrasts – based on a stakeholder co-operative trust model – offers a potentially more inclusive option. However, according to Millar (2010), the approach is less high trust than it appears and has a 'convoluted chain of command'. It involves a 'council' made up of different groups that appoints a trust, which then appoints a governing body – with no reference to elected representation or community ownership:

> The governance arrangements for the new Conservative 'free schools' are even more opaque. The website of the New Schools Network, the organisation that will deliver the new academies, suggests that although parents and teachers can campaign to start schools, they won't actually be running them. That potentially lucrative role will go to one of a number of recommended private providers, whose representatives coincidentally dominate both the NSN's trustee and advisory boards.
>
> (Millar, 2010)

As with academies, proposals for new variations of school provision based on for- and not-for-profit schooling, coincide with cuts in public services and moves to initiate charging for schooling and health. Instead of offering high trust provision that invites parents and communities to participate in new forms of school governance, the reality is one of redirecting public funds to private providers. This is being achieved through the auspices of charitable trusts that facilitate commercially minded sponsors (faith, religious, business) rather than elected representatives, with unfettered access to the private governance of the nations' schools. This shift in both capital and power in the 'ownership' of education – what is taught and learned – draws attention to a recurring theme in this volume. It concerns the nature and purpose of education in civic society, and how schools embody, reflect and critically engage with society.

The message sent by Labour and Conservatives about academies and other initiatives is mixed, controversial and unproven: it encourages the involvement of private for- and not-for-profit organisations that offer little political or parental accountability, or real partnership (see Chapters 2 and 3 in this volume). The message both intensifies concerns about the long-term impact of private sponsorship on schooling and the erosion of local autonomy and independence – values shared by academy supporters and their critics – by corporate takeover. The essential dilemma remains one of the suitability of education provision by self-selecting sponsors with particular commercial or religious interests that allow them to bring their own values and influence to bear on the schools they own and run, including the curriculum, teaching and learning conditions of pupils and teachers. For parents the process of school choice is more problematic when faced with rival value systems that are often affected by asymmetries of local supply, information and the lottery of choice that affect options, or no choice at all (Wrigley, 2006b).

Ironically Conservative pledges and cross-party support to lift obstacles, including local authority planning laws, that stand in the way of building new schools will further exacerbate this problem. It is likely to restrict parental choice by closing more schools than can be opened, thereby paradoxically reducing market options, funding and resources still further. Redefining choice and provision this way has profound implications for the way government enables society to accommodate diverse interests and cultural values that demand greater, rather than less governance, regarding the purpose of education in a plural society. While longitudinal data on academy performance will ultimately play an important part in determining academies success, it is alone unlikely to settle the political and ideological matter conclusively:

> Despite 20 years of data on Charter Schools, critics and supporters of the model continue to trade statistics. This highlights three limitations to assuming that longitudinal data will answer as to whether academies are a successful policy initiative. First, rival research methodologies will continue to produce conflicting data about school performance. Second, the

> criteria for success will continue to be disputed – in particular, how such accountability to parents and local communities should be surrendered in order to improve performance. Third, the contested data is likely to reflect a genuine heterogeneity in the cases, with averages concealing more than they reveal. Even with only a small number of academies, issues of diversity are crucially important and require further attention.
>
> (Needham *et al.*, 2006, p. 60)

One way round this is for government to initiate debate that separates off academies from commercial interests and actively includes *all* interested parties in future debates about new school developments. This will need to ensure that academy and maintained schools share parity regarding parental and community participation in governing bodies. In support of this process school funding in deprived areas requires differential funding for local rather than selected pilot schools. While supporting experimental approaches there is a need to promote freedom of information and transparency in new school developments, instead of the secrecy that has bypassed established equality and diversity policies, including workforce legislation (see Glees, 2005). Do co-operative trust and free school models possess the potential to incorporate such consensual requirements into their practices? Under New Labour up to 100 trusts with co-operative governance arrangements were considered (DCSF, 2008b; 2009a) with cross-party support. Much depends on whether the uptake will follow the academy model, or one based on greater parent and community participation. According to Glatter (2009b) such a model, if successfully implemented, offers a different democratically based schooling system, that includes significant elements of downward and lateral accountability. It also provides an alternative approach to the recent proposal from a government Minister that the best way to extend the Academies Programme to all schools would be to scrap the £2 million sponsorship entry fee – forgetting that such a measure is by default already in place. The concern remains that despite the rhetoric of parental choice and community participation driving education reform, the reality is one of the historic failure of those in power to enact popular participation in local policy-making. The irony is not in the gap between rhetoric and reality but the inefficiency of the neoliberal project to implement market policies without recourse to the use of highly centralist powers that generate far greater costs and controls than those they seek to replace.

Conclusion

To judge academies simply on the criteria of what works, measured in terms of attainment and achievement, misses the point of who and what academies are for. The issue is not that academies *per se* are the problem but rather the direction government policy is taking for *all* schools. Moreover, it is also unfair to blame academies for practices that some maintained schools engage in. On the one hand, it is possible to view the academy initiative as a highly progressive attempt to improve educational attainment in some of the weakest schools in the country. On the other, the history of academies could be construed as one in which powerful sponsors, with their own agendas and design, were handed public assets (and allegedly offered and given honours) that allowed them to define intakes, own schools and decide results. If parents are forced to choose between rival value systems in their choice of schools, rather than being able to trust their local school to equip their child to be a discerning citizen in a pluralistic society, academies will continue to lack credibility. The danger is that academies offer only a limited view of citizenship if they continue to operate outside wider systems of public accountability. Keep (2005) has likened such experimentation to a 'train set' model of policy-making that involves tinkering with other peoples lives and assets, without recourse.

To say that academies are doing no better than their non-academy peers is not to dismiss them. However, this does suggest that the political *raison d'etre* of academies is in question, both in terms of the resources expended on them (time, money, effort and energy) and the rather narrow measure of Key Stage 4 outcomes that are used to assess their performance (Gorard, 2009). In the meantime, the way the academies experiment has affected the students passing through them, and the displacement effect of academies on local schools, has been problematic (Ofsted, 2009). While resources could have been allocated differently in all deprived areas, the presumptions of institutional autonomy that underpin academies does little to rectify existing market differentiation within and between schools (NAO, 2007). Recent proposals from the Conservatives to extend parental choice and school performance by turning all high-Ofsted-rated schools into academies, or encouraging parents and communities to set up their own free schools, will do little to improve school choice without addressing the democratic deficit:

> Perhaps the most telling verdict on the Academy Programme comes from US Charter School advocate Chester Finn in response to a question from a British trade unionist . . . Told that the American Policy would soon be replicated in Britain, Finn replied that his inspiration had in fact been the old grant-maintained schools that New Labour abolished. If that remark is taken seriously, it would appear that, alongside the great expansion in school funding, Tony Blair's legacy may turn out to be having taken British education back to where he found it.
>
> (Needham *et al.*, 2006, p. 62)

With recession and cuts in public expenditure underway the wider implications of rectifying anomalies between 'winning' and 'losing' schools will not be affected by a relatively small number of academies and 'free' schools. In a recent report by the Specialist Schools and Academies Trust (Jesson and Crossley, 2007) there is recognition that there are other ways to achieve school success than becoming academies, on lines advocated in this volume. However, missing in much of this debate is the growing gap between rich and poor (Rowntree, 2009), demonstrating that poverty remains a key contributor to pupil underachievement and school failure (Raffo *et al.*, 2010). This inevitably endorses Bernstein's reminder that education alone 'cannot compensate for society' if it is not integrated within wider policies of equity, diversity and social justice (Bernstein, 1970). While those who believe that the academy experiment requires more time to prove itself, the evidence suggests that, as products of their time, their time is now up.

Acknowledgement

This chapter is based on research carried out with Catherine Needham, Brendan Martin and Rose Rickford, sponsored by the National Association of Schoolmasters Union of Women Teachers, with Catalyst and Public World. I am grateful to my colleagues and partners for allowing me to draw on, summarize and update material for this chapter from the report *Academy Schools: Case Unproven*, published in 2006.[2]

Notes

1 From a speech at the Spectator Education Conference, London, cited by Wintour, 2010, www.guardian.co.uk, 4 March 2010. Accessed 5 March 2010.

2 Available at: www.teachersunion.org.uk

Conclusion: Public Education and Academies

Helen M. Gunter

The score card?

Tony Blair's ambitions for the Academies Programme is encapsulated by his declaration that 'in a few years time when all schools will be Academies, we'll see a transformed education system' (Northampton Academy, n.d.). As the 2010 general election approaches there are challenges to the programme that will need to be addressed by an incoming administration: first, while the private sector promised and signed up for sponsorship they have actually delivered 'barely two-thirds of the £145m they are supposed to have paid towards capital costs in the seven years since the first of England's 200 Academies opened' (Mansell, 2009b, p. 1). Hence the notion and realization of sponsorship as a form of democratic renewal has to be questioned. Second, Ofsted (Office for Standards in Education) inspections of 30 academies in 2008–9 show that 'a considerable number of Academies remain below the government GCSE floor target for at least 30% of pupils to achieve five or more higher-grade GCSE passes, including English and mathematics' (Ofsted, 2009, p. 33). The idea that private sponsorship can do what the local authority failed to do and that the solution to 'failing' schools (as in the National Challenge strategy) is to turn them into academies has to be questioned. Third, it seems that academies are expected to deliver dramatic and speedy changes to student outcomes, in ways that are about justifying the policy politically as being worth the investment. The Secretary of State has made it clear that

> even though Academies are found disproportionately in the poorest areas, our expectations are not lower for Academies, they are higher for Academies. And we put a lot of investment into making sure that they deliver. We won't be softer on Academies.
>
> (Curtis, 2009, n.p.)

The political as distinct from the educational purposes of academies has to be questioned. In some ways this echoes what Edwards *et al.* (1992) said about the City Technology Colleges (CTCs) initiative, which was rushed and subjected to short-term planning, where 'many of the changes have been enforced and expedient ways of sustaining an initiative that it would have been embarrassing to abandon' (p. 102).

So in using New Labour's own measure of a scorecard, the chapters in this book, like Curtis *et al.* (2009), show that there are clearly some gains – with new provision and buildings – but also some serious and troubling issues. Each of the chapters stands alone with a specific remit and narrative regarding an aspect of the Academies Programme, but together the collection is a robust set of thinking and analysis that has things to say about systemic change and the role of the state. Specifically the evidence from this collection shows that:

- Major interventions in the legal framework of schooling have been shown by Wolfe (in Chapter 1) to have generated complexities and anomalies, and that parents of children in academies have less legal protection than those in maintained schools.
- In locations where the Academies Programme has generated debate and action there is evidence from Elliott (Chapter 3), Hatcher (Chapter 2) and Purcell (Chapter 4) that this major intervention into families and communities has revealed a demand for community participation, but the processes show and have exacerbated a democratic deficit.
- The establishment of academies opens up tensions between mainstream schooling and the academy, where Daniels shows (in Chapter 6) how such a new venture depends on knowledge, together with staffing and leadership that has been trained and developed, from within the maintained sector. Indeed Dyson and Rowley (Chapter 5) demonstrate the contradictions involved in setting up an academy in regard to the demands for both autonomy and partnerships, but within this ask whether there are approaches to sponsorship that might offer new thinking about the link between sponsors and the community.
- The authors of the PricewaterhouseCoopers (PwC) report not only outline the gains and areas that academies need to continue to work on, but also Larsen, Bunting and Armstrong (Chapter 7) identify that the longitudinal impact of academies will need tracking, particularly the way that individual schools impact on the local provision of education. Gorard (Chapter 8) and Wrigley (Chapter 9) evidence limited improvements compared with predecessor schools as well as serious damage to the curriculum. There are concerns about whether delivery and outputs make the investment worth it and whether children are being denied access to the type of curriculum that the schools they are named after (i.e. independent) provide.
- Analysis of governance by Ball (Chapter 10) shows that new forms of

networks as 'heterarchies' are developing where educational problems are reconfigured with business solutions. Glatter (Chapter 11) makes the case that rewarding schools through giving more autonomy and the ambiguities in the status of 'independence' has generated stresses and strains on the education 'system' where equity is being jeopardized.
- The globalization of the ideas outlined by Caldwell (Chapter 12), and examples of neoliberal-generated education policies in the United States presented by Goldring and Mavrogordato (Chapter 13), shows how pragmatic and hence how problematic innovation based on 'travelling' policies can be. While policy texts can look rational and coherent, it seems that decentralized systems are locally based and hence neoliberal ideas and solutions need to be critically examined. Gleeson (Chapter 14) draws together themes from within and across the chapters to show how evaluation of academies is not so much based on whether they work as to whether the reform of publicly funded education is heading in the appropriate direction.

As I come to the close of this collection there is a need to put this emerging evidence about the Academies Programme into the bigger picture and examine what it says about the relationship between the state, civil society and educational reform. In order to do this I am drawing on the conceptual work developed with colleagues regarding policy and knowledge production (Gunter *et al.*, 2010; Raffo and Gunter, 2008). From this I have deployed a conceptual architecture in order to locate the Academies Programme, where I begin with an examination of the purposes of schools. I then go on to provide a rationale for the argument by drawing on Ozga and Dale (1991) with an examination of *sources* or where policy comes from; second, *scope* or what the policy aims to achieve; and third, *patterns* or how the exercise of power operates within policy practices and cultures.

The purposes of schools

Developing perspectives about the Academies Programme needs to be located in an understanding of the purposes of education and schools: why put children of a certain age, for a prescribed number of hours and days, into a building staffed by adults trained in teaching and learning? How should education and schools be funded and controlled? In other words, why should the population as a whole fund the education of children? Such questions are located in arguments about how as a society we want to live together and make arrangements for the development of the population as citizens, as workers, and, as users and custodians of our cultural, political, economic, social, and intellectual resources. These are not matters that citizens routinely deal with every day, but the Academies Programme is a site that prompts such thinking. While strict binaries can be unhelpful, particularly since drawing boundaries can lead to essentializing in ways that disguise debates, I would argue that in reading research and theorizing about education there are two main positions. These positions are labelled as the *neoliberal* and the *civic* (Gunter *et al.*, 2010), where there is sufficient distinction to demonstrate that projects have been framed with consequent discourses in play. Newman and Clarke (2009) helpfully describe this as 'assemblages' that they identify as the 'work of enrolling ideas, images, agents, organisations, devices and technologies into something that is presented as coherent, integrated and logical' (p. 180).

By *civic* I mean that learning has a purpose that is about both individual and social development, and is about enculturating the learner with core values regarding how their agency is in ongoing negotiation with wider structural responsibilities regarding their role as citizen. As Marquand (2004) argues about the public domain:

> [I]t is a space for forms of human flourishing which cannot be bought in the market-place or found in the tight-knit community of the clan or family or group of intimates . . . In it, citizenship rights trump both market power and kinship or neighbourhood bonds; the duties of citizenship take precedence both over market incentives and over private loyalties.
> (pp. 27–8)

The debates about this within education tend to be about democratic development, how teachable moments can be recognized and used to think through difficult issues, and how choices can be open to scrutiny and through open dialogue strategies can be agreed. The projects generated from this position include, for example, secondary education for all, comprehensive education and the expansion of higher education. However, while gains have been made, reform was necessary regarding the need to challenge the impact of elites on the system. The system became overloaded, with increased demands for resources, and professionals didn't always clearly articulate a defendable model of practice to the public. Consequently, projects as dominant solutions have tended to be from the neoliberal position where private sector structures and cultures have been used to modernize education, particularly to attack teacher professionalism. Such critiques (for example, of teachers and their work as self-interested provider capture) spoke to the ordinary person as taxpayer and worker (Apple, 2006). Ultimately those who located themselves in the civic position did not fully grasp the full extent of the assault on democratic values and ways of life or how what was regarded as settled (for example, local governance of education through locally elected councillors) clearly was not. In spite of this intellectual work has continued, where Carr and Hartnett (1996) and

Ranson (1993; 1995) present education as a public good that is fundamentally changed for the worse when markets are introduced. Exiting the school market, as different from exiting a shop without making a purchase, would create a situation where 'a community is denied the possibility of clarifying its needs and priorities that are monitored, revisable and accountable to the public' (Ranson, 1993, p. 339). Indeed, Newman and Clarke (2009) report that even if the public are dissatisfied with a public service, it does not mean that they want services to be like a private business.

The language and claims made about the Academies Programme has some connections with the civic project, and hence the role of the state is to both regulate and invest. The former to secure accountability, and the latter to ensure that public education is resourced, notably so that parents who cannot exit can access a high-quality education and parents who can exit do not take this course of action because the local school meets their needs (Mandelson and Liddle, 1996). However, on balance the Academies Programme is a project that is deeply located in the value system of the neoliberal position where there is a clear rejection of public institutions because 'democratic control normally produces ineffective schools' (Chubb and Moe, 1990, p. 227) and the real problem with state education is the state (Tooley 1995; 1996). Markets are promoted as positive and productive spaces for individual choice where the parent and/or child as consumer can invest because 'human well-being can best be advanced by liberating individual entrepreneurial freedoms and skills within an institutional framework characterized by strong private property rights, free markets, and free trade' (Harvey, 2007, p. 2).

So equity is about enabling 'hard-working families' to choose the education they want for their children, with schools having 'strong leadership from heads and a distinctive ethos of their own' (Mandelson and Liddle, 1996, p. 94). It is argued that markets can bring what Marshall (2008) from ARK identifies as: first, 'contestability' where competition (or even the threat of competition) challenges the monopoly providers to improve; second, 'innovation and experimentation' where the 'system (can be) brought to life by the contrasting visions of multiple sponsors and providers'; and third, 'rapid transmission of best practice' so that schools will behave like 'companies (who) constantly try to learn from and improve upon their competitors' (p. 73). Astle (2008) goes further by arguing for a shift from the 'take over' model in the Academies Programme towards a 'start-up' model, as evidenced in Sweden. Here new schools can be established 'at a time and in the place of their choosing' and 'they are entering the system not to replace, but to compete with, existing schools' (p. 84). However, all the evidence so far shows (see Chapter 14 in this volume) that when markets are opened up it is the already advantaged who gain: 'to succeed, efforts to create an education marketplace must necessarily seek to remove control of schools from the communities they serve' (Molnar, 2006, p. 635). Finally, evidence from studies of private sector companies (e.g. Stacey, 1992) and recent experience of the 2008/09 crash, shows that companies fail and that the public may have to rescue vital services through resources and nationalization.

The Academies Programme is an example of a neoliberal project because it is based on private interests marginalizing the public domain. So what is presented as 'new', 'modern' and 'radical' is in effect highly conservative. This is because the Academies Programme is an illustration of:

- A failure to engage in democratic renewal because public institutions such as local authorities have been either excluded or turned into managerial commissioners of services: 'in effect, more and more of public policy and public decision-making is out-of-reach, either deeply entrenched in the Jacobin centre or elusively contracted-out among various private, voluntary or parastatal organisations and groups' (Ball, 2005, pp. 215–16). Indeed while the rhetoric is about partnerships and networks who through common sense management can be liberated to deliver the right type of teaching and learning, in reality what is emerging is a form of 'institutionalised governance' (Gunter and Forrester, 2009). The models of governance explained by Newman (2001) and outlined in the Introduction have produced a complex and confusing situation, and so within education the government is ensuring it can control academies through the hierarchy of public institutions such as the department, No. 10 Downing Street, the NCSL (National College for Leadership of Schools and Children's Services) and the SSAT (Specialist Schools and Academies Trust), but at the same time it needs and constructs networks of people to help with design and delivery. Regulation of governance is through the legality of contracts (such as Funding Agreements) combined with the promotion and rewarding of New Labour dispositions.
- How private interests dominate in the construction and implementation of the Academies Programme, which 'risks the creation of pedagogy of the possessed where the nature of citizen's educational experience is determined by those who can afford the purchase power' (Wilkinson, 2007, p. 268). Consequently, personal beliefs about faith, teaching, leadership and general views on how children should be raised, are given precedence because a person has wealth and/or connections with those in government. A huge financial investment has been made in courting and securing private involvement, and discourses around the normality and legitimacy of individual philanthropy or the 'diversity' that can be provided by religious groups controlling education have been accepted by the government as essential for public service provision (Beckett, 2008b).

- How the curriculum and school ethos is being redesigned to enable capitalist accumulation through the domination of entrepreneurialism as a normalized and logical way of life. Notably, this is being secured through forms of faith-based morality as a means of tempering the potential charges of training children to aspire to be greedy. So as long as a sponsor can show that they have a preferred belief system then 'doing good' is accepted as a means of indoctrinating children. This is not just through control of teaching and learning, but also through the new buildings that 'look like City offices' rather than schools (Wrigley, 2009, p. 51). Indeed, the Thomas Deacon City Academy in Peterborough is a place where the business of learning is a strong feature as it has been built without a playground because, as the headteacher states, the 'pupils won't need to let off steam because they will not be bored', and where it seems that 'those running it believe that pupils should be treated like company employees and do not need unstructured play time' (Hackett, 2007).
- The elevation of private interests based on personal wealth and cultural capital means that parents may not have the choices that they are promised and lack the institutional power of voting to secure accountability. As evidence in this book shows, local residents may not want the choice on offer, and because decision-making is out of reach then 'the only space for activist parents or "community organisers" or "political mothers" . . . within this policy is as opponents and that is where they find their authenticity' (Ball, 2005, p. 220).

I would argue that there are three main reasons for the ongoing domination of the neoliberal position with projects such as the Academies Programme. First, the *sources* of policy development are located in functionalist rather than socially critical knowledge claims; second, the *scope* of policy is based on imaginings of teaching and learning as products to be bought and sold; and third, the *patterns* of policy show the continued dominance of elite interests based on private wealth and networked associations.

Sources

The sources of the Academies Programme as a neoliberal project is complex but the roots can be traced to what Ozga and Dale (1991) identify. First, through the electoral mandate New Labour took office with a landslide victory of 418 seats, determined to speedily implement an agenda. Second, New Labour gave precedence in civil society to business entrepreneurs, and to think tanks that promoted neoliberal projects, specifically the ongoing attack on comprehensive education. Third, New Labour put emphasis on the production of human capital and education as an economic resource. What dominates thinking and policy strategy is how choice and personalization are framed as co-production as a consumer rather than as a citizen (see PMSU, 2006). Diversity is characterized in this way, and, as Barber (2007) has stated, it is outcomes and not the provider that matters, and so anyone can provide and the state will ensure that the conditions of provision do not prevent entry into the market.

What is crucial to understanding the sources of the Academies Programme is the form and practice of knowledge production. As Harvey (2005) argues, neoliberalism is both ideological and political, but the latter has dominated. Hence in education the market utopia does not always lead to projects (e.g. vouchers) and the links between projects and ideals may be unclear (e.g. national curriculum), and so the politics of change can be messy, contradictory and appear pragmatic. As Gray (2010) argues, 'in order to criticise neoliberal ideology, one must first reconstruct it' (p. 52). The types of knowledge drawn upon and the ways of knowing are a combination of both the traditional and the functional. By traditional I mean knowledge that is based on experience and beliefs, often presented as reasonable and in ways that can be difficult to challenge. By functional I mean the tendency to categorize people (poor, women, people of colour, disabled), which 'not only assume an equivalence of oppressions that ignores the specific historical roots on each, but also assumes that the categories are somehow mutually exclusive' (Newman, 2007, p. 40). So knowledge, or rather 'know-how', is about removing any dysfunctions so that the system can work better, through an emphasis on delivery and outcome measurements. Though much of the hard-edged rationality of management by targets has been made more palatable through drawing on common-sense notions of a life worth leading. Functionality is attractive because it is presented as neutral where consultants and policy advisers such as Sir Cyril Taylor, formerly of the SSAT, have served both Conservative and Labour administrations (Baker, 2009).

Scope

In launching the CTCs in 1986 the then Secretary of State for Education, Kenneth Baker, made the next wave of reform explicit:

> Education can no longer be led by the producers – by the academic theorists, the administrators or even the teachers' unions. Education must be shaped by the users, by what is good for the individual child and what hopes are held by their parents.
>
> (cited in Whitty *et al.*, 1993, p. 1)

This is very familiar, as such understandings dominate the Academies Programme and the wider New Labour strategy:

> But the key to education today is to personalise learning, to recognise different children have different abilities and in different subjects. However, personalising learning is not just about a distinctive approach to every child, it is reflected in a distinctive approach also to every school.
>
> (Blair, 2007b, p. 6)

The scope of the Academies Programme is 'framed by conceptions of what is desirable and possible for education systems to achieve' (Ozga and Dale, 1991, p. 14). Following Ozga (2005) such imaginings as speeches, emails, books, web resources, can travel to a site where there is an embedded situation that impacts on the development of what could be done. A global discourse attacking 'big' government and promoting markets has been travelling across national boundaries with comparisons between initiatives in the US with school reform projects in England (see Whitty *et al.*, 1993). It seems that such travelling is facilitated by 'a common policy community' (Whitty *et al.*, 1993, p. 166), the circulation of particular texts with the popularization of ideas (Saint-Martin, 2001; Tomlinson, 2001), and the ways in which the global economy is changing to a post-industrial model with an ever-trainable, ever-deployable, ever-disposable workforce. Reform projects tended to act 'as a source of confirmation rather than a direct model' (Whitty *et al.*, 1993, p. 166) and so policy ideas can be inspiring or provide 'what works' case study evidence rather than be borrowed lock, stock and barrel (Whitty and Edwards, 1998).

In England the school has been imagined as a firm, but reform has not been smooth or linear, with short-term trials such as CTCs and GMS (Grant Maintained Status) schools or area-specific developments such as EAZs (Education Action Zones). However, while there may have been project failures, they did, according to Walford (2000), have an importance that outweighed their reach. Specifically, such projects enabled:

- the establishment of funded educational provision as 'independent' and outside the public institutions of local governance
- the strengthening of state funding for faith-based education
- the promotion of a small-business culture through the location of the school within a quasi market combined with sponsorship and bidding
- the use of the reform project to disrupt the system through the major programmatic experiments in ways that signalled the intention to bring widespread change
- the control of the curriculum through direct investment in technology, and through both niche marketing as specialist status and central control of the product through the national curriculum
- the emphasis on renewal and regeneration through investment in education with the CTCs in urban areas and through parent power for GM schools

- the rhetoric of 'new times' that demanded a new workforce and so new methods by which to train, prepare and enculturate young people.

New Labour had learned from previous projects that: first, GMS floundered because of complex opting-out ballots that have not been a feature of the Academies Programme (Regan, 2007); and second, much of what has been done in the Academies Programme has been trialled before and even if it has failed before, and might fail again, it is enabled through manipulating the dispositions and activities of those charged with the responsibility of delivery (see McLeod, 1988).

Patterns

According to Ozga and Dale (1991) the patterns in the way power is structured and exercised is shaped by 'the *context*, the *conditions* and the *resources* within which education policy and practice related to each other' (p. 28, emphasis in original). The analysis presented so far has shown that the Academies Programme is located in ways of knowing and types of knowledge that enable existing powerful interests to not only remain but also to strengthen, and that the scope of this policy strategy is to challenge locally embedded ways of living to enable people to accept neoliberal ways of being in the world. Consequently, local areas are characterized using a globalizing discourse and lexicon as 'in challenging circumstances' and schools are 'failing' children and parents in order to accept the narratives of elite people and/or organizations who have the financial and cultural resources to 'improve' education and the school, and that the time is right for such a 'transformation'.

This is illustrated by participation in decision-making, where the emphasis is on the elite person or organization to be involved rather than the local citizen. The evidence in this book and other reports show that all the politicking is with the potential funders and that local events tend to be choreographed in ways that limit dialogue and so lead to local protests by children and parents. Hence participation is not so much about community roles and voting, but privatization is about the trading contract between the sponsor and the parent, with the government at national and local level as broker. What is happening is what Hatcher (2006) calls 'reagenting', where the old elites known as 'club culture' (see Introduction) are being reworked, new alliances formed, and new power elites are emerging nationally in the form of academy chains as well as looser networks and alliances with the SSAT and the NCSL, and locally through business and community networks cultivated to establish and sustain the academy. In this way the purpose of sponsorship is to act as a suturing device between policy requirements and powerful private interests in order 'to inject a new agency into the schools to align them with government agendas' (Hatcher, 2006, p. 612).

Making sense of policies as they unfold is, as Edwards *et al.* (1992) argue, difficult because of the need to chart and describe, as well as seek to explain through robust theorizing. Certainly this is the case with the Academies Programme because the intentions behind this initiative (as this book has illustrated) have been bold and contested, and as the programme has developed with ongoing iterations, concerns and direct opposition have been generated from within and outside (see House of Commons, 2009). What the Academies Programme is therefore illustrative of is what Pollitt (2007) describes as 'New Labour's redisorganisation' as a form of 'accelerated disruption' (p. 540) in ways that lead to 'a general loss of faith in stability and an accompanying diminution of willingness to fully commit oneself to a particular organisation' (p. 539).

Where do we go from here?

Clarke (2009) argues that

> crises always emerge as constructed, narrated and temporalised events and times. It is impossible to arrive at an 'innocent' view of crisis, since crises are always already defined and constructed as (potentially) governable objects [and] . . . crisis time also summons and empowers would-be managers or governors of the crisis – those who can intervene to protect, defend or restore.
>
> (p. 14)

He further argues that this enables particular ideas and solutions to be prominent, and enables ongoing truths to be communicated and recirculated in ways that make ideas favourable. Hence I am mindful of the potential for much politicking regarding the origins and current state of play in the 'education crisis'. The neoliberal positioning and the emerging projects have framed a crisis (with the drama of evil teachers and bureaucrats, and the sponsor as saviour) and those located in the civic position are on the back foot, where it remains challenging to present an alternative because of ongoing accusations of playing a 'politics of nostalgia' (Clarke and Newman, 2009). Angus (2004) is helpful by arguing that 'if we wish to find "spaces" for resisting and challenging dominant discourses and agendas, we need also to investigate the ways in which we knowingly and unknowingly comply with those discourses and agendas and help accomplish them' (Angus, 2004, p. 40). This raises questions for everyone, particularly the research community and how projects are designed and funded. It seems that neoliberal projects have been thoroughly researched (e.g. Ball, 2007), but, as Chapter 14 shows, the Academies Programme has generated lone academics or small groups who are often undertaking small-scale or even unfunded scholarly activity. There is a need for major research to examine the numerous experiments in education and this is fertile territory for the social sciences as theories of the state, governance and the public domain can be developed through studies of educational reform. However, there is a huge challenge: who funds independent research when significant funds are in the hands of government and competition for projects is becoming more intense as research councils face cuts? And, how does the research community enable their findings to be in the public domain and how are the public to engage to enable the very dialogue that is necessary?

While we may live and work in new dark times, the need for scholarly thinking and projects remains strong. The chapters in this book show that while the Academies Programme is meant to be about education and equity it seems that it is a political project where the economically advantaged are sustained; while rapid reform is meant to be in the interests of children, they are actually the objects of reform rather than active participants and, while choice is meant to be at the heart of the new schools, it seems that large numbers of people have been alienated. So a research imperative can be recognized through three main interlinked themes generated by the emerging evidence: the equity gap, role of children and democracy.

Wilkinson and Pickett's (2009) book *The Spirit Level* makes the equity gap visible, where it seems that educational standards do not float free of social, economic and political contexts. They argue that the issue of equity is not just something for the poor but impacts on everyone:

> National standards of health, and of other important outcomes . . . are substantially determined by the amount of inequality in society. If you want to know why one country does better or worse than another, the first thing to look at is the extent of inequality. There is not one policy for reducing inequality in health or the educational performance of school children, and another for raising national standards of performance. Reducing inequality is the best way of doing both. And if, for instance, a country wants higher average levels of educational achievement among its school children, it must address the underlying inequality which creates a steeper social gradient in educational achievement.
>
> (pp. 29–30)

The gap between rich and poor is widening with consequences for social harmony, health and general welfare. It seems that the problem of poverty should be integral with the problem of excessive wealth: '[N]or should we allow ourselves to believe that the rich are scarce and precious members of a superior race of more intelligent beings on whom the rest of us are dependent. That is merely the illusion that wealth and power create' (p. 262).

Consequently, if as a country we want to deal with educational standards and outcomes, then we need to begin with the economic and social system that produces the schools that academies were meant to improve on. The solution is not to fabricate the illusion of private privileged education through 'independence', but to examine how as a nation we want to fund the education of our children.

A second issue is children, and to illuminate this I want to begin with a story from the northern comedian, Peter Kay's, autobiography (2006), where he 'hated Mr Lawson' and, in particular, his enforcement of the school rule that coats should not be worn indoors:

> So one night, after school, myself and a few of the other lads called into a jumble sale on the way home and bought a load of ladies' coats three sizes too small . . . Bright and early next morning the seven of us turned the corner in our brand new old coats. It was like the opening scene from *Reservoir Dogs* as we strolled past the convent in slow motion. I was particularly fond of my pink PVC ladies mac with its matching tie belt and press studs. And sure enough, as we approached the gates, Mr Lawson swooped into position with a smug grin all over his fat face. He held out his hand and without even arguing we took off our coats and handed them over. Lawson was loving it . . . But we were in for the long con and three months later on the last day of term we tasted victory ourselves when we saw a furious Lawson staggering round the convent gardens carrying a mountain of ladies' coats. 'Well, they must belong to somebody', he repeatedly said to passing pupils whilst attempting to hand them a pink PVC mac. They just walked off mystified.
>
> (pp. 51–2)

This is the stuff of real schools. It was so in the 1980s when Kay was at school and, based on my observation when recently visiting an academy and a maintained school, the issue of coats as a symbol of the dominant and dominated remains. The neoliberal position would read the Kay story as one that illustrated the arrogance of professionals, and the need to use functional know-how to remove this dysfunction, not least by training teachers to deal with children as customers. Furthermore, if this school became an academy then rhetoric would be that the right type of teachers and curriculum would be on offer to parents and pupils who had actively chosen to have a better education. The patterns of power where decisions about coats had been relocated to a sponsor-controlled school would enable the right decision to be made on behalf of children. However, the potential for Kay to be just as disillusioned in 2010 as he clearly was in the mid 1980s remains, largely because there is no independent research evidence published that academies are positioning children any differently now than they were then.

The civic position would not only trouble Kay's experience but also ask about those who conform, particularly how the testing and target regime may seriously damage 'successful' children (Smyth, 2006). Evidence shows that children can be actively involved in making decisions about policy and practice in matters of choice (Walford, 1991) and policy (Thomson and Gunter, 2006). So there is a different type of future to be imagined and developed, where Touraine (2000) argues that 'we have to conceive and construct new forms of collective and personal life' (p. 15). There is a need to rebuild schools with and around children, and teachers need to develop an approach to practice that is defendable and trusted, in fact 'the independence of teachers, like the independence of the judiciary, is an essential pre-condition for the existence of democracy, whose primary task is to restrict the power of the state and social powers of all kinds' (p. 285). How democracy and professional expertise engage with each other, so that there is a respect for knowledge and practice, and for accountability is what needs our attention.

The third issue for research is the need to examine democratic renewal. That academies can be the only choice within a town is inconsistent with policy rhetoric and does not sit well with people securing control of their lives and services. Lets take the issue of admissions that has been shown to be problematic with claims of unfairness (Powell-Davies, 2008) and recognition that more than one system in operation may create complexity and confusion (PwC, 2008; West *et al.*, 2009). It seems that the rhetoric of choice as aspirational may help some children gain through new provision, but overall research evidence suggests that such selection is a 'trend in reverse' (Edwards and Whitty, 1997, p. 12) and that inequalities have been strengthened (Gorard and Taylor, 2001; Whitty *et al.*, 1993). So if we want to have good education for *all* children then we need to have a system where the interplay between the national mandate, local governance and professionals is re-designed. In doing this we need to work for political debate and activity as essential to our social and economic fabric, and as Stoker (2006) argues we have to upfront the often disappointing nature of democratic decision-making because we might not get our personal choice because the public good demands something different. So the health of our democracy depends on the public understanding and accepting this as a possibility and working for change through dialogue and political institutions. Perhaps the rehabilitation of dependency as a civic virtue would enable the stresses and strains of school admissions to be handled better so that all parents and children can rely on a good school in their neighbourhood. It could well be that as Rowley and Dyson suggest, in this volume, there are possibilities within new forms of partnerships, including new types of sponsors, for thinking differently about how the community is linked to educational provision.

While localism is vital to this agenda, what is public and what is local is open to contest (Newman, 2007). Stoker (2006) argues that our aspirations about political engagement needs to be realistic:

> Most people don't want to spend all their time on politics, they cannot and would not wish to claim the depth of knowledge and understanding available to experts, they are comfortable with a division of labour. They want to engage directly over the issues that are most salient to them but would prefer to rely on the judgements of representatives and activists over most issues, most of the time. The challenge of the twenty-first century is to design a political system that can more readily meet those aspirations. (p. 151)

The Academies Programme shows that when people are affected by decisions then they do engage, but it is a policy that is designed to appeal to self-interest, and so provokes opposition from some rather than to enable agreement. Consequently there are wider issues at stake regarding the political system, cultures and practices that require a new settlement. This involves matters such as local and regional government in England, the campaign for an English parliament with at least the same rights as Scotland, and electoral reform. Models can still come from business, where mutuality holds out possibilities for democratic development in the way that John Lewis-style partnerships operate in retailing (Stratton, 2009). But models can and should come from civic ideals and projects regarding working for a better society, and education is a good starting point, where autonomy for a school should no longer be used as a reward for delivery and compliance (Glatter, 2009b).

Consideration of these issues means that, in Apple's (2006) terms, what might a research agenda designed to 'interrupt' neoliberal projects look like? Here are some suggestions to enable and stimulate dialogue:

1. Following Vidovich's (2007) call to follow Ozga's (2000) statement that 'I want to remove policy from its pedestal' (p. 2), there is a need to shift our gaze from what the policy elites are doing, and interlink it with the realities of classrooms and school life. There is a need for more case studies of schools, and in particular of local authority mainstream schools. Interlinked with this is a need to examine the impact of the promotion of 'business values and attitudes' (Hatcher, 2008b) on children and whether human capital development as required by business has been developed through business dominating schools.
2. Wilkinson (2007) says that there are arguments 'that flexibility, inventiveness and dynamism are the preserve of business, faith groups and

charities whilst public sector professionals are regarded as impediments to reform' (p. 274). So there is a need to re-examine the nature of professionalism in terms of expertise and practice, and so we need some really in-depth ethnographies of school life.

3. Hatcher (2008b) argues that democratic accountability has eroded, but it seems to be the case that localized opposition to academies has politicized ordinary people into articulating about education in ways that could form sites for examining possibilities for civic democratic renewal. What has to be addressed is how people do or do not care for people they are not genetically or legal connected to, and what this means for our society.

The Academies Programme is an elite political project masquerading as benevolence integral to improving people's lives. The evidence shows that a school does not need to be an academy to turn around a failing school (Rogers and Migniuolo, 2007), and I would like to speculate how predecessor schools might have used the funds invested into successor academies if they and other schools had received such public investment. While no one can dispute the educational (as well as economic and social) imperative to make radical and urgent interventions to bring about pedagogical changes, it seems that publicly funded education is being dismantled. This is not happening through rapid revolution but incrementally through legislation (e.g. 1988 Education Reform Act) and through projects (e.g. CTCs), and the Academies Programme is nested within such events. In ordinary everyday terms such interventions become regularized by bringing language and behaviours into the vernacular so that neoliberal dispositions are normalized, where no other way of thinking and doing is possible. The contribution of this book is to enable the research and thinking (much of which goes back decades) about education in an unjust society to be opened up and debated. This not only examines what is going on and what it means, but also connects a particular intervention into a wider approach that is sustaining and institutionalizing injustice.

Coda[1]

A Conservative and Liberal Democrat coalition government took office following the May 2010 general election with an education policy for England clearly located in the neoliberal approach. The Thatcherite ideological commitment, often through pragmatic policies, to dismantling the welfare state and opening up public services to private market interests has re-emerged, where the level of debt caused by the banking crisis is serving as a window of opportunity to be more strategic in cutting public investment and reducing the public sector workforce. While New Labour in opposition is attempting to challenge this, their position remains vulnerable, as much of what is currently taking place has been enabled through their use of private interests to deliver education policy. It seems that Blair's prediction that opened this concluding chapter is coming true. Furthermore, the construction of alternative models by the Opposition remains problematic, as public institutions such as local authorities have been weakened through their policies with the consequent damage to the idea and practice of local democratic accountability.

In this brief addition to the Conclusion I would like to provide a summary of the key developments that illustrate the interplay between ideology and pragmatism, and the consequent strengthening of the neoliberal project. We need to remember that neoliberal ideas and practices may not be set out in a manifesto as a blueprint for action but such coherence regarding values and intention can be reconstructed through policy analysis.

The coalition has a clear commitment to extend the role of private interests in educational provision:

> We will promote the reform of schools in order to ensure that new providers can enter the state school system in response to parental demand; that all schools have greater freedom over the curriculum; and that all schools are held properly to account.
>
> . . . We will give parents, teachers, charities and local communities the chance to set up new schools, as part of our plans to allow new providers to enter the state school system in response to parental demand . . .
>
> We will ensure that all new Academies follow an inclusive admissions policy. We will work with faith groups to enable more faith schools and facilitate inclusive admissions policies in as many of these schools as possible.
>
> (HM Government, 2010, pp. 28–9)

Michael Gove, the new Secretary of State, wrote to all schools to invite them to apply for academy status, where an OfSTED (Office for Standards in Education) endorsement of 'outstanding' would lead to fast-tracking. Importantly, the scheme has been opened to primary and special schools. The terms and conditions outlined are that these academies 'will enjoy':

- freedom from local authority control
- the ability to set their own pay and conditions for staff
- freedom from following the national curriculum
- greater control of their budget
- greater opportunities for formal collaboration with other public and private organizations
- freedom to change the length of terms and school days

- freedom to spend the money the local authority currently spends on their behalf. (DfE, 2010a)

In addition to this the Free Schools policy, as discussed in Chapter 14, has been introduced, with a contention that there is parental demand to establish schools outside of local authority control. As 'all-ability state-funded schools' these can be set up by parents, charities, teachers, businesses and universities with advice from the New Schools Network (DfE, 2010b)

The coalition government is presenting support for these new initiatives with sound bites from academy principals and sponsors, and from heads who would seek to benefit.

> Patricia Sowter, Headteacher of Cuckoo Hall Primary School, indicated that her school would apply for academy freedoms:
>
> To achieve success in our school we have always been committed to effective and non-bureaucratic ways of working. I have always felt that successful schools should be given the option to adopt the same level of autonomy that comes with academy freedoms. These freedoms would allow Cuckoo Hall to continually build on its success and shape its own future by choosing our own curriculum to best meet the needs of our children.
>
> (DfE, 2010a)

In addition to this, Gove (2010) has been clear to stress two things: first, the announcement that new freedoms are very popular, with more than 1,772 schools enquiring about academy conversion; and second, that policy is underpinned by a moral purpose regarding the need for a pupil premium to fund education to close the achievement gap between rich and poor. Furthermore, there has been work done to counter the criticisms of the evidence base supporting these reforms with a 'mythbuster' document on the DfE website (2010c) outlining the positive impact of charter schools in the US, free schools in Sweden and academies in England.

The speed at which events have moved means that commentary is located in newsprint and on web pages, but these events and arguments do need to be opened up for critique.

As this book shows, the Academies Programme has gone through various iterations since its launch, and what is distinctive about the coalition shift is that the previous investment has ended and so new academies will not have new buildings (current cuts mean that all schools where contracts have not been signed face having re-building stopped) or sponsors. It seems as if what is being proposed is a mass exodus from local authority control without public consultation. Concerns are being raised by those who could be advantaged by the changes, with a cautious approach from both the Catholic

Education Service and the National Grammar Schools Association, where the latter has warned about the 'covert dangers' of leading to 'all ability intakes' following conversion (Williams, 2010, p. 17). Those who opposed the Academies Programme, outlined in the Introduction, continue to do so, with the Anti Academies Alliance leading on campaigns and evidence regarding the new developments, including free schools.

If all schools can and do move to academy status then the link between the public funding of education and public accountability for that funding through local authorities is finally broken across the system. The question to be asked is, what replaces this? Gove has made it clear that he 'has "no ideological objection" to businesses seeking profits from the new generation of academy schools and free schools' (Barkham and Curtis, 2010, p. 6), and his predisposition for this is illustrated in the Department for Education providing £500,000 for the New Schools Network (NSN), which has been given privileged status as 'the preferred route' that those interested in free schools 'must' talk with (Clark, 2010, p. 5). Millar raises issues of cronyism (Rachel Wolf, director of NSN, is a former Gove aide) but also the charity receives anonymous donations and so she goes on to say 'the NSN needs to say whether it has ever received funds from organisations with a vested interest in the drive to remove education from the maintained sector. They are well represented among its advisers and trustees' (Clark, 2010, p. 5).

Comparing the evidence and debate in this book with Gove's 'mythbusting' document shows how selectivity and silence operates in policy texts. Furthermore, since the manuscript was sent to the publisher in March 2010, the evidence to challenge the effectiveness of the Academies Programme and the free school restructuring in Sweden continues apace. There is evidence that permanent exclusions are higher for some groups of black and minority ethnic children in academies than in local authority schools (Mansell, 2010), and the evidence provided by Gorard (Chapter 8) and Wrigley (Chapter 9) regarding the impact of academies on standards and the curriculum has been further confirmed by the report that 'the Government has revealed that only 49 per cent of academies' GCSE or equivalent A*–C grades were made up of academic GCSEs last year, compared with 73 per cent for other state schools' (Stewart, 2010). Contradictions in policy-making, also evident under New Labour, are emerging where Gove (2010) speaks of a need for 'more evidence-based policymaking'; but as the Labour MP Tristram Hunt points out, in response to the report on less academic subjects being taken in academies, 'it is of real concern that the Government seems about to depart on a policy without gathering the empirical evidence of what is going on in schools' (Stewart, 2010).

The Free Schools policy is running alongside the changes to the Academies Programme, and an analysis of published evidence by Allen (2010) shows the complexity involved in using the Swedish model in an English context.

For example, she shows that there is 'a moderately positive impact of free school growth on municipality academic performance' where 'the biggest beneficiaries are children from highly educated families; the impact on low educated families and immigrants is close to zero' (p. 5). She goes on to argue that the equity gap in Sweden is not as great as in England, and so the social composition of schooling is not as great a feature. She concludes that 'so far, Swedish pupils do not appear to be harmed by the competition from private schools, but the new schools have not yet transformed educational attainment in Sweden' (p. 7), but the fall in student numbers could create a more competitive situation, and so school closure may be more of a feature. Clearly there is not enough robust evidence, and it is interesting to note that while there is no money to continue the Building Schools for the Future programme, money will be found to fund new schools opening where local authority schools already exist. Perhaps Gove (2010) should operationalize his own approach before these major reforms are implemented:

> I want to see more data generated by the profession to show what works, clearer information about teaching techniques that get results, more rigorous, scientifically-robust research about pedagogies which succeed and proper independent evaluations of interventions which have run their course.

The Academies Programme in England and the free schools in Sweden have not run their course, and this book shows the evidence about academies is at best mixed, with authors raising serious concerns about actual damage to the social fabric. The coalition has set up an Office for Budget Responsibility to break the link between data and politicking, and perhaps this should be extended with an Office for Research Responsibility.

This rapid restructuring of education is based on intellectual work and policy processes from Thatcher through Blair and currently under the Coalition Agreement. The issues raised in this book continue to resonate as the Academies Bill goes through parliament, with two chapter authors being quoted in the press on two pertinent matters. First, Hasan (2010) identifies that, while the changes are based on the rhetoric of progressive parent power, in reality power is being handed over to the centre, where David Wolfe states, 'It is hard to escape the conclusion that this bill is undemocratic . . . What it does is to remove the public process. Nobody, apart from the Education Secretary and the governors, will be able to stop the process' (p. 12). Second, anomalies are emerging, with outstanding schools who have been awarded and sustained this category under local authority control being given the opportunity to leave that control, and, as Ron Glatter (2010) notes, the Coalition Agreement (see beginning of this section, 'Coda') does not actually mention the expansion of the programme, and so he asks, 'was that because the Conservatives introduced it without consulting their coalition partners, or because the Lib Dems were too embarrassed to admit they had agreed to it?'

It seems that the neoliberal approach has crossed political boundaries in what seems to be officially post-political times, where the politics of debate and evidence are being marginalized. The coalition has maintained and accelerated the neoliberal education policies of the past 30 years, and in asking the question, 'where do we go from here?', as I write this Conclusion in January 2010 the three issues of the equity gap, the role of children and democratic renewal remain central to the agenda. Equity issues may have been raised by Gove (2010) but, as the evidence in this book shows, the market will not deliver on the type of changes necessary to make a real difference; children remain an absent presence in education policy-making, and democratic accountability based on public control of services is in mortal danger through further centralization and the handing over of public assets to private companies and interests. Indeed, Beckett (2007) has already done enough analysis of the early years of the Academies Programme to provide convincing evidence about the problems surrounding the public governance of public funds in private hands.

It seems that there is a tension between the campaign for constitutional change accelerated by the balanced parliament outcome from the May 2010 general election and the actuality of how democracy is being dismantled through a bizarre combination of stealth and celebration. However, while the research agenda remains vibrant, in the context of major spending cuts blamed on the public sector workforce rather than the bankers, it is going to be difficult to restore the public realm as a robust and necessary imaginary and way of life. This is where our attention should lie, and where alternative approaches need to be worked on. The upsurge of opposition to the Academies Programme with local and national campaigns continues apace, and demonstrates that democratic politics is alive.

But the changes are hard to get a purchase on, and this can be illustrated by the proposed reform of the National Health Service (NHS). While the rhetoric is to protect the NHS in regard to the cuts agenda, the plan is to turn GPs into commissioners of services, and not only are questions being raised about the removal of a strategic and consultation infrastructure, but Crook (2010) also asks whether GPs will 'subcontract the commissioning process to private companies involved in health care and bring privatisation to the NHS by stealth?' (p. 34). It seems that ongoing privatization generates resonances with education, particularly the lack of consultation.

Research together with 'argument and refutation', rather than 'denunciation and slander' (Bourdieu, 1998, p. 9), remain central to debates and action: ideas and evidence can be challenged and new approaches developed, and importantly we can fire back:

> [R]esearchers have a key part to play. They have to provide political action with new ends – the demolition of the dominant beliefs – and new means – technical weapons – based on research and a command of scientific knowledge, and symbolic weapons, capable of undermining common beliefs by putting research findings into an accessible form.
>
> (Bourdieu, 2003, p. 36)

While our pay may have been frozen for two years, our minds have not.

Note

[1] I would like to thank Ron Glatter, Denis Gleeson, Richard Hatcher and David Wolfe, who gave me advice and suggestions regarding this Coda. Of course, I take full responsibility for the text.

Appendix 1: Open and Planned Academies (January 2010)

1. Academies open as of September 2009

There are currently 200 academies open in 82 local authorities, and New Labour planned to open a further 100 in September 2010. The following table is adapted from a table available at: www.standards.dfes.gov.uk/academies/projects/?version=1 (accessed 4 January 2010), see p. 309.

Academy name	School	Open	Specialism	Local authority	Sponsor	History	Faith designation
Abraham Darby Academy	Co-educational 11–16	Sep-08	Performing Arts, Business and Enterprise	Telford and Wrekin	Haberdashers and the Local Authority	Abraham Darby Specialist School for Performing Arts	No
Academy 360	All through Co-educational 4–16	Sep-08	Business and Enterprise	Sunderland	Gento Group and Sunderland CC	Pennywell School	No
Accrington	Co-educational 11–16+	Sep-08	Mathematics, Sport	Lancashire	United Learning Trust (ULT)	Accrington Moorhead Sports College	Yes
All Saints Academy	Co-educational 11–16+	Sep-09	Science, Business and Enterprise	Bedfordshire	St Albans Diocese and University of Bedfordshire	The Northfields Technology College	Yes

Academy name	School	Open	Specialism	Local authority	Sponsor	History	Faith designation
Appleton Academy	All through Co-educational 3–16	Sep-09	Science and Sport	Bradford	Bradford College	Wyke Manor School	No
Archbishop Sentamu Academy	Co-educational 11–16+	Sep-08	Science (health), Business and Enterprise	Kingston Upon Hull	Diocese of York	Archbishop Thurstan Church of England Voluntary Controlled School	Yes
Ark Academy	All through 3–16	Sep-08	Citizenship, Mathematics	Brent	Absolute Return for Kids (ARK)	New school	No
Ashcroft Technology Academy	Co-educational 11–16+	Sep-07	Information Technology, Design Technology	Wandsworth	Prospect Education (Technology) Trust Ltd	ADT CTC	No
Bacon's, A Church of England Sponsored Academy	Co-educational 11–16+	Sep-07	Digital Media and Technology, Social Enterprise	Southwark	CTC Trust, Southwark Diocesan Board of Education	Bacons CTC	No
Barnfield South Academy	Co-educational 11–16+	Sep-07	Enterprise, ICT, Performing Arts	Luton	Barnfield College Further Education Co-operation	South Luton School	No
Barnfield West Academy	Co-educational 11–16+	Sep-07	ICT, Enterprise, Creative Industries	Luton	Barnfield College Further Education Co-operation	Halyard High	No

(continued)

(continued from previous page)

Academy name	School	Open	Specialism	Local authority	Sponsor	History	Faith designation
Barnsley Academy	Co-educational 11–16+	Sep-06	Science, Business and Enterprise	Barnsley	United Learning Trust	Elmhirst School	Yes
Bede Academy	All through Co-educational 3–18	Sep-09	Engineering, Enterprise	Northumberland	Emmanuel Schools Foundation	South Beach First School; Wensleydale and Delaval Middle Schools	No
Bilston Academy	Co-educational 11–16+	Sep-09	Business and Enterprise, Engineering	Wolverhampton	City of Wolverhampton FE College	Parkfield High School	No
Bexley Business Academy	Co-educational 11–16+	Sep-02	Business and Enterprise	Bexley	Sir David Gerrard	Thamesmead Community College	No
Birkenhead High School Academy	Co-educational 11–16+	Sep-09	Music, Mathematics	Wirral	GDST	Birkenhead High School	No
Bolton St Catherine's Academy	All age Co-educational	Sep-09	Business and Enterprise, Maths, Computing	Bolton	Diocese of Manchester (Church of England)	Withins School	Yes
Bradford Academy	Co-educational 11–16+	Sept-07	Citizenship, Enterprise	Bradford	Diocese of Bradford and Church of England	Bradford Cathedral Community College	No
Bristol Cathedral Choir School	Co-educational 11–16	Sept-08	Music, Maths	Bristol	No Sponsor required: School itself is the sponsor	Bristol Cathedral School (independent)	Yes

Academy name	School	Open	Specialism	Local authority	Sponsor	History	Faith designation
Bristol Metropolitan Academy	Co-educational 11–16+	Sep-09	Languages, Performing Arts	Bristol	John Cabot CTC	Bristol Metropolitan College	No
Brooke Weston Academy	Co-educational 11–16	Sep-08	Digital Media, Engineering, Production	Northamptonshire	Brooke Weston CTC Trust	Brooke Weston CTC	No
Burlington Danes Academy	Co-educational 11–16+	Sep-06	Expressive Arts, Mathematics	Hammersmith and Fulham	Absolute Return for Kids (ARK)	Burlington Danes School	Yes
Capital City Academy	Co-educational 11–16+	Sep-03	Sports	Brent	Sir Frank Lowe	Willesden High School	No
City Academy Norwich	Co-educational 11–16+	Sep-09	English, Digital Media	Norfolk	City College Norwich	Earlham High School	No
Charter Academy	Co-educational 11–16+	Sep-09	Mathematics, Music	Portsmouth	ARK, Partnered by Diocese of Portsmouth	St Luke's CofE VA Secondary School	Yes
Chelsea Academy (A Science Academy)	Co-educational 11–16+	Sep-09	Sciences	Kensington and Chelsea	London Diocese Board (LDBS)	New school	Yes
Clacton Coastal Academy	Co-educational 11–16+	Sep-09	English, Media Arts	Essex	Academies Enterprise Trust (Greensward Charitable Trust)	Bishops Park College and Colbayns High School	No
City of London Academy	Co-educational 11–16+	Sep-08	Business and Enterprise	Islington	Corporation of London and City University	Islington Green School	No
City of London Southwark Academy	Co-educational 11–16+	Sep-03	Business and Enterprise, Sports	Southwark	Corporation of London	New school	No

(*continued*)

(*continued from previous page*)

Academy name	School	Open	Specialism	Local authority	Sponsor	History	Faith designation
Castle View Enterprise	Co-educational 11–16+	Sep-09	Business and Enterprise	Sunderland	LA/Northumbrian Water	Castle View School	No
Colston's Girls	Girls 11–16+	Sep-08	Modern Foreign Languages	Bristol	The Society of Merchants Venturers	Colstons Girls' School	No
Cornwallis Academy	Co-educational 11–16+	Sep-07	Science, Technology	Kent	Cornwallis Online Learning, Kent CC	Cornwallis School	No
Darwen Aldridge Community Academy	Co-educational 11–16+	Sep-08	Entrepreneurship	Blackburn with Darwen	The Aldridge Foundation	Darwen Moorland High School	No
David Young Community Academy	Co-educational 11–16+	Sep-06	Design, The Built Environment	Leeds	Diocese of Ripon and Leeds	Agnes Stewart School and Braim Wood School	No
De Warenne Academy	Co-educational 11–19 (from 2010)	Sep-09	English, Applied Learning	Doncaster	Schools Partnership Trust	Northcliffe School	No
Dixons City Academy	Co-educational 11–16+	Sep-05	Performing Arts, Product Design	Bradford	Dixons CTC	Dixon CTC	No
Dixons Allerton Academy	Co-educational 11–16+	Sep-09	Health and Medical Sciences	Bradford	Dixons City Academy	Rhodesway School	No
Droylsden Academy	Co-educational 11–16+	Sep-09	Mathematics, Technology	Tameside	Tameside College	Littlemoss High for Boys and Droylsden School	No

Academy name	School	Open	Specialism	Local authority	Sponsor	History	Faith designation
Djanogly City Academy	Co-educational 11–16+	Sep-03	ICT	Nottingham	Sir Harry Djanogly	Djanogly CTC and Forest School	No
Eastbourne Church of England Academy	Co-educational 11–16+	Sep-07	Business and Enterprise	Darlington	Diocese of Durham and David and Anne Crossland	Eastbourne Comprehensive School	Yes
Essa Academy	Co-educational 11–16+	Jan-09	Science, Languages	Bolton	Essa Foundation and Bolton Council	Hayward School	No
Evelyn Grace Academy	Co-educational 11–16+	Sep-08	Sports, Mathematics	Lambeth	Absolute Return for Kids (ARK)	New school	No
Excelsior Academy	Co-educational 11–18	Sep-08	Business and Enterprise	Newcastle Upon Tyne	Lord Laidlaw of Rothiemay	West Gate Community College	No
Folkestone Academy	Co-educational 11–16+	Sep-07	Modern European Culture, Creative Media Arts	Kent	Roger De Haan and Kings School Canterbury	The Channel School	No
Francis Combe Academy	Co-educational 11–16+	Sep-09	English, Arts, Media	Hertfordshire	West Herts College	Francis Combe School	No
Fulwood Academy	Co-educational 11–16+	Sep-09	Technology, Arts	Lancashire	Charles Dunstone	Fulwood H.S. and Arts College and Tulketh Community Sports College	No
Gateway Academy	Co-educational 11–16+	Sep-06	Arts, Engineering	Thurrock	The Ormiston Trust	Gateway Community College	No

(continued)

(*continued from previous page*)

Academy name	School	Open	Specialism	Local authority	Sponsor	History	Faith designation
George Salter Collegiate Academy	Co-educational 11–16+	Sep-07	Language, Arts	Sandwell	Ormiston Trust and Shireland Learning	George Salter High School	No
Grace Academy, Darlaston	Co-educational 11–16+	Sep-09	Business and Enterprise	Walsall	Bob Edmiston	Darlaston Community Science College	No
Grace Academy, Coventry	Co-educational 11–16+	Sep-08	Business and Enterprise	Coventry	Bob Edmiston	Woodway Park School and Community College	No
Grace Academy, Solihull	Co-educational 11–16+	Sep-06	Business and Enterprise	Solihull	Bob Edmiston	Whitesmore School	No
Greensward	Co-educational 11–16+	Sep-08	Science, Vocational	Essex	Greensward Charitable Trust	Greensward College	No
Greig City Academy	Co-educational 11–16+	Sep-02	Technology (especially ICT)	Haringey	Greig Trust with the Diocese of London	St David and St Katherine Church of England High School	Yes
Haberdashers' Knights Academy	Co-educational 11–16+	Sep-05	ICT, Sports Science	Lewisham	Haberdashers' Livery Company	Malory School	No
Haberdashers' Aske's Hatcham Academy	Co-educational 11–16+	Sep-05	ICT, Music	Lewisham	Haberdashers' Livery Company	Haberdashers' Aske Hatcham College	No
Haberdashers' Crayford Academy	Co-educational 11–16+	Sep-09	Technology	Bexley	The Haberdashers' Federation	Barnes Cray Primary School	No

Academy name	School	Open	Specialism	Local authority	Sponsor	History	Faith designation
Heartlands Academy	Co-educational 11–16+	Sep-09	Maths, Sports	Birmingham	Edutrust Academies Charitable Trust	Heartlands High School	No
Harefield Academy	Co-educational 11–16+	Sep-05	Sports	Hillingdon	David Meller	John Penrose School	No
Harris Boys Academy East Dulwich	Co-educational 11–16+	Sep-09	Sports and PE, Health	Southwark	Harris Federation of South London Schools Trust	New school	No
Harris Academy, Merton	Co-educational 11–16+	Sep-06	Sports, Enterprise	Merton	Harris Federation of South London Schools Trust	Tamworth Manor High School	No
Harris Academy, Peckham	Co-educational 11–16+	Sep-03	Business, Performing Arts	Southwark	Harris Federation of South London Schools Trust	Warwick Park School	No
Harris Academy, Purley	Co-educational 11–16+	Sep-09	Enterprise, Sports	Croydon	Harris Federation	Haling Manor High School	No
Harris Bermondsey Academy	Co-educational 11–16+	Sep-06	Enterprise, Media	Southwark	Harris Federation of South London Schools Trust	Aylwin Girls' School	No
Harris City Academy, Crystal Palace	Co-educational 11–16+	Sep-07	Technology, Business and Enterprise	Croydon	Harris Federation of South London Schools Trust	Harris CTC	No
Harris Falconwood Academy	Co-educational 11–16+	Sep-08	Science, Enterprise, Sport	Bexley	Lord Harris	Westwood College	No
Harris Girls Academy East Dulwich	Girls 11–16+	Sep-06	Sports, Health, Enterprise	Southwark	Harris Federation of South London Schools Trust	Waverley Girls School	No

(continued)

(*continued from previous page*)

Academy name	School	Open	Specialism	Local authority	Sponsor	History	Faith designation
Havelock Academy	Co-educational 11–16+	Sep-07	Maths, Computing, Engineering	North East Lincolnshire	David Ross	Havelock School	No
John Cabot Academy	Co-educational 11–16+	Sep-07	Mathematics, Science, Technology, Digital Arts and Media	South Gloucestershire	Rolls Royce and Wolfson Foundation	John Cabot CTC	No
King Solomon Academy	All through Co-educational	Sep-07	Mathematics, Music	Westminster	ARK	New school	No
Kettering Science Academy	Co-educational 11–16+	Sep-09	Science, Business and Enterprise	Northamptonshire	Brooke Weston Foundation	Ise Community College	No
Kettering Bucceleuch Academy	Co-educational 11–16+	Sep-09	Maths, Computing, Sport	Northamptonshire	United Learning Trust (ULT)	Montagu School	No
Lambeth Academy	Co-educational 11–16+	Sep-04	Business and Enterprise, Languages	Lambeth	United Learning Trust (ULT)	New School	Yes
Landau Forte College	Co-educational 11–16+	Sep-06	Technology, Business Enterprise	Derby	Landau Forte	Landau Forte CTC	No
Langley Academy	Co-educational 11–16+	Sep-08	Science	Slough	Sir Martyn Arbib	Langleywood School	No
Leeds West Academy	Co-educational 11–16+	Sep-09	English, Performing Arts	Leeds	Edutrust Academies Charitable Trust	Intake High School	No

Academy name	School	Open	Specialism	Local authority	Sponsor	History	Faith designation
Leigh Technology Academy	Co-educational 11–16+	Sep-07	Technologies (ICT and Creative) Sports, Business and Enterprise	Kent	Leigh CTC	Leigh CTC	No
London Academy	Co-educational 11–16+	Sep-04	Business and Enterprise, Technology	Barnet	Peter Shalson	Edgware School	No
Longfield Academy	Co-educational 11–16+	Sep-08	Science, Creative and Expressive Arts	Kent	Leigh Technology Academy Trust, Kent County Council and University of Kent	Axton Chase School	No
Macmillan Academy	Co-educational 11–16+	Sep-05	Science, PE, Outdoor Education	Middlesbrough	Macmillan CTC	Macmillan CTC	No
Madeley Academy	Co-educational 11–16+	Apr-07	Sport, ICT	Telford and Wrekin	Thomas Telford School (CTC)	Madeley Court	No
Manchester Academy	Co-educational 11–16+	Sep-03	Business and Enterprise, Art	Haringey	United Learning Trust and Manchester Science Park	Ducie High School	Yes
Manchester Creative and Media Academy for Boys	Boys 11–16+	Sep-09	Creative, Media	Manchester	Manchester College (lead), Co-MCC, Microsoft	North Manchester High School for Boys	No
Manchester Creative and Media Academy for Girls	Girls, 11–16+	Sep-09	Creative, Media	Manchester	Manchester College (lead), Co-MCC, Microsoft	North Manchester High School for Girls	No

(*continued*)

(*continued from previous page*)

Academy name	School	Open	Specialism	Local authority	Sponsor	History	Faith designation
Manchester Enterprise Academy	Co-educational 11–16+	Sep-09	Business and Enterprise, Leisure, Travel and Tourism	Manchester	Manchester Airport (lead), Co-Willow Park Housing Trust, Manchester College, MCC	Parklands High School	No
Manchester Health Academy	Co-educational 11–16+	Sep-09	Health (including Bio-science), existing Sport specialism to be retained	Manchester	Central Manchester and Manchester Childrens University Hospital NHS Trust, Co-Manchester College, MCC	Brookway High School and Sports College	No
Marlowe Academy	Co-educational 11–16+	Sep-05	Business, Performing Arts	Kent	Roger De Haan and Kent County Council	Ramsgate School	No
Marsh Academy	Co-educational 11–16+	Sep-07	Business and Enterprise	Kent	Kent County Council, Microsoft and Tonbridge School	Southlands School	No
Merchants' Academy, Withywood	Co-educational 11–16+	Sep-08	Enterprise, Skills	Bristol	The Society of Merchants Venturers	Withywood Community School	No
Midhurst Rother College	Co-educational 11–16+	Jan-09	Science, Maths	West Sussex	United Learning Trust (ULT)	Herbert Shiner School, Midhurst Grammar School and Midhurst Intermediate School	Yes

Academy name	School	Open	Specialism	Local authority	Sponsor	History	Faith designation
Milton Keynes Academy	Co-educational 11–16+	Sep-09	Business and Enterprise	Milton Keynes	Edge Foundation	Sir Frank Markham Community School	No
Mossbourne Community Academy	Co-educational 11–16+	Sep-04	Technology	Hackney	Sir Clive Bourne (deceased)	New school	No
New Charter Academy	Co-educational 11–16+	Sep-08	Business and Enterprise, Sport and Health	Tameside	New Charter Housing Trust	Hartshead Sports College and Stamford High School	No
New Line Learning Academy, South Maidstone Federation	Co-educational 11–16+	Sep-07	Business and Enterprise, Vocational	Kent	Cornwallis Online Learning and Kent County Council	Oldborough Manor/Senacre	No
North Liverpool Academy	Co-educational 11–16+	Sep-06	Business and Enterprise	Liverpool	Liverpool University and Granada Learning	Anfield School and Breckfield School	No
North Oxfordshire Academy	Co-educational 11–16+	Sep-07	Media and Communications, Business and Enterprise	Oxfordshire	United Learning Trust (ULT) and Vodafone	Drayton School	No
Northampton Academy	Co-educational 11–16+	Sep-04	Sports, Business and Enterprise	Northamptonshire	United Learning Trust (ULT)	Lings Upper School	Yes

(*continued*)

(continued from previous page)

Academy name	School	Open	Specialism	Local authority	Sponsor	History	Faith designation
Northumberland CofE Academy	All through Co-educational 3–18	Sep-09	Design and the Built Environment	Northumberland	Diocese of Newcastle and the Duke of Northumberland	Hirst High School and Feeder Schools	No
Nottingham University Samworth Academy	Co-educational 11–16+	Sep-09	Health, Science	Nottingham	University of Nottingham	William Sharp School	No
Nottingham Academy	All through Co-educational 3–19	Sep-09	Mathematics, Literacy, Digital Media	Nottingham	Greensward Charitable Trust	Elliott Durham School and Greenwood Dale School	No
Oasis Academy, Brightstowe	Co-educational 11–16+	Sep-08	Business and Enterprise, Mathematics, ICT	Bristol	Oasis Community Learning	Portway Community School	Yes
Oasis Academy, Bristol	Co-educational 11–16+	Sep-08	Performing Arts, Visual Arts	Bristol	Oasis Community Learning	Hengrove Communtiy Arts College	Yes
Oasis Academy, Coulsdon	Co-educational 11–19	Sep-08	Science, Technology, Business and Enterprise	Croydon	Oasis Community Learning	Coulsdon High School	Yes
Oasis Academy, Hadley	Co-educational 11–16+	Sep-09	Mathematics, ICT, Music	Enfield	Oasis Community Learning	Albany School	Yes
Oasis Academy, Immingham	Co-educational 11–16+	Sep-07	Engineering, Business and Enterprise	North East Lincolnshire	Oasis Community Learning	The Immingham School	Yes

Academy name	School	Open	Specialism	Local authority	Sponsor	History	Faith designation
Oasis Academy, Mayfield	Co-educational 11–16+	Sep-08	Global Communication	Southampton	Oasis Community Learning	Grove Park Business and Enterprise College and Woolston School Language College	Yes
Oasis Academy, Shirley Park	Co-educational 11–16+	Sep-09	English, Performing Arts	Croydon	Oasis Community Learning	Ashburton Community School	Yes
Oasis Academy, Wintringham	Co-educational 11–16+	Sep-07	Sports, Health, Business and Enterprise	North East Lincolnshire	Oasis Community Learning	Wintringham School	Yes
Oasis Academy, Enfield	Co-educational 11–16+	Sep-07	Business and Enterprise	Enfield	Oasis Community Learning	New School	Yes
Oasis Academy, Lord's Hill	Co-educational 11–16+	Sep-08	Arts, Business and Enterprise	Southampton	Oasis Community Learning	Millbrook Community School and Oaklands Community School	Yes
Oasis Media City UK Academy	Co-educational 11–16+	Sep-08	Media, ICT	Salford	Oasis Community Learning	Hope High School	Yes
Ormiston Park Academy	Co-educational 11–16+	Sep-09	Humanities, Creative and Cultural Skills	Thurrock	Ormiston Trust and South East Essex College (TBC) The Royal Opera House as an Education Partner (TBC)	Belhus Chase Specialist Humanities College	No

(continued)

(*continued from previous page*)

Academy name	School	Open	Specialism	Local authority	Sponsor	History	Faith designation
Ormiston Bushfields Academy	Co-educational 11–16+	Sep-09	Mathematics, Sport, Performing Arts	Peterborough	Ormiston Trust	Bushfields Community College	No
Ormiston Sandwell Community Academy	Co-educational 11–16+	Sep-09	Arts, English	Sandwell	Ormiston Trust	Tividale Community Arts College	No
Outwood Grange Academy	Co-educational 11–16+	Sep-09	Science, Sport	Doncaster	Outwood Grange College of Technology, Doncaster Metropolitan Borough Council	Adwick, North Doncaster Technology Collge	No
Outwood Grange Academy	Co-educational 11–16+	Sep-09	Arts, Technology	Wakefield	Outwood Grange College of Technology (Michael Wilkins to establish a Trust to oversee Outwood and North Doncaster Tech.)	Outwood Grange College of Technology	No
Paddington Academy	Co-educational 11–16+	Sep-06	Media, Performing Arts, Business and Enterprise	Westminster	United Learning Trust (ULT)	North Westminster Community School	Yes
Pimlico Academy	Co-educatioanl 11–16+	Sep-08	Visual and Performing Arts, History	Westminster	FUTURE	Pimlico School	No

Academy name	School	Open	Specialism	Local authority	Sponsor	History	Faith designation
Q3 Academy	Co-educational 11–16+	Sep-08	Design, Enterprise	Sandwell	Eric Payne	Dartmouth High School	Yes
Parkwood Academy	Co-educational 11–16+	Sep-09	Sports, Languages	Sheffield	Edutrust Academies Charitable Trust	Parkwood High School	No
Richard Rose Academy Central	Co-educational 11–16+	Sep-08	Science, Sports	Cumbria	Brian Scowcroft, Andrew Tinkler and University of Cumbria	North Cumbria Technology College and St Aidan's County High School Specialist Sports College	No
Red House Academy	Co-educational 11–16+	Sep-09	Engineering	Sunderland	LA/Leighton Group	Hylton Red House School	No
Richard Rose Morton Academy	Co-educational 11–16+	Sep-08	Science, Creative Arts	Cumbria	Brian Scowcroft, Andrew Tinkler and University of Cumbria	Morton School	No
Rickstones	Co-educational 11–16+	Sep-08	Performing Arts, Maths	Essex	Greensward Charitable Trust	The Rickstones School	No
Saint Mary Magdalene Academy	All Age Co-educational	Sep-07	Humanities, Citizenship	Islington	London Diocese Board of Schools	St Mary Magdalene Primary School	Yes
Salford City Academy	Co-educational 11–16+	Sep-05	Sport, Business and Enterprise	Salford	United Learning Trust (ULT) and Manchester Diocese	Williamson Church of England School	Yes
Sandwell Academy	Co-educational 11–16+	Sep-06	Business and Enterprise and Sports	Sandwell	Mercers Company, Thomas Telford Online, HSBC West Bromwich Football Club	New School	No

(continued)

(*continued from previous page*)

Academy name	School	Open	Specialism	Local authority	Sponsor	History	Faith designation
Sheffield Park	Co-educational 11–16+	Sep-06	Business and Enterprise	Sheffield	United Learning Trust (ULT)	Waltheof School	Yes
Skinners' Kent Academy	Co-educational 11–16+	Sep-09	Science, Engineering	Kent	Skinners School (lead), West Kent College, HCC	Tunbridge Wells High School	No
Sirius Academy	Co-educational 11–16+	Sep-09	Science (Environmental), Sports and Leisure	Kingston upon Hull	Hull College	Pickering High School Sports College	No
Sheffield Springs	Co-educational 11–16+	Sep-06	Performing Arts, Technology	Sheffield	United Learning Trust (ULT)	Myrtle Springs School	Yes
Shelfield Community Academy	Co-educational school 11–16+	Jan-09	Sport, English	Walsall	Ormiston Trust	Sheffield Sports and Community College	No
Shireland Collegiate Academy	Co-educational 11–16+	Sep-07	Language, Arts	Sandwell	Ormiston Trust and Shireland Learning	Shireland Language College	No
Shoreham Academy	Co-educational 11–16+	Sep-09	English, Business and Enterprise	West Sussex	United Learning Trust (ULT)	Kings Manor Community College	No
Solihull 3 Academy	Co-educational 11–16+	Sep-09	Mathematics, Performing Arts	Solihull	Arden School	Park Hall School	No
South Leeds Academy	Co-educational 11–16+	Sep-09	English, Applied Learning	Leeds	Schools Partnership Trust	South Leeds High School	No

Academy name	School	Open	Specialism	Local authority	Sponsor	History	Faith designation
Spires Academy	Co-educational 11–16	Sep-07	Business, Performing Arts	Kent	Holiday Extras/Crown Products (Kent) Ltd	Montgomery School	No
Shenley Academy	Co-educational 11–16+	Sep-09	Science, Performing and Creative Arts	Birmingham	Edutrust Academies Charitable Trust	Shenley Court Arts College	No
St Albans Academy	Co-educational 11–16+	Sep-09	Maths, Engineering	Birmingham	ARK/Aston University/BMW/Cadbury's/Ove Arup	St Alban's CE Specialist Engineering College	No
St Anne's Academy	Co-educational 11–16+	Sep-07	ICT, The Built Environment	Rochdale	The Manchester Diocese and David and Anne Crosslane	Queen Elizabeth School Middleton	Yes
St Mark's CofE	Co-educational 11–16+	Sep-06	Science, Performing Arts, subject to FA variation	Merton	Southwark Diocesan Board of Education and CfBT Education Trust	Mitcham Vale School	Yes
St Michael and All Angels CofE	Co-educational 11–16+	Sep-07	Health, Science	Southwark	Southwark Diocesan Board of Education	Archbishop Michael Ramsey Technology College	Yes
St Paul's Academy	Co-educational 11–16	Sep-05	Sports, Enterprise	Greenwich	RC Archdiocese of Southwark	St Paul's RC VA	Yes
Stockley Academy	Co-educational 11–16+	Sep-04	Science, Technology	Hillingdon	Barry Townsley and others	Evelyns Community School	No
Stockport Academy	Co-educational 11–16+	Sep-07	Science, Business and Enterprise	Stockport	United Learning Trust (ULT)	Avondale High School	Yes

(*continued*)

(continued from previous page)

Academy name	School	Open	Specialism	Local authority	Sponsor	History	Faith designation
Strood Academy	Co-educational 11–16+	Sep-09	Mathematics, Business and Enterprise	Medway	University College for the Creative Arts (UCCA) and Medway Council	Temple School and Chapter School	No
Swindon Academy	All through Co-educational	Sep-07	Science, Business and Enterprise	Swindon	United Learning Trust (ULT) and (Honda UK)	Headlands School	Yes
The Academy of St Francis of Assisi	Co-educational 11–16	Sep-05	The Environment	Liverpool	Diocese of Liverpool and Archdiocese and Roman Catholic Archdiocese of Liverpool	Our Lady's Catholic High School–New School	Yes
The Aylesbury Vale Academy	Co-educational 11–16+	Sep-09	Science, Technology	Buckinghamshire	Oxford Diocesan Education Board and Buckinghamshire County Council	Quarrendon School	Yes
The Basildon Upper Academy	Co-educational 14–19+	Sep-09	Enterprise, Maths	Essex	Stanton Lane Trust	Chalvedon School and Barstable School	No
The Basildon Lower Academy	Co-educational 11–14	Sep-09	Enterprise, Maths	Essex	Stanton Lane Trust	Chalvedon School and Barstable School	No
The Belvedere Academy	Co-educational 11–16+	Sep-07	Modern Foreign Languages, Science	Liverpool	Girls' Day School Trust and HSBC	Belvedere Girls School (independent)	No
The Bridge Academy	Co-educational 11–16+	Sep-07	Maths, Music	Hackney	UBS	New school	No

Academy name	School	Open	Specialism	Local authority	Sponsor	History	Faith designation
The Bristol Brunel Academy	Co-educational 11–16+	Sep-07	English, ICT	Bristol	John Cabot Academy	Speedwell Technology College (PFI) John Cabot Legacy School	No
The Bulwell Academy	Co-educational 11–16+	Sep-09	Enterprise	Nottingham	Edge Foundation	The River Leen School and Henry Mellish Comprehensive School	No
The Bushey Academy	Co-educational 11–16+	Sep-09	Business, Communications	Hertfordshire	David Meller	Bushey Hall School	No
The City Academy, Hackney	Co-educational 11–16+	Sep-09	Business, Financial Services	Hackney	Corporation of London	Homerton College of Technology	No
The Crest Boys' Academy (CBA)	Boys 11–16+	Sep-09	Mathematics, Technology	Brent	EACT	John Kelly Boys' Technology College	No
The Crest Girls' Academy (CBA)	Girls, 11–16+	Sep-09	Languages, Technology	Brent	EACT	John Kelly Girls' College	No
The City Academy, Bristol	Co-educational 11–16+	Sep-03	Sports	Bristol	John Laycock and the University of the West of England	St George Community College	No
The Isle of Sheppey Academy	Co-educational 11–16+	Sep-09	Business and Enterprise, Sports	Kent	Dulwich College (lead), KCC, COE, (Roger de Hann donor)	Minster College, St Georges CofE Middle, Danley Middle, Cheyne Middle	No

(*continued*)

(*continued from previous page*)

Academy name	School	Open	Specialism	Local authority	Sponsor	History	Faith designation
The Corby Business Academy	Co-educational 11–16+	Sep-08	Business and Enterprise	Northamptonshire	Weston Foundation, BeeBee Development and Brooke Weston CTC	Corby Community College	No
The CTC Kingshurst Academy	Co-educational 11–16+	Sep-08	Technology, Visual Arts	Solihull	Kingshurst CTC Trust	The City Technology College	No
The Furness Academy	Co-educational 11–16+	Sep-09	Applied Maths, Sport	Cumbria	Barrow Sixth Form College, Furness College and University of Cumbria	Alfred Barrow, Thorncliffe and Parkview Schools	No
The Globe Academy	All through Co-educational	Sep-08	Performing Arts, Mathematics	Southwark	Absolute Return for Kids (ARK)	Geoffery Chaucer Technology College and Joseph Lancaster Primary School	No
The Harris Academy, South Norwood	Co-educational 11–16+	Sep-07	Business and Enterprise	Croydon	Harris Federation of South London Schools Trust and Whitgift Foundation	Stanley Technical High School for Boys	No
The Littlehampton Academy	Co-educational 11–16+	Sep-09	Business and Enterprise, English	West Sussex	Woodard Schools	The Littlehampton Community School	Yes
The Hereford Academy	Co-educational 11–16+	Sep-08	Sport, Science, Health	Herefordshire	Hereford Diocesan Board of Education	Wyebridge Sports College	Yes

Academy name	School	Open	Specialism	Local authority	Sponsor	History	Faith designation
The John Madejski Academy	Co-educational 11–16+	Sep-06	Sports	Reading	John Madejski	Thamesbridge Community College	No
The King's Academy	Co-educational 11–16+	Sep-03	Business and Enterprise	Middlesbrough	Emmanuel Schools Foundation	Brackenhoe Comprehensive School and Coulby Newham School	Yes
The Maltings Academy	Co-educational 11–16+	Sep-08	Science, Sports	Essex	Greensward Charitable Trust	The John Bramston School	No
The Open Academy	Co-educational 11–16+	Sep-08	Environmental Science, Engineering	Norfolk	Grahame Dacre and Bishop of Norwich	Heartsease High School	No
The Oxford Academy	Co-educational 11–16+	Sep-08	Maths, ICT, Sport	Oxfordshire	Diocese of Oxford, Oxford Brooks University and Adrian Beecroft	Peers School	Yes
The Petchey Academy	Co-educational 11–16+	Sep-06	Health, Care, Medical Sciences	Hackney	Jack Petchey Foundation	New School	No
The Priory City of Lincoln Academy	Co-educational 11–16+	Sep-08	Engineering, Sport, Health	Lincolnshire	The Priory Fundraising Trust	The City of Lincoln Community College	No
The Priory LSST Academy	Co-educational 11–16+	Sep-08	Science and Technology with Training Teacher status	Lincolnshire	The Priory Fundraising Trust	The Priory LSST	No

(continued)

(continued from previous page)

Academy name	School	Open	Specialism	Local authority	Sponsor	History	Faith designation
The Priory Witham Academy	All through Co-educational 3–16+	Sep-08	Performing Arts, Business and Enterprise	Lincolnshire	The Priory Fundraising Trust	Joseph Ruston Technology College	No
The Ridings Federation, Winterborne International Academy	Co-educational 11–16+	Sep-09	Modern Foreign Languages, Maths	South Gloucestershire	The Ridings Education Trust	The Ridings High School	No
The Ridings Federation, Yate International Academy	Co-educational 11–16+	Sep-09	Science, Health, Sport	South Gloucestershire	Hard Federation Pathfinder (Riding School)	King Edmund Community School	No
The RSA Academy, Tipton	Co-educatioanl 11–16+	Sep-08	Health, Citizenship	Sandwell	RSA	Willingsworth High School	No
The Samworth Church Academy	Co-educational 11–16+	Sep-08	Business and Enterprise	Nottinghamshire	David Samworth, Diocesan of Southwell and Nottingham	Sherwood Hall School and Sixth Form College	Yes
The Samworth Enterprise Academy	Co-educational 3–16	Sep-07	Business and Enterprise with a Food Technology focus	Leicester	David Samworth and Leicester Diocesan Board of Education	Soughfields Infants School and Newry Junior School – Ex Mary Linwood School – New School	Yes
The Sir Robert Woodard Academy	Co-educational 11–16+	Sep-09	Performing Arts, Maths	West Sussex	Woodard Schools	Boundstone Community College	Yes

Academy name	School	Open	Specialism	Local authority	Sponsor	History	Faith designation
The St Lawrence Academy, Scunthorpe	Co-educational 11–16	Sep-08	Sport, Science	North Lincolnshire	Diocese of Lincoln	High Ridge School Specialist Sports College	Yes
The St Matthew Academy	Co-educational 3–16	Sep-07	Business and Enterprise	Lewisham	RC Archdiocese of Southwark	St Joseph's Academy and Our Lady of Lourdes Primary School	Yes
The Steiner Academy Hereford	All through Co-educational 3–16	Sep-08	The Natural Environment	Herefordshire	Steiner School Fellowship	Hereford Waldorf School	No
The Thomas Deacon Academy	Co-educational 11–16+	Sep-07	Maths, Science	Peterborough	Deacon's Trust and Perkins Engines	Hereward Community College, Deacon's School (Beacon) and John Mansfield School	No
The University of Chester Church of England Academy	Co-educational 11–16+	Sep-09	Maths, Sports, Performance	Cheshire	University of Chester	Ellesmere Port	Yes
Tudor Grange Academy Worcester	Co-educational 11–16+	Sep-09	Science and Enterprise	Worcestershire	Tudor Grange School	Elgar Technology College	No
The Walsall City Academy	Co-educational 11–16+	Sep-03	Technology	Walsall	Thomas Telford Online and the Mercers' Company	TP Riley School	No

(continued)

(*continued from previous page*)

Academy name	School	Open	Specialism	Local authority	Sponsor	History	Faith designation
The West London Academy	Co-educational 5–16+	Sep-03	Sports, Enterprise	Ealing	Alec Reed	Compton Sports College	No
The Wellington Academy	All through Co-educational 3–19	Sep-09	Modern Foreign Languages, Business and Enterprise	Wiltshire	Wellington College	Castledown School	No
Trent Valley Academy	Co-educational 11–16+	Sep-08	Performing Arts, Technology	Lincolnshire	Edutrust Academies Charitable Trust	Castle Hills School and Middlefield School of Technology	No
Trinity Academy	Co-educational 11–16+	Sep-05	Business and Enterprise	Doncaster	Emmanuel Schools Foundation	Thorne Grammar School	Yes
Unity City Academy	Co-educational 11–16	Sep-02	Applied Technology	Middlesbrough	Amey plc	Keldholme School and Langbaurgh School	No
Walthamstow Academy	Co-educational 11–16+	Sep-06	Business and Enterprise, Science, Maths	Waltham Forest	United Learning Trust (ULT)	McEntee School	Yes
Walworth Academy	Co-educational 11–16+	Sep-07	Maths, Health	Southwark	Absolute Return for Kids (ARK)	Walworth School	No

Academy name	School	Open	Specialism	Local authority	Sponsor	History	Faith designation
Westlakes Academy	Co-educational 11–16+	Sep-08	Science, Business, Innovation	Cumbria	Nuclear Decommissioning Authority, Sellafield Limited and University of Lancashire	Ehenside Community School and Wyndham School	No
Westminster Academy	Co-educational 11–16+	Sep-06	International Business, Enterprise	Westminster	Exilarch's Foundation	North Westminster Community School	No
William Hulme's Grammar School	All age Co-educational	Sep-07	Modern Foreign Languages, Science	Manchester	United Learning Trust (ULT)	William Hulme's Grammar School (independent)	Yes
Wren Academy	Co-educational 11–16+	Sep-08	Design, The Built Environment	Barnet	Diocese of London and Birkhamsted Collegiate School	Christ Church CofE Secondary School	Yes

2. Planned academies

New Labour planned to open 100 academies in 2010. This table has been adapted from the the DCSF website which listed Academy Programme projects, available at: www.standards.dfes.gov.uk/academies/projects/development/?version=1 (accessed 4 January 2010). For the definitions of the Phases, see Appendix 2.

Project name	Phase name	Expression of Interest signed	Funding Agreement signed	Sponsors	Faith designation	Date due to open	LEA
Bedfordshire 2, The Bedford Academy, John Bunyan Upper School	Feasibility	Yes	No	Harpur Trust and Bedford College		1/9/10	Bedfordshire
Birmingham 11, Aston University 14–19 Engineering Academy	Feasibility	Yes	No	University of Aston		1/9/12	Birmingham
Birmingham 2, Birmingham Ormiston (Eastside) Academy 14–19	Feasibility	Yes	No	Ormiston Trust and Birmingham City University	No	1/9/11	Birmingham
Birmingham 3, North Birmingham Academy [College High School]	Feasibility	Yes	No	Edutrust Academies Charitable Trust and Aston Villa Football Club	No	1/9/09	Birmingham
Birmingham 5, King Edward VI Sheldon Heath Academy, Sheldon Heath Community Arts College	Feasibility	Yes	No	King Edward VI Foundation	No	1/9/10	Birmingham
Bournemouth 1, The Bourne Academy	Feasibility	Yes	No	Canford School		1/9/10	Bournemouth

Project name	Phase name	Expression of Interest signed	Funding Agreement signed	Sponsors	Faith designation	Date due to open	LEA
Bournemouth 2, The Bishop of Winchester Comprehensive School	Feasibility	Yes	No	Diocese of Winchester, University of Winchester, Bournemouth School, Bournemouth School for Girls	Yes	1/9/10	Bournemouth
Bradford 6, Greenhead High School	Feasibility	Yes	No	University of Bradford, Link Telecom and Bradford City Council (TBC)	No	1/9/10	Bradford
Camden 1, UCL Camden Academy	Feasibility	Yes	No	University College London		1/9/11	Camden
Croydon 5, Selsdon High School	Feasibility	Yes	No	Coloma Trust and Coloma Convent Girls School		1/9/10	Croydon
Dudley 3, St James's Park Academy	Feasibility	Yes	No	Oasis Community Learning		1/9/10	Dudley
East Sussex 1, Hillcrest School	Feasibility	Yes	No	University of Brighton, East Sussex CC and BT	No	1/9/11	East Sussex
East Sussex 2, Filsham Valley School and The Grove	Feasibility	Yes	No	University of Brighton, East Sussex CC and BT	No	1/9/11	East Sussex

(continued)

(*continued from previous page*)

Project name	Phase name	Expression of Interest signed	Funding Agreement signed	Sponsors	Faith designation	Date due to open	LEA
East Sussex 3, Eastbourne Technology College	Feasibility	Yes	No	Sussex Downs College (lead), East Sussex LA (co-sponsor), University of Brighton (educ. Partner), Edexcel, Peter Jones Footwear Co. (TBC potential business partners)		1/9/10	East Sussex
Gloucestershire 1, All Saints' Academy	Implementation	Yes	No	Clifton Diocese and Gloucester Diocese	Yes	1/9/11	Gloucestershire
Halton 1, Halton High School, Runcorn	Feasibility	Yes	No	Ormiston Trust (lead), University of Chester (co-sponsor)	No	1/9/10	Halton
Hammersmith and Fulham 2, Hammersmith and Fulham Academy, New Academy	Implementation	Yes	No	Mercers Company and Worshipful Company of Information Technologists	No	1/9/11	Hammersmith and Fulham
Hampshire 3, Staunton Community Sports College	Feasibility	Yes	No	South Downs FE College, Hampshire County Council, University of Portsmouth and Wildern School		1/9/10	Hampshire
Havering 1, Drapers' Academy	Feasibility	Yes	No	Drapers Company (lead) and Queen Mary University (secondary)	No	1/9/10	Havering

Project name	Phase name	Expression of Interest signed	Funding Agreement signed	Sponsors	Faith designation	Date due to open	LEA
Kent 12, The Vine Academy, Wildernesse School and The Bradbourne School	Feasibility	Yes	No	Gordon Phillips (Glen Care Group) and Sevenoaks School and Kent	No	1/9/10	Kent
Kent 13, Ashford Christ Church CoE Maths and Computing Specialist College	Feasibility	Yes	No	CE Diocese of Canterbury, Canterbury Christ Church University, Benenden School and Kent County Council	Yes	1/9/10	Kent
Kent 19, Duke of York's Royal Military School	Feasibility	Yes	No	SoS for Defence (Ministry of Defence – MoD)		1/9/10	Kent
Lincolnshire 11, St Clements School	Feasibility	Yes	No	Greenwood Dale Foundation Trust	No	1/9/10	Lincolnshire
Lincolnshire 4, Sleaford Academy, St Georges, Lafford High, The Aveland High and Coteland's School	Feasibility	Yes	No	St Georges College of Technology and University of Lincoln		1/1/10	Lincolnshire
Liverpool 3, New Heys Community Comprehensive School and St Benedict's College	Feasibility	Yes	No	Enterprise plc and Catholic Archdiocese and Church of England Diocese of Liverpool and Liverpool City Council	Yes	1/9/10	Liverpool

(continued)

(continued from previous page)

Project name	Phase name	Expression of Interest signed	Funding Agreement signed	Sponsors	Faith designation	Date due to open	LEA
Medway 2, Medway Community College and Chatham South School	Feasibility	Yes	No	CofE Diocese of Rochester, Canterbury Christ Church University and Medway Council	Yes	1/9/10	Medway
Medway 3, New Brompton College	Feasibility	Yes	No	University of Kent and Medway Council		1/9/10	Medway
Newham, Chobham Academy	Feasibility	Yes	No	Lend Lease	No	1/9/13	Newham
Northamptonshire 5, Unity College	Feasibility	Yes	No	The David Ross Foundation	Yes	1/9/10	Northamptonshire
Northamptonshire 8, Weston Favell School	Feasibility	Yes	No	ULT		1/1/10	Northamptonshire
Oldham 1, Oasis Oldham Academy, Kaskenmoor School and South Chadderton School	Feasibility	Yes	No	Oasis Community Learning Trust	No	1/9/10	Oldham
Oldham 2, Waterhead Academy, Counthill School and Breeze Hill School	Feasibility	Yes	No	The Oldham College	No	1/9/10	Oldham
Oldham 3, EACT Academy Oldham, Grange School	Feasibility	Yes	No	Edutrust Academies Charitable Trust		1/9/10	Oldham
Plymouth 1, Tamarside Community College	Feasibility	Yes	No	University of Plymouth and Cornwall College and Plymouth CC		1/9/10	Plymouth

Project name	Phase name	Expression of Interest signed	Funding Agreement signed	Sponsors	Faith designation	Date due to open	LEA
Plymouth 2, John Kitto Community College	Feasibility	Yes	No	The Exeter Diocesan Board of Education and Plymouth City Council and University College Plymouth		1/9/10	Plymouth
Poole 1, St Aldhelm's Academy, Rossmore Community College	Feasibility	Yes	No	The Church of England Salisbury Diocese and University of Bournemouth	Yes	1/9/10	Poole
Redbridge 1, Isaac Newton Academy	Feasibility	Yes	No	ARK	No	1/9/12	Redbridge
Redcar and Cleveland 1, Freebrough Specialist Engineering College	Feasibility	Yes	No	University of Teesside and Prior Pursglove College and Redcar and Cleveland LA		1/9/10	Redcar and Cleveland
Richmond 1, Hampton Community College	Feasibility	Yes	No	Kunskapsskolan and LB Richmond upon Thames		1/9/10	Richmond upon Thames
Richmond 2, Whitton School	Feasibility	Yes	No	Kunskapsskolan and LB Richmond upon Thames		1/9/10	Richmond upon Thames
Rotherham 1, Maltby Comprehensive School	Feasibility	Yes	No	U-xplore and Sheffield Hallam University (educational partner)		1/1/10	Rotherham
Somerset 1, The St Augustine of Canterbury School and Ladymead Community School	Feasibility	Yes	No	CE Diocese of Bath, Wells and Somerset County Council	Yes	1/9/10	Somerset

(continued)

(*continued from previous page*)

Project name	Phase name	Expression of Interest signed	Funding Agreement signed	Sponsors	Faith designation	Date due to open	LEA
St Helens 1, Newton Academy, St Aelred's Catholic Technology College and Newton-le-Willows High School	Implementation	Yes	No	CC of E Diocese of Liverpool, RC Archdiocese of Liverpool, Liverpool Hope University	No	1/9/11	St Helens
St Helens 2, Sutton High Sports College	Feasibility	Yes	No	St Helens College and Edge Hill University		1/9/10	St Helens
Staffordshire 2, Woodhouse High School	Feasibility	Yes	No	Landau Forte CTC Trust		1/9/10	Staffordshire
Stockton-on-Tees 1, Thornaby Community School	Feasibility	Yes	No	University of Teesside, Stockton Sixth Form College, Stockton Riverside College		1/9/10	Stockton-on-Tees
Stockton-on-Tees 2, Norton and Blakeston	Feasibility	Yes	No	Stockton PCT (lead), Stockton Riverside College, Stockton Sixth Form College, University of Durham (educ. partner)	No	1/9/10	Stockton-on-Tees
Stoke on Trent 2, Edensor Technology College, Mitchell High School and Longton High School	Feasibility	Yes	No	Stoke-on-Trent College		1/9/10	Stoke-on-Trent
Stoke on Trent 5, Blurton High School	Feasibility	Yes	No	Ormiston Educational Trust (lead) and Keele University (educ. partner)		1/9/10	Stoke-on-Trent

Project name	Phase name	Expression of Interest signed	Funding Agreement signed	Sponsors	Faith designation	Date due to open	LEA
Warwickshire 2, Manor Park Community School and Alderman Smith School	Feasibility	Yes	No	North Warwickshire and Hinckley College		1/9/10	Warwickshire
Wolverhampton 3, The Northicote School and Pendeford Business and Enterprise College	Feasibility	Yes	No	City of Wolverhampton FE College and University of Wolverhampton		1/9/10	Wolverhampton
Brighton and Hove 1, Falmer Academy, Falmer High School	Implementation	Yes	Yes	Rod Aldridge (Aldridge Foundation)	No	1/9/11	Kent
Calderdale 1, Holy Trinity CofE Senior School	Feasibility	Yes	Yes	Diocese of Wakefield and Calderdale MBC, Huddersfield University and Calderdale College	Yes	1/9/12	St Helens
Coventry 2, Sidney Stringer Academy	Implementation	Yes	Yes	Coventry City College (lead), Coventry City Council, Coventry University, Jaguar	No	1/9/11	Peterborough
Derbyshire 1, Shirebrook Academy, Shirebrook School	Implementation	Yes	Yes	All Roads DLO, Sheffield Hallam University (educ. partner)	No	1/9/11	Nottingham
Hackney 5, Skinners' Academy, The Skinners' Company School for Girls	Implementation	Yes	Yes	The Skinners Company	No	#####	Solihull
Manchester 2, Manchester Communications Academy	Implementation	Yes	Yes	BT (lead), Manchester College and MCC (co-sponsors)	No	1/9/10	Bristol, City of

(*continued*)

(continued from previous page)

Project name	Phase name	Expression of Interest signed	Funding Agreement signed	Sponsors	Faith designation	Date due to open	LEA
Manchester 3, East Manchester Academy	Implementation	Yes	Yes	Bovis Lend Lease and Laing O'Rourke (lead), Manchester College and MCC (co-sponsors)	No	1/9/10	Enfield
Manchester 5, The Co-operative Academy, Plant Hill High School	Implementation	Yes	Yes	The Co-operative Group (lead), Manchester College, MCC (co-sponsors)	No	1/9/10	Manchester
Staffordshire 1, JCB Academy, new school	Implementation	Yes	Yes	JCB	No	1/9/10	Lincolnshire

Appendix 2: The Academy Programme Process

The process for setting up an academy under New Labour has been adapted from the website, available at: www.standards.dfes.gov.uk/academies/setting_up/?version=1 (accessed 4 January 2010).

Establishing an Academy

Sponsors, Local Authorities (LAs) and other potential partners who are interested in the Academies Programme should, in the first instance, contact The Office of the Schools Commissioner (OSC) at the Department for Children Schools and Families (DCSF) for informal discussions.

For most Academies it takes between six and eighteen months from Ministers agreeing an Expression of Interest to opening. An overview of the key phases of establishing an academy in existing school buildings, whilst waiting for the academy's new or refurbished buildings is described below.

1. Brokering
   The OSC will support the development of partnerships between Sponsors and LAs to enable them and the DCSF to assess their secondary education and decide if a new Academy is the right solution for their needs.

   Once partnerships have been established, a Statement of Intent letter is issued by the Office of the Schools Commissioner to the LA. This confirms to the LA the sponsor's intention to work with them in taking forward the Academy Project.

2. Pre-Feasibility
   Once the Statement of Intent has been issued, the Sponsor and LA will work together to prepare a formal Expression of Interest (EoI) for Ministerial consideration at the DCSF. The EoI will clearly demonstrate the need for a new Academy in the area proposed and provide more details about the proposed Academy e.g. age range and pupil numbers. The DCSF provides detailed guidance on the form that the Expression of Interest should take. Once an EOI has received Ministerial approval the project will move to the Feasibility Stage.

3. The Feasibility Stage

The length of the Feasibility Phase is normally determined by the statutory process of consulting to close the predecessor school. This usually takes around 5 to 6 months. The purpose of the Feasibility Phase is to consult widely with key stakeholders to ensure the proposed academy meets their requirements of raising education standards and driving up wider community aspirations.

During this phase, the proposals in the EOI are developed further. In particular the sponsors vision and ethos for the Academy are developed into an education brief which will form the foundation of the Academy's curriculum.

A series of documents will need to be prepared to support the Academy proposal. These will allow the Secretary of State to judge whether to enter into a legally binding Funding Agreement to establish an Academy.

A project management company is appointed to co-ordinate and manage the wide range of tasks that will need to be completed ahead of Funding Agreement. A number of specialists and experts will be drawn upon to complete technical aspects such as legal work and public relations. The project management company is responsible for overseeing the work of these specialists and ensuring that work is completed on time and within the budget which DCSF has agreed.

4. The Implementation Stage

Once the Funding Agreement has been signed, the implementation phase commences and the remaining time ahead of the Academy opening will be spent preparing for a new school to open. This will include finalising management and staff appointments, agreeing the curriculum, undertaking academy marketing and collaboration activities, and supporting school development plans. Where the Principal Designate is appointed prior to opening, the Principal will be closely involved in much of this work with support from the project management company.

At the end of the phase, the Department completes final sign off on the educational plans and approves the academy for opening as an institution. Academies that open initially in the predecessor school buildings may be entitled to a small additional capital grant to cover costs such as renewed signage and other small capital projects required to open the school as an academy.

5. The Academy Buildings

The Academy buildings will usually be delivered through the Building Schools for the Future programme, or, occasionally, via a National

Framework set up by Partnerships for Schools. The LA will manage the delivery of the academy buildings and the sponsor will steer the design process. The LA will establish a Design Group which the sponsor will steer, to ensure the buildings meet the needs of the academy vision and curriculum.

6. Open
   The opening of the academy is a major milestone. However there is still much work to be done to ensure it is successful. During the initial stages of this phase a School Improvement Partner will be appointed to provide ongoing challenge and support to the academy and its leadership team in its efforts to realise the academy's vision and deliver sustainable improvements in educational standards.

References

Abrams, L. and Gibbs, J. (2002), 'Disrupting the logic of home-school relations: Parent involvement strategies and practices of inclusion and exclusion'. *Urban Education*, 37, (3), 384–407.

Adonis, A. (2006), 'Ofsted reports praise academies for raising standards in deprived areas. Results and behaviour improve as academies meet community and personal needs'. Press notice, 8 March. London: DCSF. Available at: www.dcsf.gov.uk/pns/DisplayPN.cgi?pn_id=2006_0027 (accessed 2 October 2009).

— (2007a), 'Parents back academies as report confirms they continue to improve results and make good progress'. Press notice, 19 July. London: DCSF. Available at: www.dcsf.gov.uk/pns/DisplayPN.cgi?pn_id=2007_0135 (accessed 2 October 2009).

— (2007b), 'Successful independent schools invited to sponsor or support academies'. Press notice, 2 October. London: DCSF. Available at: www.dcsf.gov.uk/pns/DisplayPN.cgi?pn_id=2007_0174 (accessed 2 October 2009).

— (2007c), 'Address to Headmasters' and Headmistresses' Annual Conference'. Speech, 2 October, Bournemouth. Available at: www.dcsf.gov.uk/speeches/search_detail.dfm?ID=681 (accessed 26 October 2009).

— (2007d), 'Academies take centre stage in Birmingham'. Press notice, 13 December. London: DCSF. Available at: www.dcsf.gov.uk/pns/DisplayPN.cgi?pn_id=2007_0237 (accessed 2 October 2009).

— (2007e), Letter addressed to Roger Titcombe, 16 October, reference 2007/0066352POAA, personal correspondence.

— (2008), foreword to Astle, J. and Ryan, C. (eds), *Academies and the Future of State Education*. London: CentreForum, pp. v–xi.

Advisory Centre for Education (ACE) (2005), *Academies: ACE Briefing*. London: ACE.

Aldrich, H. (1979), *Organizations and Environments*. Englewood Cliffs, NJ: Prentice-Hall.

Allen, R. (2007), 'Does school governance matter for pupil achievement? The long-term impact of the grant-maintained schools policy'. Paper presented at the Annual Conference of the British Educational Research Association, London, September.

— (2010), 'Replicating Swedish "free school" reforms in England'. *Research in Public Policy*, 10, (Summer), 4–7.

Andalo, D. (2007a), 'Blair appeals for more academy sponsors'. *EducationGuardian*, 14 May. Available at: www.guardian.co.uk/education/2007/may/14/schools.uk/print (accessed 27 May 2009).

— (2007b), 'Confusion over tax breaks for academies'. *EducationGuardian*, 21 March. Available at: www.guardian.co.uk/education/2007/mar/21/schools.uk4 (accessed 28 October 2009).

Anderson, A. (2005), 'An introduction to theory of change'. *Evaluation Exchange*, 11, (2), 12–19.

Angus, L. (2004) 'Globalization and educational change: bringing about the reshaping and re-norming of practice'. *Journal of Education Policy*, 19, (1), 23–41.

Anti Academies Alliance (2009), *AAA Constitution*. Available at: www.antiacademies.org.uk (accessed 28 October 2009).

Apple, M. W. (2006), 'Interrupting the Right: on doing critical educational work in Conservative times', in G. Ladson-Billings and W. F. Tate (eds), *Education Research in the Public Interest*. New York: Teachers College Press, pp. 27–45.

Ark Academies (2009), 'The ARK Schools ethos – Academic achievement: no excuses'. Available at: www.arkschools.org/pages/ark-schools/ark-academies/the-ark-schools-ethos.php (accessed 12 December 2009).

Ashworth, R. and Snape, S. (2004), 'An overview of scrutiny: a triumph of context over structure'. *Local Government Studies*, 30, (4), 538–56.

Aspire Public Schools (2009), 'Results'. Available at: www.aspirepublicschools.org/?q=results (accessed 1 September 2009).

Astle, J. (2008), 'From academies to "free schools"', in J. Astle and C. Ryan (eds), *Academies and the Future of State Education*. London: CentreForum, pp. 81–9.

Astle, J. and Ryan, C. (eds) (2008), *Academies and the Future of State Education*. London: CentreForum.

ATL (2007), 'New position on academies'. Available at: www.atl.org.uk/policy-and-campaigns/policies/new-position-on-academies.asp (accessed 30 October 2009).

Avison, K. (2008), 'Why a Steiner academy?' *Forum*, 50, (1), 85–95.

Bailey, M. (2005), 'Academies and how to beat them: "our pits, our jobs, but not our schools"'. *Forum*, 47, (1), 6–7.

Baker, M. (2009), 'Record sighting of education secretaries'. Blog, 3 March. Available at: www.mikebakereducation.co.uk/?blog=view&id=65 (accessed 27 May 2009).

Ball, S. J. (2005), 'Radical policies, progressive modernisation and deepening democracy: the academies programme in action'. *Forum*, 47, (2–3), 215–22.

— (2007), *Education PLC: Understanding Private Sector Participation in Public Sector Education*. London: Routledge.

— (2008a), 'New philanthropy, new networks and new governance in education'. *Political Studies*, 56, (4), 747–65.

— (2008b), *The Education Debate: Politics and Policy in the 21st Century*. Bristol: Policy Press.

— (2008c), 'New philanthropy and education policy'. Paper presented at the British Educational Research Association Annual Conference, Edinburgh, September.

— (2009a), 'Privatising education, privatising education policy, privatising educational research: network governance and the "competition state"'. *Journal of Education Policy*, 42, (1), 83–99.

— (2009b), 'Academies in context: politics, business and philanthropy and heterarchical governance'. *Management in Education*, 23, (3), 100–3.

Balls, E. (2007a), 'Department for children, schools and families – building on achievement, meeting new challenges'. Press notice, 10 July. London: DCSF. Available at: www.dcsf.gov.uk/pns/DisplayPN.cgi?pn_id=2007_0126 (accessed 2 October 2009).

— (2007b), 'Three new academies to get go ahead – with help of universities'. Press notice, 21 November. London: DCSF. Available at: www.dcsf.gov.uk/pns/DisplayPN.cgi?pn_id=2007_0217 (accessed 2 October 2009).

— (2008a), 'Academy programme to be further accelerated with lower set up costs and as part of new "National Challenge" programme'. Press notice, 29 February. London: DCSF. Available at: www.dcsf.gov.uk/pns/DisplayPN.cgi?pn_id=2008_0036 (accessed 2 October 2009).

— (2008b), 'Three National Challenge schools to become academies'. Press notice, 13 October. London: DCSF. Available at: www.dcsf.gov.uk/pns/DisplayPN.cgi?pn_id=2008_0227 (accessed 28 October 2009).

— (2009), '200th academy opens a year early as ministers set out new plans to open up programme to new sponsors'. Press notice, 7 September. London: DCSF. Available at: www.dcsf.gov.uk/pns/DisplayPN.cgi?pn_id=2009_0158 (accessed 2 October 2009).

Barber, M. (2003), 'Deliverable goals and strategic challenges – a view from England on reconceptualising public education', in Organisation for Economic Co-operation and Development (OECD), *Networks of Innovation: Towards New Models for Managing Schools and Systems.* Paris: OECD, pp. 113–30.

— (2007), *Instruction to Deliver.* London: Methuen.

Barkham, P. and Curtis, P. (2010), 'Gove has no "ideological objection" to firms making profits by running academy schools'. *Guardian*, 1 June.

Barnes, M., Newman, J. and Sullivan, H. (2007), *Power, Participation and Political Renewal.* Bristol: Policy Press.

Bass, B. and Stogdill, R. (1990), *Handbook of Leadership* (3rd edition). New York: Free Press.

Basu, R. (2007), 'Negotiating acts of citizenship in an era of neoliberal reform: the game of school closures'. *International Journal of Urban and Regional Research*, 31, (1), 109–27.

Bawden, A. (2008), 'Everyone loves the new kid in school'. *Guardian*, 19 August.

Becker, H. J., Nakagawa, K. and Corwin, R. G. (1997), 'Parent involvement contracts in California's charter schools: strategy for educational improvement or method of exclusion'. *Teachers College Record*, 98, (3), 511–36.

Becker, H. S. (1998), *Tricks of the Trade.* Chicago: University of Chicago Press.

Beckett, F. (2004), 'How car dealers can run state schools'. *New Statesman*, 20 September, 30–1.

— (2005), 'Blair's flagship schools and the money that never was'. *New Statesman*, 17 January. Available at: www.newstatesman.com/print/200501170021 (accessed 27 May 2009).

— (2007), *The Great City Academy Fraud.* London: Continuum.

— (2008a), 'Too much power?' *EducationGuardian*, 13 May.

— (2008b), 'Further reflections on the great city academy fraud'. *Forum*, 50, (1), 5–10.

— (2009), 'Return academies to state control'. *Guardian*, 7 September. Available at: www.guardian.co.uk/commentisfree/2009/sep/07/education-academies-sponsors (accessed 15 September 2009).

Beckett, F. and Evans, R. (2008), 'Who's making wishes come true?' *EducationGuardian*, 10 June.

Benn, M. (2007), 'What kind of future is this?' *EducationGuardian*, 23 October.

— (2008), 'Academies in action: case studies from Camden and Pimlico, 2007'. *Forum*, 50, (1), 33–40.

Bentley, T. and Wilsdon, J. (2004), 'Introduction: the adaptive state', in T. Bentley and J. Wilsdon (eds), *The Adaptive State: Strategies for Personalising the Public Realm.* London: Demos, pp.13–34.

Berends, M., Cannata, M. A. and Goldring, E. (2009), 'Innovation in schools of choice'. Paper presented at the American Educational Research Association Annual Conference, San Diego, CA.

Berends, M., Mendiburo, M. and Nicotera, A. (2008), 'Charter school effects in an urban school district: an analysis of student achievement growth'. Paper presented at the American Educational Research Association Annual Conference, New York.

Berends, M., Watral, C., Teasley, B. and Nicotera, A. (2008), 'Charter school effects on achievement: where we are and where we're going', in M. Berends, M. G. Springer and H. J. Walberg (eds), *Charter School Outcomes.* New York: Lawrence Erlbaum Associates.

Bernstein, B. (1970), 'Education cannot compensate for society'. *New Society,* 4–6 February, 344–7.

— (1990), *The Structuring of the Pedagogic Discourse: Class, Codes and Control.* London: Routledge.

Bevir, M. and Rhodes, R. A. W. (2003), 'Searching for civil society: changing patterns of governance in Britain'. *Public Administration,* 81, (1), 41–62.

Bhindi N. and Duignan, P. (1997), 'Leadership for a new century: authenticity, intentionality, spirituality and sensibility'. *Educational Management Administration and Leadership,* 25, 117–32.

Bifulco, R. and Ladd, H. F. (2005), 'Institutional change and coproduction of public services: the effect of charter schools on parental involvement'. *Journal of Public Administration Research and Theory,* 16, (4), 553–76.

— (2006) 'School choice, racial segregation and the test-score gap: evidence from North Carolina's charter school program'. *Journal of Policy Analysis and Management,* 26, (1), 31–56.

Blair T. (1999), 'Modernising public services'. Speech, 26 January. Available at: www.number10.gov.uk/output/Page1273.asp. (accessed 27 January 1999).

— (2005), 'Foreword by the Prime Minister', in DfES *Higher Standards, Better Schools for All,* Cm. 6677. Norwich: The Stationery Office.

— (2007a), 'Prime minister welcomes 200 trust school pathfinders and early adopters – and launches 400 academy prospectus'. Press notice, 14 May. London: DCSF. Available at: www.dcsf.gov.uk/pns/DisplayPN.cgi?pn_id=2007_0076 (accessed 2 October 2009).

— (2007b), 'Education, education, education – 10 years on', in T. Blair, C. Taylor and E. Reid (eds), *Education, Education, Education – 10 Years On.* London: SSAT, pp. 5–13.

Blunkett, D. (2000a), 'Blunkett sets out radical new agenda for inner city school diversity and improvement'. Press notice, 15 March. London: DCSF. Available at: www.dcsf.gov.uk/pns/DisplayPN.cgi?pn_id=2000_0106 (accessed 2 October 2009).

— (2000b), 'Blunkett announces locations for first three academies'. Press notice, 15 September. London: DCSF. Available at: www.dcsf.gov.uk/pns/DisplayPN.cgi?pn_id=2000_0396 (accessed 2 October 2009).

— (2000c), 'Transforming secondary education'. Speech to the Social Market Foundation, 15 March. Available at: www.dcsf.gov.uk/speeches/search_detail.cfm?ID=31 (accessed 18 September 2009).

— (2000d), 'Influence or irrelevance: can social science improve government?' Secretary of State's Economic and Social Research Council Lecture speech, 2 February. London: ESRC and DfEE.

Bobbitt, P. (2002), *The Shield of Achilles.* London: Penguin.

Bohte, J. (2004), 'Examining the impact of charter schools on performance in traditional public schools'. *Policy Studies Journal,* 32, (4), 501–20.

Bondi, L. (1987), 'School closures and local politics: the negotiation of primary school rationalization in Manchester'. *Political Geography Quarterly,* 6, (3), 203–24.

Booker, K., Zimmer, R. and Buddin, R. (2005), *The Effects of Charter Schools on School Peer Composition.* Working paper. Santa Monica, CA: RAND Corporation.

Bourdieu, P. (1998), *Acts of Resistance.* Cambridge: Polity Press.

— (2003), *Firing Back: Against the Tyranny of the Market 2.* London: Verso.

Brewer, D. J., Augustine, C. H., Zellman, G. L., Ryan, G., Goldman, C. A., Stasz, C. and Constant, L. (2006), *Education for a New Era: Design and Implementation of K-12 Education Reform in Qatar.* Santa Monica, CA: RAND Corporation.

Brighouse, T. and Woods, D. (2006), *The Joy of Teaching*. London: RoutledgeFalmer.
BBC News (2004a), 'Blair in academy talks with heads'. Available at: http://newsvote.bbc.co.uk/mpapps/pagetools/print.news.bbc.co.uk/1/hi/edcuation/395658 (accessed 27 May 2009).
— (2004b), 'Academies getting results at GCSE'. Available at: http://news.bbc.co.uk/go/pr/fr//1/hi/education/3602818.stm (accessed 17 November 2004).
— (2006a), 'Blair wants another 200 academies'. Available at: http://news.bbc.co.uk/1/hi/education/6157435.stm (accessed 27 May 2009).
— (2006b), 'Legal case over academy approved'. Available at: http://news.bbc.co.uk/1/hi/eduation/5148188.stm (accessed 5 May 2007).
— (2009a), 'Protesters spark academy closure'. Available at: http://news.bbc.co.uk/1/hi/england/cumbria/7846543.stm (accessed 23 January 2009).
— (2009b), 'Academies "losing independence"'. Available at: http://news.bbc.co.uk/1/hi/education/7906453.stm (accessed 1 March 2009).
Brookover, W. B. and Lezotte, L. W. (1979), *Changes in School Characteristics Coincident with Changes in Student Achievement*. East Lansing, MI: Institute for Research on Teaching, College of Education, Michigan State University.
Brown, G. (2007), 'Vision for education'. Speech, 31 October, University of Greenwich. Available at: www.number10.gov.uk/page13675 (accessed 23 December 2009).
Brush, C., Manolova, C. and Edelman, L. (2008), 'Properties of emerging organizations: an empirical test'. *Journal of Business Venturing*, 23, 547–66.
Bryk, A. S., Lee, V. E. and Holland, P. B. (1993), *Catholic Schools and the Common Good*. Cambridge, MA: Harvard University Press.
Bulkley, K. (2004), 'Balancing act: educational management organizations and charter school autonomy', in K. Bulkley and P. Wohlstetter (eds), *Taking Account of Charter Schools: What's Happened and What's Next?* New York: Teachers College Press.
— (2005), 'Losing voice?: educational management organizations and charter schools' educational programs'. *Education and Urban Society*, 37, (2), 204–34.
Bulkley, K. and Fisler, J. (2003), 'A decade of charter schools: from theory to practice'. *Education Policy*, 17, (3), 317–42.
Bullock, A. and Woodings, R. B. (eds) (1992), *The Fontana Dictionary of Modern Thinkers*. London: Fontana Paperbacks.
Burch, P. (2009), *Hidden Markets: The New Education Privatization*. New York: Routledge.
Burnett, J. (2009), 'Authentic assessment in the first Steiner academy'. *Management in Education*, 23, (3), 130–4.
Burns, J. (1978), *Leadership*. New York: Harper & Row.
Bush, T. and Glover, D. (2003), *School Leadership: Concepts and Evidence*. Nottingham: NCSL.
Caldwell, B. J. (2006), *Re-imagining Educational Leadership*. London: Sage.
Caldwell, B. J. and Harris, J. (2008), *Why Not the Best Schools?* Melbourne: ACER Press.
Campbell, C., Proctor, H. and Sherington, G. (2009), *School Choice: How Parents Negotiate the New School Market in Australia*. Sydney: Allen & Unwin.
Cannata, M. A. (2008), 'Charter schools and the teacher labor market'. Paper presented at the American Educational Research Association Annual Conference, New York.
Carnoy, M. (2000), 'School choice? Or is it privatization?' *Educational Researcher*, 29, (7), 15–20.
Carnoy, M., Jacobsen, R., Mishel, L. and Rothstein, R. (2005), *The Charter School Dust-Up*. New York: Teachers College Press.

Carr, W. and Hartnett, A. (1996), *Education and the Struggle for Democracy*. Buckingham: Open University Press.

Chavkin, N., and Williams, D. (1993), 'Minority parents and the elementary school: attitudes and practices', in N. Chavkin (ed.), *Families and Schools in a Pluralistic Society*. Albany: State University of New York Press, pp. 73–83.

Chitty, C. (2007), 'Evidence to the Committee of Enquiry into Academy Schools'. *Forum*, 49, (3), 345–6.

— (2008a), 'The academy fiasco special issue'. *Forum*, 50, (1), 3–102.

— (2008b), 'The school academies programme: a new direction or total abandonment?' *Forum*, 50, (1), 23–32.

Christensen, J. and Lake, R. J. (2007), 'The national charter school landscape in 2007', in R. J. Lake (ed.), *Hopes, Fears and Reality: A Balanced Look at American Charter Schools in 2007*. Seattle, WA: Center on Reinventing Public Education.

Chubb, J. E. and Moe, T. M. (1990), *Politics, Markets and America's Schools*. Washington, DC: Brookings Institution.

Clark, T. (2010), 'We have donors who wish to remain anonymous'. *EducationGuardian*, 6 July.

Clarke, C. (2003), *Transforming Standards in London's Most Challenging Boroughs – Clarke*. 13 November. London: DCSF. Available at: www.dcsf.gov.uk/pns/DisplayPN.cgi?pn_id=2003_0227 (accessed 2 October 2009).

Clarke, J. (2009), 'What crisis is this?' *Soundings*, 43, (Winter), 7–17.

Clarke, J. and Newman, J. (1997), *The Managerial State*. London: Sage.

Clinch, D. (2008), 'The Devon NUT campaign against trust schools'. *Forum*, 50, (1), 97–102.

Coldron, J. (2007), *Parents and the Diversity of Secondary Education: A Discussion Paper*, prepared for Research and Information on State Education. Sheffield: Sheffield Hallam University. Available at: www.risetrust.org.uk/Diversity.pdf. (Accessed 2 January 2008).

Coles, M. (2008), 'Governance and staffing', in J. Astle and C. Ryan (eds), *Academies and the Future of State Education*. London: CentreForum, pp. 25–31.

Connell, J. P. and Kubisch, A. C. (1998), 'Applying a theory of change approach to the evaluation of comprehensive community initiatives: progress, prospects and problems', in K. Fulbright-Anderson, A. C. Kubisch and J. P. Connell (eds), *New Approaches to Evaluating Community Initiatives. Volume 2: Theory, Measurement and Analysis*. Queenstown: Aspen Institute.

Conservative Party (2007), *Raising the Bar, Closing the Gap*. London: Conservative Party.

Covey, S. (2006), *The Speed of Trust*. New York: Simon & Schuster.

Crawford, M. (2007), 'Let's start at the very beginning: setting up a new secondary school'. *Management in Education*, 21, (3), 14–16.

Crook, F. (2010), 'The secret casualty'. *New Statesman*, 5 July, 34–5.

Crowther, D., Cummings, C., Dyson, A. and Millward, A. (2003), *Schools And Area Regeneration*. Bristol: The Policy Press.

Cummings, C., Dyson, A., Papps, I., Pearson, D., Raffo, C. and Todd, L. (2005), *Evaluation of the Full Service Extended Schools Project: End of First Year Report*. RR680. Nottingham: DfES Publications.

Cummings, C., Dyson, A., Muijs, D., Papps, I., Pearson, D., Raffo, C., Tiplady, L. and Todd, L., with Crowther, D. (2007), *Evaluation of the Full Service Extended Schools Initiative: Final Report. Research Report RR852*. London: DfES.

Curtis, A. (2009), 'Academies and school diversity'. *Management in Education*, 23, (3), 113–17.

Curtis, A., Exley, S., Saisa, A., Tough, S. and Whitty, G. (2008), *The Academies Programme:*

Progress, Problems and Possibilities. London: Sutton Trust and Institute of Education, University of London.

Curtis, P. (2006), 'Another school, another protest'. *EducationGuardian*, 21 November.

— (2009), 'Balls gets tough on academies'. *Guardian*, 15 January. Available at: www.guardian.co.uk/education/2009/jan/15/edballs-academies-leaguetables/ (accessed 27 May 2009).

Dale, R. (1989), 'The Thatcherite project in education: the case of the City Technology Colleges'. *Critical Social Policy*, 9, (4), 4–19.

Daun, H. (2003), 'Market forces and decentralization in Sweden: impetus for school development or threat to comprehensiveness and equity?' in D. N. Plank and G. Sykes (eds), *Choosing Choice: School Choice in International Perspective.* New York: Teachers College Press.

Davies, C. and Lim, C. (2008), *Helping Schools Succeed: A Framework for English Education.* London: Policy Exchange.

Davies J. S. (2005), 'Local governance and the dialectics of hierarchy, market and network'. *Policy Studies*, 26, (3/4), 311–35.

Davies, J. S. (2008), 'Double-devolution or double-dealing? The Local Government White Paper and the Lyons Review.' *Local Government Studies*, 34, (1), 3–22.

Davies, J. S. and Imbroscio, D. L. (eds) (2008), *Theories of Urban Politics* (2nd edition). London: Sage.

De Waal, A. (2009), *The Secrets of Academies' Success.* London: Civitas. Available at: www.civitas.org.uk/wordpress/2009/12/14/is-the-success-of-academies-a-sham/ (accessed 4 January 2010).

Dean, M. (2008), *Governing Societies.* Maidenhead: Open University Press.

Dee, T. and Fu, H. (2004), 'Do charter schools skim students or drain resources?' *Economics of Education Review*, 23, (3), 259–71.

DCSF (Department for Children, Schools and Families) (n.d.a), *Setting Up an Academy.* London: DCSF.

— (n.d.b), *Sponsorship Guide: Establishing an Academy – an Overview for Sponsors.* Available at: www.standards.dfes.gov.uk/academies/publications/?version=1 (accessed 18 September 2009).

— (2005), *Petchey Academy Funding Agreement.* Available at: www.dcsf.gov.uk/foischeme/subPage.cfm?action=collections.displayDocument&i_documentID=277&i_collectionID=190 (accessed 30 July 2009).

— (2007), *Closing a Maintained Mainstream School: A Guide for Local Authorities and Governing Bodies.* London: DCSF.

— (2008a), *Academies and Trusts: Opportunities for Schools, Sixth Form and FE Colleges.* London: DCSF.

— (2008b), 'Co-op schools to give people power over local education'. Press notice, 2008/0196. London: DCSF.

— (2009a), *What Are Academies?* Available at: www.standards.dfes.gov.uk/academies/what_are_academies/?version=1 (accessed 28 October 2009).

— (2009b), *Academies and the YPLA.* Available at: www.standards.dcsf.gov.uk/academies/news/?version=1 (accessed 28 October 2009).

— (2009c), *Every Child Matters.* Available at: www.dcsf.gov.uk/everychildmatters/ (accessed 14 September 2009).

— (2009d), *Your Child, Your Schools, Our Future: Building a 21st Century Schools System*, Cm 7588. Norwich: The Stationery Office.

— (2009e), *Why Academies?* Available at: www.standards.dfes.gov.uk/academies/what_are_academies/whyacademies/?version=1 (accessed 9 December 2009).

DCLG (Department for Communities and Local Government) (2008), *Communities in Control: Real People, Real Power*. London: The Stationery Office.

DfE (Department for Education) (2010a), 'Gove: "Teachers not politicians know how best to run schools"'. Available at: www.education.gov.uk/news/press-notices-new/academiesannouncement (accessed 2 July 2010).

— (2010b), 'Free schools'. Available at: www.education.gov.uk/freeschools (accessed 2 July 2010).

— (2010c), 'The case for school freedom: national and international evidence (*Gove mythbuster 2*) Available at: www.education.gov.uk/news/news/freeschools (accessed 2 July 2010).

DfEE (Department for Education and Employment) (2000), *City Academies: Schools to Make a Difference – a Prospectus for Sponsors and Other Partners*. London: DfEE.

DfEE/Welsh Office (1996), *Self-Government for Schools*, Cm. 3315. London: HMSO.

DfES (Department for Education and Skills) (2003a), *Petchey Foundation Expression of Interest*. Available at: www.dcsf.gov.uk/foischeme/_documents/DfES_FoI_199.pdf (accessed 30 July 2009).

— (2003b), *A Vision for Hackney Secondary Schools*. Available at: www.teachernet.gov.uk/_doc/5823/hackney.pdf (accessed 29 July 2009).

— (2003c), *Academies Marketing Toolkit*. London: DfES.

— (2004a), *What Are Academies?* Available at: www.standards.dfes.gov.uk/academies/whatareacademies/?version=1 (accessed 15 November 2004).

— (2004b), *Academies*. Available at: www.standards.dfes.gov.uk/academies/faq/?version=1 (accessed 15 November 2004).

— (2005a), *Academies Sponsor Prospectus 2005*. Nottingham: DfES.

— (2005b), *Response to the Second Annual Report from the PricewaterhouseCoopers Evaluation of the Academies Programme*. Nottingham: DfES.

— (2005c), *Extended Schools: Access to Opportunities and Services for All. A Prospectus*. London: DfES.

— (2007), *400 Academies – Prospectus for Sponsors and Local Authorities*. London: DfES.

DETR (Department for the Environment, Transport and Regions) (1999), *Local Leadership, Local Choice*. London: The Stationery Office.

Dorling, D., Rigby, J., Wheeler, B., Ballas, D., Thomas, B., Fahmy, E., Gordon, D. and Lupton, R. (2007), *Poverty, Wealth and Place in Britain, 1968 to 2005*. York: Joseph Rowntree Foundation.

Doxbury, S. (2006), 'Charter mission: Don Fisher kicks $40M to KIPP schools'. *San Francisco Business Times*, 20 March.

Duignan, P. (2004), *Authentic Educative Leadership for Authentic Learning*, Occasional paper, Australian Catholic University. Available at: http://web.ceomelb.catholic.edu.au/uploads/publications/lmatters/Duignan.pdf (accessed 29 July 2009).

Duncan, A. (2009), 'States open to charters start fast in race to the top. A statement by US Secretary of Education Arne Duncan in conference call to reporters'. Press notice, 8 June. Available at www.ed.gov/news/pressreleases/2009/06/06082009a.html (accessed 26 August 2009).

Duncan, J. S. (1990), *The City as Text: The Politics of Landscape Interpretation in the Kandyan Kingdom*. Cambridge: Cambridge University Press.

Dunton, J. (2009), 'Academy agency strife feared'. *Local Government Chronicle*, 26 February. Available at: www.lgcplus.com/news/academy-agency-strife-feared/1997670.article (accessed 1 March 2009).

Dyson, A., Raffo, C., Pearson, D., Cummings, C., Papps, I., Tiplady, L. and Todd, L. (2006), *Evaluation of the Full Service Extended Schools Initiative, Second Year: Thematic Papers* RR 795. London: DfES.

Dyson, A. and Todd, L. (2010), 'Dealing with complexity: theory of change evaluation and the full service extended schools initiative'. *International Journal of Research and Method in Education.* In press.

Economist (2008a), 'Six books a week: Harlem parents are voting for charter schools with their feet'. 10 May, 44.

— (2008b), 'Red ties and boys' pride: sowing the seeds of good schools in the mid-west'. 10 May, 44–5.

— (2009), 'The vanity of ideas: the Tories' futile quest to find an ideology'. 22 August, 46.

EducationGuardian (2008), 'Notebook'. 13 May.

Edwards, T., Fitz, J. and Whitty, G. (1989), *The State and Private Education: An Evaluation of the Assisted Places Scheme.* Basingstoke: Falmer Press.

Edwards, T., Gewirtz, S. and Whitty, G. (1992), 'Researching a policy in progress: the city technology initiative'. *Research Papers in Education,* 7, (1), 79–104.

Edwards, T. and Whitty, G. (1997), 'Specialisation and selection in secondary education'. *Oxford Review of Education,* 23, (1), 5–15.

Eisenschitz, A. and Gough, J. (1993), *The Politics of Local Economic Policy: The Problems and Possibilities of Local Initiatives.* Basingstoke: Macmillan.

Elliott, J. (2008), 'The birth of a school academy in North Norwich: a case study'. *Forum,* 50, (3), 353–66.

Elmore, R. (1990), 'Conclusion: toward a transformation of public schooling', in R. Elmore (ed.), *Restructuring Schools: The Next Generation of Educational Reform.* San Francisco: Jossey Bass.

Epstein, J. (1984), 'School policy and parent involvement: research results'. *Educational Horizons,* 62, (2), 70–2.

Evans, R (1998), *Housing Plus and Urban Regeneration: What Works, How, Why and Where?* Liverpool: European Institute of Urban Affairs, Liverpool John Moores University in association with the Housing Corporation.

ECAC (Every Child a Chance Trust) (2009), *The Long Term Costs of Numeracy Difficulties.* London: ECAC. Available at: www.everychildachancetrust.org/pubs/ECC_long_term_costs_numeracy_difficulties_final.pdf (accessed 2 January 2010).

Fearn, H. (2008), 'Vaulting Ambition'. *The Times Higher Education,* 12 June, 31–35.

File on 4 (2004), 'City Academies'. Available at: http://news.bbc.co.uk/1/hi/programmes/file_on_4/7427982.stm (accessed 23 November 2004).

Fink, D. (1997), 'The attrition of change'. Unpublished PhD thesis, School of Education, Open University.

Fiske, E. B. and Ladd, H. F. (2003), 'School choice in New Zealand: a cautionary tale', in D. N. Plank and G. Sykes (eds), *Choosing Choice: School Choice in International Perspective.* New York: Teachers College Press.

Frankenberg, E. and Lee, C. (2003), 'Charter schools and race: a lost opportunity for integrated education'. *Education Policy Analysis Archives,* 11, (32), 1–56.

Frean, A. (2009), 'Red tape is strangling our academies, say principals'. *The Times,* 24 February.

Fukuyama, F. (1995), *Trust: The Social Virtues and the Creation of Prosperity.* New York: The Free Press.

Geddes, M. (2008), 'Marxism and urban politics', in J. S. Davies and D. L. Imbroscio (eds), *Theories of Urban Politics* (2nd edition). London: Sage.

Gee, J. P. (1999), *An Introduction to Discourse Analysis: Theory and Method.* London: Routledge.

Giddens, A. (1998), *The Third Way: The Renewal of Social Democracy.* London: Polity Press.

Gill, B., Timpane, P. M., Ross, K. E., Brewer, D. J. and Booker, K. (2007), *Rhetoric Versus*

Reality: What We Know and What We Need to Know about Vouchers and Charter Schools. Santa Monica, CA: RAND Corporation.

Gillard D (2008), 'Blair's academies: the story so far'. *Forum*, 50, (1), 11–22.

Gilliland, R. (2008), 'All-through Academies', in J. Astle and C. Ryan (eds), *Academies and the Future of State Education.* London: CentreForum, pp. 41–7.

Glatter, R. (2002), 'Governance, autonomy and accountability in education', in T. Bush and L. A. Bell (eds), *The Principles and Practice of Educational Management.* London: Paul Chapman.

— (2003), 'Governance and educational innovation', in B. Davies and J. West-Burnham (eds), *The Handbook of Educational Leadership and Management.* London: Pearson Longman.

— (2009a), 'Where size does matter'. *Education Journal*, 114.

— (2009b), 'Let's look at academies systematically'. *Management in Education*, 23, (3), 104–7.

— (2010), 'Letters: academy schools. *Independent*, 29 May. Available at: www.independent.co.uk/opinion/letters/letters-academy-schools-1986228.html (accessed 2 July 2010).

Glees, A. (2005). 'Evidence-based policy or policy-based evidence? Hutton and the Government's use of secret intelligence'. *Parliamentary Affairs*, 58, (1), 138–55.

Goffman, E. (1974), *Frame Analysis: An Essay on the Organization of Experience.* Boston, MA: Northeastern University Press.

Goldhaber, D. (1999), 'An examination of the empirical evidence on achievement, parental decision making, and equity'. *Educational Researcher*, 28, (5), 16–25.

Goldring, E. and Shapira, R. (1993), 'Choice, empowerment and involvement: What satisfies parents?' *Educational Evaluation and Policy Analysis*, 15, (4), 396–409.

Goodfellow, M. and Walton, M. (2008), *The England Report.* Melbourne: ACER Press.

Goodwin, M. (2009), 'Which networks matter in educational Governance? A reply to Ball's "New philanthropy, new networks and gew Governance in education"'. *Political Studies*, 57, (3), 680–7.

Gorard, S. (2000), '"Underachievement" is still an ugly word: reconsidering the relative effectiveness of schools in England and Wales'. *Journal of Education Policy*, 15, (5), 559–73

— (2005), 'Academies as the "future of schooling": is this an evidence-based policy?' *Journal of Education Policy*, 20, (3), 369–77.

— (2006), *Using Everyday Numbers Effectively in Research.* London: Continuum.

— (2009), 'What are academies the answer to?' *Journal of Education Policy*, 24, (1), 101–13.

— (2010), 'Serious doubts about school effectiveness'. *British Educational Research Journal.* Available at: www.informaworld.com/openurl?genre=article&issn=0141-1926&issue=preprint&spage=1&doi=10.1080/01411920903144251&date=2009&atitle=Serious doubts about school effectiveness&aulast=Gorard&aufirst=Stephen

Gorard, S. and Taylor, C. (2001), 'The composition of specialist schools in England: track record and future prospect'. *School Leadership and Management*, 21, (4), 365–81.

Gove, M. (2008), 'Making opportunity more equal'. Speech delivered to CentreForum, 25 March. Available at: www.centreforum.org/events/gove-education.html (accessed 2 January 2009).

— (2010), 'Michael Gove to the National College Annual Conference, Birmingham'. Speech, 17 June, Birmingham. Available at: www.education.gov.uk/news/speeches/nationalcollegeannualconference (accessed 2 July 2010).

Gray, J. (2010), 'The nanny diaries'. *New Statesman*, 11 January, 52–3.

Green, E. (2009), 'Corporate features and faith-based academies'. *Management in Education*, 23, (3), 135–8.

Gregory, J. (2009), *In the Mix; Narrowing the Gap Between Public and Private Housing*. London: Fabian Society.

Grundy, M. (2008), 'Technology', in J. Astle and C. Ryan (eds), *Academies and the Future of State Education*. London: CentreForum, pp. 57–63.

Gunter, H. M. and Forrester, G. (2009), 'School leadership and education policymaking in England'. *Policy Studies*, 30, (5), 495–511.

Gunter, H. M., Raffo, C., Hall, D., Dyson, A., Jones, L. and Kalambouka, A. (2010), 'Policy and the policy process', in C. Raffo, A. Dyson, H. M. Gunter, D. Hall, L. Jones and A. Kalambouka (eds), *Education and Poverty in Affluent Countries*. London: Routledge, pp. 163–76.

Gunter, H. M., Woods, G. and Woods, P. (2008), 'Research and the Academies Programme in England'. *Management in Education*, 22, (4), 3–7.

Hackney Council (2006), *Implementation of the Government's Academies Programme in Hackney*, Report of the children and young people's scrutiny commission. Available at: www.hackney.gov.uk/commission-reports-academies-report-0506.pdf (accessed 10 December 2009).

Hackett, G. (2007), 'All work, no play at Blair flagship school'. *Sunday Star Times*, 6 May. Available at: www.timesonline.co.uk/tol/news/uk/article1752289.ece?print=yes&randnum=1243 (accessed 27 May 2009).

Hallinger, P. (1992), 'The evolving role of American principals: from managerial to instructional to transformational leaders'. *Journal of Educational Administration*, 30, (3), 35–48.

HOTS (Hands Off Tamworth Schools) (2008), *Putting Communities First: Education at the Heart of Tamworth*. 8 December. Tamworth: HOTS.

— (2009a), *A Response from Parents to Staffordshire County Council's 'Report on Consultation Regarding BSF in Tamworth'*. 25 January. Tamworth: HOTS.

— (2009b), *Objection to Staffordshire County Council's BSF Proposals for Tamworth*. 1 April. Tamworth: HOTS.

Hansard (2007), 'House of Commons Hansard Written Answers for 16 April 2007'. Available at: www.publications.parliament.uk/pa/cm200607/cmhansrd/cm070416/text/70416w0 (accessed 27 May 2009).

Harris, J. (2009), 'We're outsourcing the future, to be built by Thatcher and Philip K. Dick'. *Guardian*, 29 July.

Harvey, D. (2007), *A Brief History of Neoliberalism*. Oxford: Oxford University Press.

Hasan, M. (2010), 'To the schools that have, more is given'. *New Statesman*, 21 June, 12.

Hatcher, R. (2006), 'Privatization and sponsorship: the re-agenting of the school system in England'. *Journal of Education Policy*, 21, (5), 599–619.

— (2008a), 'Selling academies: local democracy and the management of "consultation"'. *Journal for Critical Education Policy Studies*, 6, (2), 21–36.

— (2008b), 'Academies and diplomas: two strategies for shaping the future workforce'. *Oxford Review of Education*, 34, (6), 665–76.

— (2009), 'Setting up academies, campaigning against them: an analysis of a contested policy process'. *Management in Education*, 23, (3), 108–12.

Hatcher, R. and Jones, K. (2006), 'Researching resistance: campaigns against academies in England'. *British Journal of Educational Studies*, 54, (3), 329–51.

Henig, J., Holyoke, T., Lacireno-Paquet, N. and Moser, M. (2003), 'Privatization, politics and urban services: the political behavior of charter schools'. *Journal of Urban Affairs*, 25, (1), 37–54.

Henry, J. (2007), 'Tony Blair's city academy £49m record cost'. *Telegraph*, 22 July.

Available at: www.telegraph.co.uk/news/uknews/1558112/Tony-Blairs-city-academys-49m-record-cost.html (accessed 27 May 2009).

HM Government (2010), *The Coalition: Our Programme For Government.* London: Cabinet Office. Available at: www.cabinetoffice.gov.uk/media/409088/pfg_coalition.pdf (accessed 2 July 2010).

Hill, P., Angel, L. and Christensen, J. (2006), 'Charter school achievement studies'. *Education Finance and Policy,* 1, (1), 139–50.

Hill, R. (2008), 'The value of partnership working'. *Education Journal,* 109.

Hodge, S. T. (2007), 'Editor's review of tough choices or tough times: the report of the New Commission on the Skills of the American Workforce by the National Centre on Education and the Economy'. *Harvard Education Review,* (Winter). Available at: www.hepg.org/her/abstract/636 (accessed 23 December 2009).

Hodgkinson, C. (1991), *Educational Leadership: The Moral Art.* Albany: State University of New York Press.

Hood, C. (1991), 'A public management for all seasons?' *Public Administration,* 69, (1), 3–19.

Hopkins, D. (2001), *Instructional Leadership and School Improvement.* Nottingham: NCSL. Available at: www.ncsl.org.uk/media/1D3/BF/instructional-leadership-and-schoolimprovement (accessed 20 July 2009).

Home Office, the Department of Health and the National Health Service (2008), *Annual Report.* Available at: www.kpmg.eu/report/5770.htm (accessed 2 January 2008).

House of Commons (2005), *Education and Skills Committee: Secondary Education. Fifth Report of Session 2004–05.* HC 86. London: The Stationery Office.

— (2009), *Academies, Oral Evidence. 1 July 2009.* London: The Stationery Office.

House of Commons Committee of Public Accounts (2007), *The Academies Programme.* HC 402. London: The Stationery Office.

Hoxby, C. (2003), *The Economics of School Choice.* Chicago: University of Chicago Press.

Hoxby, C. and Murarka, S. (2008), 'Methods of assessing the achievement of students in charter schools', in M. Berends, M. G. Springer and H. J. Walberg (eds), *Charter School Outcomes.* New York: Lawrence Erlbaum Associates.

Hoxby, C., Murarka, S. and Kang, J. (2009), *How New York City's Charter Schools Affect Achievement, August 2009 Report.* Cambridge, MA: New York City Charter Schools Evaluation Project.

Hoxby, C. and Rockoff, J. (2004), *The Impact of Charter Schools on Student Achievement.* Cambridge, MA: Harvard University Department of Economics.

Hyman, P. (2005), *1 out of 10: From Downing Street Vision to Classroom Reality.* London: Vintage.

Jencks, C. and Mayer, S. (1990), 'The social consequences of growing up in a poor neighborhood', in L. Lynn and M. McGeary (eds), *Inner-City Poverty in the United States.* Washington, DC: National Academy Press.

Jenkins, S. (2008), 'Academies, value for money and elitism'. *Guardian,* 11 June. Available at: www.educationguardian.co.uk (accessed 2 January 2009).

Jesson, D. and Crossley, D. (2007), *Educational Outcomes and Value Added by Specialist Schools, 2006 Analysis.* London: SSAT.

Jessop, B. (1998), 'The rise of governance and the risks of failure'. *International Social Science Journal,* 155, (1), 29–45.

— (2002), *The Future of the Capitalist State.* Cambridge: Polity Press.

Johnson, A. (2006), 'Parent power and new independent report give fresh backing to academies'. Press notice, 27 July. London: DCSF. Available at: www.dcsf.gov.uk/pns/DisplayPN.cgi?pn_id=2006_0114 (accessed 2 October 2009).

— (2007), 'Academies on track to give value for money says NAO. Alan Johnson says: "Academies work and are worth it"'. Press notice, 23 February. London: DCSF. Available at: www.dcsf.gov.uk/pns/DisplayPN.cgi?pn_id=2007_0028 (accessed 2 October 2009).

Johnstone, B. (2008), *Discourse Analysis* (2nd edition). Malden, MA: Blackwell.

Kay, P. (2006), *The Sound of Laughter*. London: Arrow Books.

Keating, M. (2004), *Who Rules? How Government Retains Control of a Privatised Economy*. Sydney: Federation Press.

Keep, E. (2004), 'The multiple dimensions of performance: performance as defined by whom, measured in what ways, to what ends?' *Nuffield Review of 14–19 Education and Training Working Paper* 23. Available at: www.nuffield14-19review.org.uk (accessed 10 June 2009).

— (2005), 'State control of the English VET system: playing with the biggest train set in the world'. Keynote lecture, Annual Conference of the *Journal of Vocational Education and Training* (JVET), Oxford, 14–15 July.

Kelly, R. (2006), 'Academy programme reaches halfway mark towards 200 new schools'. Press notice, 16 March. London: DCSF. Available at: www.dcsf.gov.uk/pns/DisplayPN.cgi?pn_id=2006_0036 (accessed 2 October 2009).

Kendall, S. (2008), 'The balancing act: framing gendered parental identities at dinner time'. *Language in Society*, 37, 539–68.

Kickert, W. J. M., Klijn, E. H. and Koppenjan, J. F. M. (1997), 'Managing networks in the public sector: findings and reflections', in W. J. M. Kickert, E. H. Klijn and J. F. M. Koppenjan (eds), *Managing Complex Networks: Strategies for the Public Sector*. Thousand Oaks, CA: Sage.

Kjaer, A. M. (2009), 'Governance and the urban bureaucracy', in J. S. Davies and D. L. Imbroscio (eds) (2008), *Theories of Urban Politics* (2nd edition). London: Sage.

Knight, J. (2008), 'More independent endorsement of academies' success'. Press notice, 27 November. London: DCSF. Available at: www.dcsf.gov.uk/pns/DisplayPN.cgi?pn_id=2008_0269 (accessed 2 October 2009).

Lacireno-Paquet, N., Holyoke, T., Moser, M. and Henig, J. (2002), 'Creaming versus cropping: charter school enrollment practices in response to market incentives'. *Educational Evaluation and Policy Analysis*, 24, (2), 145–58.

Ladd, H. F. (2003), introduction to D. N. Plank and G. Sykes (eds), *Choosing Choice: School Choice in an International Perspective*. New York: Teachers College Press.

Lareau, A. (1987), 'Social class differences in family-school relationships: the importance of cultural capital'. *Sociology of Education*, 60, (2), 73–85.

Larsen, J. (2001), 'Contestations, innovation and change: a case study of a new Western Australian secondary school'. Unpublished PhD thesis, Institute of Education, University of London.

Le Grand, J. (2006), 'The Blair legacy: choice and competition in public services'. Public lecture, 21 February, London School of Economics. Available at: www.lse.ac.uk/collections/LSEPubliclecturesAndEvents/pdf/20060221-LeGrand.pdf (accessed 2 January 2007).

Leithwood, K., Jantzi, D. and Steinbach, R. (1999), *Changing Leadership for Changing Times*. Buckingham: Open University Press.

Liberal Democrats (2009), *Equity and Excellence: Policies for 5–19 Education in England's Schools and Colleges*. Policy Paper 89. London: Liberal Democrats.

Lubienski, C. (2003), 'Innovation in education markets: theory and evidence on the impact of competition and choice in charter schools'. *American Education Research Journal*, 40, (2), 395–443.

— (2006), 'School diversification in second-best education markets: international

evidence and conflicting theories of change'. *Educational Policy*, 20, (2), 323–44.
Lubienski, C., Gulosino, C. and Weitzel, P. (2009), 'School choice and competitive incentives: mapping the distribution of educational opportunities across local education markets'. *American Journal of Education*, 115, (4), 601–47.
Lupton, R. (2001), *Places Apart? The Initial Report of CASE's Areas Study*. London: Centre for the Analysis of Social Exclusion, London School of Economics.
Macaulay, H. (2008), *Under the Microscope: Leading in a Climate of Close Public Scrutiny. Research Associate Report*. Nottingham: NCSL.
Machin, S. and Wilson, J. (2009a), 'Academy schools and pupil performance'. *CentrePiece*, (Spring), 6–8.
— (2009b), *Academy Schools and Pupil Performance*. London: Centre for Economic Performance, London School of Economics.
Mackenzie, R. and Lucio, M. M. (2005), 'The realities of regulatory change: beyond the fetish of deregulation'. *British Journal of Sociology*, 39, (3), 499–517.
McLeod, J. (1988), 'City Technology Colleges – a study of the character and progress of an educational reform'. *Local Government Studies*, January/February, 75–82.
Malloy, C. L. and Wohlstetter, P. (2003), 'Working conditions in charter schools: what's the appeal for teachers?' *Education and Urban Society*, 35, (2), 219–41.
Mandelson, P. and Liddle, R. (1996), *The Blair Revolution: Can New Labour Deliver?* London: Faber & Faber.
Mansell, W. (2009a), 'The unofficial opposition'. *EducationGuardian*, 5 May.
— (2009b), 'A ludicrously expensive con-trick'. *Guardian*, 1 December.
— (2010), 'Threat hangs over appeals panels for excluded children'. *Guardian*, 29 June. Available at: www.guardian.co.uk/education/2010/jun/28/school-exclusion-appeal-panels-threatened (accessed 2 July 2010).
Marinetto, M. (2005), 'Governing beyond the centre: a critique of the Anglo-governance school'. *Political Studies*, 20, (3), 592–608.
Marjoribanks, K. (1979), *Families and Their Learning Environments: An Empirical Analysis*. London: Routledge & Kegan Paul.
Marley, D. (2007), 'Academies preach to the unconverted'. *The Times Educational Supplement*, 9 November.
Marquand, D. (1981), 'Club government – the crisis of the Labour Party in the national perspective'. *Government and Opposition*, 16, (1), 19–36.
— (2004), *Decline of the Public*. Cambridge: Polity Press.
Marshall, P. (2008), 'Primary academies', in J. Astle and C. Ryan (eds), *Academies and the Future of State Education*. London: CentreForum, pp. 72–80.
Meikle, J. (2007), 'Steiner school to join state academy ranks'. *Guardian*, 23 January.
Meyland-Smith, D. and Evans, N. (2009), *A Guide to School Choice Reforms*. London: Policy Exchange.
Metz, H. (1990), 'Real school: a universal drama amid disparate experience', in D. E. Mitchell and M. E. Goertz (eds), *Education Politics for the New Century*. New York: Falmer Press.
Miliband, D. (2002), 'David Miliband opens Unity City Academy in Middlesbrough'. Press notice, 13 September. London: DCSF. Available at: www.dcsf.gov.uk/pns/DisplayPN.cgi?pn_id=2002_0290 (accessed 2 October 2009).
Miliband, R. (1973), *The State in Capitalist Society*. London: Quartet Books.
— (1982), *Capitalist Democracy in Britain*. Oxford: Oxford University Press.
Millar, F. (2006), 'Parents go to court'. *New Statesman*, 31 July, 18.
— (2008), 'Just tell us the truth about academies'. *EducationGuardian*, 12 February.
— (2010), 'Beware private empire building parading as parent power'.

EducationGuardian, 9 March. Available at: www.guardian.co.uk/education/2010/mar/09/schools-governors-democratic-private-companies (accessed 9 March 2010).

Miller, T. and Miller, J. (2001), 'Educational leadership in the new millennium: a vision for 2020'. *International Journal of Leadership in Education*, 4, (2), 181–9.

Mills, S. (1997), *Discourse*. London: Routledge.

Miron, G. and Nelson, C. (2002), *What's Public about Charter Schools? Lessons Learned about Accountability and Choice*. Thousand Oaks, CA: Corwin Press.

Molnar, A. (2006), 'The commercial transformation of public education'. *Journal of Education Policy*, 21, (5), 621–40.

Morris, E. (2000), 'Two more city academies to boost standards in Haringey and Middlesbrough – Morris'. Press notice, 12 October. London: DCSF. Available at: www.dcsf.gov.uk/pns/DisplayPN.cgi?pn_id=2000_0433 (accessed 2 October 2009).

— (2002), 'Morris sets out the London Challenge: standards, behaviour, choice'. Press notice, 1 July. London: DCSF. Available at: www.dcsf.gov.uk/pns/DisplayPN.cgi?pn_id=2002_0134 (accessed 2 October 2009).

Morris, H. (1924), *The Village College. Being a Memorandum on the Provision of Educational and Social Facilities for the Countryside, with Special Reference to Cambridgeshire*. Available at: www.infed.org/thinkers/et-morr.htm (accessed 2 May 2005).

Moynihan, D. (2008), 'Sponsors', in J. Astle and C. Ryan (eds), *Academies and the Future of State Education*. London: CentreForum, pp. 14–24.

Muller, K. (2008), 'Hey! Bankers! Leave those kids alone: the fight to save Islington Green School'. *Forum*, 50, (1), 71–83.

NASUWT (National Association of Schoolmasters Union of Women Teachers) (2009), 'Academies'. Available at: www.nasuwt.org.uk/InformationandAdvice/NASUWTPolicyStatements/PolicyStatement1/NASUWT_000263 (accessed 30 October 2009).

NAO (National Audit Office) (2007), *The Academies Programme*. London: The Stationery Office.

NAHT (National Association of Headteachers) (2009), *Academies*. Available at: www.naht.org.uk (accessed 6 November 2009).

National Centre on Education and the Economy (2007), *Tough Choices or Tough Times*. San Francisco: John Wiley & Sons.

NUT (National Union of Teachers) (n.d.), *Privatisation of Education: The Future?* Available at: www.teachers.org.uk (accessed 27 May 2009).

— (2007), *Academies, Looking Beyond the Spin. Why the NUT Calls for a Different Approach*. London: NUT.

Neal, D. (2009), 'Private schools in education markets', in M. Berends, M. G. Springer, D. Ballou and H. J. Walberg (eds), *Handbook of Research on School Choice*. New York: Routledge.

Needham, C., Gleeson, D., Martin, B. and Rickford, R. (2006), 'Academy schools: case unproven'. Independent study. Birmingham: NASUWT.

Nelson, F. (2008), 'Made in Sweden: the new Tory revolution'. *Spectator*, 27 February. Available at: www.spectator.co.uk/the-magazine/features/526631/made-in-sweden-the-new-tory-education-revolution.thtml (accessed 26 August 2009).

Newman, J. (2001), *Modernising Governance*. London: Sage.

— (2005), 'Participative governance and the remaking of the public sphere', in J. Newman (ed.), *Remaking Governance*. Bristol: Policy Press.

— (2007), 'Rethinking the "public" in troubled times'. *Public Policy and Administration*, 22, (1), 27–47.

Newman, J. and Clarke, J. (2009), *Publics, Politics and Power*. London: Sage.

Northampton Academy (n.d.), 'Tony Blair visits Northampton Academy'. Available at: www.northampton-academy.org/news/tony-blair-visits-northampton-academy (accessed 27 May 2009).

Nuffield Review of 14–19 Education and Training in England and Wales (2009), *Education For All: The Future of Education and Training for 14–19 Year Olds.* London: Routledge.

O'Hear, P. (2008), 'Community', in J. Astle and C. Ryan (eds), *Academies and the Future of State Education.* London: CentreForum, pp. 48–56.

Ofsted (Office for Standards in Education) (2009), *The Annual Report of Her Majesty's Chief Inspector of Education, Children's Services and Skills 2008/09.* London: Ofsted.

Orfield, G. and Lee, C. (2006), *Racial Transformation and the Changing Nature of Segregation.* Cambridge, MA: Civil Rights Project.

OECD (Organisation for Economic Co-operation and Development) (2007), executive summary in *The Programme for International Student Assessment (PISA): PISA 2006 – Science Competencies for Tomorrow's World.* Paris: OECD.

— (2008), *Education at a Glance 2008: OECD Indicators.* Paris: OECD.

Osborne, D. and Gaebler, T. (1992), *Reinventing Government.* Reading, MA: Addison-Wesley.

Ozga, J. (2000), *Policy Research in Educational Settings: Contested Terrain (Doing Qualitative Research in Educational Settings).* Buckingham: Open University Press.

— (2005), 'Modernising the education workforce: a perspective from Scotland'. *Educational Review,* 57, (2), 207–19.

Ozga, J. and Dale, R. (1991), *Module 1. Introducing Education Policy: Principles and Perspectives.* Milton Keynes: Open University Press.

Panel on Fair Access to the Professions (2009), *Unleashing Aspiration: The Final Report.* London: Cabinet Office.

Pennell, H. and West, A. (2007), *Parents in the Driving Seat? Parents' Role in Setting Up New Secondary Schools.* London: Research and Information on State Education Trust.

Pike, M. A. (2009), 'The Emmanuel Schools Foundation: sponsoring and leading transformation at England's most improved academy'. *Management in Education,* 23, (3), 139–43.

Podgursky, M. (2008), 'Teams versus bureaucracies: personnel policy, wage setting, and teacher quality in traditional public, charter and private schools', in M. Berends, M. G. Springer and H. J. Walberg (eds), *Charter School Outcomes.* New York: Lawrence Erlbaum Associates.

Pollitt, C. (2007), 'New Labour's re-disorganisation: hyper-modernism and the costs of reform: a cautionary tale'. *Public Management Review,* 9, (4), 529–43.

Powell-Davies, M. (2008), 'Haberdashers' Aske's: the campaign against academies in Lewisham'. *Forum,* 50, (1), 61–9.

Power, A. and Mumford, K. (1999), *The Slow Death of Great Cities? Urban Abandonment or Urban Renaissance.* York: York Publishing Services.

PricewaterhouseCoopers (PwC) LLP on behalf of the Department for Children, Schools and Families (DfES) (2003), *Academies Evaluation: First Annual Report.* London: DfES. Available at: www.standards.dfes.gov.uk/academies/pdf/Annualreport2003.pdf?version=1

— (2005), *Academies Evaluation: Second Annual Report.* London: DfES. Available at: www.education.gov.uk/research/programmeofresearch/projectinformation.cfm?projectid=14965&resultspage=1

— (2006), *Academies Evaluation: Third Annual Report.* London: DfES. Available at: www.standards.dcsf.gov.uk/local/pdf/3rdannualreport.pdf

— (2007), *Academies Evaluation: Fourth Annual Report.* London: DCSF. Available at: www.standards.dfes.gov.uk/academies/pdf/FourthAnnualPwCReportfinal.pdf?version=1

— (2008), *Academies Evaluation: Fifth Annual Report.* London: DCSF. Available at: www.standards.dcsf.gov.uk/academies/pdf/Academies5thAnnualReport.pdf?version=1

Prime Minister's Strategy Unit (2006), *The UK Government's Approach to Public Service Reform – a Discussion Paper.* London: Public Service Reform Team/Cabinet Office.

Punt, B., Nusche, D. and Moorman, H. (2008), *Improving School Leadership, Vol. 1, Policy and Practice.* Paris: OECD.

Purcell, K. (2008), 'Academies: Neoliberal educational institutions?' Unpublished paper presented to the RGS–IBG Annual International Conference, London, 29 August.

Quinn, B. (2008), '40 Pupils excluded in Academy 360 discipline crackdown'. *Sunday Times,* September 18. Available at: www.timesonline.co.uk/tol/life_and_style/education/article4776352.ece (accessed 18 September 2008).

Raffo, C., Dyson, A., Gunter, H. M., Hall, D., Jones, L. and Kalambouka, A. (eds) (2010), *Education and Poverty in Affluent Countries.* London: Routledge.

Raffo, C. and Gunter, H. M. (2008), 'Leading schools to promote social inclusion: developing a conceptual framework for analysing research, policy and practice'. *Journal of Education Policy,* 23, (4), 363–80.

Ramnarayan, S. and Rao, R. M., (1994), 'Leaders in action: some illustrations and inferences'. *Vikalpa,* 19, (2), 3–12.

Ranson, S. (1993), 'Markets or democracy for education'. *British Journal of Educational Studies,* 41, (4), 333–52.

— (1995), 'Public institutions for cooperative action: a reply to James Tooley'. *British Journal of Educational Studies,* 43, (1), 35–42.

— (2008), 'The Changing Governance of Education'. *Educational Management Administration and Leadership,* 36, (2), 201–19

Ranson, S. and Crouch, C. (2009), *Towards a New Governance of Schools in the Remaking of Civil Society.* Coventry: University of Warwick Institute of Education and Institute of Governance and Public Management for the CfBT Education Trust.

Rao, H., Morrill, C. and Zand, M. N. (2000), 'Power plays: how social movements and collective action create new organizational forms'. *Organizational Behaviour,* 22, 239–82.

Rawlings, L., Harris, L. and Turner, M. A. (2004), 'Race and residence: prospects for stable neighborhood integration'. *Neighborhood Change in Urban America,* 3, March 2004. Washington, DC: Urban Institute. 1–9. Available at: www.urban.org:80/UploadedPDF/310985_NCUA3.pdf (accessed 2 January 2005).

Raywid, M. A. (1985), 'Family choice arrangements in public schools: a review of the literature'. *Review of Educational Research,* 55, (4), 435–67.

Regan, B. (2007), 'Campaigning against neo-liberal education'. *Journal for Critical Education Policy Studies,* 5, (1), n.p. Available at: www.jceps.com/index.php?pageID=article&articleID=82 (accessed 27 July 2007).

Richardson, E. (1975), *Authority and Organisation in the Secondary School.* London: Macmillan.

Ringen, S. (2007), *What Democracy Is For: On Freedom and Moral Government.* Oxford: Princeton University Press.

Rogers, M. and Migniuolo, F. (2007), *A New Direction: A Review of the School Academies Programme.* London: TUC.

Rose, G. (2001), *Visual Methodologies: An Introduction to the Interpretation of Visual Methods.* London: Sage.

Rowntree (2009), *Monitoring Poverty and Exclusion.* York: Rowntree Foundation.

Rutter, M., Maughan, B., Mortimore, P. and Ouston, J. (1979), *Fifteen Thousand Hours: Secondary Schools and Their Effects on Children.* London: Open Books.

Ryan, C. (2008), 'The history of academies', in J. Astle and C. Ryan (eds), *Academies and the Future of State Education*. London: CentreForum, pp. 1–13.

Saint-Martin, D. (2001), 'How the reinventing government movement in public administration was exported from the U.S. to other countries'. *International Journal of Public Administration*, 24, (6), 573–604.

Sass, T. R. (2006), 'Charter schools and student achievement in Florida'. *Education Finance and Policy*, 1, (1), 91–122.

Seldon, A. (2008), 'Boarding', in J. Astle and C. Ryan (eds), *Academies and the Future of State Education*. London: CentreForum, pp. 64–71.

Sheppard, B. (1996), 'Exploring the transformational nature of instructional leadership'. *Alberta Journal of Educational Research*, 42, (4), 325–44.

Shepherd, J. (2008), 'How's business at Thomas Deacon plc?' *EducationGuardian*, March 4.

Silverman, E., Lupton, R. and Fenton, A. (2006), *Attracting and Retaining Families in Inner Urban Mixed Income Communities*. Coventry: Chartered Institute of Housing for the Joseph Rowntree Foundation.

Sinnott, S. (2008), 'Academies: a breakthrough or yet more spin?' *Forum*, 50, (1), 41–7.

Skelcher, C. (1998), *The Appointed State: Quasi-Governmental Organisations and Democracy*. Buckingham: Open University Press.

Skelcher, C. (2000), 'Changing images of the state – overload, hollowed out, congested' *Public Policy and Administration*, 15 (3), 3–19.

Skidmore, P. and Bound, K. (2008), *The Everyday Democracy Index*. London: Demos.

Smrekar, C. (2009), 'The social contest of magnet schools', in M. Berends, M. G. Springer, D. Ballou and H. J. Walberg (eds), *Handbook of Research on School Choice*. New York: Routledge.

Smith, A. (2008), 'Should universities and colleges sponsor academies?' *UC*, October, 12–13.

Smithers, A. and Robinson, P. (2008), *HMC Schools: A Quantitative Analysis*. Buckingham: University of Buckingham for the Headmasters' and Headmistresses' Conference.

Smyth, J. (2006), 'Educational leadership that fosters student voice'. *International Journal of Leadership in Education*, 9, (4), 279–84.

Smyth, J. and Gunter, H. M. (2009), 'Debating New Labour education policy', in: C. Chapman and H. M. Gunter (eds), *Radical Reforms: Perspectives on an Era of Educational Change*. London: Routledge, pp. 182–95.

Speakman, S. (2008), 'Back to the future: sustaining an equitable public-private model of school funding', in M. Berends, M. G. Springer and H. J. Walberg (eds), *Charter School Outcomes*. New York: Lawrence Erlbaum Associates.

SSAT (Specialist Schools and Academies Trust) (2007), *City Technology Colleges: Conception and Legacy*. London: SSAT.

Stacey, R. (1992), *Managing Chaos*. London: Kogan Page.

SCC (Staffordshire County Council) (2008a), *Readiness to Deliver*. Stafford: SCC.

— (2008b), *Manifesto for Change*. Stafford: SCC.

— (2008c), *Consultation Proposals for Tamworth*. Stafford: SCC.

— (2009a), *Report on the Consultation Regarding BSF in Tamworth*. Stafford: SCC.

— (prepared by Step Beyond) (2009b), *Tamworth BSF Consultation Meetings: Independent Report*, January 2009 (incorrectly dated 2008). Stafford: SCC.

Starratt, R. J. (2004), *Ethical Leadership*. San Francisco: Jossey Bass.

Stein, M., Goldring, E. and Zottola, G. (2008), *Student Achievement Gains and Parents' Perceptions of Invitations for Involvement in Urban Charter Schools*. Nashville, TN: National Center on School Choice.

Stewart, J. (2006), 'Transformational leadership: an evolving concept examined through the works of Burns, Bass, Avolio, and Leithwood'. *Canadian Journal of Educational Administration and Policy*, 54, (June), 1–29.

Stewart, W. (2010), 'Less than 50% of academies' passes are academic'. *The Times Educational Supplement*, 2 July. Available at: www.tes.co.uk/article.aspx?storycode=6049288 (accessed 7 July 2010).

Stoker, G. (2006), *Why Politics Matters*. Basingstoke: Palgrave Macmillan.

Stratton, A. (2009), 'Labour's plan for 'John Lewis' public services'. *Guardian*, 11 November. Available at: www.guardian.co.uk/society/2009/nov/11/labour-manifesto-public-services-sector (accessed 6 January 2010).

Stuart, T. E. and Sorenson, O. (2007), 'Strategic networks and entrepreneurial ventures'. *Strategic Entrepreneurship Journal*, 1, (1), 211–17.

Sullivan, H. and Skelcher, C. (2004), *Working Across Boundaries* (*Government Beyond the Centre*). Basingstoke: Palgrave Macmillan.

Sutton Trust (2008), *Wasted Talent? Attrition Rates for High-Achieving Pupils between School and University*. Available at: www.suttontrust.com/reports/wastedTalent.pdf (accessed 2 January 2009).

Tannen, D. and Wallet, C. (1987), 'Interactive frames and knowledge schemas in interaction: examples from a medical examination/interview'. *Social Psychology Quarterly*, 50, (2), 205–16.

Taylor, M. (2005), Private academy produces worse results than schools it replaced. *Guardian*, 19 May. Taylor, M. (2006), 'Parents rebel at Dickensian school run by millionaire evangelist friend of Blair'. *Guardian*, 30 May.

Terry, R. W. (1993), *Authentic Leadership: Courage in Action*. San Francisco: Jossey Bass.

Teske, P. and Schneider, M. (2001), 'What research can tell policymakers about school choice'. *Journal of Policy Analysis and Management*, 20, (4), 609–31.

Thomson, P. and Gunter, H. M. (2006), 'From "consulting pupils" to "pupils as researchers": a situated case narrative'. *British Educational Research Journal*, 32, (6), 839–56.

Thornhill, J., and Kent-Smith, J. (2009), *Housing, Schools and Communities*. Coventry: Chartered Institute of Housing.

Thrift, N. (2005), *Knowing Capitalism*. Sage: London.

Tikly, L. (2003), 'Governmentality and the study of education policy in South Africa: an analysis and critique of post-election government policy'. *Journal of Education Policy*, 18, (2), 161–74.

Titcombe, R. (2008), 'How academies threaten the comprehensive curriculum'. *Forum*, 50, (1), 49–59.

Titcombe, R. and Davies, R. (2006), 'Discover the truth about GCSE league tables'. *The Times Educational Supplement*, 13 January.

Tomlinson, S. (2001), *Education in a Post-Welfare Society*. Buckingham: Open University Press.

Tooley, J. (1995), 'Markets or democracy for education? A reply to Stewart Ranson'. *British Journal of Educational Studies*, 43, (1), 21–34.

— (1996), *Education Without the State*. London: IEA.

Touraine, A. (2000), *Can We Live Together?* Stanford, CA: Stanford University Press.

UNISON (2006), *Academies Called to Account*. London: UNISON.

US Department of Education (2008), *Making Charter School Facilities More Affordable: State-Driven Policy Approaches*. Washington, DC: US Department of Education.

van Beuren, E. M., Klijn, E.-H. and Koppenjan, Joop F. M. (2003), 'Dealing with wicked problems in networks: analyzing an environmental debate from a

network perspective'. *Journal of Public Administration Research and Theory*, 13, (2), 193–212.
Vidovich, L. (2007), 'Removing policy from its pedestal: some theoretical framings and practical possibilities'. *Educational Review*, 59, (3), 285–98.
Walford, G. (1991), 'Choice of school at the first City Technology College'. *Educational Studies*, 17, (1), 65–75.
— (2000) 'From City Technology Colleges to sponsored grant-maintained schools'. *Oxford Review of Education*, 26, (2), 145–58.
Webb, A. (1991), 'Co-ordination: a problem in public sector management'. *Policy and Politics*, 19, (4), 229–41.
West, A., Barham, E. and Hind, A. (2009), *Secondary School Admissions in England: Policy and Practice.* London: RISE.
West, A. and Currie, P. (2008), 'The role of the private sector in publicly funded schooling in England: finance, delivery and decision-making'. *Policy and Politics*, 36, (2), 191–207. Available at: www.guardian.co.uk/education/2009/apr/25/conservatives-school-policy-primary-academies (accessed 25 April 2009).
Whitfield, D. (2006), *New Labour's Attack on Public Services.* Nottingham: Spokesman Books.
Whitty, G. and Edwards, T. (1998), 'School choice policies in England and the United States: an exploration of their origins and significance'. *Comparative Education*, 34, (2), 211–27.
Whitty, G., Edwards, T. and Gewirtz, S. (1993), *Specialisation and Choice in Urban Education: The City Technology College Experiment.* London: Routledge.
Wilby, P. (2008) 'Referee on an uneven playing field'. *Guardian*, 26th February. Available at: www.guardian.co.uk/education/2008/feb/26/schooladmissions.schools (accessed 26 February 2008).
Wilby, P. (2009), 'The real problem with academies'. *Guardian*, 10 February.
Wilkinson, G. (2007), 'Pedagogy of the possessed: the privatization of civic education and values under New Labour'. *Educational Review*, 59, (3), 267–84.
Wilkinson, I. R., Caldwell, B. J., Selleck, R. J. W., Harris, J. and Dettman, P. (2006), *History of State Aid to Non-Government Schools in Australia.* Canberra: Department of Education, Science and Training.
Wilkinson, R. and Pickett, K. (2009), *The Spirit Level.* London: Allen Books.
Williams, P. (2002), 'The competent boundary spanner'. *Public Administration*, 80, (1), 103–24.
Williams, R. (2010), 'Grammar schools warned of "covert dangers" in seeking academy status'. *Guardian*, 24 June.
Wilshaw, M. (2008), 'Curriculum', in J. Astle and C. Ryan (eds), *Academies and the Future of State Education.* London: CentreForum, pp. 32–40.
Wintour, P. (2010), 'For-profit schools drive up standards, say Swedish educationalists'. *Guardian*, 4 March. Available at: www.guardian.co.uk/education/2010/mar/04/swedish-free-schools-conservative-education (accessed 4 March 2010).
Wintour, P. and Watt, N. (2009), 'Tories plan to create thousands of primary academies'. *Guardian*, 25 April. Available at: www.guardian.co.uk/education/2009/apr/25/conservatives-school-policy-primary-academies (accessed 25 April 2009).
Witten, K., Kearns, R., Lewis, N., Coster, H. and McCreanor, T. (2003), 'Educational restructuring from a community viewpoint: a case study of school closure from Invercargill, New Zealand'. *Environment and Planning C: Government and Policy*, 21, (2), 203–23.
Woods, P. A., Bagley, C. and Glatter, R. (1998), *School Choice and Competition: Markets in the Public Interest?* London: Routledge.

Woods, P., Woods, G. and Gunter, H. M. (2007), 'Academy schools and entrepreneurialism in education'. *Journal of Education Policy*, 22, (2), 237–59.

Wrigley, T. (2003), *Schools of Hope: A New Agenda for School Improvement*. Stoke-on-Trent: Trentham Books

— (2006a), *Another School Is Possible*. London: Bookmarks/Stoke-on-Trent: Trentham Books

— (2006b), 'Schools and poverty: questioning the effectiveness and improvement paradigms'. *Improving Schools*, 9, (3), 273–90.

— (2007), *Academic Success of the Academies Programme*. Edinburgh: Edinburgh University.

— (2008), 'School improvement in a neo-liberal world'. *Journal of Educational Administration and History*, 40, (2), 129–48.

— (2009), 'Academies: privatizing England's schools'. *Soundings*, 42, (Summer), 47–59.

Yu, C. M. and Taylor, W. L. (1997), *Difficult Choices: Do Magnet Schools Serve Children in Need?* Washington, DC: Citizens' Commission on Civil Rights.

Zhao, Y., Ni, R., Qiu, W., Yang, W. and Zhang, G. (2008), *Why Not the Best Schools? The US Report*. Melbourne: ACER Press.

Zimmer, R., Buddin, R., Chau, D., Daley, G., Gill, B., Guarino, C., Hamilton, L., Krop, C., McCaffery, D., Sandler, M. and Brewer, D. (2003), *Charter School Operations and Performance: Evidence from California*. Santa Monica, CA: RAND Corporation.

Zuboff, S. (2009), 'The old solutions have become the new problems'. *Business Week*, 2 July. Available at: www.businessweek.com/managing/content/jul2009/ca2009072_489734.htm (accessed 23 December 2009).

Zuboff, S. and Maxmin, J. (2004), *The Support Economy*. New York: Penguin Books.

Index